PHILOSOPHY & LOGIC FOR EVERYBODY
Solution to your Problem

WILLIAM I. AMAM

PHILOG VENTURES

ATLANTA USA

© Copyright 2017 by William I. Amam

All rights reserved

For information about permission to reproduce selections from this book, Contact Philog Ventures at: philogventures@gmail.com

For information about special discounts for bulk purchases, please Contact Philog Ventures at: philogventures@gmail.com

Library of Congress Cataloging-in-Publication Data
Amam, William I.
Philosophy and Logic for Everybody: Solution to your Problem
William I. Amam
Includes bibliographical references and index

ISBN (Paperback USA): 978-1-68026-050-2

1. Philosophy 2.Logic 3. Society, Law and Religion

Published by Philog Ventures
Printed and Bound in the United States
Premier Graphics & Communication,
2505 Meadowbrook Pkwy,
Duluth, Georgia, USA 2017

A wise man is mightier than a strong man and a man of knowledge than he who has strength. Hence, the pen is mightier than the sword and the gun.

DEDICATION

This work is dedicated to the evergreen memory of my father, Late Mr. Maurice Amam, for his unalloyed and unflinching effort in my education for which I am well pleased.

TABLE OF CONTENTS

1. Understanding Philosophy: Demythologization of Philosophy........9
2. The Nature and Significance of Philosophy..............................25
3. Philosophical Methodology: Types of Philosophical Methods......45
4. Fundamental Problems of Philosophy and their Solutions 78
5. Metaphysics: The Horizon of the Question of Being 153
6. Epistemology: The Search for the Meaning of Truth 173
7. Ethics: The Morality of Human Actions 191
8. Aesthetics: The Criteria for Value Selection............................225
9. Branches of Philosophy: Thoughts on Society, Law, Religion, Science and History 230
10. Human Thought Patterns: Naturalism, Materialism and Supernaturalism 265
11. Schools of Philosophy: Empiricism and Rationalism 280
12. Schools of Philosophy: Idealism and Realism..........................288
13. Schools of Philosophy: Existentialism and Marxism 299
14. Schools of Philosophy: Pragmatism and Logical Positivism 319
15. Logic: The Instrument of Philosophy......................................335
16. Fallacies in Logic: The Errors of the Human Mind 358
17. Main Streams of Philosophy: Western and Eastern Philosophy......399
18. African Philosophy: The Different Senses of the Concept "African" 412
Notes 456
Index 492

FOREWARD

There is no doubt that a crying need exists for books on philosophy in many countries of the world. This is because the importance of philosophy as a veritable tool for sustainable human and national development has gained international prominence. This also explains why all developed countries still emphasize and insist on the teaching and learning of philosophy in schools. Third World countries, since independence, have made considerable progress in initiating and sustaining sound philosophical programs for their citizens. Specialized aspects of philosophical principles and ideas have been pursued but with varying degrees of success. Our suggestion here is that a lot more is required to put philosophy and the study of it at the center stage of national life and programs. This call is both emergent and urgent.

The book 'Philosophy and Logic for Everybody: Solution to your Problem' is remarkably very auspicious by its contemporaneous relevance – coming at a time when the battle cry of governance by governments of the time is 'reform, transparency, due process and small government' all of which drive their being and sustenance from ethical principles which philosophy readily espouses. By this book, the author has brilliantly thrown a very bright and illuminating light on these aspects of national and international aspirations.

The book deals with such sub-themes as the nature and significance of philosophy, philosophical methodology, problems of philosophy and their solutions, branches of philosophy, schools of thought. It also deals with such topics as Logic as instrument of philosophy, fallacies, other philosophies including Oriental and African Philosophy. The eighteen chapters of the book are well written and informative; one chapter flows into the next in such a way that they are well linked.

In terms of comprehensiveness and depth of coverage, the book has fully satisfied these requirements. Suffice it to say that it is written in sufficiently simple language as much as the subject can allow, and the issues dealt with therein are ones that would contribute immensely to advancing the intellectual and ethical frontiers of not only students of philosophy and others in tertiary institutions pursuing other fields of study but also the civic and philosophic awareness of the fairly literate segment of the public. Since the book has all the qualities of a good book, I strongly recommend the text to readers from all works of life not just in the United States of America and the United Kingdom but the entire world.

David G. Stones
Philosopher and Attorney,
London, United Kingdom

PREFACE

Today, there is need for philosophy to occupy a center stage in our educational pursuits and aspirations. This is based on the discovery of late that the world is in dire need of a guiding philosophy that would bring about common sense solutions to our problems and encourage sustainable personal and community development. Presently, many tertiary institutions all over the world are taking up the teaching of philosophy especially the introduction to philosophy and logic. This was consequent upon the directive of ministries of education and university commissions in many countries that the teaching of philosophy should be made compulsory in all academic departments in community colleges and universities. Some child welfare advocates in many countries have also encouraged the introduction of philosophy in early childhood education. The reasons for these decisions and directives are obvious.

Socrates had warned many years before Christ that any nation that does not value the unique knowledge, wisdom, courage and prudence that are gained from learning philosophy is doomed. Plato in many of his epic works also had explained vividly the importance of philosophy in the building and sustenance of a stable polity. For him, a man without some tint of philosophy is no doubt dangerous, in fact doubly dangerous. First, to his own person, because he gropes in the dark and may never find his way, and second, to the society because he could be likened to a ship without a rudder, plan or compass. He can hardly tolerate, co-exist and live well with other people in the society.

Plato therefore called on all nations and peoples of the earth warning them that unless philosophers become kings (leaders) or by design or accident, kings and leaders learn and become philosophers, that there would be no end to the problems of the world. Plato could not have been more prophetic.In our own times, recorded experiences have demonstrated the powerful role philosophy can play in both human and national development. The best recorded world leaders and thinkers were philosophers. Abraham Lincoln, Karl Marx, Charles Darwin, Francis Bacon, Mao Tse Tung, Mahatma Gandhi, Franklin Roosevelt, Winston Churchill, Martin Luther King Jr. and Nelson Mandela were model philosophers and world leaders.

The United States of America is a developed and stable country today due to the immense contributions of Abraham Lincoln, J.F. Kennedy, Franklin D. Roosevelt, J.S. Mill and Martin Luther King Jr.to liberty, freedom and equality. And the philosophy of education of John Dewey and the pragmatism of Charles Sanders Peirce and William James helped to reshape the thinking of Americans as a practical, skilled and result - oriented people.

Before the breakup of the Soviet Union (USSR), the youths and adults of that country were initiated into Marxist and Communist ideologies through their educational system. The guidelines of these ideologies were laid out and propelled by the philosophy of Karl Marx and Friedrich Engels in the Communist Manifesto. The practical application of this philosophy in spite of its obvious shortcomings in individual freedom, civil liberties and free enterprise, still accounts for the development of Soviet Union and presently, Russia as a world power.

Furthermore, Chinese development as a world power and later as the second largest economy in the world after the United States is absolutely attributed to its adherence to the principles of Mao's philosophy as documented in the Little Red Book, which has become after the Bible one of the most printed books in history. The same could be said of Gandhi and the development of India. His nonviolent resistance - which is akin to that of Martin Luther King Jr. - played a great role in getting the independence of India from the British. In the same way, Dr. Luther King Jr's nonviolent protest philosophy helped improve civil rights situation in America. It is also on record that the Empiricism of John Locke, the religious wager and the calculating machines of Blaise Paschal were the forerunners of modern computers, while the scientific methods of Francis Bacon and Rene Descartes, the social contract of J.J. Rousseau and Thomas Hobbes assisted in transforming the nations of Europe to first world countries. Likewise, the ethics of Spinoza, Leibniz and Kant contributed greatly to the moral development and conscientization of Europe and America that ended incessant civil and ethnic wars in the West.

In the continent of Africa, some of the foremost statesmen and nationalists were philosophers. African nationalists like Jomo Kenyatta of Kenya, Julius Nyerere of Tanzania, Nnamdi Azikiwe of Nigeria, Kwame Nkrumah of Ghana, Leopold Sedar Senghor of Senegal and Nelson Mandela of South Africa were carriers of African thought and molders of African philosophy. Philosophy shaped the course of actions of these individuals, and up till today they are still remembered fervently by their people.

The point here is that a businessman, politician, manager, marketer or accountant who is opportune and fortunate to learn philosophy would definitely have an edge over his colleagues who have no iota of philosophy. In the same vein, a leader who has keen interest and knows much about philosophical inquiries would logically and reasonably perform better than his counterparts who are bereft of philosophy. Even a teacher or a preacher who learns philosophy and loves to philosophize is always an inspirational speaker and attracts more followers than any other.

Generally, this book *Philosophy and Logic for Everybody: Solution to your Problem* seeks to introduce the undergraduate in tertiary institutions, the man on the street as well as professionals to the double-barreled discourse on Philosophy and Logic.

Specifically, it is designed to expose in meticulous detail solutions to some fundamental problems that worry the mind of everybody who is of age. These prescriptions and knowledge of philosophy and logic are essential to students and professionals in all fields of human endeavor - law, mass communication, political science and sociology, engineering and Medicine, and of course those in management sciences (accountancy, marketing, banking, finance and management), would find the book most valuable and significantly pertinent. Hence, the book is honestly written for everybody.

The author pays due regard to several eminent authors, publishers and owners of copyright materials consulted in the course of writing this book most of which were duly acknowledged. The author's appreciation and gratitude also go to his family members and friends for their encouragement. Finally, if this book succeeds in initiating and provoking the reader into more erudite philosophical inquiries, it would have succeeded in discharging its gratuitous assignment. The overall glory, however, goes to God, the author and finisher of our being.

William I. Amam (MBA, MA)

1

UNDERSTANDING PHILOSOPHY
Demythologization of Philosophy

WHAT PHILOSOPHY IS NOT

To know and understand philosophy, we have to consider first and foremost what philosophy is not. This involves separating the chaff from the substance, removing accidents and trivialities from the substance of philosophy. This is for philosophy to stand out and present itself unadulterated with myths, mysticism and misconceptions. It will ultimately make people see philosophy for what it is and be able to source from philosophy common sense solutions to daily problems of life.

Myths about Philosophy

Myths are stories handed down from olden times, especially concepts or beliefs about the early history of a race or culture. They contain explanations of natural events such as the seasons, and causes of natural phenomena like hurricanes, earthquakes, tornadoes, severe drought, etc. Many of the concepts and beliefs that are found in myths are imaginary, fictitious and invented. Philosophy, from the ancient times through the middle ages to the modern and contemporary periods, has gathered and intermingled with some myths, and has been wrongly identified with these myths making philosophy sometimes a strange subject.

The word "philosophy" often strikes fear in some people just as Marxism, communism and capitalism do to some people. Philosophy seems to connote some strange ideas of gravity, mysticism, religion, or some sort of self-imposed sanctity or esoteric activities. People often associate philosophers with seclusion, inflexibility and aloofness. Others still associate philosophers with cultism, mysticism, atheism and some lukewarm religious tendencies. Philosophers are sometimes seen as a chaotic bunch of confused people groping in the no-man's land between religion, theology and science.

Again, it is rather unfortunate that until now philosophy is regarded as an unprofitable course of study, a very difficult and impractical subject. For many people, philosophy has no cash-value in a world in which what you are as a person is determined by the size of your pocket and bank account. In their view, philosophy is a discipline far removed from the affairs of everyday life and usual interests. It offers no solution to everyday problems, and to that extent, it is not for an average person.

Furthermore, it is erroneous that people had regarded the philosopher as someone who sits with head in hand pondering over abstract and abstruse matters which have no practical relevance to life. It is on the basis of this kind of erroneous belief that Herbert Spencer, an English Sociologist of the 19th century regarded philosophy as a specific gift bestowed by some higher divine power on "chosen" people, mostly those of Western Europe. In Spencer's opinion "blacks were by nature incapable of abstract thinking." According to Spencer, "a black man thinks in concrete images only, and his emotions prevail over his reason. Neither can he perceive sophisticated philosophical ideas."[1] It is this faulty thought current that miseducated and derailed some early African scholars such as Kwasi Wiredu of Ghana and Leopold Sedar Senghor of Senegal.

It was Wiredu who once surmised and suggested that Africans were colonized not because of their color or geographical location, but only because Africans could not think logically. Leopold Sedar Senghor, on the same line of thought with Wiredu, opined that "the Blacks have been endowed with emotions and the Greeks with reason." This means that African thinking is imaginative and poetic, but not philosophic. From a holistic point of view, it means that Africans are incapable of creating their own philosophy and science. This myth is untrue and has no place in philosophy. We know undoubtedly that the Creator created all humans in his own image; he created them equal and free, and endowed them with the capacity for reason and emotions. The image of God has no color. Black and white colors are just two extremes in the spectrum of human skin color. Some black people believing that virtue stands in the middle of two extremes bleach their skin and some whites tan theirs in effort to come to the middle of the spectrum – probably applying Aristotle's Doctrine of the Mean. And according to the renowned cultural anthropologist, Erich von Daniken in one of his three epic works, *According to the Evidence, the Signs of the Gods, and the Chariots of the Gods,* the Arabs including the Egyptians in their customs and traditions assert that they have the most perfect color as theirs approximate to the mean of the skin color spectrum. But, we believe the idea of a perfect color is a matter of choice and that skin color has nothing to do with who is rational or who is emotional.

Another myth spread and perpetuated by some scientists today is that philosophy has nothing to do with scientific knowledge. According to them, in the past, philosophers anticipated certain scientific discoveries (e.g., the atomic theory, the law of gravity and the theory of electricity), but now philosophers are "out of a job," since concrete, "positive" knowledge has replaced philosophical meditations. For them, since the cognition of the real world has been divided among concrete sciences, philosophy is left with nothing concrete. The only sphere it now has is that of imagination, utopia, and myth. The philosopher turns out to be a dreamer who destroys by force of his imagination, the world as it is, i.e., the real world, and creates another world - the world as it should be, the utopian world which precipitates endless and fruitless discussions. This also is a false opinion of philosophy.

Demythologization of Philosophy

Philosophy, we make bold to say, is not any of the above misconceptions. Philosophers have been grossly undervalued and misrepresented.

First and foremost, philosophy is not religion. This is clearly confirmed by the view of Merriam Webster that religion is a concern over what exists beyond the visible. It is differentiated from philosophy in that it operates through faith or intuition rather than reason, and generally it includes the idea of the existence of a single being, a group of beings, an eternal principle or a transcendent spiritual entity that has created the world, governs it, controls its destinies, or intervenes occasionally in the natural course of its history, as well as the idea that ritual, prayer, spiritual exercises, certain principles of everyday conduct are expedient, due, or spiritually rewarding, or arise naturally out of an inner need as a human response to such a belief, principle, etc.[2] Similarly, Albert Sidney Hornby sees religion as the belief in the existence of a supernatural ruling power, the creator and controller of the universe, who has given to man a spiritual nature which continues to exist after the death of the body. Religion also is considered as the various systems of faith and worship along with their beliefs; it includes Christianity, Islam, Buddhism and Confucianism, to mention but a few.[3]

It is clear from the above that philosophy is not religion. Religion takes the path of belief, faith and dogma, while philosophy deals with experience and reason. Philosophy deals with rational and logical methods which necessarily lead to sound theories and reliable principles.

Religion, etymologically, comes from the Latin word *re-ligare* which means to bind with or bound with the absolute (God) with faith. But philosophy suggests rather the continuous search for the absolute with the human reason. The fact that philosophy departments in some universities in the world are merged with or mounted in the department of religion should not be misconstrued as an identification of one with the other.

Furthermore, we affirm here that philosophy is not mysticism as erroneously taken by some. Mysticism concerns the beliefs and the experiences of a mystic. It is the teaching and belief that knowledge of God and of real truth may be obtained through meditation or spiritual insight independently of the mind and the senses. Philosophy, on the other hand, works and operates on the functionality of the human mind and reason. Even philosophic intuition as a source of knowledge does not work outside the mind. Anything outside the realm of the mind is outside the confines of philosophy. Granted of course, that a philosopher could be a mystic or vice versa in the same sense in which a scientist, an engineer or a medical doctor can be a mystic or vice versa. The position is clear that mysticism cannot be synonymous with philosophy nor it can be with engineering or medicine.

Philosophy is not atheism. Many uninformed people very often think of philosophers as atheists or people who do not believe in anything. Even when they have been persuaded or forced to believe, they are lukewarm in stance. In Plato's *Apology*, Socrates asserts that this myth comes from the erroneous belief by many people that a wise man who pursues inquiries and speculates about the heavens, and who examines into all things that are beneath the earth, and make worse appear the better reason never believe in the gods.

However, atheism is a belief that there is no God. It suggests that if God exists, He could not be known by any human or natural means.[4] Philosophy on the other hand espouses the existence and continued control of the universe by an unmoved mover; an uncaused cause, a supreme being – God. Philosophy has articulated and marshaled out some praise – worthy proofs of the existence of God. One of the proofs that appears persuasive and most convincing and which has been accepted by some physical scientists, is the existence of intelligent and efficient designs in nature and natural things. The acceptance of efficient designs in the natural order of things called for the belief in and acknowledgement of the existence of an efficient designer – God. Even the imperfections of our own designs remind us of the existence of the most efficient and perfect designer of all things.

Philosophy is not theology. Theology is the formal study of the nature of God, His attributes and of the foundations of religious belief. Theology is regarded as "divine wisdom which treats of God and His activity in the world on the basis of a supernatural revelation."[5] To put it succinctly, theology is an application of reason to faith. On the other hand, philosophy is not wisdom supernaturally infused into our souls which man possesses in virtue of a superhuman illumination, but it is wisdom of man as man acquired with difficulty by the labor of the human intellect and reason. However, we must say that philosophy is *"ancilla theologiae."* This is to say that philosophy is the handmaid of theology. It renders service to theology by sharpening the mind and expecting the understanding of revealed truths and systematizing them as science. Thus, philosophy has a symbiotic rapport with theology, but it is not identifiable with it.

We acknowledge that some philosophical problems were first formulated in myths, but they soon burst out of this tight shell just as other sciences in their early stages. And we affirm that the fundamental concepts of philosophy have taken shape and should be dissociated from puzzles and bewilderments of age-long myths and mysticism. Other misconceptions about philosophy will be projected and taken care of as we go into the definition and nature of philosophy.

WHAT IS PHILOSOPHY?

Etymological Definition

Philosophy as a concept has two Greek words: *"Philein,"* to love and *"Sophia"* wisdom. So, the derivative meaning of philosophy is "love of wisdom." Even the Latin compound *"philosophia"* from which philosophy is derived also is translated as "love of wisdom." How does the phrase "love of wisdom" explain what philosophy is all about? We can behold this by conducting some analyses of the philosophic conception of love and wisdom.

The Meaning of "Love" in the Definition

Love has always been known commonly as a feeling of strong attraction and inseparability toward someone or something. Philosophic love is higher in excellence than the common love. The common love could be a passive emotion that does not go anywhere and does not achieve anything. The philosophic love is "a designated activity rather than an emotion - the activity of pursuing wisdom rather than the emotion motivating that pursuit."[6] It is a kind of active friendship with wisdom.

Love as an activity or a pursuit is best illustrated by its symbolic letters L.O.V.E. The "L" signifies that loves comes from heaven (God) and goes to the world. This concerns God's love for man and the environment. "O" means love goes round the world or as the Chinese would say love makes the world go round. "V" means love goes back to heaven (God), it neither stops nor ends in the world, it signifies man's love of God and things that are Godly, and the "E" means love is a transformer; it can step up positive things as well as step down negative things. Love covers a multitude of sins say the scriptures. Love is the greatest creative force known to man especially when it works with wisdom. Thus, philosophic love involves actions directed to a specific goal. It is a show of overwhelming quest for wisdom or knowledge which a person needs to make his life and the world better – *Plato's Symposium*. The essential question that we need to consider is what exactly is the wisdom that the philosophic love seeks?

The Meaning of "Wisdom" in the Definition

Generally, wisdom is regarded as the right application of knowledge in solving human problems. It is one of the four cardinal virtues. In fact, it is taken as the greatest of the cardinal virtues of justice, courage and prudence. We have to know what justice, courage and prudence are to exercise them very well and recognize each when we see it. In the early Plato's dialogues, we see Socrates searching for definitions of the virtues, motivated by the view that one must know what, for example, justice is before one can hope to act justly. In the middle ages, Aquinas sees wisdom as the father of all virtues (including the theological virtues such as faith, love, hope, and holiness) in the sense that it is the cause, measure and form of all virtues. Without wisdom we cannot recognize holiness in a person or in a thing when we see one.

Specifically, wisdom is the habit or disposition to perform action with the highest degree of adequacy under any given circumstance. This implies a possession of knowledge or the seeking thereof in order to apply it to given circumstance. It involves an understanding of people, things, events, situations and the willingness as well as the ability to apply perception, judgment, and action in keeping with the understanding of what is the optimal course of action. It often requires the control of one's emotional reactions (passions) so that the universal principle of reason prevails to determine one's action.

Succinctly, wisdom is insight, hindsight and foresight geared toward finding the truth. It also goes with an optimum judgment and decision making as to what action should be taken in order to deliver the correct outcome and with courage to carry it out to a logical conclusion.

For Aristotle, wisdom is the understanding of causes, that is, knowing why things are a certain way which is deeper than knowing that things are a certain way. Wisdom is hence regarded as the capacity to realize what is of value in life, for oneself and for others. The significance of philosophic wisdom is seen when we contrast wisdom with ignorance on one hand and foolishness on the other.

Philosophic Wisdom Contrasted with Ignorance

For Melvin Rader, the word wisdom can be looked at from two points of view. "Wisdom" is first of all "contrasted with ignorance; the wise man is he who knows and therefore is not ignorant."[7] At this level, Philosophy and other sciences such as Engineering, Medicine, Law, Political Science, Sociology and other academic disciplines are at the same level because they all aim to replace ignorance with knowledge. This is seen in the compendium of knowledge they all have produced over the years, and more is being generated every day. This means that at this level, philosophy cannot be distinguished from other sciences, and the philosopher cannot be differentiated from other scientists. They work to extend the frontiers of knowledge and increase the body of knowledge in existence. They all research and produce research works. They do their businesses, and work in private and public institutions to earn a living. Scientists and philosophers work to extend the frontiers of knowledge to make the world a better place for man to live in and be happy.

Philosophic Wisdom Contrasted with Foolishness

In the second and higher sense, "wisdom is contrasted with foolishness; the wise man is he who has good judgment and therefore is not foolish."[8] The fool may have a great deal of knowledge about ordinary matters of facts, but he lacks the right use of the knowledge. He lacks the balance and maturity and ripe insight that make it possible not only to live but to live well with other people in a given society.

When philosophy is seen as the pursuit of wisdom contrasted with foolishness, it is marked off and differentiated from other sciences such as physics, chemistry, biology, zoology, medicine, engineering, mathematics, political science, law, sociology, etc. The subject matter of science is facts, and science attempts to discover verifiable laws, that is, regularities among these facts. These laws give a description of facts without any value judgment such as good or bad, right or wrong. For Rader, it is obvious that the physicist does not talk about wicked atoms or beneficent motions, and even the sociologist, in his purely scientific role, tries to describe rather than to evaluate the behavior of social groups.[9]

When philosophy, on the other hand, takes the gab of wisdom contrasted with foolishness, it becomes a critical activity concerned with appraisals and evaluations. It goes with the power of seeing something with the mind; the power of sudden perception that gives understanding and helps the individual to make good judgment and carry out informed decisions as to what is right or wrong, true or false in a given situation. It uses the various agents for determining moral standard to prescribe or assess a given human conduct.

Thus, a philosopher must not only contribute to increasing the body of knowledge and extending the frontiers of knowledge, he must also have good insight and judgment, make informed decisions and live well with fellow human beings with the principles of good moral conduct as a guide.

When a scientist goes beyond the description of facts and figures to make value judgment on what is before him, he ventures into the arena of moral philosophy. To that extent the scientist can be regarded as a philosopher. In the history of thought there are many scientists who are renowned philosophers and there are philosophers who are great scientists. This is what Plato had in mind when wrote about philosopher – king as a solution to societal problems. Whatever endeavor one is concerned with, he or she needs a tint of philosophy to excel in life.

Authoritative Definitions of Philosophy

Apart from the above etymological definition and conceptual explanation, many experts, scholars and authors in the field have evolved numerous definitions, all aimed at making clearer the meaning of philosophy. Some of these definitions were given by authorities in philosophy in the ancient period, modern period and contemporary time. We shall here enumerate as many as possible.

Definitions of Philosophy by Ancient Philosophers

- Socrates: Philosophy is the spectator of anytime and all existence.[10]

- Plato: Philosophy is the passion to seek the truth.[11]

- Aristotle: Philosophy is the knowledge of the truth.[12]

- Democritus and Lucretius: Philosophy is the science of nature and its qualities.[13]

- Cicero: Philosophy is the art of life.¹⁴

- Epicurus: Philosophy is an activity which secures the happy life by means of discussion and argument. ¹⁵

Definitions of Philosophy by Modern Philosophers

- Ducasse: Philosophy is the general theory of criticism.¹⁶

- John Dewey: Philosophy is the criticism of criticisms. It is the act of thinking which has become conscious of itself.¹⁷

- Jacque Maritain: Philosophy is the science which by the natural light of reason studies the first causes or highest principles of all things. ¹⁸

- William James: Philosophy is the thinking of generalities rather than particulars.¹⁹

- Martin Heidegger: Philosophy is the science of the correspondence to the being of Being.²⁰

- A. J. Ayer: Philosophy is an activity of analysis.²¹

- Wittgenstein: Philosophy is the logical clarification of thought.²²

- Thomas Hobbes: Philosophy is the study of material things and their causal relations.²³

- Lenin: Philosophy is theoretical knowledge that resolves the most general issues relating to world outlook.²⁴

- Avicenna: Philosophy is the wisdom with perfect knowledge and perfect action.²⁵

Definitions of Philosophy by Contemporary Philosophers

- Satischandra and Datta: Philosophy is the wisdom of an enlightened life led with far-sight, foresight and insight.[26]

• Nicholas Omoregbe: Philosophy is the rational search for answers to the questions that arise in the mind when we reflect on human experience.[27]

• Kirilenko and Korshunova: Philosophy studies the most general laws governing the universe, man and humanity as a whole; it studies the very foundations of the unity of man and society of man and nature.[28]

• John Herman Randall Jr: Philosophy is the criticism of the fundamental beliefs in any man's great cultural enterprises, science, art, religion, the moral life, social and practical activity, when some new idea or some altered experience has impinged upon them and generated intellectual tension and maladjustment.[29]

• Paul Edward and Arthur Pap: Philosophy is the critical reflection on the justification of basic human beliefs and the analysis of basic concepts in terms of which such beliefs are expressed.[30]

• G.N. Garmonsway and J. Simpson: Philosophy is the study of ultimate nature of existence, reality, knowledge and goodness, as discoverable by human reasoning; any specified system of thought on these matters; general mental and moral outlook on life, wisdom, rationality and calmness.[31]

• Charlie Dunbar Broad: Philosophy is a science that reflects on the outcome of other sciences with a view to reach some general conclusions as to the nature of the universe, and as to our position and prospects in it.[32]

Comprehensive Definition of Philosophy

Each of the above authoritative definition contains an element of truth of what philosophy is. Actually, no single definition can articulate everything about philosophy; each can only reflects one or two aspects of philosophy. However, there is need to search for the most holistic definition that can articulate the essentials of philosophy. We found this in Titus Harold, Marilyn Smith and Richard Nolan conceptions of what philosophy is.

They gave five conceptions of philosophy:

- Philosophy is a personal attitude towards life and the universe.

- Philosophy is a method of reflective thinking and reasoned inquiry.

- Philosophy is an attempt to gain a view of the whole.

- Philosophy is the logical analysis of language and the clarification of the meaning of words and concepts.

- Philosophy is a group of problems as well as theories about the solution of the problems.[33]

One of the difficulties confronting philosophers is perhaps how to agree on a specific definition of the subject matter of philosophy. We must acknowledge that the definitions by Harold, Smith and Nolan, present to us a comprehensive view of what philosophy is all about, as a result we will give it more elucidation for clearer meaning and understanding.

- Philosophy is a set of attitudes or beliefs towards life and the universe which are often held uncritically. Harold, Smith and Nolan referred to this meaning as the informal sense of philosophy or "having" a philosophy. It is often called the philosophy of life of a person or the guiding principle of life of a person. Usually, when a person says "my philosophy is," he is referring to an informal personal attitude toward whatever topic is being discussed. When a person goes through some crisis or unusual experience, often we inquire, "How does he take it?" or "How does it affect him?" Sometimes, the answer is, "He takes it philosophically."[34] This means that he thinks outside the box; he looks at the problem in its broad perspective, sees the big picture and takes it as a part of a larger scheme of things; hence he faces the situation calmly and reflectively, with poise and composure. Some people have adopted some axioms, maxims or principles as their philosophy of life because these principles have proved to be effective for managing certain situations. One of such principles is the golden rule; do onto others the way you will like to be done onto. Others like it include; No condition is permanent. Every dark cloud has a silver lining. A stitch in time saves nine. The hull mark of a gentle man is not to be a burden unto others. Don't saw the sawdust, it is already sawed. Maxims like these and many others have helped many people pull through and overcome tough situations in life. This is why such maxims and principles are framed and placed at strategic positions in homes, offices and vehicles.

- Philosophy is a process of reflecting upon and criticizing our most deeply held beliefs and attitudes. This is the formal sense of "doing" philosophy, that is, philosophy as an intellectual activity. These two senses of philosophy – "having" and "doing" philosophy – cannot be treated entirely independent of each other, for if we did not have a philosophy in the informal, personal sense, then we could not do philosophy in the critical and reflective sense. This leads to the notion that philosophy is a world view or world outlook of a person or people which comes from reflective thought. Moreover, it is also a conviction, a belief in the necessity for action on the basis of the acquired knowledge. Simply "having" a philosophy of life or a personal philosophy is not sufficient for doing philosophy or engaging in philosophical activity. A genuine philosophical attitude is a search and critical attitude; it is open-minded and tolerant, that is, being willing to look at all sides of an issue without prejudice. To philosophize is not merely to read and know philosophy; there are skills of argumentation to be mastered; techniques of analysis to be employed and a body of material to be appropriated by the individual such that he becomes able to think and feel philosophically.[35]

Thus, philosophers in the formal sense are reflective and critical. The formal sense of doing philosophy brings out the true essence of not only philosophers but also of the subject they criticize and reflect on. They take a "second look" at the material problem presented by common sense. They attempt to think through these life's problems by looking at all the facts involved.

There are different approaches to doing philosophy and that is why some philosophers in their critical evaluations often times differ. Philosophers also disagree, first because they view things from different points of view and their personal experiences, cultural backgrounds and training may vary widely. This is especially true of people living at different times and in different places. Secondly, philosophers disagree because they live in a changing universe. People change, society changes, and nature changes. Some people are responsive and sensitive to change; others cling to customs, traditions and the status quo, and to systems that were formulated long time ago and were declared to be authoritative and final. A third reason philosophers disagree is that they deal with an area full of ideologies; an area of human experience in which the evidence is not complete, discoveries are made continually. The evidence we do have may be interpreted in various ways by different people. In spite of these disagreements, however, philosophers continue to probe, examine and evaluate the world with the hope of presenting consistent principles by which a person can live his life happily in a world full of problems.

• Philosophy is an attempt to gain a view of the whole. Here, philosophy seeks to combine the conclusions of the various sciences and human experience into some kind of consistent world view. Many philosophers concur with this position when they assert that philosophy studies the most general laws governing the universe, man and humanity as a whole; it studies the very foundations of the unity of man and society, of man and nature. So, the philosopher wishes to see life, not with the specialized slant of the scientist or the businessman or the artist, but with the overall view of someone cognizant of life as a totality. At this point the philosopher is involved in speculative activity.

In differentiating "speculative philosophy," from "critical philosophy," C.D. Broad in his work, *Scientific Thought* says that the object of speculative philosophy is to take over the results of the various sciences to add to them the results of the religious and ethical experiences of mankind and then to reflect upon the whole. The hope is that, by this means, we may be able to reach some general conclusions as to the nature of the universe and as to our position and prospects in it.[36] Hence, the task as well as the objective of speculative philosophy is to give a view of the whole life, to produce a worldview and to integrate the knowledge of the sciences with that of other disciplines to achieve some kind of consistent whole.

• On the critical aspect, philosophy involves the logical analysis of language and the clarification of the meaning of words and concepts. Explaining this function of philosophy, Harold, Smith and Nolan affirmed that nearly all philosophers have used the methods of analysis and have sought to clarify the meaning of terms and the uses of language. There are some philosophers, indeed, who see this as the main task of philosophy, and a few who claim this is the only legitimate function of philosophy. Such philosophers consider philosophy as a specialized field serving and aiding in the clarification of language rather than a broad field reflecting upon all of life's experiences.

It is important that we acknowledge here that this outlook is recent and has gained considerable support from the logical positivists of the 20th century. The outlook would limit what we call knowledge or statements to observable facts and their interactions and also confines them to the business of various sciences rather of philosophy. According to this narrower point of view, the aim of philosophy is to expose confusion and nonsense in language, and to clarify the meaning and use of terms in sciences and everyday affairs.

- Philosophy involves a group of perennial problems which interest mankind and for which philosophers have always sought answers. Again, throwing light on this definition of philosophy, Harold, Smith and Nolan asserted that philosophy presses its inquiry into the deepest problems of human existence. Thus, some philosophical questions raised in the past have been answered in a manner satisfactory to the majority of philosophers. For example, the existence of atoms has been proved scientifically, and the existence of innate or inborn ideas has been refuted in the modern period. Many questions, however, have been answered only tentatively and many problems remain unsolved.

Sometimes, we stop and ponder because of a startling event, and often out of simple curiosity to think seriously about some fundamental issues. Why there is something rather than nothing? What is the place of life in this great universe? Do things operate by chance or through mechanism, or are there some plans or purpose or intelligence at the heart of things? Is my life controlled by outside forces or do I have a determining or even a partial degree of control? The above questions and countless others are all philosophical problems that worry the mind of any person who has come of age.

To provide answers or solutions to the above problems and many others, schools, theories and systems of thought have arisen in the field of philosophy, such as empiricism, rationalism, idealism, realism, pragmatism, analytical philosophy, existentialism and phenomenology. Without these great philosophical schools, systems, the solutions they offered, and the thinkers associated with them, human thought in general and philosophy in particular would not have the rich content they have today. Humanity is where it is today in the modern period because of the immense contribution of philosophy. This is aptly demonstrated by Greenblatt in his recent work, *Swerve: How the World became Modern*, which espouses that modernity has its source and basis on the philosophy of atoms as presented by Lucretius in his epic work, *On the Nature of Things*. Even though we may be unconscious of the fact, we are constantly influenced by ideas that have come down to us from the various schools of thought in philosophy. These ideas have helped and will continue to help to a great extent in solving problems of life.

2

THE NATURE AND SIGNIFICANCE OF PHILOSOPHY

The nature of philosophy is revealed when we look at it from the following points of view.

Philosophy as a Science

Etymologically, the word science comes from the Latin word *"scientia"* meaning knowledge. For Merriam Webster, science is a branch of knowledge or study dealing with a body of facts or truths systematically arranged and showing operation of general laws.[1]

Specifically, science is knowledge obtained by observation and testing of facts, and the pursuit of such knowledge. Generally, as a systematized body of knowledge, scientific knowledge includes not only the ones from the natural sciences, e.g., botany, zoology, and the physical sciences, e.g., physics, chemistry; but also those of the social sciences, e.g., psychology, sociology, political science and philosophy.[2]

Sometimes, we see people who hold the view that philosophy cannot be considered a science, since throughout its history, it has tackled the same set of questions, while each concrete science, having solved a problem, never returns to it but poses and elaborates new ones. But we must assert here that philosophical problems are called "eternal" not because they cannot be solved, but because each epoch poses them in its own way. And each philosophical problem can only arise at a certain stage of development of the individual and the society. The method of posing and resolving these philosophical problems is closely connected with the level of development of the society and all its aspects – economics, political relations, science and culture. Philosophy epitomizes its age and it is that age's consciousness, the quintessence of human thought and of everything that was created by mankind at any stage of its development.

Aristotle saw philosophy as a science. For him, "all sciences pursue special aims, except philosophy which alone of all the sciences is free, for only this science exists for its own sake."[3] Further, Cicero asserted the significance of philosophy as science when he said, "thou we are turning to, thou we are asking for help oh philosophy, the Lodestar of life, neither we nor human life itself could exist without you."[4]

On the origin of philosophy as a science, we must state that man's ability of operating with abstractions which appears with the development of mathematics is an important precondition of philosophy, for each philosophical category is an abstraction, too. Again, the ability to make generalization required knowledge of how to differentiate between the necessary and the accidental, the cause and the effect. This ability did not appear immediately. Both arithmetic and astronomical knowledge were first developed in the orient - in Egypt, Assyria, Babylonia and Phoenicia. Philosophy as science started in these places to help unite scattered information about the world into a single whole and to provide other sciences with a methodical and firm theoretical base.

Aristotle was a unique personality, in whose works all branches of contemporary philosophical and scientific knowledge found reflection. According to Melvin Rader, "apart from Aristotle's numerous philosophical works which influenced the development of philosophy in the whole world, he wrote treaties on socio-political problems and questions and a detailed system of formal and symbolic logic which also deals with the forms of thinking used today in computerizations."[5] Aristotle also wrote on natural science e.g. on the heavens, physics, animal parts, meteorology, etc. which were very important in the advancement of other sciences such as astronomy, chemistry, biology and medicine.

From the works of Aristotle, Epicurus, Lucretius, Democritus, Descartes, Alfred North Whitehead, Russell, Sanders Peirce and Karl Popper, we know that when philosophy wears the garb of science, it is distinctive. For example, Lucretius was not only primarily concerned with the hypotheses of atoms and evolution as scientific descriptions of the nature of things, he also was concerned with the right way to think and live in the sort of universe that he regarded as real, empirical and quantitative. Philosophy resembles science not so much in its aim as in its method. Both employ reason and evidence as means to the discovery of truth and the clarification of meaning. Both are forms of inquiry, other sciences being an inquiry into the laws of nature; philosophy an inquiry into the norms of criticisms. The faith of the philosopher, like that of the scientists, is that inquiry or research is worthwhile in a world that is constantly changing.

Philosophy as an Art

An art is defined as activity or production in which imagination and personal taste are more important than exact measurement and calculation.[6] Examples of arts include history, journalism, music and literature, etc. Although philosophy strives to take the approach of science, it is not taken as exact science because first, it is not involved in strict experiment, observation, measurement and calculations of results.

Seemingly, philosophy as love of wisdom is perfect knowledge and behavior, that kind of knowledge which helps men to choose which path to take in life, and not that which is abstract and far removed from vital human needs. This is why Cicero defined philosophy as an art of life. So, the aim of philosophical wisdom is not merely the satisfaction of intellectual curiosity, but mainly an enlightened life led with farsight, foresight and insight.[7] Thus, philosophy as an art involves the conviction and belief in the necessity for decision making and action on the basis of the acquired knowledge. And this decision-making and action; the final choice from alternatives (by which philosophy becomes complete) is an art that is based on insight and judgment.

The lives of people like Abraham Lincoln, Franklin Roosevelt, Wilson Churchill, Martin Luther King Jr., Nelson Mandela, and J.F. Kennedy, Charles de Gaulle, Mao Zedong, Joseph Stalin, Mother Theresa and Pope John Paul II, to mention but a few, are embodiment of this notion of philosophy as an art. Thus, philosophy at best is a combined approach/synthesis of some sciences, molded carefully with some pragmatic art. There is no better way in which to grasp the personal import of philosophy as an art than to study the life and character of Socrates. More than anyone else in the history of thought, he represents the very type and ideal of philosophy. According to Rader, Socrates' portrait drawn by the genius of Plato has for more than two thousand years been the standard by which all philosophy and philosophers have been measured. No one has loved wisdom more fervently than Socrates, and no one lived more truly according to the dictates of reason. In him, philosophy is not merely a way of thinking but a way of living – a way of life.[8] Thus, the beauty of philosophy as an art is expressed in the lives and works of reputable philosophers from the ancient to the contemporary period.

Universality of Philosophy

The question of universality of philosophy is a key one in the context of the objectives of this book. This is based on the ongoing controversies whether Africans as a people have a philosophy or not. This debate came on the heels and as a result of a variety of prejudices and misconceptions by Europeans in particular and the West in general about Africans, their thinking and traditional ways of life. Consequently, Africans were reluctant to think and write on "African Philosophy" side by side Greek, German, American, or English or Oriental philosophies. According to Barnabas Chukwudum Okolo, even African scholars themselves colored by the same prejudice most likely as a result of training and scholarship in Western philosophy and tradition for instance, entered the debate on the existence of African philosophy on a very skeptical note.[9]
They were not really sure of themselves. Prof. Henri Maurier kicked off his own debate in his inviting question: Do we have an African philosophy? He answered this question in the negative "NO! Not yet."[10] Some scholars and many professional philosophers concurred with Maurier's answer. Such professionals include Kwasi Wiredu, P. Bodunrin, and Erik Ruch. For Ruch, "what goes under the name of African philosophy is nothing more than cultural anthropology decked out for the occasion in the cloak of philosophical jargons.[11]

Scholars and professionals like C.S. Momoh, Onyewuenyi and Okolo argued in favor of the existence of African philosophy. According to L.C. Onyewuenyi, philosophy is a universal experience. Every culture has its own worldview.[12] Supporting this view, Momoh posited that in traditional and ancient African societies, there were generally medicine men, priests, rulers, military leaders and sagacious elders whose position in the group corresponds roughly to the position occupied by the scholars and thinkers in modern societies.[13]

Concluding this view, Nicholas Omoregbe opined that the ancient kingdoms of Africa might well have had her own Socrates, Plato, Descartes, Hegel, but unfortunately, due to the absence of records and writing in Africa until recent times, the philosophical reflections of African thinkers were not preserved and transmitted effectively.[14] So, if we regard philosophy as a worldview as well as worldwide phenomenon, Africa has a share in it.

The fact that God created all men equal and free and endowing them with inalienable rights (to life, liberty and pursuit of happiness) implies that God also endows them equally with the capacity to think and reason and to express emotions and feelings. Because the idea of rationality and reasoning belong to man as man, the interpretation of experience and criticism of worldviews are activities we all do at different levels of maturity. As a result, we can rightly talk of different types of philosophy; namely: Western philosophy, Oriental philosophy and African philosophy.

Philosophy as a Discipline: An Area of Study

Philosophy is a systematized body of knowledge. Along with other sciences it aims at replacing ignorance with knowledge. Hence, in some developed countries, like the United States and Britain for example, thousands of people are studying philosophy in one form or the other in a university or college.

In these countries, philosophy is introduced to new students through a number of approaches; namely:

By reading classical works by philosophers like Plato, Aristotle, Democritus, Epicurus and Lucretius, etc. from the ancient period, Augustine and Aquinas from the medieval period, Descartes, Locke, Kant, Hume, Hegel, Spinoza, Berkeley, Leibniz, Marx, Heidegger, Bentham, Mill, Rousseau, Hobbes, among others from the modern period. There are also works by contemporary thinkers.

It can also be introduced by studying the history of philosophy from the ancient period to the medieval period, the renaissance period, modern period and contemporary period. By studying the history of philosophy, we are immediately acquainted with the thoughts of great philosophers and how they fit into the time they lived and further development of such thoughts in time and space.

It also can be introduced by asking and answering rhetorical questions. Life is full of philosophical questions, ones that task the mind of anyone of age. This book is replete with such questions and your mind gives you notice whenever you come across them because they are questions that ginger the mind and evoke some thoughts about problems we all face in life. And answers to them are not lacking here.

It also can be introduced by way of dialogue and discussion with professionals and students in the field. Through discussions the terms, concepts and systems in philosophy are made known to students.

There is also the systematic approach which emphasized the study of certain philosophical problems and attempts made by philosophers to resolve the problems. This approach has been recognized by some scholars like William H. Halverson in his work, *Concise Introduction to Philosophy*[15] as one of the best for learners. For instance, the philosophy of atoms as the basic stuff of things can be traced from the ancient philosophers to modern philosophers and scientists.

In Asian countries such as India, China, Japan, Indonesia, Malaysia etc., thousands of people are also engaged in the study of both Western and Oriental philosophy through these approaches. Also, in Africa and other developing countries, thousands of people have joined the trend to read philosophy in their various universities and colleges. Research grants are being given to students by some agencies like the African Studies Association (ASA) and the Council for the Development of Social Science Research in Africa (CODESRIA) to carry out some research on contemporary philosophical issues and the outcome of these researches is superb. Many books and journals on philosophy are published all over Africa and other developing countries. So, philosophy is a recognizable area of academic study for the advancement of reflective thinking and interpretation of our experience.

Some scholars have tried to modify this view about philosophy as a discipline and a course of study when they said that one can teach about philosophy but cannot teach philosophy, that one can learn to philosophize, but he cannot necessarily be taught philosophy. But this has not affected the view that philosophy is an area of study, a discipline par excellence which has the widest scope and the oldest and longest running history in human thought. What they are saying is that the methods of philosophizing which are scientifically based can be taught, but the choice of action in relation to what is taught and learned, which is based on judgment, is an art that cannot be wholly taught.

Philosophy as a Profession

On the question of whether philosophy is a profession, many disagree that philosophy is a profession just as engineering, medicine and law, while some agree. One may want to ask, what is a profession? A profession is an occupation, especially one requiring advanced education and special training. Following this definition, we can say that there are thousands of people all over the world who have doctorate degrees in philosophy, and we know many who are professors of philosophy. Many of them are in the teaching profession and some are either in government or are special advisers to those in government. And for these people philosophy have served them as an occupation either permanently or temporarily.

The Sophists of ancient Greece paraded themselves as professional philosophers and they went about the Greek empire and beyond teaching people for a fee. The courses they taught their students included grammar, oratory, argumentation, semantics, hermeneutics, dialectics and sophistry.

Pythagoras (582 – 497 BC), the great mathematician and philosopher was born in Samos in Ionia. He opened a philosophical school in Croton, Italy, and was reputed to have been the first to use the word "philosophy." In reply to Leon's question as to what his vocation (profession) was, he called himself a philosopher – a lover of wisdom. He pointed out that since wisdom belongs in the strictest sense to him alone; a philosopher is not only a possessor of wisdom but also a lover of wisdom. Consequently, as a lover of wisdom, the guiding principle is not only to possess it but also to spread it.

Of course, wisdom does not dwell permanently in any human being rather it comes and goes like the waves of the sea. This necessitates the continuous search for wisdom through reason, experience, intuition and revelation, etc. When a person gets wisdom or is endowed with it, wisdom grows if the conditions are favorable and stays as long as possible. When it is active in a person, the person's actions and words are perfect; the person is on top of his game, but when it is passive the person fumbles and bungles and makes mistakes in whatever he is doing.

Joseph Omoregbe acknowledges the existence of professional philosophers as opposed to students of philosophy. We regard a professional philosopher as person who has been able to transmit and preserve his reflections by way of writing, in the form of books published by him or books on his ideas written and published by other people. Professional philosophers, more often than not, are philosophers who deliver lectures and conduct seminars and conferences on topical and burning issues of their time, and these lectures most often appear in journals of wide readership. Through this medium, reflections of philosophers are preserved and transmitted intact, and the philosophers whose reflections are so preserved and transmitted, are identified and known individually. In this way, it is possible to know the philosophers who are the original authors of certain ideas or views.

Europe and America were able to have many professional philosophers than other parts of the world because of their early advancement in the culture of writing. They were able to produce professional philosophers such as Socrates, Plato, Aristotle, Kant, Hegel, Descartes, Hume, William James, Karl Marx, Santayana and Russell to mention but a few. As a result of the preservation and transmission of their ideas through publications, we are now able to dialogue with them when we read their works. Descartes declares this fact in the opening chapter of his *Discourse on Method,* when he said, "the reading of good books is, as it were, to engage in talk with their authors, the finest minds of past ages, artfully contrived talk in which they give us none but the best and most select of their thoughts."[16] So, here we are asserting that professional philosophers are people who have published their ideas and efforts to give unity to human arts and sciences by their critical examination of the grounds of our meanings, values and beliefs. The guiding principle of these professional philosophers is that ideas should be published or they perish with their authors. The graveyard is regarded as the richest place on earth because many have died and gone to grave with their best and richest ideas.

There are, however, certain characteristics or criteria that confer a disci pline, an association or a person a professional status. These include:

• Formal education in a specialized body of knowledge: Philosophy is involved in this. Many great philosophers were products of renowned universities like Oxford, Harvard, Columbia, Cambridge, Yale, Princeton, etc.

• Unselfish service motive which every philosopher should have but not all philosophers have it.

• Controlled entry (not everybody who studied philosophy should be regarded as a professional philosopher, one should at least be an authority in the field maybe by having a doctorate degree or being a professor, or to have published up to seven articles in international/ professional journals)

• Universal ethical code: Philosophers are yet to have a code, such as patient-doctor confidentiality, client-attorney confidentiality.

• A sanctioning organization (some philosophers belong to national associations but they have not developed such organizations as a body with power to admit professional philosophers and disqualify any if he breaks a code of conduct either in writing or in administration as a public servant or government official). A good example of this kind of body was the 20th century Austria's Vienna Circle. This school or body of professional philosophers espoused logical positivism as thought current. Professional philosophers such as A.J. Ayer and Rudolf Carnap gained their prominence from this school that was founded by Moritz Schlick to build a master mind on topical issues and to encourage cross fertilization of ideas among professional philosophers in the western world.

Similar associations of professional philosophers exist in Oxford University, London and the University of Berlin Germany where professional philosophers such as Hegel and Karl Marx featured and rose to fame. It is on record that some philosophers never gained professional status because of their misdeeds while some professional philosophers lost their teaching positions or professional status because of the views and opinions they held and propagated. For instance, some professors that propagated Marxist views are regarded and treated as "Communist dogs".

MODES OF PHILOSOPHIZING

From the various definitions of philosophy, we have come to understand that philosophy just like any other science cannot be subsumed under one definition. Philosophy, on one hand, is such an easy notion that practically everybody thinks he has a good idea of it. But philosophy, on the other hand, is such a difficult notion, that perhaps, only the beatific vision can acquaint us with true and complete notion of the subject. This discipline is full of paradoxes; for one thing, one might see in philosophy the denial or a condemnation of a part or the whole of philosophical propositions/ statements as nonsensical and meaningless. This discipline therefore, cannot be subjected to a procrustean bed. It defies all streamlined definitions, for one reason that it is basic to human nature and human nature is inexhaustibly mysterious.

Again, philosophy cannot be defined with regard to genius and specific difference just as "man" can, for instance, were it an object, it could be described but unfortunately, it is not. What Thomas J.M. van Ewijk said of freedom could be said of philosophy, that it is "strictly speaking, impossible to be given a description or a definition."[17] Therefore, the combination of the different activities of philosophy will broaden our own idea of it. Hence, it becomes necessary for us to go into some modes or styles of philosophizing. Among others, we are interested in three modes of philosophizing, namely, the speculative, the prescriptive and the analytical-synthetic.

Speculative Philosophy

Speculative philosophy is a way of thinking systematically about everything that exists. When we read a book, look at a painting, or study an assignment, we are concerned not only with particular details but also with the order or pattern that gives those details their significance. The opinions reached on the matters are obtained through meditation and reflective thinking. According to C.D. Broad, the object of speculative philosophy is to take over the results of the various sciences, to add to them the results of the religious and ethical experiences of mankind and then to reflect upon the whole in attempts to reach some general conclusions as to the nature of the universe, and as to our position and prospects in it.[18] Speculative philosophy then is a search for order and wholeness applied not to particular items or experiences but to all knowledge and all experience. This is in line with the view of William James that philosophy deals with the principles of explanation that underlie all things without exception, the elements common to gods and men and animals and stones, the first whence and the last whither of the whole cosmic procession, the conditions of all knowing, and the most general rules of human conduct.[19] So, it deals with what is general.

Succinctly put, speculative philosophy is the attempt to find coherence in the whole realm of thought and experience. It tackles questions such as: what is good life? What is the relation between mind and body? Do we have free will? Is there a God? Is the world fundamentally material or spiritual? Can we know the ultimate nature of reality? What is the ultimate nature and relationship between time and space? Why is there something rather than nothing? These are some of the basic questions involved in the general interpretation of the universe.

Prescriptive Philosophy

This seeks to establish standards for assessing values, judging conduct and appraising art. It examines what we mean by good and bad, right and wrong, beautiful and ugly, truth and falsehood. It asks whether these qualities are inherent in things themselves or whether they are just expressions of our minds. The prescriptive philosopher seeks to discover and to recommend principles for deciding what actions and qualities are most worthwhile and why they should be so. And then, since prescriptive philosophy gives order and direction, it is said to be normative, that is to say, according to D.D. Raphael it makes provision for theories, doctrines, or ideologies and sets up norms or ideal standards for individuals, society and government, telling us what ought to be the case or what we ought to do.[20]

An example of prescriptive philosophy is found in Plato's epic work, *Republic,* a partial utopia which depicts an ideal society, with the purpose of criticizing the existing society and promoting the understanding of general social concepts such as justice, freedom, war, peace and security, etc. Prescriptive philosophy recommends proper definitions and usages of these value laden concepts in making value judgments. For instance, Socrates in Plato's *Republic* says that "good is the harmonious development of all parts of the soul under the control of reason, and that the good of the state is the harmonious development of all classes under the control of wise men." Plato himself raised the notion of philosopher king and asserted that there will be no peace in the world until philosophers become kings or kings become philosophers. Aristotle in his *Nicomachean Ethics* outlined the meaning of truth succinctly; to say what is, is and what is not, is not, that is to say the truth. Conversely, to say that what is, is not and what is not, is, is to lie.

Analytical Philosophy

Analytic or critical philosophy as it is often called, seeks to analyze and define our most fundamental and general concepts, such as "goodness," "truth," "reality," and "causation."[21] It involves the analysis and systematic study of meaning - the pursuit of meaning, so to speak. Those who adopt this interpretation such as Schlick, sometimes cite Socrates as an example of an analytic philosopher. In employing his favorite conversational method of giving questions and receiving answers, he is usually trying to analyze the meaning of some basic concepts, such as "knowledge," "freedom," "justice," "courage," "friendship" or "beauty." For Rader, this notion is narrow in the sense that Socrates and analytical philosophers in general not only pursue meanings but also truth. He concludes, however, that Broad was right when he said that analytic or critical philosophy includes not only the clarification of concepts but the resolute criticism of our fundamental beliefs.[22] Analysis as a philosophical method is most often complemented with synthesis. An embodiment of analytic philosophy would be seen when we highlight the analytic/synthetic method in philosophy.

BASIC USES AND FUNCTIONS OF PHILOSOPHY

Of what use, function, value or utility is philosophy? Who will benefit from philosophy? Why is the study important? Such are questions of significance which need due consideration. We shall answer from various perspectives.

Philosophy as a part of Natural Education Process of Rational Beings

First and foremost, philosophy begins from wonder and wonder is the feeling of a philosopher. Philosophy according to Titus Harold, Marilyn Smith and Richard Nolan constitutes a part of the natural being. The four-year-old child asks extraordinary questions, sweeping in scope and perception. "How did the world begin?" Or "what is everything made of?" Or "what happens to a person when he dies?" "Where do we come from and where are we going?" These are existential problems. He or she desires to know and there is need for guidance and explanation.[23] Philosophy is better placed than other disciplines to provide these explanations in all their ramifications. As a result, governments and institutions of higher learning are articulating philosophy of education for children that would assist early child education to make sure no child is left behind in holistic education that involves knowledge of self and the world.

Philosophy deals with the Basic Practical Problems of Life

For most of its history, philosophy has been committed to dealing with the basic problems of human life. Everyday human situations are characterized by diverse problems such as childlessness in marriage, divorce, abortion, suicide, war, hunger, disease, ill-health, illiteracy, unemployment, poverty, crime and racism to mention but a few. Philosophy gives insights and directions that can assist individuals and the society to manage these problems of life. These solutions can be found in philosophical books, journals, colloquies and magazines that came out of conferences, symposia, workshops and seminars organized for these societal problems.

Explication of Conceptual problems

Philosophy also is involved in the explication and clarification of terms for clearer meaning. It analyzes and defines concepts that are often misused by common sense, prejudice and the society. Such concepts include "goodness," "truth," "causation," "determinism," "freedom," "liberty," "love,"etc. These concepts are used by other sciences without explanation of what they mean, and tendencies exist for the miscarriage of their real meanings.

Philosophy attacks Errors and Contradicting Ideas

Philosophy undertakes to attack errors and contradicting ideas of any society. It highlights and denounces anomalies. Because of this, philosophy necessarily creates disturbances for those involved in these anomalies so that they could have a rethink and change for the better. Basically, we know that error can occur but error has no right to exist. Errors may occur as a result of what Francis Bacon in the Book 1of his epic philosophical work; *Novum Organum,* prominently called "idols of the mind." These idols are:

- Idols of the Tribe – these are deceptive beliefs inherent in human minds. Thus, men are prone to recognize evidence and incidents favorable to their own side or group (tribe, race or nation or religion). Here, errors arise from the abstractions and the tendencies to exaggerate, distort or extrapolate to give things imaginary qualities, and over time, facts and fiction will mix and form compounds of ideas.

- Idols of the Cave – human minds are like caves in which thoughts move about at random. These thoughts are modified by habit, temperament, training, environment and education. Within this cave environment, men tend to see themselves as being the center of the world. Thus, they stress their own limited outlook and interpret everything according to their interest.

- Idols of the Market Place – these errors arise from false significance given to words. Thus men are influenced by the words and phrases which they are familiar with in everyday discourse, but do not have deep knowledge of and as such they make fallacies out of them. For example, some people often are led astray or deceived by the use of emotionally toned words and phrases like military dictatorship, radicals, conservatives, progressives, independents, conspiracy theory, hidden agenda, ideology, democracy dividends, socialist, communist manifesto, imperialist expansion, capitalist exploitation, racism, etc.

- Idols of the Theatre - these errors arise from sophistry or false learning or miseducation. They could arise from our attachment to parties, creeds or beliefs, cults, fads, fashions, schools of thought in philosophy and science. These things which are like stage plays, lead men into imaginary worlds and biased conclusions. And because they come from learned men and celebrities, they are accepted by the masses without question. It is the function of philosophy to detonate these idols that lead to errors and contradictions.

Philosophy inspires Healthy Living

Philosophy inspires the wise to prudent action. It makes the gullible less credulous and hence less vulnerable. It causes the lily-livered to become stout-hearted. It gives courage, which is the strength of the mind. It gives knowledge that inspires confidence. According to Bertrand Russell, the chief value of philosophy is philosophic contemplation which liberates human beings from the thralldom of narrow hopes and fears. It does this not by encouraging evasiveness, and the use of defense mechanisms to evade responsibility. Philosophy does not make a person become introversive visionary like the case of James Ngugi's Njoroge, the hero of the first English novel from Kenya, *Weep Not Child,* who, besieged by the enormous problems of the moment, did nothing and made no effort to solve the problems but took refuge and relied only in the hope of a brighter tomorrow. Rather, philosophy encourages the formation of a master mind that is action oriented, smart, proactive and pragmatic in solving problems of the moment.

Thus, philosophy is opposed to any form of "cargo cult mentality"[24] – the tendency of inhabitants of a port city (or crude oil producing communities hosting multinational oil companies) to wait by the shore in vain hope that an imaginary ship with variety of goodies will one day dock for them to partake in the free goodies instead opting for hard work to earn a decent living and change the circumstances of their lives – a situation which Chinua Achebe decried in his book, *The Trouble with Nigeria.* Barack Obama made a similar remark that angered some Midwest voters in America when he said at a San Francisco fundraiser Sunday speech in 2008 that "our challenge is to get people persuaded that we can make progress when there's no evidence of that in their daily lives. You go into these small towns in Pennsylvania, and like a lot of small towns in the Midwest, the jobs have gone now for 25 years and nothing's replaced them. And they fell through the Clinton administration, and the Bush administration, (they fell through Obama administration too and as a result Donald Trump won the 2016 elections) and each successive administration has said that somehow these communities are going to regenerate and they have not. And it is not surprising then they get bitter, they cling to guns or religion (or hip- pop music or reggae music or alcohol or drugs or violence or crimes or their votes) or antipathy toward people who are not like them or anti-immigrant sentiment or anti-trade sentiment as way to explain their frustrations."

The statements by Ngugi, Achebe and Obama cannot be true of the entire population but they definitely reflect how some of us who are bereft of philosophy live in times of problems. We resort to all kinds of defense mechanisms that do not solve the problem. And we know that the easiest way of going about a problem is most often not the best way of resolving them and the tendency to follow the line of least resistance makes rivers and men crooked. One of the lessons we can drive from the seemingly hash views of Achebe and Obama among other things is that people should not see unemployment, poverty, diseases, infertility, misfortunes, etc., as the will of God or the will of government rather they should look for commonsense solutions and meaningful ways of solving these problems. Philosophy makes us aware that the will of God or the will of government has for ages been the refuge of ignorance, laziness, poverty, misfortunes and other vices. Lao Russell in her epic philosophical work, *God will work with you but not for you: A Living Philosophy* demonstrated the fact that God helps those who help themselves.

Philosophy enlightens Other Sciences

Philosophy is useful because it makes people broadminded. It expands one's perception and horizon. Most other sciences are narrow-minded. They do not give us a holistic view of the world and the purpose of man in it. This is seen often confessed by many scientists. For instance, Niels Bohr, 1922 Nobel Laureate, asserted that we can admittedly find nothing in physics or chemistry that has even a remote bearing on consciousness. Yet all of us know that there is such a thing as consciousness simply because we have it ourselves. Hence, consciousness must be part of nature, or more generally, of reality, which means that quite apart from the laws of physics and chemistry as laid down in quantum theory, we must also consider laws of quite a different kind.[25]

Following the same line of thought, Albert Szent-Gyorgyi, 1957 Nobel Laureate, Physiology and Medicine, confirms thus, "in my search for the secret of life, I ended up with atoms and electrons, which have no life at all. Somewhere along the line, life has run out through my fingers. So in my old age, I am now retracing my steps." Also, Thomas H. Huxley, a Biologist and Humanist said "it seems to me pretty plain that there is a third thing in the universe, to wit, consciousness, which ... I cannot see to be matter or force, or any conceivable modification of either ..."[26] Max Planck, one of the founders of Quantum theory asserts that "all matter originates and exists only by the virtue of a force which brings the particles of an atom to vibration and holds this most minute solar system of atom together. We must assume behind this force the existence of a conscious and intelligent Mind. This Mind is the matrix of all matter."[27] This Mind also could account for "Chance", the scientists' god of the gaps which they use to explain away anything they could not observe in their empirical investigations and experiments. Furthermore, the year 2013 was remarkable for the discovery of many planets outside the solar system, but scientists were consternated by a number of them that revolve around their star from a distance billions of light years away. This tends to throw doubts or better calls for further studies on the stipulations of the Big Bang theory and its use to explain stars and planetary formations. This discovery once again throws up the idea of design and the existence of a supreme Mind who could be responsible for this awesome arrangement.

Hence, the Quantum theory and the Big Bang theory cannot fully explain the universe as we now know it in 2016. In the light of the above revelations, philosophy should respond to science and technology to enlighten and direct them because as William Brett puts it, "the uncertainties of a whole technological civilization, which even as it wields its great technical powers, is unsure of its limits or possible consequences."[28]

Philosophy makes Leaders and Followers Insightful

Philosophy as an art of critical and systematic thinking deals a lot with clarification of ideas and concepts. This is very important for clear thinking and insight. It fosters a true understanding of issues. Critical vision and discernment involve reflecting over matters, i.e. going back to things. It is this going back to reality and seeing beyond superficial appearances that make somebody a philosopher, says Edmund Husserl in his phenomenology. Today, the motive of studying philosophy should include seeking answers to turbulent development problems, the lack of progress in some parts of the world and specifically backwardness in education, endemic ethnicity/racism, injustice, corruption, human right abuses, political marginalization, economic powerlessness, terrorism, over population, mass poverty and suffering in many countries including the advanced ones. Philosophy calls for a thoughtful examination and analysis of data and viewpoints on these facts of our lives. Our leaders should avail the opportunity provided by the existence of professional philosophers and their critical evaluation of information and conflicting beliefs, and use them to try to work out some systematic, coherent and consistent picture of our problems and their solutions. Philosophy gives a sense of direction and stimulates leaders to prudent action.

In many things of life, it is a fact that quantitative increases lead to qualitative change just as quantitative increases in temperature turns water to gaseous vapor. We can confidently assert that quantitative increases in philosophic knowledge were responsible for the qualitative changes in history when basic shifts took place in human thought, values and practice such as in the Greco-Roman civilization, the Renaissance, the Reformation, the Industrial Revolution, Information Technology and Globalization Era. For Jacques Maritain "philosophy reminds men of the supreme utility of those things which do not deal with means, but with ends, for men do not live by bread and vitamins and technological discoveries alone."[29] They also live by values and realities which are above time and worth knowing for their own sake. These things redirect the people to their self-realization.

MOTIVES FOR PHILOSOPHICAL APPROACH TO OUR PROBLEMS

Phoenix Wright suggests six motives for philosophical approach to our problems. They are:

Curiosity
By nature, man is a curious being and because of this he makes rea-

sonable inquiries about the meaning of things. This is confirmed by Aristotle in the opening sentence of his great work, *Metaphysics,* where he asserted "Man by nature desires to know."[30] Thus, philosophy seeks to provide man with the satisfaction that the understanding of the meaning of things would bring.

Symbolic Interest
Man has pronounced interest in symbols, varieties of forms, patterns and the arrangements which these patterns can assume particularly, linguistic symbols and various forms of meaningful language. Philosophy provides excellent occasion for the *homo loquens* - "the talking being" to get involved in hermeneutics and semantics to get the satisfaction of talking with one another (in dialogues about their problems) or in themselves (in contemplations) to explore the shades of differences and feel "the shock of contradiction and the harmony of synthesis."

Search for Meaning
Man lives in a vast complicated universe, and in the world which Fredrick Nietzsche intoned *"Requiem aeternam deo,"* and declared "God is dead."[31] For Nietzsche, God was killed by human scientific ingenuity and innovations and was buried in the church. So, in a world in which advances and automation of science and technology stand in sharp contrast with the failures of big governments, the crises of failed states, domestic and international terrorism, the individual finds it difficult to come to grips with the pressing intellectual and moral problems of life. Philosophy tries to reduce the anxiety of these multiplicities to a comprehensive and comprehensible pattern to create peace of mind for the individual in midst of crisis.

Drive for Completion
Man is a psychosomatic unity and prefers wholeness to partiality. Philosophy, being an all-embracing discipline, shows promise of the comprehensiveness and wholeness as we see in the body of this work. Philosophy gives something of everything than everything of something.

Drive to Solve Problems
Philosophy has always helped us to solve our problems as it makes us ever ready to analyze underlying assumptions, allow criticisms, imbibe tolerance and make informed decisions. These always facilitate solutions to daily problems.

Need for Inspiration
From age to age, philosophy has inspired people from different walks of life. It satisfies the desire to gain comprehensive insight, to see relationships, purify language, to stretch the imagination, to overcome contradictions and to be caught up in a vision of ideal possibilities. These are just a few of the motives. Many more are revealed in this work.

3

PHILOSOPHICAL METHODOLOGY
Types of Philosophical Methods

Philosophical Methods
A method is the way of doing something. It involves the techniques and procedures of investigation. It concerns the system and orderliness in a course of study. We study a discipline methodically when we approach it with a plan, work out its particular areas, organize the various bits of knowledge logically and bring out as many relationships as possible. Philosophical methods, therefore, designate systematic ways through which an ordered totality of critically-tested knowledge is acquired and built up.

It must be noted here also that the thing to be studied often conditions and determines the methods to be used. In other words, methods differ, because the various objects of study are different and as such they determine the proper methods to be used in the investigations. For instance, every philosophizing is a fresh discussion and, therefore, cannot be reproduced as such, while every scientific result can be reproduced using the same method and procedure.

Again, since philosophy does not in the strict sense deal with measurement and calculations, it cannot conveniently use the method of experimentation which an empirical science like chemistry uses. The aspects of reality which philosophy treats, e.g., general principles of being like determinism, freedom and moral responsibility, are neither quantifiable nor measurable in the laboratory. Another factor that determines the method to be used in a study is the way in which a person perceives the particular object to be studied. That is, whether the object of study is a matter for sense perception or that of deductive reasoning which transcends the sensible order. Thomas Aquinas paved the way for this distinction with his teaching on the three degrees of abstraction in human knowledge. Actually, he developed this view out of some of the insights of Aristotle. According to Aquinas, in addition to the abstraction proper to the physical sciences, and that which is proper to mathematics, there is also the metaphysical abstraction which considers the existent in so far as it is or has existence. Philosophy culminates in metaphysics which is the study of realities beyond the physical realm. Thus, the third degree of abstraction belongs to philosophy.

Kinds of Philosophical Methods

Numerous methods are available in philosophy for use. The method to be employed in any situation depends on the object in view and the philosopher concerned. Here, we shall consider some of these methods that are still in vogue.

Socratic Methods

Socrates was made popular by the methods he used in his philosophical inquiry. Melvin Rader described the Socratic Method as the art or process of "examining an idea, theory, etc., by question and answer between two or more people."[1] This Socratic Method is known to be of two kinds:

Socratic Ironic Method

Socratic irony is one of the well-known ancient methods of philosophy. The Socrates of the early dialogues typically strikes up a conversion with one or two interlocutors which eventuates in a question about the nature of some virtue or other: what is justice, what is piety, what is courage, what is truth or what is temperance? The interlocutor attempts an answer. Socrates then subjects the answer to critical analysis, usually showing that the answer is inconsistent with something else held by the interlocutor to be true or that the answer leads to some confusion or is plainly lacking in some respects. The Greek word for this pattern of questioning, responding and scrutinizing is "elenchus," and Socrates is a master in it.

Socratic irony as a philosophical method consists in cornering one's opponent in a discussion or debate/controversy with questions that make him or her choke in his or her own contradictions. By means of this method, one exposes the inconsistencies in another person's opinion through close questioning, while at the same time, feigning ignorance or pretending one doesn't know much about the issue in question. Socrates' questioning and teaching were characterized by the use of these ironies. He claimed to have a low opinion of his own knowledge and repeatedly asserted that he did not know anything. He believed that a wise man is he who knows that he knows nothing. And a fool is the person who knows nothing and does not know that he knows nothing. The possibility of error, ignorance or lack of knowledge should always make one to ask questions and the answers received clear one's mind. Through this, one would not advertise one's ignorance as knowledge or being oneself.

Questions and answers being used today in conferences and seminars and the benefits derived from them are traceable to their Socratic use. In conferences, sometimes more is revealed and achieved during the question-and-answer sessions than during the paper presentation. In the political arena, any news briefing by the president or governor or any other politician without the question-and-answer session annoys not only the journalists and newsmen, but also every other person expecting answers to nagging problems of the state.

Socratic Dialectic Method

Socrates was a town hall teacher who used to lecture in the city center of Athens, the capital of ancient Greece. Different caliber of persons, politicians, teachers and students came from surrounding small towns to listen to him and take lectures from him. He employed dialectics as his teaching pedagogy as opposed to the rhetoric method of the sophists. This is a mode of instruction by question and answer which Socrates used to elicit from his pupils truths which he considered to be implicitly known by all rational beings. Socrates used the method of andragogy to make his students active participants in his discussions. He saw them as adults who have reached the age of reasoning, and thus, he sits in their midst during this process of learning. The method of Socrates reduces to absurdity people's wrongly held notions or beliefs.

This method is opposed to sophists' pedagogic method which confines the listeners to a passive role in the process of learning. Sophistry only allows one to listen to the delight of the knowledge of the speaker who is either standing or sitting in front facing one, and most often than not reduces to absurdity notions we generally and rightly held as true and certain. The sophists taught and emphasized more on the power of oratory than the power of knowledge. For them, there is no certainty in knowledge for man is the measure of all things. There is nothing the mind cannot doubt.

Rader noted that the method of Socrates was not a product of chance but something borne out of a studious life style. Socrates studied under Archelaus, the first native Athenian philosopher, and he also was familiar with the teachings of the sophists – some humanistic philosophers and paid educationists who traveled from city to city in the ancient world. But preferring intellectual leisure to lucrative employment, he was too poor to take formal instruction from the sophists, whose "wisdom," moreover, he regarded as somewhat hollow. Socrates studied science, becoming familiar with the doctrines of the Sicilian Empedocles about cosmic and biological evolution, the theories of the Italian Alcmacon about the brain as the organ of mental life, the mathematical doctrine of Pythagoras and Zeno, and the theory of Diogenes of Apollonia that everything consists of "air." Socrates soon became disillusioned by the flat contradictions of such rival tenets and when one day he read in the book of Anaxagoras (the first important philosopher to live in Athens) that "mind" is the cause of the natural order. The concept struck him with the force of revelation. Reading on, he discovered that Anaxagoras introduced a cosmic mind to explain only the initial impetus and potentialities given to matter and then employed mechanical principles to explain the general structure of reality. Socrates, in contrast, vowed that he would try really to understand the mind and its place in the cosmos. Hence forth, his main endeavor was to search his own mind and the minds of his fellow citizens in an attempt to discover the essence of man and of goodness.[2]

Socrates nursed the sense of obligation and felt capable of the venture based on the fact that in Plato's *Apology* he saw it as God bidding and hence a service to God. This is consequent on the fact that he has been declared the wisest man by the greatest and most important oracle in Greece at the time, the Delphic Oracle. According to one legend, Chaerephon asks the Oracle at Delphi whether anyone is wiser than Socrates, and the surprising answer is that no one is wiser. Socrates was astonished and flabbergasted when he heard about the proclamation of the Delphic Oracle. According to Plato's Apology, Socrates asserted, "When I heard of the oracle I began to reflect: What can God mean by this dark saying? I know very well that I am not wise, even in the smallest degree. Then what can he mean by saying that I am the wisest of men? It cannot be that he is speaking falsely, for he is a god and cannot lie." So in the light of this, Socrates set out to prove the Oracle wrong by approaching those who are reputed to be wise and those who profess wisdom and asked them about virtues. The purpose according to Socrates is if anywhere, he could prove the Oracle wrong, he would be ready to point out to the Oracle its mistakes, and say, "You said I am the wisest of men, but this man is wiser than I am"

Socrates examined a number of men, first he started with a politician of great repute and knowledge, and he found out that though a great many persons thought that the politician was wise, and much more the politician regarded himself as wise, yet he was not wise. After conversing with and cross- examining the politician, Socrates thought to himself "I am wiser than this man: neither of us probably knows anything that is really good, but he thinks that he has knowledge, when he has not, while I, having no knowledge, do not think that I have. I seem at any rate to be a little wiser than he is on this point: I do not think that I know what I do not know." After the dialogue with the politician, Socrates went to other men reputed to be wiser than the politician and believing he is carrying out God's mandate and command in spite of making many enemies along the line he cross-examined and tested these men and found out that the men whose reputation for wisdom stood highest were nearly most lacking in it; while others who were looked down on as common people were much better fitted to learn.

During the entire investigation, Socrates cross-examined the poets of his time – the equivalent of the journalists, writers and authors of our time - and asked them questions on their works and he found out that some bystanders can talk on the works of these poets better than the poets themselves. Socrates realized that the poets write not much by wisdom but much more by certain natural powers and inspiration, like soothsayers and prophets who say many fine things but understood nothing of what they say. Also because of their proficiency in their poetry, the poets thought that they were the wisest of men in other matters too, while they were not.

Socrates also tested the artisans, if you like the engineers, lawyers, doctors and scientists of our days, and he found out they have real knowledge of their professions which of course Socrates did not have and they produce fine things but they made the same mistakes made by the politician and the poets for each of them believed himself to be extremely wise in matters of great importance because he was skillful in his own art: and this mistake of theirs threw their real wisdom into the shade. When Socrates had reduced each of them to confusion, he concluded that "the oracle was right."[3] In a way, Socrates knew he didn't know anything worthwhile, whereas others were wrong in thinking they know.

Nevertheless, the bystanders always thought Socrates was wise in any matter wherein he convicted another man of ignorance. But Socrates believed that only God is really wise: and by this oracle God meant a man's wisdom is worth little or nothing. Thus, Socrates did not think the oracle meant that he was wise. The oracle only made use of Socrates name and used it as an example, as though he would say to men "He among you is the wisest, who, like Socrates knows that in every truth his wisdom is worth nothing at all." For instance, from a star, billions of light years away, man and his knowledge and wisdom count as nothing at all. Man becomes an infinitesimal speck of the universe.

Socrates also confessed that some of his students who were sons of wealthy persons went out and tried this method testing others to know whether they are wise. Eventually, they came out with the same result that they found great abundance of men who think they know a great deal, but when they were taken, weighed and measured they were found wanting as they know little or nothing. The above method used by Socrates to prove right the Delphic Oracle portrays the dialectic method, the conflict of ideas that paves way for the reign of superior argument. It is the ancient pioneering effort for modern dialectical method concerning conflict of opposites, thesis and antithesis leading to synthesis as well as modern scientific hypothesis statement and testing. With the Null hypothesis as "Socrates is not the wisest man" the Alternative hypothesis as "Socrates is the wisest man." And samples of acclaimed wise men were taken and tested, and none was found worthy of the term wise. Hence, the Alternative hypothesis "Socrates is the wisest man" was taken to be true.

In essence, his technique for achieving his goal consisted in the artful use of proper questions so that by the help of clear inductive examples, he could induce those conversing with him to arrive at proper conclusions on their own and thus they do their own thinking and reasoning, instead of accepting conclusions on the authority of someone else. Through this procedure, he tried to bring his audience to the recognition of eternal, unchangeable essences of both virtues and things, thereby performing the function of a mental, intellectual and spiritual midwife. Socrates in pursuing this "mission" was trying to explore the human mind to know its nature and processes and its relationship with the external world of physical things. He wants to know about mental processing such thinking and reasoning, and what it means to be a rational being. Essentially, he wants to reach the truth by dint of question and answer, dialogue and debate. This give and take method of investigation by discussion, the conflict of ideas and opposites in the process are called "dialectic" or "the Socratic method". It is still the essential method used by philosophers and some other people like teachers, investigators, the police, lawyers, judges and administrators seeking to find out the truth about something. It may be carried on between two or more persons or within the mind of a single inquirer, as he puts questions to himself and wrestles with his answers.

On the essence of the Socratic Method, Rader holds that the objective of the individual who is involved in this exercise is to establish a definition, to fix in mind the essential reality of some basic value or property. Each proposed definition, is tested by a process of critical examination. Is it internally consistent? Does it fit the facts? Does it agree with what we already know? In formulating and testing the definition, the philosopher continually refers to the particular data of experience; but he examines the particulars as instances of a type and he defines the type - the "idea," "form," or "universal"– by establishing its significance in the particulars. The same thing happens when two or more people are involved. The process is also controlled by experience, and it is more of inductive generalization.

Apart from the intellectual and epistemological importance of the method, it is of great significance for healthy living in human society for the reason that the knowledge secured is necessary for making right choices in life. Unless we know what justice is, how can we possibly hope to act justly? Again, how can we love right if we do not have the correct meaning of love? The same applies to other things like: truth, peace, prudence, courage, hope, freedom, faith, wealth, happiness, knowledge, beauty, goodness, loyalty, holiness, kindness, etc.

The Socratic Method is often criticized for asking loaded questions, i.e., the type of questions which compel the person being questioned to give the kind of answers which the interrogator required to suit his purposes. Such questions are called leading questions in a law court, and no advocate willingly permits a counsel to use them while interrogating his client, because they make the client who can only answer "yes" or "no" to condemn and convict himself out of his own mouth. The questions of the prosecutor lead the defendant to the answer which the prosecutor needs to clinch his case.

However, for Socrates, the aim of the exercise is not merely to get definition of something like truth, justice or peace; perhaps the activity of joint inquiry itself is the aim; the examination itself is of value. It may be that Socrates finds value not only in getting at the truth, but also in looking for it in conversation. Essentially, Socrates thinks that instilling in his companions not only truth but the desire for truth was of paramount importance.

The Socratic dialectic is still being used today in symposia, seminars, conferences and lectures where discourse takes the center stage, question and answer follow. Hence, discussions have always been a way of solving problems. Great crisis, protracted war and conflict could be avoided by mere sitting and having a round table dialogue. Dialogues solve a lot of problems; they prevent wars, save lives, save businesses and avoid wanton destruction of property. Peace treaties are reached through dialogues. Thus, most solutions of problems are found through dialogues. The dialogue can be in the reflections of our minds or in discussions with others about the problem. We could also say that examination involving questions and answers has become the nucleus and back bone of modern educational system; many thanks to Socrates who first brought it to limelight as the best test as well as the true test of knowledge.

Modern Dialectic Method

Dialectics is a well-known philosophical method in the history of modern thought. It is a critical analysis of mental processes; art of logical disputation. It is usually a conflict in the form of logical dispute between innovators, progressives and conservatives or ruling party and opposition party. Literally, dialectics is the art of conversation. It is the practice of assessing the truth of an opinion by discussion or logical argumentation. Even though it was in use before Socrates, he was the one who gave it its classical form. He wanted to bring men to the essences of things through a gradual clarification of concepts. Plato's dialogues also propelled this effort further as they attempted to dig out the essence of things through a process of statement and contraction, and so prepare for the ascent to the primordial reality - the world of ideas. Thus, for Plato, dialectics is the method of metaphysics involving the third degree of abstraction.

The scholastic method used in medieval metaphysics was somewhat similar to dialectics. The disputations were conducted as colloquies or dialogues on diverse issues such as free will, reason, liberty, God, faith, soul and immortality, etc. Dialectics have the same character which determined the structure of the scholastic question. In each case, the dynamism of the *sic et non* (yes and no) propels thought forward. The scholastics or the schoolmen as they were then called employed dialectics in the production of epic treatises that still occupy a special place in contemporary thought such as Saint Thomas Aquinas' *Summa Theologica and Summa Contra Gentiles.*

In the modern period, dialectics struck its apogee and zenith in the philosophy of Hegel. Inspired by some of the insights of Heraclitus, the philosopher of evolution, revolution and change, Hegel developed the concept of dialectics further. In him, dialectics emerged as the Algebra of Revolution. The insight Hegel got from Heraclitus stems from the fact that Heraclitus was the first to put forward the idea that everything is in a state of flux; change is the only permanent feature of the universe of reality, and as such, men are fools to trust in the stability of their false happiness. For Heraclitus, you cannot step into the same water twice for fresh water is forever flowing upon you. He saw in discord and strife - the conflicts of opposites - the innermost essence of reality, and for him reality is change or becoming.

Hegel inherited this idea from Heraclitus, and went further to propose that the real is essentially becoming, which moves on from stage to stage in the triple pace of thesis – antithesis – synthesis. This, he called the dialectical process. He therefore opined that our thinking and reasoning too must proceed in the same way. The Hegelian dialectic is an interpretative method in which the contradiction between a proposition (thesis) and its antithesis (like the opposite) is resolved at a higher level of truth (synthesis). This is precisely why people are wiser after arguing than they were before they argued out a point with someone else. The pros and cons of an issue get synthesized at the end of an argument to the mutual enrichment of the two parties in the polemic. The resolution becomes another thesis and the process continues.

Hegel's dialectical method is based on his firm belief in absolute idealism. Hegel contended that "Berkeley is correct in maintaining that reality is spiritual but incorrect in maintaining that God is distinct from men and each spirit distinct from every other. Hegel maintained always that "the universe is an integrated system and all spirits are members one of another." This view of Hegel shows that reality involves total integration of being. The whole reality is a system in which each part is related to one another. In this relativity or relational position, no part can be understood in isolation just as a single line in a well-integrated painting cannot be understood and appreciated in isolation from the rest of the painting. Also, a single theorem in geometry cannot be understood in isolation from the geometrical system of which it is a part. Thus, for Hegel, to see things together, in their interconnection and unity, is to see them truly; to see things apart, as isolated, fragmentary and contradictory, is to see them falsely.[4]

Consequently, Hegel evolved a new kind of dialectical logic which would take account of the conflicts, continuities and gradations of reality. Some scholars based on the above facts have surmised and suggested that Hegel borrowed much of his dialectics from the Bible; the transition from the thesis to antithesis and to the synthesis is comparable to the transition from God the father of the Old Testament, to God the Son of the Biblical New Testament and God the Holy Spirit of the Acts of the Apostles as summed up in the beginning of Gospel of John Chapter 1:1-18.

The traditional logic following the theory of Aristotle, conceived opposition as the contradiction of a positive and negative: "X is Y" being opposed by "X is not Y." From this opposition, no new synthesis can spring. Hegel did not accept Aristotle's view of opposition. Hegel thought of the characteristic way in which argument develops. He conceived of opposition, not as the juxtaposition of a positive and a negative, but as the opposition of two positive terms, the thesis and antithesis which implicate, and yet in a sense, negate each other, their mutuality and opposition forcing us to reconcile them in a wider thought - construct (the synthesis). For Hegel, "in turn, the synthesis tends to become a new thesis, and the process begins anew. Thus, each new idea, not being the whole truth, is inevitably tainted with falsehood and must be gathered up and transformed in a more comprehensive whole." In contextualizing and concretizing the above theorem in the human society, "the contradiction and its resolution in the realm of thought are paralleled by a similar movement in nature and human affairs. Here, too, there are antithetical tendencies, each bent upon destroying its opposite, and producing a kind of crisis by its inordinate one-sidedness. The clash of these tendencies exposes the logical ridiculousness of each factor taken in isolation, and thus releases corrective forces which restore the balance."[5] In this way, the whole process leads on to more coherent and comprehensive state of equilibrium. These movements characterize what we call progress and development in the society.

The simplest way of understanding the Hegel's dialectical method is to see it from this point of view, namely: a problem as the thesis, reaction to the problem as the antithesis and solution to the problem is synthesis. And since every solution over time constitutes another problem or the basis of it, so the solution becomes another thesis and the process continues ad infinitum. Karl Popper was one of the critics of Hegel. He accused Hegel of being responsible for the rise and growth of contradictions like totalitarianism and fascism in Europe. For Popper, Hegel's method encouraged and justified irrationality like dictatorship of those in government or wanton civil disobedience and unrest in the name of conflict of opposites. Popper claimed that Hegel's dialectics and absolutism inspired the totalitarianism of the 20th century liberal and stable Europe. For Hegel taught that absolutism is the only true expression of reality. This literally juxtaposes absolute authority with freedom and civil liberty. And the outcome is usually conflicts and strife as freedom resists and wrestles with absolutism. But what Popper did not say is that Europe emerged from those anomalies and crises to become one of the most advanced and most stable parts of the world.

Immanuel Kant was another philosopher who applied the method of dialectics in his thought. In the third part of his *Critique of Pure Reason,* Kant proposed what he called *transcendental dialectics.* For him, dialectics means the attempt to determine or know objects beyond the limits of experience by the use of the categories and the principles of understanding. In Kant's view, the classification of sensible intuitions, performed by the intellect through its categories, does not attain perfect unity. It remains always in the world of phenomena, in a phenomenal series which extends itself indefinitely in space and time. Kant contended that within us, however, "there is a tendency to achieve a definite unification of phenomena, and as a consequence, there arise in us certain 'ideas' which serve as a point of reference and organization for the totality of phenomena."[6] These ideas that serve as the center of unification and convergence for all phenomena are three, namely; personal ego (which is the unifying principle of all phenomena regardless of their origin), the world and God.

Kant regarded these three supreme realities of traditional metaphysics as things that belong to the noumenal world as realities-in-themselves, super sensible and unconditioned beings – the unconditioned condition. Kant's transcendental dialectics attempts to investigate and unmask all knowledge of super reality or transcendental reality (i.e., personal ego or soul, the world and God) and sees them as a kind of deceptive appearance of things that are not there. This means the mind wrestles with these super sensibles and makes effort to know and understands them but it could not because they are beyond the powers of the mind. The mind is always conflicted whenever it tries to know the unconditioned condition. This makes metaphysics, which has these objects as an area of study look impossible and beyond human knowledge and clear understanding. This Kant's argument, which attacks and rejects the possibility of metaphysics or knowledge of transcendental realities, featured prominently in his work, *The Prolegomena of All Future Metaphysics.* So, Kant's dialectics tried to x-ray the nature of human knowledge and the limits of human understanding in order to answer the question, what actually can we really know about life and the world.

Dialectics as a method and as well the Algebra of revolution became a practical reality in the philosophy of Karl Marx and Friedrich Engels.

Before them, people have always dreamed of improving life, eliminating poverty and suffering, injustice and arbitrary rule, but the underlining principle for achieving this was not clear to them. They lack advocacy and affirmative action that would engineer change, start something or make things happen. It is this affirmative action that Marx discerned and offered in his dialectics.

For Marx, the principle of dialectics is traceable and can be found in historic conflicts that changed people's lives and the way things were done. Historical themes are replete with these endeavors made by different personalities that changed the status quo of people's lives. For instance, History accounts have it that during the *Third Servile War* (109 - 71 BC) in Ancient Rome, slaves rebelled against their masters, the slave owning aristocracy in the Roman Republic to regain their freedom. Spartacus of Rome was well known for leading such a rebellion against the lords and the ruling aristocrats. His effort brought freedom to many in his days and changes to the society as well. And he transformed himself from being a slave to a warrior and became a legend.

History is also full of accounts of conflicts and wars between nations to resolve issues. These wars, whether they are just or unjust, involved a kind of clash of opposites involving may be a just aggressor or an unjust aggressor against a nation. Dialectics does not presuppose or meant that war is good or is the best way of resolving issues. It only supposes that some wars are necessary means for reaching a synthesis, a higher level of development in a particular issue concerned. And so most often they are not freely chosen. It was a Roman army commander, General Vegetius, who said in Latin, "*Igitur qui desiderat pacem, praeparet bellum*" - if you want peace prepare for war. This war is regarded by many in our modern period as a necessary war for justice.

Dialectics or conflict of opposites is also seen in the past struggles between peasants and land owners. Peasants were known to have staged actions against landowners and forced them to change their obnoxious farm practices. Some landowners were even forced to give up some of their lands in a kind of land redistribution agreement or land for peace arrangement.

Conflict of opposites continued with the advent of industrial revolution and the coming of modernity in Europe and America as new forms of deplorable conditions emerged over time in work places. Workers were exploited by factory owners. They were not paid a living wage. The standard of living of the masses was poor while business owners lived in affluence. Many generations passed, but things did not improve; there was no progress and development in the Western world. The gap between the rich and the poor continued to widen in an alarming rate.

However, the first opportunity to change and improve things came with the emergence of literate and organized working class in Britain, France, Germany, America, Canada, etc. In these countries, the ability and the action of the working class – the most organized and politically conscious – to change the shape of things was spontaneous. The workers acted on the awareness that through changing a man's consciousness, his thoughts and views it is possible to change an unjust system. They tried to convince the rich to engage in a collective bargaining and to give up some of their wealth to the poor believing that social evil could be alleviated in this way but no remarkable result was being achieved in the process. Consequently, in many countries, workers struck and destroyed factories and machines to encourage collective bargaining and get improved working conditions from employers and business owners. Whenever workers matched their words with action, things took a turn for the better in Europe and America. Most often, when workers or the masses use civil disobedience, the nonviolent resistance and dialogue components of dialectics to seek for better condition of living much more is achieved as in the modern cases of Martin Luther King Jr. in America and Mahatma Gandhi in India.

Thus, history becomes one of struggle between the oppressed and the oppressors. This clash of opposites played a pivotal role in the transformation of ancient and medieval periods to the modern societies. Marx and Engels relied on this dialectical materialism, modern science and the experience of the international revolutionary movement to create a philosophy which reflected the interests of the working masses. For Marx and Engels, dialectical philosophy concerns self-development as an internal source of evolution, and hence for them, it is an instrument and a weapon for transforming the world.

This mode of thinking put into action led to the emergence of communism in the former Soviet Union, and socialism in countries like China and North Korea. For Karl Marx as "dialectical philosophy finds its material weapons in the proletariat – the working masses, the proletariat finds its spiritual weapons in philosophy."[7] According to him, history is nothing but the dialectical development of the human society from the ancient-feudal relationships to socialism and scientific communism.

In the contemporary society, conflict of opposites is reflected in workers' power of collective bargaining which more often than not enhances working condition and workers' welfare in particular and the society in general. It also is reflected in the affirmative action of civil societies which also help to create awareness and a new state of affairs in most of their endeavors. What is always a controversial issue is whether the synthesis that results after the clash of thesis and antithesis presents a better state of affairs than what exists at the thesis level. It is just like asking after colonialism are Africans better off? After the Iraqi war are the Iraqis or the world better off in terms of terrorism? Answers vary widely according to individuals and their perspectives.

Those who believe in the Modernist theory of development tell us that colonialism was a civilizing venture that was beneficial to African development, and that the present African underdevelopment is the result of bad governance and corruption which have eaten into the fabrics of African states. Those who believe in the Marxist theory hold a contrary view. For them and for many African scholars, colonialism and neocolonialism, that is, western imperialism and racism, are the root cause of African underdevelopment. Walter Rodney's monumental work, "*How Europe Underdeveloped Africa*" is an epic and a classical Marxist theory of African underdevelopment. His thesis in the work is quite magnificent and formidable and could make interesting reading to anyone who wants to know what actually happened to Africa.

In a wider sense, contemporary dialectics is identical with formal logic, which is the study of the forms and laws of thought as such. It is also regarded as the theory of the negation of the negation; the thesis is a negation (i.e. a problem) while the antithesis (a solution) comes to negate the problem to create normalcy, a stability that start up a new paradigm shift.

In periods of intellectual decline, dialectics has been misused to foster rhetoric and sophistries so that sometimes and in some respects dialectics also signifies sophistry. It lost much of its potency and importance in this area. Politicians employ sophistries to win votes in elections but after the elections the people would see the emptiness of such statements. It could be in form of slogans such as President Obama's 2008 slogans "Power belongs to the people, if you love your health insurance plan you can keep it." Yes, you can!

Again, dialectics as the algebra of revolution has no blue prints for *hic et nunc* – here and now implementation, and it lacks definitive procedure and results. But as a principle and fact of nature, the dialectics in conflict of opposites is still very much in operation in every human society, and most often it brings about a new state of affairs. It is the closest principle that explains and accounts for progress in any society. Politically, it is expressed in the operation of the ruling party and the opposition party in the Congress of the United States, the Parliament in Britain or any given state in the world that has effective opposition party and pressure groups. Civil rights groups and trade unions still use it in their collective bargaining with government to achieve specific objectives.

In fact, multinationals firms and big businesses like big media houses such as CNN, BBC, Time Magazine, Newsweek Magazine, Wall Street Journal and New York Times do not allow crises to go waste; they often use them for business. For many of them, crisis and anomalies are good for business. For instance, defense industries in the United States could get big contracts from Europe if they project directly or indirectly that the present 2014 annexation of the Crimea part of Ukraine by Russia is the beginning of revitalization of the former Soviet Union and the setting up of Eurasia by President Putin, and urge European countries to increase their defense budget and be ready for the coming conflict with resurgent Russia. In fact, dialectics as a principle is expressed in every conflict both violent and nonviolent. But taking advantage of a crisis or benefitting from it depends on a number of variables like the actors, space, time and matter. If one is able to handle these variables and manipulate them, one can be able to surf on any crisis and come out with something positive, as it is, making lemonade from a lemon.

Deductive Method/Intuitive Method

Generally, deduction is an argument in which conclusions are reached by reasoning from general laws to particular cases. This process of reasoning is used especially in logic and mathematics. In these disciplines, specific conclusions necessarily follow from a set of general premises.

Deduction is therefore an inference from the universals to a less universal or particular, as opposed to induction which is an argument that involves inference from particular instances to particular conclusion or from particular instances to general laws or conclusions. We cannot discuss deduction without talking about induction for they are like the two sides of a coin or better two rivers flowing in opposite directions.

In simple terms, inductive reasoning involves a transition from information about a given set of objects or situations to a conclusion about some wider and more inclusive set. Inductive reasoning is a kind of reasoning from samples to a general conclusion, that is, drawing inferences and conclusions from a given number of samples. Sometimes, it is experimental and empirical, and hence it is a valid method for science but not for philosophy. It is widely believed among philosophers that deductive method is the only really reputable mode of reasoning, for it is the only strict method in which the conclusion follows by logical necessity from the premises. According to Rene Descartes, "there are two ways by which we arrive at the knowledge of fact namely; by experience and by deduction."[8] Some examples of deduction include:

All trees can be cut down. Oak is a tree. Therefore, Oak tree can be cut down. All men are mortal. Socrates is a man. Therefore, Socrates is mortal.

The two conclusions above "the oak tree can be cut down" and "Socrates is mortal" all followed necessarily and logically from the two premises before them. This means the conclusions are deduced or inferred from the premises necessarily.

On the other hand, an example of induction is seen in the following estimation by the Environmental Protection Agency (EPA) and Chevy Volt production manager that the first samples of Chevy Volt tested for fuel efficiency show that each car does 35 miles per gallon (mpg) on city/ 40mpg on highway gas. Second samples tested also show that each car does 35 miles per gallon on city/ 40mpg on highway gas and the third 120 samples of 2015 Chevy Volt show that each car does 35mph on city/ 40 mpg on highway gas. Therefore, it is our knowledge that every Chevy Volt will do 35mpg on city/ 40mpg on highway gas. It is induction if from the few samples of Chevy Volt tested; a general conclusion on gas efficiency is drawn for all Chevy Volt produced during the year 2015 and beyond.

William Whewell (1794-1866), a British philosopher, scientist and educator, drew a comparison between induction and deduction to bring out their clearer meaning and differences. According to Whewell, "it has been said that inductive and deductive reasoning are contrary in their scheme; that in deduction, we infer particular from general truth; while in induction, we infer general from particular: that deduction consists of many steps, in each of which we apply known general propositions in particular cases; while in induction, we have a single step in which we pass from many particular truths to one general proposition." Furthermore, Whewell said that contrary to the above notion of deduction and induction, the two are the operation of the same mind traveling over the same ground. According to him, deduction is a necessary part of induction. Deduction justifies by calculation what induction had intelligently guessed. Induction recognizes the core of truth by its weight; deduction confirms the recognition by chemical analysis. Every step of induction must be confirmed by rigorous deductive reasoning, followed in such a detail as the nature and complexity of the relation (whether of quantity or any other) render requisite. If not justified by the supposed discoverer, it is not induction.

Rene Descartes was one of the greatest protagonists of deduction as a method of philosophy. In his *"Rules for the Direction of the Mind,"* Descartes asserts that "in any subject we propose to investigate, our inquiries should be directed, not to what others have thought, nor to what we ourselves conjecture, but to what we can clearly and perspicuously behold and with certainty deduce; for knowledge is not won in any other way."[9] So for Descartes, all knowledge is based on two mental processes, intuition and deduction. Intuition for him is not the fluctuating testimony of the senses, not the misleading judgment that proceeds from the blundering constructions of imagination. Rather, he sees intuition as the conception which an unclouded and attentive mind gives us so readily and distinctly that we are wholly free from doubt about that which we understand. Succinctly put, intuition is the undoubting conception of an unclouded and attentive mind, and it springs from the light of reason alone. Descartes concludes that intuition is more certain than deduction, in that it is simpler, though deduction, as we have noted above, cannot by us be erroneously conducted. Thus, each individual can mentally have intuition of the fact that he exists and he thinks; and that the triangle is bounded by three lines only and that $2 + 2$ amount to the same as $3 + 1 = 4$.

Descartes went further to explain why we have besides intuition taken to deduction as a supplementary method of knowing. He expressed the view that by deduction we understand all necessary inference from facts that are known with certainty. He said we could not avoid deduction because many things are known with certainty though not by their selves evident, but only deduced from true and known principles by the continuous and uninterrupted action of a mind that has a clear vision of each step in the process. It is in a similar way that we know that the last link in a long chain is connected with the first, even though we do not take in by means of one and the same act of vision all the intermediate links on which that connection depends, but only remember that we have them successively under review and that each single one is united to its neighbor, from the first even to the last.

Descartes also distinguished mental intuition from deduction. For him, the difference lies in the fact that in the concept of deduction there is a certain movement or succession while in that of intuition there is not. Furthermore, deduction does not require immediately presented evidence like intuition possesses; its certitude is rather conferred upon it in some way by memory. We must acknowledge at this point that Descartes not only sees intuition as a source of knowledge but also as a method of attaining certainty in knowledge, and thus, it is a foundation for deduction.

However, Henri Bergson's conception of intuition differs slightly with the view of Descartes. The word "intuition" which is derived from the Latin word *"Intuere,"* means to look at. And here, the looking or directness of the insight is its fundamental mark and characteristic. Bergson agrees with Descartes that intuition is a method of attaining knowledge. But Bergson conceives it in contrast as "the direct apprehension by a knowing subject of himself and of his mental states, or of anything with which he is immediately acquainted."[10] For Bergson, intuition is more akin to sympathetic imagination than to abstract reasoning, and valued more for its own sake than as a foundation for deductive inference. Bergson sees it further as a realization of the real rather than the fictitious. The position of Descartes on intuition is that it is the immediate grasp of truths, for example, that three men are more than two men. Also, as a source of axiomatic truths, intuition provides the premises from which deduction draws by a process of logical inference, the conclusions which necessarily follow.

John Locke tends to agree with Descartes' position on intuition. Locke sees intuition as the instance when the mind perceives the truth just as the eye dots the light only by being directed toward it. However, the greatest criticism of Descartes on intuition was Charles Peirce. He rejected Descartes' individual intuition, or "clear and distinct perception," as the test of truth and method of attaining certainty in knowledge. Peirce says this substituted or removed the social criterion of truth i.e. the other minds that may have something different. This is to say that other people may not be in agreement with what an individual mind perceived through intuition to be true.

Again, Descartes' asserts that intuition is the individual mind's immediate insight into self-evident truth and as such it is the ultimate source of knowledge. Peirce has objections to this view of Descartes. This is because Descartes' assertion involves a two-term relation between the knowing mind and the known truth, and hence it is a relation that takes no account of other minds or other truths. Succinctly put, we can say that Descartes did not take into consideration the "third term" relation, that is, the social criterion of truth and the relationship of one truth with other facts known to be true.

However, it also can be argued that if the grasp of intuited truth would depend upon the agreement of other minds, or upon connections with other truths, it would lose its immediate and intuitive character. What guarantees the reliability of intuition is not only its immediacy but its clarity.

Still, Peirce insisted that any interpretation of inquiry based on Descartes' notion of intuition is radically false. According to him, Descartes failed to distinguish between an idea that seemed clear and one that really was so, or a proposition that seemed self-evident and one that really was so. Peirce remarks that philosophers have notoriously disagreed about what really is clear or self-evident. Hence, the appeal to intuition simply results in assertion and counter assertion. Peirce says to assert as Descartes did, that whatever is clearly and distinctly perceived is true is to abandon all tests of truth beyond individual opinion. He concludes that "ideas" moreover, "may be ever so clear without being truth" – a fact Descartes apparently did not grasp.

Rader summarized Peirce as proposing a quite different approach to truth and clarity. First, Peirce maintained that "the way in which to clarify the meaning of an idea or proposition is to envisage its practical consequences. We establish clear meaning by testing an idea in use - by tracing out its concrete application and consequences rather than by intuitive inspection or abstract definition."[11] But we know that not every idea can be tested in such a way. Some ideas of value such as immortality of the soul and goodness of God cannot be subjected to concrete test and application but we still know they are true ideas.

Secondly, Peirce contended that truth is established by public agreement rather than private insight - and not just the agreement of ignorant minds but the agreement of qualified investigators converging towards an ideal limit of accuracy and objectivity. The ultimate test of truth is that it is verified by facts open to inspection and admitted to be such by all qualified observers. So, as long as intuition remains the object of a single individual's perspective and is not submitted to the test of social verification, there is nothing to guarantee its reliability. "Truth is public," Peirce concluded. But we still believe that there may be what individuals could regard as private truth, that is, things that work for them which may not work for other people. Individual differences are a fact in many things of life. The role of the individual in the acquisition of intuitive knowledge can never be denied.

Thirdly, Peirce denied that we "ever grasp ideas and statements in isolation and immediately discern their truth or clarity."[12] For him, thinking is fundamentally contextual - we understand things when we relate them to other things; we connect the immediately given with the non-given. Peirce concludes that even a very simple perception, such as your awareness of "this moment," involves such contextual interpretation. In that you are aware that it is this moment, a particular instance of a universal and you are aware that it is this moment only because it stands in contrast to a moment ago, which you now remember, and the next moment, which you anticipate.

According to Rader, Peirce reaffirms in his theory of inquiry that we can "establish the truth of statements only by fitting them into the context of our beliefs and of socially verified perceptions and judgments."[13] So for him, the discovery of truth should take the experimental, social and contextual approach instead of the intuitive individualistic and isolationist approach of Descartes.

Before we conclude, we want to remind the reader that further attacks on the Cartesian method by Peirce would be discussed under Rationalism as a school of thought in philosophy. Again, we must state clearly that Peirce attacks on intuition and deduction could not be said to have dismantled intuitive and deductive method as a source of certain knowledge. This is because evidences abound to support intuition and deduction both in the sciences, mathematics and human experience and we should not tamper with evidences or facts because they are sacred. Rather, Peirce's criticisms appear to sharpen intuition as one of the unique foundations of certainty in knowledge.

Analytic Method and Synthetic Method

The word "analysis" means to examine something in order to learn what it is made up of. It involves splitting up a sentence (or a concept, or an idea) into its grammatical parts with the motive of studying in order to learn about it. Analysis is the process of detailed examination of a physical whole or an abstract whole in order to discover its meaning and essential features. In a similar sense, analysis is the separation of a book, a character or a situation, etc. into its parts and possibly ends with the passing of comments and judgments not only on the parts but also on the whole. In essence, to analyze a thing is to break it down to its constituent parts in order to determine their relationship and value.

As a philosophical method, analysis signifies and involves the method of mental division of a whole - either an actual whole or some mental construct - into its components. In this way, the parts which at first are known implicitly in their undivided unity, are singled out and known explicitly. To a great extent, 20th century philosophers, chiefly English and American, employed the analytic method. Their philosophy came to be known as analytic philosophy.

However, as a method, analysis is philosophically neutral in the sense that it can be used to clarify and often support quite varied philosophical positions. Some philosophers who rely on the analytic techniques insist that the philosopher must go beyond mere analysis and aim at synthesis. For them, analysis should pave the way for synthesis. As a result, views are varied as to what analysis should target. This is seen from their different conceptions of analysis as a philosophical method.

For Bergson, "analysis is the operation of the mind which reduces the object to elements already known, that is, to elements common both to it and other objects."[14] To analyze, therefore, is to express a thing as a function of something other than itself. All analysis is thus a translation, a development into symbols, a representation taken from successive points of view from which we note as many resemblances as possible between the new object which we are studying and others which we know already. In his estimate, Bergson says, analysis in its eternally unsatisfied desire to embrace the object around which it is compelled to, multiplies without end the number of its points of view in order to complete its always incomplete representation, and ceaselessly varies its symbols that it may perfect the always imperfect translation. Bergson concludes that analysis can go on ad infinitum (to infinity).

Wittgenstein, Gottlob Frege and Bertrand Russell were among the philosophers who were very much interested in the analytic method. According to Gilbert Ryle, it was the analysis of Wittgenstein, who studied under the tutelage of Frege and Russell, of what it is to make sense, that is, to be true or false, that led to the famous principle of verifiability, by which the logical positivists ostracized as nonsensical, the pronouncements of metaphysicians, theologians and moralists.[15] The logical positivists like Rudolf Carnap, A. J. Ayer, M. Schlick, etc. deriving their ideas also from David Hume, tried to enunciate and illustrate a theory of verification and meaning that provided a foundation for subjectivist ethical conclusions. Their argument runs as follows: For a statement to have cognitive truth or meaning, it must be either analytic or empirically testable. If the statement is analytic, it must be confirmed or unconfirmed by the test of logical consistency, and it then has logical meaning. Examples include the propositions of pure mathematics and formal logic. If the statement is empirical, it is verifiable by observation and it then has factual meaning. Examples include statements of fact of the empirical sciences. To understand a factual statement is to know how to obtain evidence for or against it. When there is no conceivable way to find such evidence, the statement is factually meaningless.

In the writings of Kant, the analytic method is epitomized. Here, analysis is seen as the separation of a concept from another that contains it. In Kant's words, "we need to distinguish two kinds of judgments or statements: analytic, in which the predicate merely analyses the subject;

and synthetic or amplifying in which the predicate adds something to the subject."[16] Kant illustrates these with examples. According to him, if A is the subject of a statement and B is the predicate, there are two choices. If B is contained in A, the statement is analytic; If B is not contained in A but is related to it otherwise, the statement is synthetic or amplifying. Kant continues and asserts, "If I say, "all bodies are extended," this is an analytic statement or judgment. I need not go beyond the very idea of "body" to find the idea of "extension." Still more, a square has four angles is an analytic statement. The angles which are implicitly contained in the square are made explicit as the predicate of the subject "square." This is said to be analytic, because the predicate from the beginning is not only thought of as belonging to the concept of the subject, but it is necessarily deduced from the content and so represents an "essential characteristic" or a "property" of the subject. Again, a proposition which is necessarily true by reference to its meaning alone, being independent of fact or experience is considered analytic, e.g., all spinsters are unmarried or this cripple is lame. The predicate does not give any new information which the subject does not already embrace.

On the other hand, synthesis means "putting together." It is the process of combining objects or ideas into a complex whole. In Kant's Critique of Pure Reason, synthesis is seen as the unification of one concept with another not contained in it. A proposition is termed synthetic when it has a truth value that is not determined solely by virtue of the meaning of the words, as in "all men are smart." The idea of smartness is not contained in the notion of men. In the same sense, it must be noted that if we say, "all bodies are heavy," the predicate "heavy" is quite different from what I think in the idea of "body" as such, and the addition of this kind of predicate to the subject makes the statement synthetic.

Thus, synthetic or amplifying statement is the opposite of analysis and its necessary completion. By means of synthesis a complex concept grows out of basic ones. Unlike analytic judgment, a proposition is referred to as synthetic judgment when the predicate adds something to the notion of the subject. This new element is not something already embodied in the notion of the subject as in the case of analytic judgment. If the predicate is added on the basis of experience and observation, the judgment is termed "synthetic a posteriori", but if it is added independently of experience, but on account of insight or reason that flows from the content of the subject, it is termed "synthetic a priori."

We can illustrate the above two kinds of judgment thus:

    analytic ====== a priori (Knowledge based on reason alone)

    synthetic ====== a posteriori (Knowledge based on experience alone)

Hume's epistemology recognizes this classification of judgments. Hume and Kant are in agreement that analytic judgments do not give us any new knowledge of reality. They are only expressions of what is already there in the concept of the subject. Hume and Kant are also in agreement about the existence of synthetic a posteriori judgments. According to Hume, these are judgments that deal with nothing else than that which our senses provide us. Kant, went further to affirm the possibility of a third kind of judgment, namely; judgments which are both synthetic and a priori - that is to say, judgments where the predicates state something about the subject that is not already contained in the concept of the subject, and where that which is predicated is nevertheless necessarily true, is necessary and universally valid. For Kant, the third type of judgments that can be made is synthetic a priori. For Kant, it has the most certain knowledge the human mind is capable of getting for man.

This knowledge is based on both reason and experience as shown in the diagram below.

    Analytic====// a priori

             //

    Synthetic //==== a posteriori

By maintaining that there are synthetic a priori judgments as seen in the above illustration, Kant affirms ipso facto that knowledge cannot consist exclusively in the receiving of sense impressions. For him, any judgment or a report about sense impressions we have received (i.e., an empirical judgment or a judgment of experience) can only be synthetic a posteriori propositions. And synthetic a posteriori statements cannot be universally true or necessarily true. This is because the statements are space and time determined. But, in any case where there are judgments that are both synthetic and a priori, it follows as Kant says that even if the knowledge begins with sense experience, it does not come exclusively from it. Or to put it in another way, even if sense experience is a necessary condition of the knowledge, it is not a sufficient condition. Among those judgments that are synthetic a priori, include, according to Kant mathematical judgments. An example is the mathematical statement that says: $7 + 5 = 12$. First of all, this mathematical proposition is a priori (i.e. universally valid and necessary, and therefore independent of verification by experience), for if a man knows that he had seven items and knows that he has just got five more, then he does not need to count them in order to assure himself that he now has twelve in all. If he were afterwards to count them and come to a result other than twelve, no one would take this as proof that $7 + 5$ are not after all (or in any case not always) 12, but that there were not seven to begin with, or that he did not in fact get five other items but some other number instead, or that he had counted incorrectly. Secondly, this judgment is synthetic, for the predicate "12" is not contained in the subject "$7 + 5$." This latter concept contains only the notion that these two numbers shall be added but contains nothing as to what the result is. Hence, the above mathematical statement is a synthetic a priori statement.

As a further illustration of this point, Kant cited the proposition from geometry that "a straight line is the shortest distance between two points." This statement is a priori, for it would be a misunderstanding to attempt to verify it by measuring; we know that the proposition is correct independent of any possible measurements. If by measuring we were to discover that it is not the shortest distance, we would not take this as evidence that we had discovered an instance where a straight line is not the shortest distance. We would regard it as evidence either that we had not measured correctly in the first place or that it was, after all, not a straight line. And the judgment is synthetic, because the concept "straight" does not contain anything about distance.[17]

Kant tried to show from the above that analysis as a philosophical method should be complemented with the method of synthesis. And the best method is one that involves reason and experience. This is the method that gives certain knowledge. The implication is that form (reason) without matter (experience) is empty and void; while matter without form is blind. After determining the three kinds of judgments we can possibly make about the world, as we have seen above, namely; judgment based on experience – a posteriori, judgment based on reason – a priori, and judgment based on experience and reason – synthetic a priori, Kant went further to use these judgments to assess the possibility of gaining certain knowledge from the sciences as we know them. Thus, in his book, *Critique of Pure Reason*, the assessments were done as follows:

Transcendental Aesthetic

Kant investigates the elements of sensible knowledge with reference to a priori forms of space and time. He wants to find out the contribution of sensation to the act of knowing. He identified space and time as the form of appearances as well as the contribution of sensation to cognition. But Isaac Newton asserts that space and time have real existence, that is, they exist independent of our awareness. The aim of transcendental aesthetics is to prove mathematics as perfect science. In mathematics, reason interlocks with experience to produce exert knowledge.

Transcendental Analytic

This is an inquiry into the reality of intellectual knowledge. It examines the means by which the mind categorizes data from sense experience. For Kant, the subject inherently possesses the underlying conditions to perceive spatial and temporal presentations. Kant sees space and time as the limits within which appearances can count as sensible. Thus, the object of transcendental analytics is the physical world and its scope is the justification of the natural sciences especially "pure physics" - mechanics - as a perfect science that does not go beyond space and time in its stipulation. Kant rejected the conception of space and time in Aristotle as well as the Isaac Newton's notion of space and time. But, a hundred years after the publication of Kant's *Critique of Pure Reason*, Albert Einstein gave the world a new notion of space and time. In Einstein's theory of relativity, space and time become space-time relation. Einstein findings tend to support the statements of Kant on the concept of space and time; even though Bertrand Russell refuted this idea. Einstein went further than Kant to give the relation between space-time some observable and verifiable footings. Einstein avoided the thing- in-itself of Kant which is neither observable nor verifiable but which for Kant is the cause of that which appears in space and time.

Transcendental Dialectic

This has for its object that reality which lays beyond our experience, namely, the essence of God, the essence of man and the essence of the world. Kant reduces these objects of traditional metaphysics to "ideas" about which reason fruitlessly revolves without hope of ever arriving at any definitive result and knowledge except on the moral level. Thus, Kant discussed the nature and impact of this morality on man in his *Critique of Practical Reason*. According to him, the two greatest realities or wonders are: the starry heavens above and the moral law below. Thus, it appears for Kant the existence of God can only be accepted on moral ground.

Phenomenological Method

The word phenomenon has to do with things that appear to or are perceived by the senses. A phenomenon can be a remarkable person, thing, happening/event, etc. Phenomenology as a method of inquiry was originally founded by Edmond Husserl as a movement that concentrated on the detailed description of conscious experience, without recourse to explanation, metaphysical assumptions and traditional philosophical questions.

In his works; *Philosophy of Arithmetic* and *Logical Investigations*, he criticized the methods of the past and then philosophers as inadequate source of certain knowledge. In the first part of his second work known as *Prolegomena of Pure Logic,* he criticized psychologism and relativism from an intellectualist and objectivist stand point as courses that do not give certain knowledge. In his later book: *Ideas pertaining to a Pure Phenomenology and Towards a Phenomenological Philosophy*, he gives phenomenology the status of "first philosophy" and is related to the study of knowledge in general. Like Descartes, Husserl sought for truths on which all other human knowledge rested. He often refers this unshakable foundation of human knowledge as the *"Archimedean Point."* It was Archimedes who demanded a fixed and immovable point in his popular request, *Da mihi locum movebo terrae stantes* "Give me a place to stand and I will move the earth."

For Husserl, the situation in philosophy during the 19th century was an impasse between realism and idealism. Both sides seemed to have compelling reasons on their sides; the idealist in his insistence that we never get beyond mind since every object known to exist is known through consciousness; the realist urging and asserting the conviction of common sense that we are creatures of a world that quite clearly exists independently of human consciousness. Husserl felt that what was needed was a *"third way"* out of this impasse between idealism and realism. The Third Way has to be a fixed and immovable point. That Third Way has to be the discipline of phenomenology which would be a rigorous and purely descriptive study of what was given in experience without making any metaphysical postulate in the fashion of realism and idealism. Such metaphysical speculations, as Husserl puts it are to be "bracketed," that is, simply set aside though not declared meaningless, as the positivists did.

For Husserl, instead of metaphysical speculation, and the incessant and fruitless dialectic that ensues from such speculation, let the philosophers turn to the things themselves to see what it is that is really given in experience when we scrutinize without any obscuring and empty preconceptions. Philosophy is supposed to be descriptive rather than dialectical. Where then does the process of this scrutiny begin? According to Husserl, the ultimate legitimate source of all rational statement is being or as he puts it "that prime consciousness which presents the giving immediately."[18]

It is imperative we get to things themselves; that is the first and fundamental rule in the phenomenological method. "Things" are simply taken to mean whatever is given, that which we "see" in consciousness, and this "given" is called "phenomenal" in the sense that it appears to our consciousness. The world indicates that there is an unknown thing behind phenomena; but such an unknown does not come into question for phenomenology which is content to start with whatever is given to the consciousness without trying to decide whether this given thing is a reality or an appearance – at least, it is there, it is given. Hence, phenomenological method is neither deductive nor empirical; it consists in pointing to what is given and describing it. It neither explains by means of laws nor deduces from any principles, instead it fixed its gaze directly upon whatever is presented to the consciousness, that is, its object at any particular moment.

Consequently, the sole direction of phenomenology is towards the objective, and although the activity of a subject can itself become an object of investigation in its own right, it is neither this activity nor the subjective concept which immediately interests the phenomenologist but rather what is known, doubted, loved, hated and so forth. Even in the case of fancy, the act of imagination must be distinguished from what it imagines; when we imagine a golden mountain, for example, this golden mountain is quite distinguishable as an object from our mental act. Similarly, the number 2, a figure or a circle and so forth are objects and not mental acts.

For Husserl, every sensible individual object possesses an essence. The proper object of phenomenology is essence (*eidon*) of things. It has to be attained by what Husserl calls *Epoche* - the suspension of judgment. This means that the essence of things can be attained when we bracket certain elements of what is given by not giving any attention to them. The *Epoche* can be historical when it sets aside or reduces every philosophical doctrine of the past. After this, the next to be bracketed or reduced is the individual existence of the object in question (this is called the eidetic reduction) since it is the essence which phenomenology is searching for. Husserl's phenomenology culminates in his transcendental reduction. This consists in not only bracketing existence but also everything that is not a correlate of pure consciousness. All that remains of object after this is the essence of the object.

Paul Ricoeur, another phenomenologist posits three clearer progressive steps in the phenomenological method. The first procedure is the phenomenological description which consists in the analysis of the language or cultural heritage of a given people (i.e. the reality) as disinterestedly and dispassionately as possible. The second phase is the transcendental phenomenology which is an interpretation of the reality as one sees it. The third step is philosophy of the reality as one sees it. This is the philosophical reflection, which involves existential personal reflection, an appropriation of the results of the hermeneutic recreation of event arrived at in stage two. In other words, the philosopher makes the interpretation his or hers and applies or uses it when necessary.

Eclectic Method

Eclectic comes from the Greek word, *eklektikos* meaning selective. It means choosing and accepting freely ideas or things from various sources and putting them together and blending them to produce a consistent whole. For the *New Encyclopedia Britannica,* it is a practice of selecting doctrines without adopting the whole parent system. It is the attempt of combining concepts to form a pattern of philosophical thought.[19] Eclecticism is a term used in philosophy to identify a composite system of thought which incorporates ideas selected from other systems. It does not modify but blend the opposite views. Its essence is the refusal to follow blindly one set of formula and conventions with a determination to recognize and select from all other sources those elements which are good or true either in the abstract or in the concrete, so far as they are practicable and useful.

For V.M. Martin, irrespective of the constructive criticism leveled on eclectics, it should be conceded that it is a study of the opinions and theories of others so as to discover a new dimension in the frontiers of philosophy that would be agreeable and enlightening. In this respect, it forms a part of philosophic method. But it cannot pretend to be a doctrine of its own right.[20]

The German thinker, Gottfried Wilhelm von Leibniz (1646-1716) was an eclectic philosopher. In his philosophy, he welded the scholastics with the modern theology and morals with the dictates of reason. He was able to raise his own ideas such as *monadology* and *occasionalism* which became topical issues in philosophy.

The German philosopher, Martin Heidegger incorporated Greek thought and theology to form his philosophy. He was able to cause a stir in metaphysics with his epic book, *"Being and Time"* which has emphasis on *Sein* (Being), *Dasein* (man - the interpreter and shiner of being) and *seindes* (other things).

Thomas Aquinas (1225-1274) tried, to reconcile faith (theology) with reason (philosophy). He showed much interest in Plato and Aristotle and used their ideas in building his theology and philosophy. He sees philosophy as the hand maid of theology and he worked to reconcile Christian faith with philosophy. He enriched the Christian faith with his eclecticism. In fact, Aquinas is regarded as the father of eclecticism; he gave it recognition in his works before others. This is evidence in his works *Summa Contra Gentiles (On the Truth of the Catholic Faith against the Unbelievers)* and *Summa Theologica (Summation of Theology)*. Aquinas asserts that truth can be arrived at through reason as well as through revelation. And more importantly, he asserts that reason can arrive at some revelatory truths and most often he used Aristotle's method to show it.

In the renowned views of Nnamdi Azikiwe, eclecticism is not syncretism because it does not attempt to reconcile or combine irreconcilables. Rather it leaves the contradictions unresolved but blends compatibles to make them practicable for utilitarian purposes. By this method of eclectics, one can add, subtract, multiply or divide any idea and adapt it to situations or historical circumstances.[21]

Zik of Africa used eclectic method to mediate between socialism, capitalism and welfarism to form *Neo-welfarism*. He advocated it for Nigeria when the country was searching for a system of government to adopt after her failed attempt at parliamentary democracy from 1960 to 1966 and many years of military rule from 1966 to 1979, but Nigeria rejected it and opted for the presidential system of democracy. This is inline with the views of McHenry that eclecticism is naturally more apt to manifest itself when established systems are losing their novelty or having their defects revealed by changes of historical circumstances.

In his work, *Eclectic Philosophical Hermeneutics of African Personality*,[22] Horace Emeagwara adopted the eclectic method in his philosophical hermeneutics of African personality and by being eclectic in the examination he felt free to blend and adopt ideologies to periscope African personality, identity and experience. Hence, for him African personality includes everything that has something to do with Africa. It includes, but is not limited to the following: African communalism, African socialism, enslavement and colonial experience, Black power, Black pride, Negritude, PanAfricanism, African Union, African freedom and nationalism, African militarism, African security and development. At present, African personality will relate also to the emergence of Barack Obama as the first black president of the United States and his policies during his two terms in office as leader of the free world.

Hermeneutics as a Method

Etymologically, hermeneutics comes from the Greek work, *hermenuetili* which means it is concerned with interpretation especially as distinguished from exegesis or practical exposition. While exegesis is a critical explanation of the meaning of words and passages in a literary work; hermeneutics is the art or science of interpretation, especially of scriptures. However, one can say that hermeneutics and exegesis are closely related to each other. Both of them are involved in the exposition and interpretation of scriptures. By extension, we have philosophical hermeneutics and exegesis of concepts and passages of literary works. It is concerned with philosophical interpretation of beliefs and world views whether it is the religious or the cultural, the socio-economic or the political. Here, hermeneutics assumes the form of anatomy or dissection of concepts, beliefs, principles, hypothesis, laws and world view of a people.

In concluding this chapter, we must say that no philosopher can successfully use anyone of these methods all through to the exclusion of the others. Clarity of thought has greater importance in philosophy than any method used. Any of these methods which can help a philosopher achieve this objective is welcome. But all said and done, argumentation is central to all these philosophic methods. Philosophy is highly argumentative. The philosopher argues as he or she writes, raises questions, proffers solutions, answers objectives and clarifies issues in the bid to stave off and ward off intellectual mediocrity and ideological bigotry and to lead the human mind to great heights, broad - mindedness, tolerance and peaceful co-existence. Even in certain situations when the philosopher is silent, we can figure out that he has already philosophized "*Si dixerit se non philosophari est philosophantium.*" If he says he would not philosophize, he has philosophized.

4

FUNDAMENTAL PROBLEMS OF PHILOSOPHY AND THEIR SOLUTIONS

Right from the ancient period, many problems have confronted philosophers in particular and mankind in general. In as much as there is life, there will be problems, and there will be solutions; as it is in other sciences so it is in philosophy. However, it is remarkable that in philosophy, a problem could often receive many competing reviews and solutions. As some of these problems are perennial in nature, they must always remain with man as a matter of fact, just like some problems in other areas of life. For example, problems of education, culture, religion, economy, health, politics, etc., will always remain with man on this planet. The only difference is that the problems of philosophy are fundamental, in that at one time or the other, these problems arise and confront the mind of everyone who has reached the age of reasoning. In other words, these problems are distinctly human problems and it is hard to be human without wondering about them at some point. And the decisions one makes based on any of these problems usually turn around and make the person the type of human being he will be in the society. Here, solutions offered by philosophers and other great minds to these fundamental problems are given so that the individual or society confronted by these problems may get a clear vision to believe better, know and choose better, and act better to be better.

Fundamental Problems of Philosophy and Their Solutions 79

The Nature of Reality

The first major problems of philosophy and ones that often bug the minds of many persons who are mature or have reach the age of reason include: What is the nature of reality as such? Is reality mere appearance? Or is there something substantially real behind the appearances? We shall consider the solutions that have been offered to these problems.

What is the Nature of Reality?
Solution:

Absolutism

This view holds that reality is basically "constant, unchanging, fixed and dependable." This view tells us that appearances are not reality. Appearances are in constant flux and changing. We know from experience that things are not always what they seem. Instances abound where appearances have been shown not to be real just as all that glitters is not gold. Consider the following instances: The earth appears flat; the sun appears to move from the east to the west every day; our shadows appear in different sizes, heights and shapes at different times of the day; the moon appears to have the light of its own; the sky appears blue and the cloud looks like a smoke fog. And from a distance, a pool of water appears to be on an asphalt road on a sunny day, a stick in a pool of water appears bent and the floor of the pond appears less in depth and atoms appear indivisible. We can continue ad infinitum to enumerate but the fact here is these instances or situations are not a reflection of reality. Parmenides was the first philosopher to articulate and produce a systematic answer to the effect that "reality is constant, unchanging, fixed, one and eternal."[1] Plato also supported the view that reality is eternal and unchanging. For Plato, the changing things we see around us are not realities but only appearances, in other words, they are reflections of realities. Since reality and being tend to be synonymous, more views on the absolute nature of reality would be provided under the question of being.

Relativism

This view holds that reality is fleeting and changing. Reality is always relative. The apostles of this solution are not as many as we have in absolutism of reality.

Heraclitus was the forerunner of the philosophy of change. According to him, the only thing that is permanent and constant is change. He asserts that you cannot step into the same river twice for fresh water keeps running unto you. For him, reality is always changing; it is only change that does not change. *Pythagoras* was another philosopher who buys the idea of relativism in reality. According to him, man is the measure of all things. This means there is nothing absolute in any field of life and since man is not an absolute being; his measurements are bound to be dependent and relative.

The Ultimate Constitution of Reality

The question of what reality is made up of has always being a thorny issue in the history of thought and no one satisfactory answer has been given. However, the diverse views give us a deeper understanding of reality and its constitution.

Solution:

Monism as a Solution

This view holds that reality is one unified whole or entity. And as for its ultimate constitution, it is variously held to be only, namely: matter, mind, energy, will or spirit. Let us consider each of them briefly.

Matter as the ultimate Constituent of Reality

The early materialists see reality as constituted of matter. For them, everything is made up of atoms, indivisible particles of every element. Democritus and Lucretius as materialist philosophers were the forerunner of systematized materialism. They maintained that matter is the ultimate constituent of reality. On the genesis of this view, Stephen Greenblatt rightly pointed out that Democritus was the excellent student of Leucippus of Abdera in the Fifth century BC, and that Democritus propagated "the incandescent idea that everything that has ever existed and everything that will ever exist is put together out of indestructible building blocks, irreducibly small in size, unimaginably vast in number."[2] The Greeks called these invisible building blocks atoms, which are things that as they conceived them at that period could not be divided any further.

In Lucretius' epic work, *On the Nature of Things (De Rerum Natura)*, he expounded the view that the basic stuff of the universe is an infinite number of atoms moving randomly through space, like dust motes in a sunbeam, colliding, hooking together forming complex structures, breaking apart again in a ceaseless process of creation and destruction. There is no escape from this process. Lucretius included in this treatise the vision of his master Epicurus known for his powerful knowledge of the nature of things. Epicurus's meditations on the nature of things prompted him at the age of twelve to seek from his teachers the explanation for the meaning of chaos he saw in the nature of things such as birth and death, generation and disintegration, association and disassociation, composition and decay, coming into being and going of being. His teachers failed woefully to provide explanation to the existence of chaos in the world, and Epicurus's intellectual odyssey led him to the old teachings of Democritus on atoms and he imbibed them as a plausible explanation to the problem of chaos in the world of matter.

Epicurus supposed that in constant motion, atoms collide with each other and in certain circumstances they form larger and larger bodies. The largest observable bodies – the galaxies, the stars, the planets, the moons and the asteroids - are made of atoms, just as are human beings and water-flies and grains of sand. There are no super categories of matter, no hierarchy of elements. Heavenly bodies are not beings that shape our destiny for good or ill, nor do they move through void under the guidance of gods. They are simply part of the natural order, enormous structures of atoms subject to the same principles of creation and destruction that govern everything that exists. And this means, according to Greenblatt in his epic work, *The Swerve: How the World became Modern,* "if the natural order is unimaginably vast and complex, it is nonetheless possible to understand something of its basic constitutive elements and its universal laws. Indeed, such understanding is one of human life's deepest pleasures."[3] As it has revolutionized the way we see a lot of things and the way we do a lot of things in the contemporary period.

Modern scientists brought empirical proof to the two- thousand year-old speculation of Democritus on the existence of atoms as the basic constituent of matter. However, the idea of indivisibility of atoms held by Democritus, Lucretius and Dalton's atomic theory has been repudiated by modern science. According to modern empirical scientists, atoms are known to have three particles, namely the electrons, neutrons and protons. And the application of the knowledge of atoms in nuclear technology and its military use in the *Manhattan Project* ended the Second World War and saved the world from possible fascist dictatorship and other enemies of freedom. The weaponisation of atomic knowledge by some countries especially the world powers has maintained a balance of power in the world. Currently, modern empirical scientists are investigating the existence and nature of other aspects of this reality such as dark matter and antimatter. For Thomas Hobbes, the ultimate constituent of reality is matter. He believes that conscious life is nothing but sensations, movements in the brain and nervous system that could be explained without appeal to any non-physical principles. For him, human beings are physical objects. He compared the human body to sophisticated machines made up of wheels, nuts, bolts and springs. Human actions can also be explained similarly as physical pressures. Likewise, Karl Marx maintains that matter is the ultimate constituent of reality. For him, "the mind is matter that has reached or attended a level of consciousness."[4]

Mind as the ultimate Constituent of Reality

Most of the idealist philosophers assert that the mind or the spirit is the ultimate constituent of reality. George Berkeley sees his own idealist philosophy as immaterialism and holds that nothing but minds and their ideas exist. To say that a thing exists means that it is being perceived by the mind. According to him, *Esse est percipi* "To be is to be perceived."[5] For Friedrich Hegel, the absolute spirit is the ultimate constituent of reality. According to him, all parts of the universe are included in one all-embracing order, and he attributed the unity to the Absolute Mind or Spirit. He maintained that thought is the essence of the universe. In his words, "the universe is an unfolding process of thought."[6]

Energy as the ultimate Constituent of Reality

This is a school of thought found among the modern materialists. It propagates the concept of *"energism."* The adherents affirm that everything can be reduced to a form of energy such as chemical, mechanical, electrical, nuclear, etc. They also assert that certain phenomena can be explained in terms of energy. They claim that "the universe, including all energy, matter, force or motion, have always existed and always will exist."[7] This is to say that the universe has no beginning in time and will never have an end in time. Energy will outlast every other thing because it is eternal.

Dualism

This is the view that reality is composed of two antithetical primordial principles: Matter and Sprit or Body and Mind. Dualism also involves by extension polar concept, that is, the idea that reality is constituted of two forces or pairs of forces, e.g. good and evil, right and wrong, beginning and end, life and death, male and female, light and dark. One of the two principles is usually considered superior to the other. Few thinkers consider them equal and opposite.

Rene Descartes proved himself to be the greatest protagonist of dualism. For him, reality is composed of *'res cogitans'* and *'res extensa,'* the *res cogitans* is the unextended thing which is the mind while the *res extensa* the extended thing is the body. "The intrinsic quality of mind is thought while that of matter is extension."[8] As a result; Descartes recognized two distinct realms of reality. One is the world as described by physics and the other reality is the world whose essence is thought - perception, feeling, reasoning, imagining and the corresponding ideas or mental representations.

John Locke acknowledged matter and mind as the ultimate constituent of reality. He spoke of the mind as a blank piece of paper, "a tabula rasa" that experience writes on. At the same time, he denied that the mind has innate ideas. However, he acknowledged that the mind has inherent faculties which it brings into the world with it. He also accepted that "the mind has innate powers, but experience makes these powers to be manifested."[9] Locke also asserts the existence of external world of matter, which is for him the source of sensations and ideas we have in our minds.

The Trilogy of Reality

This is a conception of reality as a trilogy that concerns mind, matter and antimatter. There are current investigations around the world into the nature and functions of antimatter as one of the constituents of reality that is related to matter and mind in an impact bound way. It has been established by the European Organization for Nuclear Research *(CERN)* that "for any particle of matter there exists corresponding antimatter and that when matter and antimatter come into contact they annihilate and disappear in a flash of energy."[10] This implies we can also think of reality in terms of three components, namely: mind, matter and antimatter. In this *'trilogism'*, sufficient knowledge of antimatter and its practical applications will revolutionize how we see things, do things and travel in the future.

Pluralism and Diversity

This is the view that fundamental realities are many, namely, minds, matter, antimatter, energies, forces, spirits, etc. These realities are considered equally real, and to a certain degree, independent. For the pluralists, the world or reality consists of indefinite number of separate elements or substances. Pluralists stand in contrast with both the monists and dualists. According to Canon Fernand Van Steenberghen, the radical monists assert that "diversity is only apparent, superficial and phenomenal, while the real is fundamentally one, undivided, indistinct and unique because everything is being under every aspect."[11] The radical pluralists, on the other hand, deny all unity in the real. According to them, diversity imposes itself on us, we observe particulars, and this being is opposed entirely to that being. No element of this universe has any other element. There is no intrinsic underlying unity among them such as being or existence, and no one source at least knowable to us. Unifying terms like being and existence are mere mental abstractions, verbal conceptual devices of our minds for joining things together to speak conveniently about them in our limited vocabulary. Thus, Martin Flyn observed that we may claim that the concept of being synthesizes the diversity, but that concept is only a label, a word, a *nomen* (nominalism) or at least a mental representation without objective value, an artifice of the mind to unify phenomena - 'conceptualism'.[12]

The critics of the pluralists have accused them of committing fallacy of false exclusion that is excluding the vital part of the question or the problem instead of explaining it. *Zeno and Plato* were philosophers who

Fundamental Problems of Philosophy and Their Solutions

came nearer to the idea of pluralism of reality. Plato understood being or reality in terms of plurality of natures but certainly not the same as Zeno's plurality of units. However, Aristotelian view recognized the Platonic forms of nature and the unity of being as well as Zeno's unity of parts as constitutive of a plurality.[13] This means for Aristotle that there is plurality of reality.

Pythagoreans ridiculed Parmenides for maintaining that reality is one and indivisible. They asserted that reality is not one but many. According to them, reality is made up of infinite divisible units just as a line is made up of infinite number of points. From this, we can infer that if it is made up of infinite divisible units, then it must be innumerable for what is infinite is innumerable.

The Problem of Being and Existence

This problem raises questions such as: What is being? What does it mean to have being? What are characteristics of being? What is the nature of existence as such? These questions raise the problem of being and existence to an ontological level quite apart and above the physical things we see in the world. Several solutions have been offered by philosophers and scholars from the ancient period to the modern period. We shall consider some of the most important solutions.

On the Problem of Being

The question that often arises here is: what is being? This is one of the greatest questions in human thought.

Solution:

Being as One, Eternal and Unchanging

This is the position of Parmenides. For him, whatever is, whatever exists is being. He maintained that being as being is one, eternal and unchanging. In the view of Nicholas Ikhu Omoregbe, this position of Parmenides means that the things we see around us which change are not being as such because they are transient, temporal and always changing whereas the real and actual being is eternal and unchanging.[14] So, for Parmenides, reality is one, being is one, not multiple. It is only in the senses and appearances that reality seems to be multiple and changing but reason tells it is one. For Plato, being as being is one and unchanging. The changes we see in the physical world of things according to Plato are appearances and reflections of realities.

Being as Multiple

This view holds that being as being is multiple, not one. A member of this school of thought is Plato. He differed from Parmenides by maintaining that being or reality is multiple and many. For Plato, beings or realities are found in the world of forms or world of ideas. There they exist as forms or ideas. He concluded that the form of good is the ultimate of all other forms or ideas. The realists are among philosophers who hold the view that being or reality is many and physical.

Being as Atomic

Actually, the idea of the atom and its characteristics was first conceived in the Fifth century B.C. by Leucippus and his exceptional student, Democritus. But Democritus' conception of an infinite number of atoms that have no qualities except size, figure and weight - particles then that are not miniature versions of what we see but rather form what we see by combining with each other in an inexhaustible variety of shapes was a fantastically daring theory of being and a solution to the problem of basic stuff that make up the universe which worried the mind of previous ancient thinkers. It became part of the speculative philosophy of the time and raised the question of the basic stuff of being to a higher level than air, earth and water but without much application to human life.

But, Epicurus in his search for a root cause of chaos in life; the composition and decomposition of things thought of the old atoms of Democritus as solution. He started applying it to explain human problems and the result is a compendium of account of the universe and a philosophy of human life. Epicurus expounded magnificently the old idea of Democritus. He brought into it a supreme vision that commands attention and an intellectual authority that is worthy of acknowledgement. He espoused that in constant motion, atoms collide with each other and in certain circumstances they form larger and larger bodies. The largest observable bodies, the galaxies, the stars, the sun, the planets and the moons are made of atoms, and the same applies to human beings, plants, animals, and a drop of water and a grain of sand. And as we noted before, there are no super categories of matter, no hierarchy of elements. Heavenly bodies are not beings that shape our destiny for good or ill, nor do they move through the void under the guidance of gods. They are simply part of the natural order, enormous structures of atoms subject to the same principle of creation and destruction that governs everything that exist.

Furthermore, according to this atomic theory of being, as we mentioned earlier, if the natural order is unimaginably vast and complex, it is nonetheless possible to understand something of its basic constitutive elements and its universal laws. And for Greenbelt, such understanding is one of human life's deepest pleasures. Indeed, this pleasure is perhaps the key to comprehending the powerful impact of Epicurus' philosophy; it was as if he unlocked for his followers an inexhaustible source of gratification hidden within Democritus' atoms. He went further to say "for us, the impact is rather difficult to grasp. For one thing, the pleasure seems too intellectual to reach more than a tiny number of specialists, for another, we come to associate atoms with fear than with gratification."[15]

This fear came from the advancement in the studies of atoms of different elements and great capacity and danger of atomic radiation of some these natural elements like uranium, plutonium, etc., to life in terms of their military use as atom bomb, nuclear bomb or hydrogen bomb, and their misuse in health facilities as x-rays, cancer radiation treatment and in chemotherapy. This was enough to displace the idea of Epicurus that smooth atoms are the source of sensual pleasure while rough atoms give pains. Hence, smooth atoms should be desire over rough ones in relation to the human body and as a key to enduring peace of mind and happiness. Thus, pain and pleasure become agents that determine moral standard and guide human behavior. It was this Epicurus of Greece gratification and pleasure philosophy that Lucretius of Rome in his epic work, "*On the Nature of Things*" tried to bring to his Roman audience as a tribute to his master Epicurus and for the encouragement of the Roman public and its army which most often than not was engaged in imperial wars with other nations. Epicurus believed that the cancellation of the role of the gods and demons in controlling our destiny, the removal of the fear of death and the absence of some horrendous punishment waiting for one afterlife would enhance the life of the people and the development of the Roman Empire. For the reason that the soldiers would not need to fear death during imperial wars, and the Roman Army would not be a respecter of the gods or have mercy on rebellious colonies on the basis of piety to the gods.

In fact, Lucretius projected Epicurus as the intellectual messiah of the world and his thought on being as godlike in wisdom, vision and courage. He took him as a philosophical savior who came when humanity was wallowing in ignorance and superstitions, and brought intellectual redemption to the world through the power of his intellect and reason. With this, the materialistic philosophy of Epicurus spread throughout the Roman Empire and its colonies. To a great extent, Epicureanism and Stoicism were regarded in many quarters as the official philosophies of the Roman Empire.

Lucretius wanted Romans and foreigners who visited their temples and gardens to accept and imbibe their article of faith and the motto of Epicureanism which is expressed on the inscription on the gate of Epicurus garden: "Pleasure is our summum bonum." It urged visitors to linger on in the garden for "here our highest and ultimate good is pleasure." This pleasure is regarded by many as more of peace of mind that comes from frugality, simplicity, friendship and charity as opposed to the pleasures of sensuality and its attendant variations like an unbroken succession of sexual love, drinking, enjoyment of meat and fish in the best of cuisines. Nevertheless, antagonists of epicurean philosophy see the inscription as pointing to carnal pleasures. They based this view on the fact that Lucretius has "urged the person who felt the prompting of sexual desire to satisfy it for a dash of gentle pleasure soothes the sting of being human."[16]

Being as God

This school of thought holds that being is the foundation of all things. The major members of this thought current include Aristotle and Thomas Aquinas. For Aristotle, Being as Being, Being *qua tale* is God. He is the Pure Being, the Unmoved Mover and the Uncaused Cause. Aquinas also affirmed that being as being, being as such is God. He demonstrated the existence of this being in his *Quinque Viae;* Five Ways of proving the existence of God. Thomas' argument on the existence of God from design stands out as the most apt demonstration of the existence of God. He also holds that individual things are being in the analogical or derivative sense of the word. The scholastics call the pure being a necessary being while the analogical being e.g. man, they call a contingent being.

Being as Man

It was Martin Heidegger who pummeled the traditional philosophers as having lost the trend and the meaning of being in their metaphysical speculations over many centuries. For him, there is urgent need to recapture the meaning of being and save it from getting lost forever in that drift to oblivion. First and foremost, he sees being as man and he calls man "*dasein*", a being-in-the-world and describes man as the presenter and shiner of being. This means man is the only being capable of discussing the being of other things as well as the being of man. Man himself is a finite being thrown into the world without consultation by an infinite being. At the same time, at birth man is irrevocably propelled towards death. In his epic work, 'Being and Time,' he proposes that man and the human condition should take the center stage in any discussion on the question of being. However, he acknowledged the existence of other things "*seindes*" which are meant to be used by man to overcome self-alienation in his journey towards authentic existence and death.

Being as a Concept

The nominalist school of philosophy holds that being is just a mere concept which includes among other things, God, man and other individual things. In this sense, being becomes a univocal concept that accommodates every reality both being and becoming. Within this thought current, we have philosophers like Duns Scotus, William of Ockham, John Locke, Rene Descartes, Immanuel Kant, etc. Even within this concept of being, non-being is discussed. For instance, one can ask; why is there something rather than nothing? How is something created out of nothing as opposed to the maxim "out of nothing, nothing comes"?

Being as Substance

In the modern period of philosophy, being is regarded mainly as substance. Descartes sees being as a concept that contains two substances, the *res extensa* and *res cogitans*. In other words, there two kinds of substance, namely: the extended thing which is the material or physical things and the unextended thing which is the mind. On the extended physical things it is believed that there is in them the substratum (the thing that stands under) which the accidents adhere to. The substratum therefore holds together the particles of things and the accidents in things which include: color, smell, taste, hotness, coldness, etc.

Being as Attributes

Another school of thought identifies being with attributes. According to them, we cannot grasp being as being or being as a whole rather we know being by its transcendental attributes, namely: unity *(unum)*, truth *(verum)*, goodness *(bonum)*, beauty *(pulchrum)*, thing *(res)* and otherness *(aliquid)*. These transcendental properties are in co-existence with being, through these attributes and in them, being manifests itself and reveals what it actually is. Just as being is never found without such attributes, so these are inseparably bound up with one another in the sense that they include and interpenetrate each other. Thus, according to the measure and manner in which a thing (or a person) possesses being, it partakes of unity, truth, goodness, beauty; and it becomes a thing separated or differentiated by otherness. The nature of these attributes is considered under metaphysics as a division of philosophy.

Being as Dialectic

In the modern philosophy of Hegel, the idea of being took a turning point. Being is seen as dialectic. The idea of non-being and becoming is juxtaposed with the idea of being. This gives rise to what Hegel calls Thesis, Antithesis and Synthesis respectively. Consequently, being and non-being become moments in the process of becoming. Being is therefore always open and not a closed entity. This openness of being is an infinite continuum. Hence, becoming is a process that will go ad infinitum. This idea was bought over by Jean Paul Sartre and he affirms in his work, *'Being and Nothingness"* that being by its very nature is contingent. This is to say that being is an unfinished project; it is always evolving just like any work in process and this evolvement continues indefinitely. The physical universe is an ever expanding entity and so will be human development.

Being as a Mystery

Gabriel Marcel, a modern existentialist philosopher sees being as a mystery. It is a mystery that encloses every human. And because it engulfs every one of us, one needs to be out of it to comprehend it. Since we could not and cannot be out of it or go beyond it and remain what we are, it is therefore ordinarily incomprehensible. According to Marcel, faced with questions about freedom, the meaning of life, the existence of God, etc., no objective standpoint can be found from which a universally valid answer may be discovered.

However, this does not mean that this mystery is unknown or unknowable or lies in the realm of vague feeling over which thought has no grasp. Rather, knowledge of mystery presupposes an immediate participation in what Marcel calls a "blind intuition" but this participation is understood only with the aid of a conceptual process. An unaided intuition is not an adequate philosophical instrument. Hence, second reflection penetrates into the mystery of existence and being only when it works in conjunction with love, fidelity, faith and the other "concrete" approaches. It yields a kind of knowledge and truth which is unverifiable, nevertheless is confirmed as it illuminates our lives.

For Marcel, being is not a problem since for him; a problem is something external to us and can be solved. A problem is a question which can be considered purely objectively, a question in which the being of the questioner is not involved, e.g., in a mathematical problem, the solver is out of the picture. In a mystery, the distinction between the subject and object, between what is in me and what is before me breaks down. This is to say that in a mystery you cannot differentiate between the subject and the object, they become interwoven, intermingled and intertwined.

What is the Nature of Existence?

Solution:

Nature Theory: Space and Time

This is the view that nature is existence. Whatever occupies space and time exists. To be matter or physical energy is to exist. This solution was offered by naturalism and physical realism. The naturalists represented by Democritus, Epicurus and Lucretius, and in the modern time by Baruch Spinoza and George Santayana, propagated this view of space and time as the basis of being and the sole conditions of existence. Their view would be given the much space it deserves later in this work.

Also, the physical realists assert the above position. For them, being is what is real or is reality. And the real is the actual, or the existing. The concept of "being" refers to things or events that exist in their own right; as opposed to that which is imaginary or merely in our thought. So, reality refers to what is physical. For them, the objects of our senses are real in their own right, they exist within space and time independent of their being known to, perceived by or related to the mind. In the modern time, Samuel Alexander also espoused this view in his work, *Space, Time and Deity*.[17]

Idealist View: Existence as Mind Dependent

Most true idealists will hold that Spirit, God or Mind is existence. To exist is to be a mind or spirit, or to be dependent on mind or spirit. This is the position of George Berkeley's subjective idealism. Hegel, an absolute or objective idealist, expressed the view that Berkeley is correct in maintaining that reality or being is spiritual but incorrect in maintaining that God is distinct from man and each spirit distinct from every other. For Hegel, the universe or being is an integrated system and all spirits are members of one of another. For him, God is the absolute Spirit or Mind.

The Sceptics view: Existence as a Category

This solution expresses the view that existence is just a category. Everything is constantly in a flux; nothing is to be ultimately attributed to existence. This position is well expressed in the philosophy of David Hume, who had a huge influence on thinkers like Adam Smith and Charles Darwin. He sees no being as ever present to the mind but perceptions are. According to him, "we may observe a conjunction or a relation of cause and effect between different perceptions, but can never observe it between perceptions and objects."[18] Hume asserts that all the content of experience is fleeting and effervescent. For him, therefore, there is no identical self or personal ergo, no spiritual substance or material substance, and no identical thing. There are no entities or a substratum behind the flux of experience. There is only a constant change. Hence, there is no pure identity. There is no lasting unity of being.

The Problem of Substance

In the history of philosophy, the problem of substance is as thorny as the problem of being. The question that arose in the mind of thinkers is: what is substance? Etymologically, substance comes from two Latin words *"sub"* which means under and *"stans"* means standing. So, substance literally means "standing under" or that which stands under. It stands under to hold all particles in a unity of being. It holds together qualities like color, taste, cold, heat, solidity, liquidity, extension, etc. of matter and form. Substance is taken to be the unifying power, force or energy in a thing. This binding power cannot be seen but reason tells us it is in anything that has particles.

What is the Nature of Substance?

We know that what substance is could be found in its nature, so we ask: What is the nature of Substance?

Solution:

Substance as Essence

Philosophically, substance is conceived by some scholars as the essence of a thing. The essence of a thing is seen as that which constitutes the specific nature of a thing. It is that which makes a thing what it is. The essence of the pen is to write and this differentiates a pen from a ruler used for measurement. The essence of man is taken to be rationality. It is this rationality that distinguishes man from other animals and things.

Aristotle distinguished substance from accidents. For him, accidents represent the qualities that inhere in the nature of a thing such as color, size, taste, height, smell, heat, cold, etc. Aristotle also distinguished a "primary" and a "secondary" substance. In the primary sense, a substance is an absolutely individual thing: this man, this dog, this apple, etc. In the secondary sense, a substance is a class of things, e.g., "man," "tree," "dog," "apple," "rock." In both senses, substance is distinguished from the changeable qualities (accidents) that attach themselves to things and do not show the essence of a thing.

Substance as Material Stuff

In the modem science, substance is generally seen as the material stuff which a thing is made up of. In this regard, any matter or material that is used in the making of a thing is taken as the substance of that thing. This includes things like wood, water, iron, clay, gold, silver, bronze, copper, aluminum, etc. This is similar to Locke's material substance which he sees as the reality that underlies or supports qualities such as the color, size, height, taste and smell we see or perceive in things.

Substance as Self-Existence

In ancient and modem philosophy, substance is also taken to mean self-existent or independent existence; that is, whatever exists on its own. It does not depend on another to maintain its existence. It is on this basis that Descartes distinguishes three self-existent substances, the *res cogitans* (the mind), *res extensa* (the bodies) and God. He asserts that a human being as a compound of mind and body belong to the two realms of substance.

Gilbert Ryle rejected this dualism of substance in his famous polemic against the *"Deus ex machina"*- "the ghost in the machine." He calls it a categorial - mistake to regard both minds and bodies as things of the same logical geography, logical type or as substances. This means it is a fallacy to conjoin two terms of different categories as if they were of the same. Thus, there is a logical absurdity in the concept of the mind having a parallel, non-material existence of its own corresponding to the material existence of the body. In other words, by postulating mental operations as a correlate of physical processes, we are led into a category-mistake. To think there is something called the mind over and above a person's behavioral dispositions leads one into this fallacy. Spinoza identified God as the only self-existent substance. According to him, it is only God who requires nothing but himself to exist. He went further to state that God, nature and substance are three different names for the same reality. This reality has infinite attributes but we know only two: matter and spirit. Spinoza's idea of substance leads to pantheism, which means God is everything and everything is God.

Substance as "Atomic" Spiritual Reality

The history of philosophy is replete with ideas that substance is atomic in nature. In his philosophy, Leibnitz asserts that Monads are simple substances. These monads are the building block of all things as well as their smallest conceivable units. For Leibnitz, their indivisibility and infinitesimal smallness endow the monads inwardly with spiritual quality and by extension all things they make up. This position of Leibnitz tends to come down to the position of Berkeley that there are spiritual substances which he called spirits. Hegel and right wing Hegelians and neo-Hegelians went further to assert that all substances are united in one comprehensive and absolute substance that is the universe and that it is spiritual in character but material in appearance.

Substance as the Thing-in-Itself

Kant brought a new description of substance to the philosophical lexicon. According to Kant, it is the thing-in-itself that underlies or supports the qualities of things we see. However, the thing-in-itself or the substratum or the dark matter is imperceptible as it belongs to the noumenal world of Kant as opposed to the phenomenal world of physical things we see in space and time. For Kant, in his *Critique of Pure Reason,* the noumenon in the negative sense means something which is not an object of sense and so is abstracted from awareness but in the positive, it is an object of non-sensible awareness. Kant concludes that what the mind acquires through the idea of noumenon is negative extension. The mind is not then limited by sense but rather, it limits sense by applying the term "noumena" to things-in-themselves, which are not phenomena. It also limits itself, since noumenal beings are not to be known by means of mental categories. They can be thought of only as unknown something- the dark matter.

The Problem of Essence

In philosophy, there have been hair-splitting arguments by philosophers on the nature of Essence, whether Essence is prior to existence, that is, the primacy of essence over existence. They also raised the question: Can there be Essence without Existence? To end this controversy, solutions have been offered by philosophers past and present.

Solution:

Essence as Prior to Existence

The scholastics maintained that the distinction made between essence and existence is only possible in the field of contingent or dependent beings. For them, Essence is the very nature of a thing. It is that which makes a thing that particular kind of thing which it is and which differentiates and distinguishes it from other things.

Essence is prior to existence in dependent beings. This is based on the fact that one can imagine the essence of a thing that has not come into existence. For Omoregbe, "even if a being does not actually exist, it is possible to think of or imagine its essence."[19] It could be said that most artists and sculptors conceive the essence of an art work before they go on to bring it into existence in form of drawings, paintings, carvings, or moldings. Most times, we imagine the essence of a dish before we prepare it. We also imagine the essence of a write up before we put our pen on the paper to write it. Existence may only bring secondary or added essence to the primary essence. In philosophy, phenomenology is the science of essences "*eidetic science*." It agrees that while essence is actualized by existence, existence on the other hand is limited by essence. For instance, the primary essence of a pen is to write but if a pen can no longer write, the existence is in trouble. The essence of salt is taste but if salt loses its taste, the existence is no longer worthy. It has out lived its usefulness. It is thrown away if we cannot find a secondary essence of it.

Essence as Identical to Existence

The distinction between essence and existence is impossible in a Necessary Being. And the only Necessary Being is God. So, the essence of God is identical with his existence. The existence of God is as well his essence. Under theism and philosophy of religion, Descartes and St. Anselm based their ontological proofs of the existence of God on the fact that essence is identical to existence in a necessary being. They moved from the idea of a highest conceivable being to the necessary existence of God. While Descartes on his own part argued from the point of view of God as a perfect being to reach a conclusion on the necessary existence of God. This means that he sees existence as part of God's perfection.

Kant rejected the above proof because existence was not actually proved but was treated as a predicate. This amounts to a separation of essence from existence which Kant sees as identical in any idea of being. Some philosophers rejected Anselm argument because for them one can imagine or conceive the idea of a perfect island which does not actually exist anywhere.

Existence as Prior to Essence

In modem philosophy, a system of thought came up to repudiate the idea that essence is prior to existence. The existentialists among them Jean Paul Sartre and Friedrich Nietzsche argued from the vantage point of existence philosophy. Nietzsche, the "mastermind" of existentialism lays emphasis on life, instinct and power. He recognized the "Will to Power" as the basic human motive. And he wanted to make way for the "higher man," (the super-man) who would embody higher values, not the virtues of mediocrity that Nietzsche found exhibited in Christianity, democracy and nineteenth century bourgeois morality. Thus, Nietzsche believes man can achieve whatever he wants to be including making a superman out of himself. He believes where there is a will there is a way. This means man exists first and then he makes his essence and he can make out of himself a superman in as much he has the will and courage.

Building upon this philosophy, Jean Paul Sartre contended that existence precedes essence. According to Sartre to argue that man was created with a fixed essence is tantamount to denying man of his freedom. That is to say that man is not free to decide what he wants to be. For the existentialists, man is a bundle of possibilities, an open entity and uncompleted project. The idea of fixed essence also implies the impossibility of auto-transcendence or self-transcendence. It also throws spanners to the notion of self-actualization and self-realization.

In his dialectics, Sartre sets out to defend man, his existence and freedom. He first of all rejected the old dualism of body and mind, mind and matter, physical necessity and free will, reality and appearance as artificial separation of what in reality is a whole. He accepted Edmund Husserl's concept of intentionality, according to which consciousness is always the consciousness of something. This, of course forms a much closer link between man and his world than the earlier interpretation of a subject with a "pure" consciousness. Pure consciousness which might or might not focus on its world gave the individual an aura of detachment.

Sartre accepted Heidegger's Being-in-the-world (*Dasein*) as man without accepting his being(s) (*Seindes*) or other things and insists on the inseparability of man from his world. Sartre realizes that there must first be a man of flesh and blood before consciousness can appear. In each act of consciousness, man is aware both of an object outside of himself and also of himself. And of each moment, consciousness creates the meaning of both I (the Ego) and the world. Meaning or essence thus emerges only with man. The world with all its thousands of beings carries no meaning in itself without man. For Sartre, individuals have no essential selves. Existence precedes essence, we exist first, the self that we subsequently become is a construct that is built and rebuilt out of our experiences and behavior. This means the self can be changed, it can be lost or it can be reconstructed. This is partly the function of education and training in all facets of human endeavor.

Sartre went further to state that the world will be meaningless without man. Succinctly, it would be said thus: first there was being, and being became consciousness, and then there was light. Man, in Sartre's view is in the midst of a world which silently stares at him. It is this theme which Sartre develops in his famous dualism of the *en-soi* (in-self) and the *pou-soi* (for- itself) which could be translated to self-contained being and conscious being. The *En-soi* signifies all the objects around man. They are impermeable and dense, silent and dead. From them, comes no meaning or essence. They only are. They only exist. All hopes that behind these appearances must be an essence, a "Ding an sich" (thing-in-itself) or any other vehicle of meaning are futile. Even living beings (except man) are mere passivity and instincts upmost. The world of the *en-soi* is absurd, *de trop*. It finds meaning only through man, the one and only *pour-soi* (conscious being). For Sartre, compared to the *en-soi,* man is a strange being. He has no fixed nature and his characteristics cannot be listed. *Pour-soi* is forever incomplete, fluid, vacuous and lacking in determinate structure. Sartre affirms that man first of all exists and then decides his essence by deciding what he wants to become.

The moral choices that individuals make are theirs and theirs alone,and they are fully responsible for them. He acknowledged that man has the givens, which is, fixed characteristics that cannot be changed which Sartre called facticity such as age, height, sex, and genetic dispositions. For Sartre, these are limiting factors to the fact of freedom and existence, and a pointer to the fact that there is no absolute freedom, and the fact that man is free but everywhere in chains. Regarding the issue of choice, man is condemned to choose for when he refuses to choose, he has already chosen not to choose so he has chosen. He always has a choice. Therefore, for Sartre, it is bad faith for anyone to pretend that he or she has no choice in any particular situation. Wherever you are in life, directly or indirectly, it is your choice that brought you there. For him, one can only avoid choice in life by choosing death, that is, suicide. But suicide is not only awful and it is cowardice.

Finally, it has been argued that Sartre confused man's essence with his moral character. It is true that every man chooses freely his moral character but it is not true that every man chooses freely his essence. For Omoregbe, "man's essence is man's nature and we know that human nature is not something which everyone chooses by himself. Man's essence (nature) is the same for all men and it is given to all men by the creator of all men."[20] This means that right from the beginning of time man has only one nature and hence one essence and man can never be able to change it. If the natural and primary essence of man changes, man will no longer be man, he becomes something else.

The Problem of Universals

In the history of thought, the problem of universals has been an enigma to the human mind. Debate upon debate has been centered on the nature of universals, whether they have concrete existence or are they conceptions of the human mind.

To be precise, questions raised in relation to these universals include: Is there anything like love itself, in other words, what is love? What is justice? What is peace? What is freedom? These questions are asked on the basis that there is a difference between love and instances of loving acts, between justice itself and instances of just acts, between peace and a particular peaceful situation, between freedom and instances of free acts, between beauty and instances of beautiful things.

Thus, freedom, peace, love, beauty, justice, etc., are the universals while their instances are regarded as the particulars. So, we ask, why are universals always there even as the particulars come and go? How can this be explained?

Solution:

The Doctrine and Theory of Participation

The earliest a fortiori explanation of the nature of the universals was given by Plato with his doctrine of participation. He posited this theory as a solution to the problem of the one (universals) and many (particulars). He asked questions such as, what is the first cause of all reality. In whose existence and reality do all other beings take part? What is it that is permanent and not changing, that could stand for the basis of all beings? How does the many relate to the one? The word "participation" is derived from the Latin verb *"participare"* meaning "to take part" with its four principal parts as: *participo, participare, participari, participatum*. The term is also a combination of the Latin word "pars - parties" meaning "part" or "side" and the Latin verb *"capio, capere, capi, captum"* meaning "to take." So, the etymological derivative or literary meaning of participation is "to take part" as the above analyses show.

In the technical and philosophical sense of participation, the sensible world is conceived as full of temporal beings, none of which has the essence of its existence in itself. This is the modality of existence in finite beings, and the urge to explain the necessity of their "to be" has strongly influenced many philosophers especially Plato to think and work out some ultimate and metaphysical foundation from which to give fundamental explanations for the temporality and finitude of sensible realities. In the process, philosophers have come to identify the ultimate and metaphysical foundation with the absolute being which is immutable, necessary, eternal and irreducible to any more primordial being or source of being. Succinctly then, the term "participation" in its philosophical meaning is the theory, whereby finite beings according to their respective ontological perfections are said to share in the one ultimate and infinite being whose essence is existence.

Thus, all reality in whatever modality of existence or perfection is regarded as an expression or mirroring of the infinite being whose act it is to be in itself. It was Plato who first used the term participation in his doctrine of being and theory of participation. According to S.E. Stumpf, Plato believed that, "every concrete or actual thing in some degree participates in the perfect model of the class of which it is a member, and in some measure is an imitation or copy of the form."[21] The good is the supreme reality whose being and perfection every other thing shares in. Hence, for Plato what we have in the world are the copies or the imitation of the perfect copies or ideals in the world of ideas or world of forms which he held to be eternal. Thus, beautiful things share in the universal beauty or ideal beauty. This notion pervades the whole period after Plato as the true state and relation of things.

Plotinus (204-270 AD), an adherent of Plato's philosophy, used the Emanation theory to explain participation, and hence the relation between one and many, the universals and the particulars. According to Ivan Frolov, the emanation theory holds that the world process begins with the incomprehensible divine one which is the eternal sources of all beings and emerges first as the universal reason then as the world soul and later as individual soul as well as individual bodies including matter.[22] This doctrine of Plotinus has come to be known as ultra-realism or exaggerated realism. According to Bertrand Russell, this position is easy to pass on into mysticism. We may hope in a mystic illumination to see the ideas as we see objects of sense, and we may imagine that the ideas exist in heaven. For him, these mystical developments are very natural, but the basis of the theory is in logic, and it is as based in logic that we have to consider it thoughtful.[23]

Nominalism: Universals as mere Labels

The nominalists assert that the universals are not entities or realities and as such they are nothing but names used in designating things that have or share certain similarities. For instance, everything that all desires is said to be good, everything that appeals to the eyes is said to be beautiful and all that is calm is said to be peaceful. But there is no object called good, beauty or peace existing somewhere independently. William of Ockham was one of the protagonists of this view and he used his *Ockham's razor* to repudiate and oppose ideas that have no basis in reality including the universals. According to the principle of plurality of Ockham's razor, plurality should not be posited without necessity, and its principle of parsimony states that it is pointless and vain to do with more what is done with less. Literally, it tells us that the simplest explanation is usually the right one. Most often people say the error is in the details and it is a good principle to explain a phenomenon by the simplest hypothesis.

Hence, there is the need to eliminate complex and unnecessary postulates in our thought system. It is because of this that Russell advised whenever possible substitute or replace inferences to unknown entities for constructions out of known entities. Elucidating the views of nominalists, Steenberghen says that we may claim that the concept of universals synthesizes the diversity in nature but the nominalists assert that the concept is only a label, a word, a name, a *'nomen'* and as such it is nominalism.[24]

The nominalists went further to say that the universals are mental representation without objective value, an artifice of the mind, a mental construction to unify phenomena and to that extent it should be regarded as conceptualism. This view has been regarded as another extreme position with monstrous implications. By denying the concept of being on a universal level, it has dealt a mortal blow on metaphysics, the science of being as being. It refutes also the formal object of the intellect thereby denying intelligence. Finally, it reduces the real universe into a confused mass of absolutes, hence rendering it unintelligible.

Radical Pluralism

This view denies all unity in reality. Only the plurality and diversity of things are real. According to them, diversity imposes itself on us, we observe only particulars. This being is opposed entirely to that being. No element of this universe has any intelligible relation or real similarity with any other element. There is no intrinsic underlying unity among them such as being or existence, and no one source at least knowledgeable to us. The mind invents unity where there is none to enable it deal conveniently with the multiplicity of things that exist in nature. Unifying terms like "being" or universals are mere mental abstractions, verbal conceptual devices of our minds for joining things together in order to speak conveniently about them in our limited vocabulary. The above view is the foundations of nominalism and tends to be synonymous with it.

Moderate Realism

The moderate realists assert that the universals actually exist but not as independent realities different from individual or particular things. They are not separate from the instances of objects or events. Boethius, Abelard, and Thomas Aquinas were among those who offered this solution to the problem of universals. For Aquinas, participation simply put, is the act of receiving existence or becoming from the *Ipsum esse subsistens*, the being whose act it is to be in itself, the unparticipated source of all reality.

Thus, for Aquinas, the ultimate foundation in which everything participates is the fullness of God who as existence actually contains within himself all perfections in the highest degree according to all possibilities.[25] Further, he says that participation means not having something by nature but as received from above(from that which is of absolute value). Therefore, all other being are being by participation and so made by God.[26] God is the unmoved mover and His essence is to exist and his existence is his essence. The God whose being is self-subsistent is the unparticipated source. This leads us to the idea of God as the *Ipsum esse subsistens:* the unparticipated source of Aquinas, the being whose act it is to be in itself, the pivot of existence of all participants and all created beings.

The Problem of Change and Permanence

The reality of "change" and "permanence" has constituted a glaring metaphysical problem in philosophical thought. The Greek thinkers in Richard Popkin's view were impressed with two basic features of the world, the occurrence of natural change and the continuance of certain apparently permanent conditions.[27] The questions that are raised here include: How true is it that what we call change really takes place? Why do things still remain the same (permanence) despite the occurrence of change? For Heraclitus and Cratylus, the only permanence is the principle or law of change, only the universal principle that everything changes remains unaltered.

The Parmenidean argument, on the other hand, is since everything is consistent, any more attempt to divide, separate the unchanging, the unchangeable and immutable nature of the world would indicate change, therefore that which is, is (exists) while that which is not, is not (does not exist). Parmenides' contention is that since we can know what is commonly regarded as past, it must, in some sense, exist now (in the present). Hence for him, "there is no such thing as change when you recollect, the recollection occurs now which in the present is identical with event recollected."[28]

Whatever exists is born by death of something else. There is unity in the world, but it is a unity formed by the combinations of opposites (two contraries) death has its origin in life and life in death, sleep has its origin in waking and waking in sleep, and the whole has its origin in part and part in whole. Therefore, the world has its harmony in tensions of opposites. In change, what takes place is neither annihilation nor creation but the transition of being from one state to another. Wherever there is change, it presupposes the reality of that which changes. Therefore, there is permanence and there is change. Let us consider briefly each of the problems and solutions offered by philosophers.

Solution:

Change as the Primary Feature of the Universe

The word change etymologically comes from the Latin word *"muta-*

lia" meaning to become something else or to pass from one state to another. Change is practically considered as to leave one place and enter another, take off something and put something else on. For the *hoi polloi* – the layman, change could be understood concretely as not being at one place or not found in the same location or position, like a student transferring from one institution to another or a worker moving from one job to another.

To think of change as the primary feature of reality is to reason philosophically as Heraclitus did. For Heraclitus, the first theoretician of change, everything alters and changes - "Omnia flux," "All changes," this means everything in the world is in flux. This affirmation of change in all things in the universe by Heraclitus is climaxed with his famous aphorism: "It is not possible to step twice into the same river, for fresh water constantly runs upon you." Heraclitus thereby equates reality with a river which flows or changes always. Change for him is the coming into being and passing away of things in the cosmos.

Again, he maintains that in this fluidity of things, the only thing that remains unaltered or permanent is the universal principle that everything changes. So, for Heraclitus, change or becoming is quantitative, a transformation of one phase into another. He holds extremely that permanence is an illusion; nothing is permanent in this universe. Hence, "all things pass away and naught abides." Kingdoms and empires rise and fall, seasons come and go, plants and animals live and die, the sun rises and sets, asteroids and comets come and pass, the universe moves on. The motion of the universe does not permit permanence. We cannot be in a moving vehicle and not be moved.

Heraclitus went further to assert that the essence of all things is fire, and that the law of opposites keeps the universe in harmony. So, the harmony is a product of a delicate balancing act. It is this harmony that gives us the illusion of permanence in things we see in the universe. Hence, Bertrand Russell writes "He (Heraclitus) regarded fire as the fundamental substance; everything is like flame in a fire, is born by death of something else, mortals are immortal, and immortals are mortal, the one living the other's death and dying the other's life. There is unity in the world but it is a unity formed by combination of opposites."[29] That is to say that every apparent stable thing is just like a river which maintains its level by taking as much as it loses; or fire which continues to burn by feeding on new matter.

With the arrival of Hume on the philosophical scene, the problem of change took a new complexity and became complicated. According to Hume, change exists, but only as a mere succession of ideas, that is, series of ideas with no causal relation. This thought of Hume indeed awoke many philosophers such as Kant from the dogmatic slumber of their minds and urged them into more critical reflections on the twin issues of change and causality. For Rader, Hume's thought on change and denial of causality made him to anchor his ship of knowledge at the shore of skepticism and allowed it to decay there. So, his theory of knowledge did not raise fire but it made a spark through which fire can be rekindled.

Nietzsche x-rayed the problem of change and asserts that being and permanence are fictions invented by those who suffer from becoming and those who are afraid of changing and becoming something bigger than what they are at presence. For Nietzsche, change is the only reality. This is well-manifested in his evolutionary philosophy where all is evolutionarily heading to become the superman, to attain the highest virtue which is "the will to power." However, William James in reaction against Hume's position states that "thought is not a series; it is a stream, a continuity of perception and feeling in which ideas are passing nodules like the corpuscle in the blood."[30] That is to say that everything is in flux and consciousness is not an entity, not a thing but a flux and system of relation. For him, whoever holds the doctrine of monism suffers from the "natural disease of philosophers who hunger and thirst not for truth but for unity."[31]

Henri Bergson demonstrated the above view when he claims that every moment is new but some unforeseeable change is far more radical than we supposed. At least for conscious being to exist is to change, to change is to mature, to mature is to go on creating oneself endlessly.[32] The logic of evolutionary doctrine and its fidelity to change as the ultimate reality of all things is well exposed here. Life is much more a matter of time rather than of space; it is not a position as it changes, and it is a fluid and persistent creation.

For Karl Marx, history has shown that social and economic orders are in a process of change. The purpose of his dialectical materialism was to show also that the material world is primary; it is the basis of what is truly real; there are no stable, fixed points in reality because everything is involved in the dialectical process of change. With this view, Marx rejected the notion that somewhere there are stable, permanent structures of reality or certain eternal verities. He argued that all the natural things, from the smallest thing to biggest, from the grain of sand to the sun ... to man is in a ceaseless state of movement and change.[33] Again, Marx asserts that history is the process of change from one epoch to another in accordance with the vigorous and inexorable laws of historical motion. According to him, change is not the same with mere growth. A society does not simply mature the way a boy becomes a man. Nor does nature simply move in an eternally uniform and constantly repeated circle. For him, change is emergence of new structures, novel form.[34] From all these, we can see that the affirmation of change as the ultimate reality throws the truth of permanence into abyss and the search of the truth by the intellect seems problematic.

Permanence as the Absolute Truth of Reality

Permanence is seen by the layman as being always in the same place and time, as not possessing the potentiality to change. In philosophy, Parmenides insists that permanence is the absolute truth of reality. For him, change is an illusion. His affirmation is that "being is, non-being is not" and that only the unchanging belongs to the world of being. There is no motion or movement from non-being to being because from non-being, nothing comes - *"ex nihilo nihil fit,"* out of nothing, nothing comes. Parmenides did not define permanence but he upheld it and affirmed that reality is one; hence he was one of the early protagonists of the doctrine of monism. Before Parmenides, some philosophers have supported the reality of permanence in various arguments.

Thales affirmed the reality of permanence in his postulation of water as the single substance or the ultimate stuff out of which the material universe was made. For him, at the basis or within the changing universe, is something that remains permanent and this is water.

Following his master, Anaximander propounded that the boundless or the infinite is the basic stuff out of which everything comes. He said that everything comes from a single stuff- boundless infinite, and for him, this is a real manifestation of permanence in nature.

Anaximenes in trying to solve the problem of permanence in nature or what is at the root of every changing thing affirms air as the basic stuff behind the coming to be of everything, thereby demonstrating the reality of permanence. He believes that air is the only thing that is everywhere occupying space and at the same time moves around.

The reality of permanence for Pythagoras is manifested in the number *"ONE"*. For him, everything consists of numbers but the number ONE is that from which all other numbers were created. If there is no number ONE, there will be no other number, there will be nothing. The implication is that all things in the universe are diversified but since they flow from the ONE, it implies that the ONE is permanent. In the midst of those diversities, the ONE remains, and it is the source of numbers as well as other things, hence permanence is realized in the number ONE. It is the basis of unity among things.

The above Milesian philosophers attempted to explain reality as unity in diversity, but Parmenides did not share with his predecessors the view that the ONE can become many and diverse at the same time. He therefore rejected the notion of change on the ground that if there is a single substance behind all things, the concept of change is absurd logically.[35] Parmenides saw the notion of change in the sense of something coming into being or going out of being. The phenomenon of change becomes absurd if the Milesian thinkers and Heraclitus held that reality is one. This is because the concept of one and many are logically exclusive of each other. Something cannot be one and many at the same time. This is inferable from the metaphysical concept of identity. If anything is "P" then it is "P." If anything is being then it is being. This makes the notion of change logically unthinkable or inexpressible.

Parmenides justified that whatever is cannot not be. This is to say that whatever is, simply is and cannot without any degree of inconsistency be said not be. For him, whatever exists in reality exists absolutely. He affirmed that being is (in an absolute sense) and nonbeing is not (also in an absolute sense). If it is, it is being, if it is not, it is nonbeing. In fact, he maintained that being is and nonbeing is not. Building on this premise, he concluded that change is impossible. His argument runs like this: "You cannot say about anything that it ever had non-being, for if you can think of an "it," it already exists and, consequently, there is no "non-being" from or into which a thing or a state of a thing could change."[36] According to Parmenides, the concept of change is the result of the assumption that something can change from being to non-being or from being to being.

In the contrary, Parmenides has consistently maintained that change is impossible. Revealing further the absurdity of change, he argued as follows: if we are to hold as the Milesian philosophers and Heraclitus held that a thing comes into being, then it must either come out of being or non-being, if the former, then, it already is, in which case it does not come to be. On the other hand, if it is the latter, it is nothing since out of nothing, nothing comes. What Parmenides is saying in effect is that what is already in existence cannot be said to come into being since it already exists.

In the whole, Parmenides arrived at the conclusion that being is one, immutable, indestructible, eternal and unchangeable. Spinoza being much influenced by this static monism applied it in his philosophical work on the notion of substance as absolute being. For him, substance exists as one; while other things are merely its modes and attributes, and these attributes or qualities are perceived by the senses. For him, all in the physical world are not real except in God's thought.

The Middle Position: Change and Permanence Co-exist

The first man to appreciate the absurdity of the two opposing extremes of Heraclitus and Parmenides was Empedocles. For him, none of the either extremes is totally devoid of truth and untruth. In fact, his merit consists in his attempt at a synthesis. By deciphering some vestiges of truth in both arguments of Heraclitus and Parmenides, the ground was set for the synthesis. According to Empedocles, although Parmenides was right to conceive being absolutely, he missed the mark by declaring this being to be one. Being is rather many and it is this "many" that are changeless and eternal. This "many" are the material particles he depicted as water, air, fire and earth. These changeless material particles enter into the constitution of objects, through the mingling and interchange of what has been mingled and thus necessitate change.[37]

For Empedocles, the objects we see or experience do come into being and are as well destroyed. The reason for this change is due to the composition of these objects by the many material particles (water, air, fire, earth). Change thus consists in the mingling and interchange of these material particles. This mingling is accomplished by forces of love and hate. He concluded that although objects can change, as Heraclitus had said, the particles of which they are composed do not change but are as Parmenides had said about being, changeless.

Plato posited the physical and the ideal worlds to explain the problem of change and permanence. He espoused the idea of participation to explain the relationship between the two worlds, as we have discussed before. His student, Aristotle sees both change and permanence in a particular being or entity. Synthesizing change and permanence are tenable in a particular being. A being which is first in potency is acted upon by the actualizing principle, bringing it to act, so it has changed from potency to act. Therefore, the world of becoming is a world of realization, of reduction, of potency to act. It is a world in which actuality or being is constantly realized in matter.[38]

With the emergence of Aristotle's doctrines of Hylemorphism, act and potency and Aquinas doctrine of *Essence* (being-in-potency) and *Esse* (Pure act) the problem of change and permanence seems to have been resolved. Kant introduced another dimension to the problem of change and permanence by his doctrine of phenomenal world and noumenal world. In the phenomenal world, that is, the physical world there is change but in the noumenal world, that is, the world of things-in-themselves, permanence and unity are found.

The Problem Concerning the Three Aspects of Being and Reality

Having raised the ultimate problems of reality and existence, philosophy identifies three basic aspects of being and reality, namely: the cosmos (world or universe), man and God. Accordingly, we shall consider concisely these three fundamental groups of problems.

The Cosmos as a Basic Aspect of Being and Reality

The following questions are often raised:

What is the Origin of the Cosmos?

Solution:

Evolutionary Theory

Evolution is the term for the process of change in the universe. Evolution- or the theory of evolution is the interpretative conception of how the process proceeds. This theory holds that the cosmos evolved of its own accord by chance. The Big Bang Theory is one important aspect of the evolutionary theory. The big bang theory is a cosmological model which espouses that the universe came into being by chance about 13.798 Billion years ago. The galaxies with their stars and planets came into existence as a result of explosion in the universe which ab initio was in extremely hot and dense state. The explosion occurred when the hot and dense universe started to expand rapidly. The explosion sets off a chain of events in which energy given out were converted to sub atomic particles, namely electrons, protons and neutrons. Simple atomic nuclei were formed within the first three minutes after the big bang, but thousands of years passed before the first electrically neutral atoms formed.

The majority of the atoms produced by the explosion are hydrogen, helium and lithium. Giant cloud of these primordial elements later coalesced through gravity to form stars and galaxies. The evolutionary trend continued with formation of heavier elements within the stars and during supernovae. And the universe up till today continues to expand as the distances between the galaxies continue to increase.

The Big Bang Theory did not give us a complete picture or rather it has no description of the initial state or condition of the universe before the expansion and explosion. It did not tell us what caused the universe to expand and explode. It did not inform us how the thing that exploded came to exist and how long it has existed before the explosion. The theory only describes some of the chain of events that followed the explosion many of which are still under investigation in many laboratories across the world like the Hadron Atom Collider in Switzerland.

The idea of evolution of the universe (cosmic evolution) can be "differentiated into stellar, geological, atomic, organic and cultural evolutions."[39] The Cosmic evolution was very much popularized in the Copernican worldview known as the Copernican Revolution. A renown group of scientists and philosophers such as Copernicus (1473-1543), Galileo (1564-1642), Newton (1642-1727) and Charles Darwin (1809-1882) upheld this view of cosmic evolution which existed before them. The publication of the *Origin of Species* in 1859 and the theory of Natural Selection by Charles Darwin also espoused further and brought to limelight the idea of organic evolution which followed the cosmic evolution.

Creationism

The cosmos (the world or universe) was made by a creative cause, mind or personality. Many reasons have been given to attest to this fact. One such reason is the fact of intelligent design in the nature of the cosmos. There appear to be reason and purpose in the nature of things. Thomas Aquinas demonstrated through his Five Ways or *Quinque Viae* that the universe is the product of an uncaused cause, unmoved mover, intelligent designer and efficient being.

In each case, the argument runs backwards from empirical facts accepted by all – facts of motion, causation, change and qualities – to something responsible for the lot, something rendering intelligible the world around us. St Augustine surmised and suggested *seminal reason* as the principle underlining creation. According to him, God created the original stuff and gave it the initial impetus and potentiality to develop into other things that existed in the past, things that exist today and those that will exist tomorrow. It can be inferred from this that God's creative art is an infinite continuum and this accounts for the emergence of new forms and species in the world and the birth of new galaxies, stars and planets in the universe. This also underscores the fact that the universe is not a product of chance as some scientists want us to believe. Augustine's position is akin to Plotinus' view of creation by emanation in which he held that God created the original stuff and gave charge for other things to come from it. But everything is before him in an eternal presence. He sees them in an eternal now; the everlasting and infinite present.

What is the nature of Cause?

This is the problem of cause and effect relationship. It was Isaac Newton who said anything that moves is moved by something and that bodies remain in a state of inertia, rest or constant motion until they are acted upon by a force. The statement raised exponentially the issue of cause and effect in the history of thought. It urges us to examine temporal priority and spatial proximity to see whether they are integral elements of causality. It also urges us to differentiate between causality and determinism. Human free actions are not caused but are determined by the individual will and choice, and as such the individual is responsible for his actions. Diverse opinions have been offered as to the exact relationship between cause and effect. Some of these views are compelling and possibly true while others are plausible but possibly false as we shall see in false cause fallacy in chapter sixteen.

Solution:

Regularity Theory

This is called the empiricist theory. This is the view that causation is simply regular sequence. Generally, causation is a principle or rather a theory which holds that every effect has a cause. For A.R. Lacey, causation may also be defined roughly as the relation between two things when the first is necessary or sufficient or both for the occurrence of the second.[40] However, the empiricists see causation in the form of one thing following the other regularly as fire is the cause of smoke. For David Hume, "the only connection or relation of objects which can lead us beyond the immediate impressions of our memory and senses is that of cause and effect. It is the only one thing in which we can find a just inference from one object to another."[41] He maintained that the notions of succession, continuity and constant conjunction in causality can be defended but that of necessary connection cannot be verified and defended.

Entailment Theory

This is also called the Rationalist theory. It holds that causation is like the connection between premises and conclusion in a valid and sound argument. In the same way, there is necessary connection between cause and effect. The theory is applicable to every finite being, namely any being which cannot account for or explain its own being. It owes whatever belongs to it to another higher being. Whatever is finite is by this very fact the effect of a cause. And since every finite being, considered as such, carries with it a real structure of potency and act, we can likewise formulate this principle: *"Omne compositum causam habet"* meaning "every composite being is a being that is caused."

In the above Entailment theory, the word "cause" would be conceived in several but closely related perspectives. In the first instance, a cause may be defined as anything capable of changing something else. It may also be taken to mean that which produces something and makes something happen. It is further regarded as that which brings about the occurrence of something without which that thing would not have resulted. A cause of an effect may be thought of as the same for a multitude of relevant conditions none of which, exclusive of others, can be called the cause. Therefore, the cause of an effect may be defined, according to Peter A. Angeles in his book *"A Dictionary of Philosophy,"* as those conditions each of which are sufficient for its occurrence, and which precede the event in time. Schematically, when "A" occurs and "B" invariably follows, then "A" is said to be the cause of "B" and "B" the effect of "A."

A cause, according to Richard Taylor, in the *Encyclopedia of Philosophy,* has traditionally been thought of as that which produces something and in terms of that which is produced; its effect can be explained. The effect of a cause, therefore, is that which derives from the efficiency of the cause, and which cannot share in being without the latter. The effect is not self-existent, and cannot define itself as such without reference to the cause. In order that one could have a scientific knowledge of the effect, the cause must first of all be known.

On how the effect is related to the cause, Racymaeker opined that the cause is an efficient principle; it gives birth to, it produces the effect, it is the source of a new reality which is distinct from this latter. This effect, therefore, is not a part of the cause; to produce effect does not signify to distribute parts of itself and in so far as to impoverish itself; but the effect is a reality which results from the efficiency of the cause.[42]

Activity Theory

This theory holds that cause involves activity. Activity involves a will. Thus, cause is a will, a mind or spirit. For George Berkeley, it is God. God is the cause of all the ideas we have of ourselves and of things in the physical world. In Berkeley's words, "there is a mind which affects me every moment with all sensible impressions I perceive. And, from the variety, order and manner of these, I conclude the Author of them to be wise, powerful, and good and beyond comprehension."[43] For Hegel, the universe is a spiritual reality. It is an integrated system and all spirits are members of one another. In this total integrated system of the universe, activity or causality is the essence of the minds or spirits. This is a view that is well reflected in Hegel's work, *The Phenomenology of Spirit*. In his view, the idea of self leads progressively to the absolute spirit or mind.

The Problem of Space and Time

One of the wonders of nature is the phenomenon of space and time. Man has not being able to grasp in its entirety these twin issues. Man is also limited by space and time, and he has not being able to overcome them. He cannot travel far into space and he cannot live long enough. Will the discovery and application of antimatter and understanding of dark matter help to overcome space and time? Nobody is sure yet. But our hope is they will. Hence, questions that are raised here include, what is the nature of space and time and their relationship?

Solution:

Materialism: Space and Time as Things and Events

This is the view that space and time are vast receptacles of things and events respectively. This view portrays space and time as container that is empty and therefore could contain things. The things can be put away or keep out of sight. For Lucretius, if there is no vacuity, that intangible and empty space, things could not move at all. This position of Lucretius is elaborated in his epic work, *On the Nature of Things*.

Space and Time as Pure Forms of Mental Intuition

Here space and time are regarded as ways of looking at things and events and their relations. For Kant, space and time are pure forms of intuition. According to him, there is a sense or sensitivity of the mind, by which we reach out to things and see them located in external space. For him, space is the visualization which is necessary to the mind, and the basis of all external perceptions.

One might imagine space with no objects to fill it, but it is impossible to imagine that there should be no space. Space is therefore a condition of the possibility of phenomena and not a form required by them. It is a subjective, a visualization which precedes all external experience. That is to say, it is a mental awareness that is not derived from experience. It is essentially one and of infinite quantity. For Kant, time like space is a form of perception, not a thing perceived. Just as phenomena are spread out in space, above or below, near or far, to the right or the left, so likewise are they ordered in time, before, after, or simultaneous with other events. Anything experienced as spatial is thought of as belonging to the outer world, but temporal order applies to one's psychological acts of apprehension. Hence, time is the form of inner sense, that is, of our awareness of us and our own inner states. But both space and time are necessary forms of human perceptions and cannot be ascribed to objects in themselves apart from experience.[44]

We must add that by mere looking at our wrist watches or any other time piece like a wall clock or the movement of our shadows on a sunny day we may not grasp actually the understanding of time as reflected by Kant. We will get only the fact that time is transient in nature, and it appears to be material in nature but it is not. We can touch the time piece but we cannot touch time. Hence, time is a form of mental perception and awareness of something of transient quality.

Likewise, space appears as something that can be measured with measuring instruments because it appears to have three dimensions, namely length, width and height, but we cannot grasp the actual meaning of space in this way. We can better see space as form of mental intuition, perception or awareness of something of spatial quality.

Euclidean Non- Relativistic Space and TimeTheory

Euclid was a Greek (300 B.C) mathematician who lived and studied in Alexandria Egypt. He was regarded as the father of Geometry. Euclid epic work, *Elements* popularizedGeometry and was later called Euclidean Geometry. Archimedes acknowledged Euclid as the author of the

Elements and that this pioneering and clear presentation of geometric knowledge had great influence on him. Archimedes asserted in his popular quest for a lever, "give me a place to stand and I will move the earth." Under Euclidean conception of our universe, he treated space and time as consisting of three geometric dimensions, namely: length, width and height, and he saw time as consisting of one dimension, which was regarded as the 'fourth dimension'. Under this Euclidean scheme, time is treated as universal and constant, and as such it was regarded as being independent of the state of motion of an observer. In other words, it held the view that motion, speed, acceleration or velocity does not affect time in any way. This view was later regarded as the non-relativistic view of space and time and was used in classical mechanics until the 20th century when new discoveries rendered the view obsolete.

Relativity Theory of Space - Time

Philosophy of science gives us the contemporary understanding of space and time. It was in the 20th century that great minds like Max Planck and Einstein took a second look at the issue of space and time and updated the Euclidean conception of space and time. For Einstein, space and time should be considered together and none should be treated in isolation of the other. Thus, space and time are joined together to be space-time.

In Einstein's *Special Relativity theory* he outlined the following views, namely:

• Relativity of simultaneity: this holds that two events simultaneous for one observer may not be simultaneous for another observer if the observers are in relative motion.

• Time dilation: Moving clocks are measured to tick more slowly than an observer's stationary clock in the ground station.

• Length of contraction: Objects are measured to be shortened in the direction that they are moving with respect to the observer.

• Mass-energy equivalence: Energy and mass are equivalent and transmutable.

- Maximum speed is finite: No physical object, message or field line can travel faster than the speed of light in a vacuum.[45]

What is essential to grasp from the above is that in the relativistic scheme time cannot be separated from the three dimensions of space. This is based on the fact that the observed rate at which time passes for an object depends on the object's velocity relative to the observer and also on the strength of the gravitational fields which can slow the passage of time for an object as seen by an observer outside the field.

Succinctly put, time slows down at higher speed. This time dilation was demonstrated in the slowing down of time of the atomic clocks aboard a space shuttle relative to another synchronized clock in the ground station.

Does the Cosmos or Universe have a Purpose?

Solution:

Non-teleological Views of the Universe

First, teleology as a term comes from the Greek word *"teleo"* which means "end," or "purpose." Non-teleological views hold that there is no purpose in the operations and working of the universe. The world came about as a result of chance, accident or blind mechanism, and so has no purpose in view. No end is discernible from its existence.

Generally, Lucretius championed the view that there is no discernible purpose in the universe and went further on to assert that the stars, the planets and their moons are not created by the gods but are due to unpredictable and unexpected moving of matter he called swerve. For him, the universe has no master plan, it is not designed and there is no purpose toward which it moves. This means therefore the universe has no divine architect and no intelligent designer. Lucretius refused to accept Aristotle's description of Unmoved Mover God as the source of the universe.

Specifically, Lucretius asserts the existence of a non-designer god. For him, the gods exist as part of the scheme of things in the universe. Just as the seasons come and go so also the gods manifest themselves in some scheme of things. In his poem in honor of Venus, he says spring comes and Venus, preceded by Venus' winged harbinger, and mother flora, following hard on the heels of Zephyr, prepares the way for them, strewing their entire path with a profusion of exquisite hues and scents. According to Lucretius, the gods go about their own business in their level of existence including having and encouraging sexual inclinations in certain respect. Even in this direction, the gods too are concerned with their own pleasures. Lucretius in this poem in honor of Venus the goddess of Love, sees Venus as coming in spring to scatter the clouds, flood the sky with light, and fills the entire world with frenzied sexual desire.

For Lucretius, the gods exist but by virtue of being gods, they could not possibly be concerned with human beings or with anything that we do. By their divine nature the gods enjoy eternal life and peace entirely untouched by any suffering or disturbances in the world and so they are indifferent to human actions, and nothing we do or not do could possibly interest them. We must add that what Democritus, Epicurus and Lucretius missed or left out in their thoughts about the gods, was supplied by the idea of the existence of a Supreme Being, God the Creator of the universe and personal God in the theistic philosophy of St Augustine and Thomas Aquinas.

On the nature and purpose of universe, Lucretius departed from the tradition of seeing one element such as water, air and fire as the basic stuff of nature. He looked beyond to think of what these elements are made of themselves. He asserted that the universe is made of infinite number of atoms. The universe came into being from the clash of atoms in an infinite void of space. According to him, there are infinite number of atoms moving randomly through space, like dust notes in a sunbeam, colliding, hooking together, forming complex structures, breaking apart again, in a ceaseless process of creation and destruction. When we look up at the night sky and feeling unaccountably moved, marvel at the numberless stars, we are not seeing the handiwork of the gods or a crystalline sphere detached from our transient world. We are seeing the same material world of which we are a part and from whose elements we are made. There are no master plan, no divine architect, and no intelligent design. All things including the species to which we belong have evolved over vast stretches of time. The evolution is random, though in the case of living organisms it involves a principle of natural selection. That is, species that are suited to survive and reproduce successfully endure, at least for a time; those that are not so well suited die off quickly. But nothing – from our species to the planets on which we live to the sun that lights our day - lasts forever. Only the atoms are immortal. Nothing at all is able to escape this power of creation and destruction because it is the live wire of an infinite universe in which everything is interconnected and intertwined.

Modern science has even shown that atoms are subject to this fact of creation and destruction. Atoms are destructible and have particles such electrons, protons and neutrons. Scientific researches on these particles are continuing and findings are not definitive and final. There is no doubt that the issue of a universe being formed out of the clashes of atoms in an infinite void has the gained acceptance of modern scientific thinking and researches being conducted to prove this include the Large Hadron Collider (LHC) of the European Particles Physics Laboratory, CERN, near Geneva, Switzerland which is the most powerful particle accelerator ever built.

On the purpose of man, Lucretius opines that man is not a special creature in the world. The universe is not all about us, about our behavior and our destiny; we are only an infinitesimal speck of something inconceivably larger. Man's body and soul are solely made of atoms. The body is made up of heavy atoms while the soul is composed of light atoms like the fragrance of a perfume. For him, in a universe so constituted, there is no reason to think that the earth or its inhabitants occupy a central place, no reason to set humans apart from other animals, no hope of bribing or appeasing the gods, no place for religious fanaticism, no call for ascetic self-denial, no justification for dreams of limitless power or perfect security, no rationale for wars of conquest or self-aggrandizement, no possibility of triumphing over nature, no escape from the constant making and remaking of forms.[46]

Furthermore, Lucretius advised that "human beings should conquer their fears, especially of death because death is nothing to us. It is folly to spend our existence in the grip of anxiety about death, and those who inflict such anxiety on others are dubiously manipulative and cruel."[47] To allow death to cast a shadow over our life is sure to let our life slip from us incomplete and unenjoyed. For Lucretius, in place of the thought of death, we should see every encounter in life as transitory. When we see every state of mind as transitory then we will be open to the glories of the world and ready to embrace the beauty and pleasure of it. For many other forms of fear, it is often advised "Do the thing you fear and death of fear is certain."

However, Greenblatt asserted that it is difficult to understand how Lucretius idea that we are made of the same matter like the stars and the seas, and all other things offer us a consolation and make us live a happy life. There is no reason to accept that we would have serenity of mind and pleasure if we accept that the dream of God, angels and afterlife are mere illusions. Except that Lucretius believed the nonexistence of God, angels, demons, afterlife heaven and hell would give way for us to devote ourselves solely to the pursuit of pleasure as the ultimate good.

Here, Lucretius followed the path of his Greek master and mentor, Epicurus (342 B.C.) who advocated two centuries earlier the idea that everything that has ever existed and everything that will ever exist is put together out of indestructible building blocks, irreducibly small in size, unimaginably vase in number and that pleasure is the ultimate good and should be desired for its own sake. For Lucretius, the real messiah of the world was Epicurus who used the pleasure principle to cure the miserable condition of the man, who bored to death at home rushes off frantically to his country villa only to find that he is just as oppressed in spirit. He asserted that when human life lay groveling ignominiously in the dust, crushed beneath the grinding weight of superstition, one supremely brave man, Epicurus arose and became the first who ventured to confront it boldly with pleasure principle projected with the power of intellect and vision.

The Implications of Non- teleological Views for the Modern Period

The revival of learning during the renaissance made many people in Western Europe especially the Romans to go back to the forbidden and forgotten pagan classics. Thus, materialism and its non-teleological views surfaced again in Western Europe. Hence, works like Lucretius,' *On the nature of things* which was heading toward oblivion, made a U-turn and came back to reckoning to animate the spirit of the renaissance period. The Western world has tested two conflicting values namely pleasure and pain doctrines both bodily and intellective and has seen the consequences of both. Pleasure appears to have encouraged education, innovativeness, freedom, progress and development. There was this realization that the whole goal of education, science and technology was not to increase human pains but to reduce them. The essence of acquiring knowledge is not for pain and suffering to abound but rather it is for them to subside. Hence, in our contemporary time, poverty and self-mortification – the Mother Teresa's (1910 -1997) type of *Imitation of Christ* - is regarded as old school spirituality. For modern man, poverty and suffering should be eradicated and not alleviated and celebrated in any guise or form. The fact that pain theology contributed to the Dark Ages while pleasure philosophy assisted in the emergence of the Enlightenment and Modern Periods is not in doubt. Romanticism - a movement in the arts and literature emphasizing inspiration, subjectivity and the primacy of the individual - was a pointer to this fact.

For Greenblatt, this was most evident in the works of art, and this change from one way of perceiving and living in the world to another was not restricted to aesthetics: it helps to account for the intellectual daring of Copernicus and Vesalius, Giordano Bruno and William Harvey, Hobbes and Spinoza. The transformation was not sudden or once-for-all, but it became increasingly possible to turn away from the preoccupation with angels and demons and immaterial causes to focus instead on things in this world; to understand that humans are made of the same stuff as everything else, and are part of the natural order; to conduct experiments without fearing that one is infringing on God's jealously guarded secrets; to question authorities and challenge received doctrines; to legitimate the pursuit of pleasure and the avoidance of pain; to imagine that there are other worlds beside the one we inhabit; to entertain that though the sun is only one of the stars in an infinite universe of stars; to live an ethical life without reference to postmortem rewards and punishments; to contemplate without trembling the death of the soul.[48]

The above spirit marks the transition from the Medieval and Dark Ages to the Renaissance and the Modern Periods. With it is born the scientific spirit, free thinking and the age of researches, discoveries and inventions. Hence, are born the Leonardo da Vinci's scientific and technological explorations, Galileo's vivid dialogues on astronomy, Francis Bacon's ambitious research projects and projections on inductive reasoning as a scientific method, Charles Darwin's thesis on the Origin of Species and the theory of natural selection, Hume and Montaigne's philosophical thoughts on God's existence and the problem of evil in the world, Isaac Newton's scientific thoughts on the Laws of motion, Einstein's scientific thoughts on mass, energy and the theory of relativity and the Machiavelli's analysis of political power and strategy, Thomas Hobbes' sovereignty of the Leviathan and John Stuart Mill's Individual liberty and private morality, to mention but a few.

In our contemporary period, the list is continuing with various inventions and the use of microchips by information technology and telecom companies like Apple, Samsung, Google, Yahoo, U-tube, Twitter, Facebook, etc. These have produced enormous intellectual pleasure for the modern period. Relatively, with all these preoccupations, the fear of some horrendous punishment waiting for one in a realm beyond the grave no longer weighs heavily on most modern men and women as it did during the Ancient and Medieval Periods.

Teleological Views of the Universe

These views assert that from the beginning of the universe, there has been a purpose, or that a purpose is discernible in its progress. For them, the sun, the moon, the oceans, plants and animals have a purpose. Without the sun light plant and animal life will not be here or at least will be different from what we know today. Then without plants and animal the continued existence of man on the planet will be in doubt.

Overall, we know that without water there will be no life in this planet earth. The purpose of water is to support life. Thomas Aquinas provided a good description of purposeful universe in his philosophy and theology, a purpose we can perceive in everyday life, activities and events, and see in our relationships with other people and things of this world. Some people see God and purpose in nature, some in wonders and mysteries in the universe, some in religious worship and fellowship, some in civic duties and services, some in loving relationships and others see God in the problems and sufferings of life.

Actually, the advent of Judeo-Christianity as official religion of the Roman Empire brought a counter proposition to a purposeless universe and the quest for pleasure. Christianity projected the existence of a creator, loving and merciful God, the existence of heaven and hell, the enthronement of suffering, pain, sacrifice and piety as salvific symbols worthy of emulation and the imitation of Christ in his redemptive work, in his suffering and death on the cross. Other religions like Islam, Buddhism and Confucianism as we shall see later also professed similar teleological views of the world in Asia and the Middle East.

Epicureanism or pleasure seeking was one of the outcomes of the belief in a purposeless universe. But the advent of Christian vision of God's providential rage for pleasure seekers gave rise to the emergence of hatred of pleasure seeking and these became the death knells of Epicureanism which was at the time the guiding philosophy of the Roman Empire. So, in one of the greatest religious metamorphosis cum cultural transformations and value change in the history of the Europe, the pursuit and acceptance of pain and self-sacrifice triumphed over the pursuit of pleasure. With these antitheses, materialism took a downward spiral and so did the Roman Empire as materialism was the source of strength of the empire. The vast empire over time could not withstand the paradigm shift in thought, and the relentless rebellion and attacks from the Barbarians, the Goths, and other Germanic tribes made the Western Roman Empire go down slowly until its last emperor, Romulus Augustus (475-476) was forced to resign in 476AD. This marked the beginning of the middle ages in Europe. This forced resignation of Emperor Augustus (often nicked-named unofficially as Augustulus which means Little Augustus) can be likened in modern time to the case of Mikhail Gorbachev who has no alternative than to resign with the collapse in December 1991 of the Soviet Union and its communist materialistic philosophy as a result of the glasnost (openness to western ideas and goods) and perestroika (allowing limited market incentives) reformation. The destruction of pagan literatures by Christians, and the burning of Roman libraries and archives by the Barbarians threw the wholeWestern world into the dark ages. The invading Germanic tribes have no interest in preserving learning and its material traces. As a result of incessant attacks from the enemies of the empire, the primary and secondary education became unsustainable and they crumbled with time, and with it schools closed, private and public libraries shut down, public lectures and symposia stopped. Teachers were out of work and they looked for alternative modes of livelihood. Prohibition by the invaders of classical works by thinkers like Plato, Aristotle, Cicero, and Lucretius as pagan literatures was the last stroke for the death of learning.

However, Christianity by design through the instrumentality of the monasteries - where monks are required by scriptures and community regulations to embrace learning including reading and writing - was able to preserve the stock of books in their domain and salvage some of those left behind by the invading armies of the barbarians and the Goths. At that time the number of monasteries had skyrocketed not only because of the triumph of self-mortification over self-gratification and pleasure seeking but also for the reason that the monasteries were the only safe place in the empire to hide both human and material resources as some of the invaders were Christians and as such ignored most of these inaccessible monasteries and spiritual castles.

Succinctly put, as a result of the shift in the way of life of the Roman Empire from pagan pleasure to Christian belief that redemption comes through mortification and suffering, pain and self-sacrifice, many people in the western world opted for ascetic and monastic life. By the year 600 AD, according to Greenblatt, there were about three hundred monasteries and convents in Italy and Gaul. These institutions served among other things the purpose of preserving the books that provided the base for the reawakening of learning and revival of education that marked the renaissance and modern periods.

Experimentalist Views of the Universe

Some experimentalists believe there is no inherent purpose in the universe; but purposeful activity can impose purpose on it. Darwin, Stevenson, and Whitehead believe that a purposeful activity gives purpose where there is none like when a river is channeled to irrigate a large area of farm land or used to generate electricity through hydropower. For some of the experimentalists, the perceived order or purpose in the universe is imposed by the human mind.

However, the opponents of this view have argued that the mind has the idea of purpose built into its structures by the maker; hence it is able to engage in purposeful activity. For nothing produces what it does not contain, and *Nemo dat quod non habet*. Nobody gives what he doesn't have.

Furthermore, we accept the uniformity of natural laws like the law of gravity and the law of constant motion and that life in this present form cannot be possible without oxygen, carbon dioxide, water and sunlight. Hence, the waters of oceans and the light of the sun are here for a purpose namely to support life. Even the body systems and the organs of the body have purpose assigned to them. No system or organ exists in vain in the body. We do not assign purpose to them but their maker did. But we assign purpose and function to those things we make.

Man as a Basic Aspect of Reality

Topical issues that are raised here include:

The Essential Nature of the Self

Solution:

The Self as a Soul

This view holds that the self is a spiritual being. It is a soul. This is the position of some idealists, existentialists and the spiritual realists. Some of these idealists and spiritual realists believe in the immortality of the soul while others hold the view that the soul is mortal, it does not survive death, it disassociates with the body at death.

The Self as the Same with the Body

This position holds that the self is essentially the same as the body.
It is not an entity distinct from the body and cannot exist outside or independent of the body. This is the position of naturalism and physical realism. For them, the self has no spiritual overtone.

The Self as a Social-Vocal Phenomenon

This position is held by the experimentalists. For John Dewey, the emphasis should not be on what self is or the value of self but on the valuation of self. This means that they are more interested in the process of appraisal of self than the qualities appraised. This valuation, Dewey insists should be in accordance with the method of experimental logic. For him, living well is an experiment and there should be flexible reappraisal and reorientation as the experiment progresses. The experimentalists are against all stereotyping of self and profiling of a group as nobody would like to be defined by the worst moments of his life. Somebody that is bad today could be good tomorrow and vice versa. Thus, everybody deserves a second chance or a second look in any assessment of self and character evaluation.

The Relation of Mind and Body

Right from the ancient period, thinkers have wondered on the relationship between the mind and the body. This led some of them to localize the mind in the body organs like the brain, heart, liver, lungs and kidneys. However, the relationship problem has been considered in different ways and solutions have been given.

Solution:

Interactionism

Body and mind are different substances but they have causal interaction. This is the position of the dualists. Philosophers such as Rene Descartes hold tenaciously to this view that the mind and body are distinct substances but they influence each other. This is to say that body and mind are things that belong to different logical geography and are subject to different natural laws. But they always interact. They always have a relationship. What happens to the body affects the mind and vice versa. This is why the Latin says, *Mens sana in corpore sano* "A healthy mind lives in healthy body."

Parallelism

This position holds that there is interaction between the mind and the body in the sense that series of mental and bodily events correspond; not because of causal relationship but because they are different sides of the same thing. In his work, *"The Concept of Mind,"* Gilbert Ryle laid out this view on the relation between the body and the mind, and he criticized any attempt to separate the mind from the body and vice versa to see them as two different entities. Any attempt to do so he calls it a categorial mistake and a fallacy.

Experimentalist View

This espouses the position that man is neither free nor determined. For them, man is not automaton but at the same time he not free. Man is subject to the law of gravity and the laws of motion. Man is also guided by some genetic factors and made to behave in some certain ways without his knowledge, choice and permission.

God as a Basic Aspect of Reality

Issues about the nature and attributes of God are very much discussed in philosophy of religion and theodicy i.e. the defense of the existence of God against the problem of evil in the world. Many questions have been raised in these areas. Some of them include: What is the nature and operation of God?

Solution:

Atheism
There is no ultimate reality spiritual or otherwise that created the universe and controls it. Philosophers such as Nietzsche, Johann Wolfgang von Goethe, Hegel and Sartre seem to share this view judging by their views. It was Goethe who on his death bed when pressured by relatives and friends to believe in the existence of God exclaimed "Oh God! If there is God save my soul if I have any." This exclamation is assumed to be his final testament of unbelief in God's existence and doubts about the existence and immortality of the soul.

Consider this topical view of Nietzsche on "The Death of God."

The Death of God

Lovejoy in his work, "Joyful Wisdom," has Nietzsche tell the story of a madman who appeared in the market place in search of God and through the madman's mouth; Nietzsche putforth the notion of the death of God. The passage is fully quoted below:

The Madman: Have you ever heard of the madman who on a bright morning lighted a lantern and ran to the market place calling out unceasingly. "I seek God! I seek God!" As there were many people standing about who did not believe in God, he caused a great deal of amusement. Why! Is he lost? One asked. Has he strayed away like a child? Asked another? Or does he keep himself hidden? Is he afraid of us? Has he taken a sea-voyage? Has he emigrated? The people cried out laughing, all in hubbub. The insane man jumped into their midst and transfixed them with his glances. "Where is God gone?" he called out. "I mean to tell you! We have killed him, you and I! We are all his murderers! But how have we done it? How have we done it? How were we able to drink up the sea? Who gave us the sponge to wipe away the whole horizon? What did we do when we loosened this earth from its sun? Whither does it now move? Whither do we move, away from all suns? Do we not dash on unceasingly, backwards, sideways, forwards, in all directions? Is there still above and below? Do we not stray, as though infinite nothingness? Does not empty space breathe upon us? Has it not become colder? Does not night come on continually, darker and darker? Shall we not have to light lanterns in the morning? Do we not hear the noise of the grave-diggers who are burying God? Do we not smell the divine putrefaction? - For even Gods putrefy! God is dead! God remains dead! And we have killed him! How shall we console ourselves, the most murderous of all murderers? The holiest and the mightiest that the world has hitherto possessed has bled to death under our knife, who will wipe the blood from us? With what water could we cleanse ourselves? What instruments, what sacred games shall we have to devise? Is not the magnitude of this deed too great for us? Shall we not ourselves have become Gods, merely to seem worthy of it? There was never a greater event, and on account of it, all who are born after us belong to a higher history than any history hitherto! Here the madman was silent and looked again at his hearers, they also were silent and looked at him in surprise. At last he threw his lantern on the ground, so that it broke in pieces and was extinguished. "I come too early," he then said, "I am not yet at the right time." This prodigious event is still on its way, and is traveling; it has not yet reached men's ears. Lightning and thunder need time, the light of the stars needs time, yet further then, the furthest star, and yet they have done it! It is further stated that the madman made his way into different churches on the same day, and there intoned his *Requiem aeternam deo*. When led out and called to account, he always gave the reply. "What are these churches now, if they are not the tombs and monuments of God?"

One of positive inferences we can draw from the above passage is the fact that Nietzsche wants to remind this new generation that most people live daily as if God is dead and at the same time in religious settings they behave like angels. In some government offices, market places and in interpersonal relationships, God is murdered by many people in their words, actions, thoughts and omissions. Take a look at some countries where Christianity and Islamic religion are flourishing and see the existence of conflicts and corruption side by side with each religion. This shows that God is actually "dead" in many people's lives. And for Nietzsche, the churches and the mosques have become the "grave yards and monuments of God." This means that God's existence is seen only in the churches and mosques and religious gatherings. Even these days, life within and outside the churches and mosques revolves on the thumb rules "survival of the fittest, the end justifies the means." And most people that are offered front seats in the churches are known to be persons who have "murdered" God in one way or the other as government officials or as businessmen. These corrupt persons are those Nietzsche described as murderers of God, and ironically they are just in the churches to rejoice and sing *Requiem aeternam deo* - a burial and condolence hymn for the dead God.

However, the above exegesis does not make Nietzsche a believer in God for he regarded himself as an atheist and a free spirit who was consternated by the moral decadence of his time. And Nietzsche was specifically flabbergasted and amused as well by the hypocrisy of Christians and other believers in God which he experienced directly as his father was a Lutheran minister and with his mother, Franziska who was the daughter of a Lutheran minister too. His father lost his mind when Nietzsche was five years old, and this might have contributed to Nietzsche's despondency and negative outlook on God and life. Nietzsche asserted, in fact, we philosophers and "free spirits" feel ourselves irradiated as at the new dawn by the report that the "old God is dead," our hearts overflow with gratitude, astonishment, presentiment and expectation. At last, the horizon seems open once more, granting even that is not bright; our ships can at last put out to sea in the face of every danger; every hazard is again permitted to the discerner; the sea, our sea, again lies open before us; perhaps never before did such an "open sea" exist.[49] This means Nietzsche was happy with the wide spread secularization that came with modernity and its scientific innovations.

Having denied God existence, Nietzsche grounded his philosophy on the shore of nihilism which holds the view that values have no justification and meaning. He formed a negative view of all moral standards. For him, there are no moral standard of right and wrong, good or bad. And truth has no moral value. He also presented a scathing view of religion and sees it as something decadent and dying, threatened with extinction as in the West where many churches and mosques are being closed to open industries. He sees secularization and scientific innovations as the new world order and free thinking as something in vogue, the new norm and the new direction. According to Jeremy Stangroom and James Garvey, Nietzsche argued that "the Western world intellectual and interpretive scaffolding and its underlying concepts which we all use to arrive at judgments of value can no longer sustain us. Perhaps it was possible for human beings, once, to buy into the idea that value has a basis in something beyond this world (say God or the absolute), but no longer."[50] Nietzsche believes we are on the verge of spiritual crisis and something new is needed to sustain us, otherwise we will plummet into the horrors of nihilism or worse.

Thus, Nietzsche viewed this crisis with euphoria and ecstasy because he thinks it is a unique opportunity for a new kind of freedom, the freedom for everyone to find value for himself and the catchphrase for this crisis of value is "God is dead." In his work, *"Thus Spoke Zarathrustra"*, Nietzsche surmised and suggested that the dead of God will create space and opportunity for the enthronement of the *"Ubermensch"* the Superman or the Overman. This enthronement will necessitate Western moral and value reconstruction, a value system that would only express what is excellent in the individual, and in each human person.

For Nietzsche, the Superman is that being which has overcome what has so far defined us as humans, the now-crumbling system of value. Humanity as it is now is something to be overcome, and the Superman is the lightning out of the dark cloud of man, the new ideal of which to aim. Nietzsche labeled as "human all too human," the religious or transcendental hopes and illusions that characterized our current dying scheme of value (morality and spirituality), the belief that virtue consists in obeying (and doing) the will of a dead God, that the fictitious rewards of the next life somehow excuse subjugation in this one and so on. For Nietzsche, the Superman has to renounce and reject all these too human variables and carve out his own unique place in the world according to his own will.[51]

These free thoughts of Nietzsche are based on the fact that he believes that the will to power is the ultimate reality and the ultimate good as well. In his work, *"Beyond Good and Evil"*, he sees the will to power as the essence of everything, the constitutive element of everything, and the elemental force underlying all reality. For him, the will to power is the fundamental explanatory cause of all things. The Superman should of necessity exercise this will to power to a logical conclusion, and he would not be submerged in the dogmatic slumber the rest of mankind has been thrown into.

Nietzsche's philosophy and his great quest for the superman have inspired in some quarters the search for the superman. Some looked to the direction of glorified Aryan hero or the African American Buffalo soldier while some others looked for Aristotle's man of virtue or the philosopher king of Plato; still some others search for a modern religious saint, many awaits the Parousia i.e. the second coming of the Christ, while some are looking for the anti-Christ. These searches are epitomized in movies and in film productions like the Spiderman, Batman, Ant-Man, the Incredible Hulk, the Terminator, the Wonder Woman, the Superman, the IronMan, Man of Steel, the Transformers, the Star Trek, Star Wars, etc. It is also reflected in the desire of some people in Astronomy for deep space exploration, the Mission to Mars and the new search for alien existence, the extra-terrestrial beings and the Unidentified Flying Objects (UFO).

For Rader, "the Nietzsche account of the death of God epitomizes the feelings of many thoughtful persons that our civilization has become overwhelmingly secular (and corrupt) and the rise of science, technology, (social media) and urbanization, and the collapse of traditional religion (and morals) are now the hallmarks of our era."[52] Thus, there are false pretenses in every quarter both religious and political. International terrorism and mass murder have become the order of the day and are carried out everywhere. There are no corridors of peace in the world anymore, and as such nobody is safe, nowhere is sacred and secure.

Theism: The Existence of God

Etymologically, theism comes from a Greek word *"theos"* which means God. Theism as a position holds that there is an ultimate reality, a personal God, more than the universe through whom the universe exists. This God continues to intervene in the universe and in personal life of the individual and the community. His words and actions are inspired and revealed to humans and are found in the sacred scriptures of different religions of the world. Many philosophers have tried to prove his existence. Foremost among them were Thomas Aquinas, St. Anselm, Rene Descartes, etc. St. Thomas Aquinas' *Quinque Viae* – (The Five Ways) are excellent efforts in demonstrating the existence of God on the bases of things accepted by believers and non-believers like the fact of causation, existence of intelligent designs in nature, the fact of motion, etc.

Monotheism

This view asserts that there is only one God. The Jews (Judaism), Islam and Christianity hold this view also. These religions acknowledge the existence of angels, demons and spirits but these are not regarded as gods. Most often they are seen as messengers of God.

Polytheism

This view states that there are many Gods. This means that God is more than one. Polytheism as a belief system existed in Ancient Greece and Roman Empire. African Traditional Religion (ATR) is also polytheistic in nature. ATR accepts the existence of one supreme God, the Supreme Being and the creator of the universe and all that it contains. However, it acknowledges the existence of other minor gods. Some people and cultures in Africa see the minor gods as deities and messengers of the supreme God. Sacrifices are still offered to these deities in some of their shrines manned by their priests up till today.

Pantheism

This is the view that everything is God and God is in everything. God and nature (the cosmos or universe) are identical. Pantheism is very much expressed in the philosophy of Baruch Spinoza. For him, there is only one substance with its attributes and modes. These are the only things that exist in reality. According to him God exist and is abstract and impersonal. He believes that everything that exists in the universe is one reality hence one substance. He disagreed with Descartes' Dualism that mind and body are two substances. He rejects the idea of mind being in the body, literarily as kind of *"Deus ex machina"* i.e., the ghost in the machine. For Spinoza, mind and body are different modes of the same thing. Nature and God are two names for the same reality – the single fundamental substance. All other entities are mere modes, attributes or modifications of this substance. God has infinite attributes of which thought and extension are two of them. These two attributes of God are known to the human mind. According to Spinoza, God does not rule over the universe by providence, and as such God does not bring changes in the universe because He is a part of a system that is wholly determined. So for him, those who rely on the will of God do so out of ignorance. Hence, he asserts "the will of God is the refuge of ignorance." Spinoza sees God or nature as a deterministic system, and hence human free will is not possible. Everything is a part of the long chain of cause and effect. Our actions are guided by natural impulses and what we call freedom is our knowledge that we not free.

In our contemporary time, there is no organized religion that is purely pantheistic in nature. However, pantheism more often creeps into a number of personal beliefs of an individual or thought current of a particular people or epoch by way of free thinking or through the misconception of causality and determinism. There is need to differentiate the two here. To say an action is free is by no means to say that it has no cause. It is true, perhaps, that every action has a cause. But then the cause does not determine an action. It takes a (human or God's) will to determine an action. If I am hungry and decide to eat, my action of eating has a cause, and this cause is hunger. Yet it is a free action, for I freely decided to eat. I could have refused to eat in spite of the fact that I was hungry. I could decide to starve or decide to eat. There is free will, hence there is free choice. Again when the Syrian conflict broke out in 2012, many Syrians moved out of the conflict zones, their action of relocating was caused by the war, but it was a free action, the result of a free will and free decision.

Some Syrians, of course, decided to stay within the conflict zones as others moved away to safety. So, contrary to the position of Spinoza we determine our actions, causes or impulses do not determine them.

Deism

Etymologically, deism come from the Latin word "*Deus*" which means god. Deism is a position that there is an ultimate reality, objectively existent, quite distinct from the physical universe and human beings. He created everything. He is the author of all natural and moral laws. However, he does not interfere with the established order which runs based on natural laws. So, the deist seems to believe like some people do that God has created the world and turned his back on it. Deism goes further to assert that the existence of this God can be known through reason and observation of the natural world rather than through revelation, authority of religions and their scriptures.

Deism is known to be the religious thoughts of the renaissance in the 17th and 18th centuries. The age of enlightenment is known for its rejection of medieval church authorities in favor of the modern science in Britain, Germany, France and America which have advanced the course of humanity far better than the organized religions of the middle and the dark ages. For the deists, organized religions inspired most of the conflicts and wars in history and the attendant loss of lives and property, and as such they have lost credibility in terms of directing people to God. Many deists are found in the wisdom religions of today. The theist criticized deism for projecting a reluctant God, one that is not personal, has no interest and does not get involve in human affairs. From this, theism apologetics can surmise and suggest that it is a waste of time and pointless too to offer prayers and sacrifices to a reluctant God.

God's Emergence Theory

This is a general view that God is still emerging or evolving with the cosmos. God is the end towards which the cosmos is tending, not the end from which it came. This is the experimentalist's conception of God and some scientists hold this view as it aligns with the Bid Bang Theory and the expanding universe.

On the Problem of Human Knowledge

Many questions that are asked on human knowledge border on the possibility, nature, source and types of human knowledge. We take some of them and the solutions offered.

Is Knowledge Possible?

The human senses are imperfect in nature and reason is also fallible. These make one wonder whether what we call knowledge is possible and reliable at all, whether we can point at any particular thing that is certain to all and not doubtable to any person in any way.

Solution:

Agnosticism

The word comes from Greek word "*Agnosco*" meaning "I do not know." This is a position that certain, conclusive and indubitable knowledge of ultimate reality is not possible. This kind of undecided position is portrayed in Herbert Spencer's view that "about the fundamental nature of things or their origin, my position is that I know nothing about them, hence I am satisfied with my ignorance. I deny nothing and I affirm nothing." Some agnostics express different views; some maintained that man cannot know more than he learns through his senses while others reduced cognition to that which is sensually experienced. Still others assert that it is possible to know a phenomenon but not its essence. It is from this kind of spirit that one of the well-known agnostic, Gorgias declared that nothing exist, nothing is, and assuming that being is, it cannot be known, even if it is knowable, no communication of what is known is possible.

Skepticism

This is the position that doubts the possibility of any knowledge. The adherents of skepticism argue that our daily lives may be a kind of sleep in which we dream that we know something and as well we are conscious of ourselves. They assert that the justification for and proof to their position include the existence of conflicting and erroneous ideas, and the contention that there are fluctuations and lack of uniformity on the views of philosophers and scholars on many pressing and vital issues of life.

They therefore see the human mind as incapable of attaining any genuine knowledge about logical and ontological realities. Again, to buttress their position, the skeptics pointed at the impossibility of getting a criterion for determining what knowledge is. Sextus Empiricus, one of the protagonists of skepticism was of the opinion that any person who thinks he has acquired knowledge must have done so through one of the following three ways; either the person proves his judgment by a proof which needs another proof and so on to infinity. And infinity does not provide us any final proof. He can also stop at a certain proof which he does not prove or cannot prove but only assumed at that point to be true. Finally, he can prove his statement with some principles and later prove this principle with his original statement. After this analysis, Sextus contended that certain knowledge cannot be achieved in any of these ways. Hence, any knowledge based on any of these ways is doubtable. With this, the skeptics grounded their ship of knowledge at the shore of skepticism and allowed it to vegetate and decay there.

The Affirmation of Knowledge

The view generally accepted by many is that knowledge is fractional never total. And this knowledge is functional in a particular field where it is needed. This is a view widely held by the experimentalists.

What are the Kinds of Knowledge?

Solution:

A posteriori Knowledge

This is the kind of knowledge based on experience and observation. That the sun is shining or the rain is falling or sky is cloudy and snowing concerns knowledge based on observation.

Experimental Knowledge

First and foremost, it is knowledge derived from experiment. This knowledge is also called empirical knowledge because it is based on experience. It is not exactly a posteriori knowledge because it is validated from observation and sometimes from induction. For instance that every volt car makes 34 miles per gallon of petrol is not knowledge based on purely experience but a fact of induction. All volt cars in existence were not tested to prove or reach the above conclusion. But the number of experiments on some volt cars warranted the conclusion.

A priori Knowledge

This is a self-evident knowledge or principle. It is knowledge based on reason, and is recognized to be true without any need for proof through observation or experiment. This is called rational knowledge. For example, if A is bigger than B and B is bigger C. Therefore, A is bigger than C.

What are the Sources of Knowledge?
Solution:
Empiricism

This is the view that all knowledge come through sensation or sense perception or experience. John Locke and David Hume were the protagonists of this system of philosophy.

Rationalism

This view holds that reason is the major avenue of gaining knowledge. Rene Descartes was the chief exponent of rationalism.

Intuitionism

This view states that knowledge can be gained by an immediate and sudden insight or awareness. Henri Bergson was an advocate of intuitionism.

Authoritarianism

This is the view that knowledge is gained through indisputable authority, for instance, the church, the state, experts in a field or discipline, etc.

Revelation

This is the view that God reveals Himself in Holy books like the Bible, Koran, the Vedas, etc. and through the churches and to individuals.

What is the Nature of Thought/the Process of Valid Reasoning?

The nature of thought and the process of valid reasoning are given more elucidation in the chapters of this work dealing with philosophical methods, logic and fallacies.

Solution:

Induction

This view holds that thought process proceeds from premises that are particular to a conclusion that is universal.

Deduction

This holds that thought-process proceeds from universal premises to a particular conclusion.

Syllogism

This is the structure or form of deductive reasoning comprising three propositions: two premises (major and minor), and a conclusion.

Hypothetic - Deductive Reasoning

This is also called Reproductive Experimental Reasoning or Problem-solving. This reasoning process is mostly inductive, but also deductive.

It starts with a problem, we observe all the data about the problem, formulate hypotheses, and test them to reach a workable solution to the problem.

Dialectic

This is a method of reasoning that gets to the truth by contrasting conflicting ideas. Dialectics for Hegel passes through three stages: thesis, antithesis and synthesis.

On the Problem of Value

The issue of value has been a topical one for many people because of the divergence of opinion on the nature of value and the criterion for value determination and selection. Here questions that are asked on axiological issues include:

What is the Nature of Value?
Solution:

Interest Theory

This view holds that values are simply what a person has interest in and enjoys. No value exists except what the perceiver desires. This suggests that the beauty of a thing (e.g., a work of art or the beauty of a woman) resides in the eyes of beholder.

The Existence Theory

This is a view that values have objective existence distinct and independent of the perceiver. This means that values actually reside with the object of value and not in the eye of the observer. Values are essence and existence with foundation in existence. We can surmise here that beauty resides in the beautiful woman and not in the eyes of the beholder.

The Experimentalist Theory

This view of value states that a valuable thing is that which yields a greater sense of happiness now and also opens the way for further goods. An inventor values his invention because it gives him joy and opens the door for recognition, wealth and wellbeing of others.

The Part-Whole Theory

The key to realizing and enjoying value is by relating the parts to the whole. For instance, an individual is said to be of great value if he relates well and becomes useful to the community. But the individual loses value if he cuts himself off from the community. Again, the chain is said to be as strong as it weakest link. This indicates the importance of parts to the whole. Peaceful individuals make a peaceful family, peaceful families make a peaceful community, peaceful communities make a peaceful state, peaceful states make a peaceful country and peaceful countries make peaceful world.

The Problem of Value in Ethics

This raises questions on the problems of good and evil, and of human conduct. Is life worth living?

Solution:

Pessimism

Arthur Schopenhauer (1788-1860) was regarded as a great advocate of philosophical pessimism. He was well known for brooding on the misery of things. In his work, *The World as a Will and Representation*, he espoused the view that the world is essentially a will. He went further than Kant who asserted that the world we perceive is constituted and constructed by the mind. For Schopenhauer, it is the will that makes us to reach out for anything or do anything. Hence, the world and all that we see are manifestations of a will, and as such it is an embodiment of a will; the exteriorization of the will.

However, Schopenhauer reduced this philosophy of will to pessimism when he asserts that the will in the abstract is the will-to-live or will-to-exist, and it manifests itself particularly as a constant throbbing of desire, striving and yearning with no particular goal or object. It is merely an undirected, blind, irrational want which drives everything or better which is everything. Thus, the human life is actuated by nothing as it is a constant craving, occasionally fleetingly satisfied but more often than not thwarted. When the will actually manages to satisfy itself, "life-benumbing boredom" quickly sets in and the striving is reawakened. The will does nothing but vainly keep itself willing until death. Thus for Schopenhauer, life is something which ought not to be, and this world is the worst of all possible worlds.

At the zenith of his pessimism, Schopenhauer insisted that existence is constant hurrying of the present into the dead past, a constant dying, that even our walking is admittedly merely a constantly prevented falling, the life of our body is only a constantly prevented dying, an ever postponed death. Finally, in the same way, the activity of our mind is constantly deferred ennui or boredom. Every breath we draw wards off the death that is constantly intruding upon us. Thus, life becomes a theatre of the absurd described by Albert Camus in his work, *The Myth of Sisyphus*, which illustrates a world full of paradoxes and miseries and as such a world without meaning.

Schopenhauer went further to suggest that the way to overcome this tyranny of the will and its cravings is through ascetic contemplation and saintly renunciation of life. In this way, one can grasp the essential futility of all life, see life for what it is, the blind craving of a single, unified Cosmic Will.[53] Schopenhauer joined other atheists and pessimists in asserting that if they could claim omnipotence and assume omniscience, they would create a far beautiful and better world than the one we live in.

This view of existence is negative, as it says life is not worth living. It is partly the outcome of the problem of evil and suffering in the world. So, some proponents hold this view because there are a lot of evils around us and life seems meaningless, and as Shakespeare would put it in *Macbeth, Act 5 Scene 5* that life is a tale told by an idiot, full of sound and fury signifying nothing.

Thus, they suggest we should find a way to escape life. This escape is most often achieved by many pessimists through loss of self-regulating capacities, dependence on Alcohol and drug addiction. Some pessimists escape life through loss of joy in living which often culminates in neurosis. Others get lost in a paranoid way of life in which they fear and dread everything ranging from their neighbors, the government, the media, aliens invasion and heavenly bodies like asteroids, etc. They think these are monitoring them and are out to destroy them. They become conspiracy theorists. They build fortified dungeons and store food, water and arms for the impending Armageddon, apocalypse or nuclear holocaust. Some others escape life through loss of contact with reality and the individuals can end up a victim of psychosis or schizophrenia.

In extreme cases, the pessimist escape could result to a loss of alternative modes of being and the pessimist could commit suicide. In suicide, the pessimist misconceives death as the ultimate freedom from the constant throbbing of the will and from the vicissitudes of life. At the highest point of pessimism, sudden and painless death is considered as the ultimate good. Suicide bombers, terrorists, serial killers and mass murderers are known to be extreme pessimists.

Optimism

Leibniz was one of the best known philosophical optimists. It was Leibniz who asserted that this world is the best of all possible worlds. He argued that if God as the most perfect being and the highest conceivable being exists; since He is perfect, it is inconceivable that He could have made things better than He has; therefore, this world is the best of possible worlds.

Leibniz went further to examine the problem of evil in the world vis-à-vis the existence of all powerful, loving God. Since evil is antithetical to a good and happy world, Leibniz wonders whether human happiness is necessarily the right measure for assessing the goodness of the world. Thus, for him, the world is the best of all possible worlds because it is the richest in phenomena. The biblical book of Genesis holds that God created the world and saw that it is good. It has the highest multiplicity of things and the appreciation of these things and God creative ingenuity is the root of happiness in the world. Thus, life is good and it is worth living. There is no need to escape life through alcoholism, drug addiction or suicide.

Meliorism

This school of thought holds that good or evil in existence is inconclusive. This means that the world tends to improve and we as human beings can and do play a role in raising the standard of goodness in the world. And we should continue to work to better the world and not escape life or bring more evil into the world. Meliorism runs on the Latin adage, *Bonum sit faciendum et malum vitandum,* which means "Good must be done and evil must be avoided." William James was one of the protagonists of meliorism as a mid-point between metaphysical optimism and pessimism. He believes that human effort contributes in improving the natural order in the world as well as bettering the human condition. This conception is often seen as the foundation and the basis of contemporary liberal democracy and human rights which aim at improving the human condition and making the world a better place than we saw it.

Evil is a Privation

This view holds that there is no evil in the world actually. Concretely for this view, "evil" or "bad" designates something which lacks some proper particular good which it should have according to its kind. Taken abstractly "evil" or "badness" is privation itself; that is, the absence of something which is due. An example is the hypothetical case of a bird without wings, or the biblical "salt" without a taste.

Privation itself is not a real being but a being of reason. For Klubertanz, an evil thing, of course, in the concrete sense is a real being with the reality of the thing which lacks the good that it should possess according to its nature.[54] Moral evil proceeds from human volition or free-will that lacks the good proper to it while physical evil like natural disasters, drought, famine and diseases are the result of adverse interactions among the multiplicity of things in existence.

What is the Highest Good (Summum Bonum)

The question of what should be the purpose of life or what should be the end of every human action has always been a burning issue. This raises the stake of what is the highest good to seek in life.

Solution:

Hedonism: Pleasure as the highest Good

This is the view that pleasure is the highest good. The word "Hedonism" comes from the Greek word *"Hedone"* meaning "pleasure." The theory says that pleasure is the final end of man and it is what every man seeks in his actions. According to Hedonism, pleasure or pleasant consciousness and this alone, have positive ultimate value; it is intrinsically good and has no parts or constituents which are not intrinsically good. Equally for the Hedonist, displeasure or unpleasant consciousness, and this alone have negative ultimate value; it is intrinsically bad. Those who advocated this position include Aristippus of Cyrene (435 BC), the founder of the Cyrenaic School and his followers. They hold that pleasure is the supreme and only good: everything, even virtue, is good only as a means of procuring and maintaining the maximum of pleasurable emotion together with a minimum of painful emotion.

Epicurus (341-270 BC) founder of the Epicurean School believes also, that pleasure is the only unconditioned good; and everything else including virtue has only a relative value. For him, life is not necessarily made manifest in the acquisition of the greatest number of pleasure but it lies in the serenity of mind. This peace of mind he offered drives from the fact he believes that the body and soul are made of atoms and at death the body, the soul do not survive the dissection and disintegration. For Epicurus, belief in the mortality of the soul saves one the worries of afterlife events such as punishment in hell with the dread of suffering, and perishing and the scare stories associated with them.

Hence, liberated from such eschatological superstitions, Epicurus taught, we would be free to pursue pleasure. But Cicero rejected this epicurean view by saying it is difficult to understand why Epicureans think that they are offering any palliative, to be told that one perishes completely and forever, soul as well as body, is hardly a robust consolation.[55] Epicurus also went further to support intellectual pleasure, and holds that the pleasure of a good conscience is supreme to sensitive pleasure. However, Lactantius in his polemics against the epicureans asserted that Epicureanism or the pleasure principle is an empty doctrine but it still has many followers not because it brings forward any truth but just because the attractive name of pleasure invites many.

In the modern period, Thomas Hobbes, a 17th century English Political Philosopher, an egoistic hedonist revived the pleasure principle and claims that intrinsically nothing is good or evil but is being rendered such due to our disposition or feelings towards it. For him, man is a sensitive being; it follows with necessity that pleasure is man's supreme good. Whatever therefore agrees with man's appetite or desire is morally good. Whatever man's appetite abhors, he calls evil.

Utilitarianism: Happiness as the highest Good

Bentham was the chief proponent of Utilitarianism. For him, people act in their own interests, and those interests consist of getting pleasure and avoiding pain. Similarly, individual human happiness consists in achieving a greater balance of pleasure over pain for the greatest number of people. According to this utilitarian principle, the highest good is the greatest happiness of the greatest number. This is different from egoistic hedonism in the sense that it advocates for altruistic or universalistic pleasure which by implication seeks or concentrates on the pleasure of the greatest number of human beings. The proponents of this view include philosophers like John Stuart Mill, Henry Sidgwick, Thomas More and Steven Smart. For many of these utilitarian thinkers, happiness is the end of every human action and that is what everybody seeks. Money is important because it contributes to happiness, and happiness is good for its own sake.

Bentham opines that good acts are those which produce the greatest happiness for the greatest number of people. John Stuart Mill went further to assert that the only purpose for which power can rightly be exercised over any member of a civilized community, against his will, is to prevent harm to others. His own good, either physical or moral, is not a sufficient warrant. For Mill, any society that abides by this rule of private morality would have happy citizens.

Perfectionism: Self-realization as the highest Good

This position holds that self-actualization, self-realization and self-fulfillment; the perfection of the self is the ultimate good. This is also reflected in Abraham Maslow's pyramid of needs where it occupies the highest point in the hierarchy of needs. Self-perfection most often goes with hard work to achieve a high standard one sets for oneself, and so it does not exclude pain entirely from the notion of ultimate good. Thus, no cross no crown is an intrinsic principle that runs with perfectionism.

The problem with perfectionism is that most often the standard set is an ideal and as such is very difficult to reach. Perfectionism sometimes has social reference. In this regard, the highest good is a certain ideal social order. Plato in his work, *The Republic*, tried to present an ideal social order, a perfect human society but the scheme he presented appeared unrealistic to modern minds.

The Problem of Criterion for Human Conduct

This deals with problems regarding human conduct. Whatever conclusion one makes about what is the highest good, a further problem about the criterion of human conduct would be raised.

Solution:

Kant's Categorical Imperative: The Means justifies the End

Kant's work, *Grounding for the Metaphysics of Morals,* contains the first formulation of the categorical imperative which states: "Act only according to that maxim whereby you can at the same time wills that it should become a universal law without contradiction." For example, the proposition "it is permissible to steal" cannot be universalized and it cannot be a universal law because it is contrary to the notion of property and ownership. It is not workable both in conceivability and in practicality.

Second Formulation of Kant's categorical imperative states: "Act in such a way that you treat humanity whether in your own person or in the person of any other never merely as a means to an end, but always at the same time as an end."

Third formulation of Kant's categorical imperative states: "Therefore, every rational being must act as if he were through his maxim always a legislating member in the universal kingdom of ends." Kant's moral legislation is anchored on duty and good will. For Kant good will is the ultimate good. It is the only thing that is good without qualification. It has no adulteration. People of good will are the best humans.

Spencer and Machiavelli's Principle: The End justifies the Means

Spencer holds that an action is right if it is conducive to self-preservation. This is well elaborated by Niccolo Machiavelli in his epic work, *The Prince*. For Machiavelli, there is a gap between how one lives and how one ought to live, anyone who abandons what is done for what ought to be done learns his ruin than his preservation: for a man who wishes to make a vocation of being good at all times will come to ruin among so many who are not good. Hence, it is necessary for a prince who wishes to maintain his position to learn how not to be good, and how to use his knowledge or not to use it according to necessity.

Based on the above principle, Machiavelli advised political gladiators never to forget that serious politics requires strength, fortitude and the capacity to act quickly and decisively. Machiavelli insisted that political gladiators should desire to be feared than to be loved for permanent honor and glory come from being feared than acting virtuously and being loved. Again, Machiavelli asserts that men are less hesitant about harming someone who makes himself loved than one who makes himself feared because love is held together by chain of obligation which, since men are a sorry lot, is broken on every occasion in which their own self-interest is concerned; but fear is held together by a dread of punishment and unpleasant experiences which will never abandon you. He went further to say that the excessively merciful prince, by tolerating disorder, will often bring greater harm to a state than the cruel prince who creates harmony through fear.

Thus, Machiavelli advised the prince to set aside moral considerations when making political decisions but rather should strive for goals of honor and glory as these are the measure of the prince's virtue. And the prince should be willing to do whatever is necessary in the face of unpredictable fortune to achieve honor and glory.

Machiavelli contended that the prince (i.e., the politician, administrator, leader, ruler or any person in authority) should not in an attempt to get honor and glory apply cruelty after cruelty for this can only bring great power but it cannot bring glory. According to him, well used are those cruelties that are carried out in a single stroke, done out of necessity to protect oneself, and are not continued but instead converted into the best possible benefits for the subjects. Badly used are those cruelties which, although being few at the outset, grow with the passing of time instead of disappearing.

Machiavelli urged the prince to have the strength of a lion and the cunning of a fox. In a world full of political enemies and antagonists, the prince cannot afford to lose in the game of self- preservation; he has to be a master in this survivalist game. The game theory for the prince according to Machiavelli is: the prince has be a lion to be able to scare away wolves and a fox to be able to dictate traps. The combined strengthens of the two animals minus their weaknesses (for the reason that the lion is susceptible to traps and the fox is endangered by the wolves) literally gives the prince an edge over his adversaries.

Descartes' Principle: The Methodic Doubt

Descartes urged all scholars that in any rational inquiry they should accept nothing as true without investigation and methodic doubt. Complex problems should be divided into as many smaller problems as possible and begin with what is most simple and easily understood and build on this by degrees to which is presented to the mind so clearly and distinctly that there is no reason to doubt it. Finally, the scholars should review the entire chain of thinking to ensure nothing is omitted.

Dewey's Principle: Human Beings are Products of their Environment

Discover the probable consequences of what you can consider doing (pragmatism). John Dewey was very much influenced by Darwin's theory of organic evolution – the origin of species and natural selection. According to Stangroom and Garvey, in the pre-modern world, species and organisms were seen as immutable, perfectly defined entities, the product of a benevolent designer. But Darwin's theory blew this idea apart, showing that the natural world is in fact dynamic and fluid and that organisms and species are ever-changing as they interact with environment.[56]

Based on the above fact, Dewey rejected the idea that human beings have fixed essence. Rather, he went on to assert that human beings are constituted in their interaction with the multiple aspects of their environment. For him, human beings are product or consequences of their lived practice.

Succinctly put, Dewey projects the view that we should be conscious of the environment we live in and the choices we make because they have consequences. When we make a choice, our choice will turn around and make us the person we will be now and projected into the future as well.

Pascal's Religious Wager: The Rationality of Belief

Pascal wants to make our belief reasonable. He asserts: live your life on the basis that there is God, at the end if there is no God, you have nothing much to lose rather than to live as if there is no God, at the end if there is God, you will have infinite loss of eternal happiness.

This is the position of Pascal in his work, Thoughts (Pensees), and his decision theory runs like this: Either God exists or He does not. We have to choose one way or the other on the issue; it is an unavoidable existential dilemma. If God does not exist, then we lose very little by believing that he does exist. If he does exist, then we stand to gain an awesome lot by believing that he does, and to lose an awful lot by thinking that he doesn't. Therefore, it is sensible to wager that he does exist, and to behave appropriately. As Pascal put it: "I should be much more afraid of being mistaken and then finding out that Christianity is true than of being mistaken in believing it to be true." This statement could also be made about other world religions like Islam and Buddhism, etc.

The above argument could lead us to accept the religious principle that we should obey the will of God and commit ourselves completely to the fulfillment of God's purpose for us and the world.

The Hobbes' Principle: Follow the Dictates of Reason

The natural condition of ungoverned human beings (literally, like those in the world of gangsters, illegal drug trades, crimes, terrorism, failed states and civil conflicts) is war, every man against every man. For Hobbes under this condition no one would enjoy life, no one would be happy but one could console oneself that one's suffering would be short as one probably would not last very long. For Hobbes in this state of nature, there is no knowledge of the face of earth; no account of time; no arts; no letters;

no society; and which is worst of all, continual fear, and danger of violent death; and the life of man is solitary, poor, nasty, brutish, and short. According to Hobbes, the only way to change this situation is for those concerned to follow the three laws of nature, namely:

- They must follow the dictates of reason to desire and seek the peace. This is to say that rationality coupled with the fear of violent death demands that people who find themselves in the state of nature must wish to get out of the state of nature to live better lives and have some measure of security.

- If the people must seek peace then they have to give up a share of their natural rights, their unfiltered liberty and contented with so much liberty against other men, as he would allow other men against himself. For Hobbes, peace is not possible if everyone has an equal share in liberty, an equal right to everything and the means simply to take it. Their pledge according Hobbes must read like this: "I authorize and give up my right of governing myself to this man or assembly of men (e.g., legitimate government with power and authority), on this condition that thou give up thy right to him, and authorize all his actions in like manner."

- The next rational requirement for these people who want to emerge from the state of nature is that they must keep their covenant to come out from the state of nature. For Hobbes, covenants without a sword are mere words and so to ensure that people keep their covenant to come of the state of nature, the guarantor of the covenant and the resultant social contract must be a sovereign with an absolute (constitutional government) power – the great Leviathan, that mortal God, to which we owe under the immortal God our peace and defense.[57]

The lessons we can drive from the above position of Hobbes include among other things, the necessity of seeking justice and peace at all times, the realization that there is nothing like absolute freedom for the individual, and then there is the need to obey the laws of the state and recognize and obey legitimate and constituted authority of the state officials. These are essential dictates of reason we need to live and survive in any city.

The Problem of Ultimate Motivation of Human Action

Every human action has a motive. So, what are those things that are incentives to perform or not perform an action?

Solution:

Altruism

This view holds that the interest of others or society is the motive of individual's actions. It is based on the notion that self-sacrifice with good will is the highest moral good. It is also guided by the belief in some quarters that man has no right to exist for his own sake, that service to others is the only justification of his existence. We know that some serve because they think they are born to serve, some are forced to serve, some serve because of the material gains while the ultimate service are rendered by those who think by serving others and their fatherland they serve God.

Egoism

Self-interest is the ultimate motive of human action. Psychological egoism holds that man by and according to his natural constitution and make up does everything (including prayers, charity and philanthropy) out of self-interest. Jeremy Bentham grounds all decision making on the psychological fact that people act in their own interest, and those interests consist of getting pleasure and avoiding pain.

Lastly, there are other questions asked about values, aesthetics, religion, education, society, politics, economy, etc. What we have presented, however, is just a panoramic outline of some problems of philosophy. It should also serve as a guide for understanding some of the solutions to our problems.

5

METAPHYSICS
The Horizon of the Question of Being

Philosophy has attempted to comprehend all that existed in our world; it was one unified body of endeavor to acquire general knowledge. Philosophy is like the tree of knowledge; the individual sciences grew out of it as the society developed and factors of production emerged and progressed. But as a discipline and a field of study, philosophy has major divisions. They include the following:

Metaphysics: This investigates the structure of being and reality.

Epistemology: This discovers what is in our power to know.

Ethics: This investigates the rules of human conduct, and

Logic: This establishes the canons of valid reasoning.

The Meaning and Origin of Metaphysics

Metaphysics has been defined from many perspectives by many scholars. However, their definitions boil down to almost one denominator, that is, the study of being as being; the science of reality. In metaphysics, we examine the three major aspects of being and reality, namely the world – cosmos and its constituents, man and his nature, God and His attributes.

Succinctly put, metaphysics is the theory about the nature of man and the world which he lives in. It deals with man's behavior and the cause of such behavior. It goes beyond that at times to deal with hidden and abstract topics of matter. In the words of Cardinal Mercier, metaphysics is "the science as well as a discipline disengaged by thought from the conditions of matter, as of things which are by their nature untrammeled and unhampered by such conditions."[1] Succinctly put, it is the science of things whether negatively or positively immaterial. This means that the object of metaphysics is the individual substance.

Metaphysics as an organized discipline got its name when Andronicus in the 1st century B.C. organized the works of Aristotle dealing on material things like plants and animals, the world and other planetary bodies like the stars, the moon and the sun, etc. These, he called the Aristotle's physics, then, he saw a collection of Aristotle's works on immaterial objects, things that are not within experience such as soul, God, the causes and the universals, and since they came after the physics of Aristotle, he called this collection, metaphysics, which means "after physics."[2]

The Division and Subject Matter of Metaphysics

Metaphysics as a discipline and course of study has been divided into two, the Traditional metaphysics and Pure metaphysics.

Traditional Metaphysics

This is metaphysics as done by the early philosophers. The Ionian and Greek philosophers reflected on the nature of reality, the ultimate constituent of being, and the problem of change and permanence, etc. Philosophers like Thales, Heraclitus, Parmenides, etc., were among the earliest traditional metaphysicians. Traditional metaphysics reached its summit in Plato and Aristotle. The problem of particulars and universals, one and many, act and potency, being and essence, substance and accidents, causality and participation including permanence and change, to mention but a few, were the subject matter of their works.

Pure Metaphysics

The term pure metaphysics distinguishes the subject matter from that of traditional metaphysics that was weighted down by ancient reflections on the basic stuff of reality. With modernity, metaphysics came of age and took a distinctive form. Pure metaphysics is divided into two branches, Special Metaphysics and General Metaphysics.

Special Metaphysics

This distinction rests on the following basis: We have a tendency to classify things according to their resemblance, and thus, we group natural beings as living and non-living, we distinguish living things as plants and animals, and among these we reserve a special place for man. The particular philosophical study of each of these groups belongs to special metaphysics. Special Metaphysics consists of two major branches, namely: Cosmology and Rational psychology. Cosmology is the philosophy of the inorganic world. It studies the universe as a whole, its birth, formation, growth, shape, size, age, future development, etc. Thus, things like astronomy and astrophysics are part of this study, and they have as subject matter heavenly bodies like the galaxies, the stars, the planets and their moons, asteroids, comets etc.

Rational Psychology, on the other hand, is the philosophical study of the corporeal living beings and especially of man. Today it is called Philosophical Anthropology. It deals with things like language, culture, knowledge, human person, work, human will and freedom, passion, determinism, causality, creationism, auto transcendence, death and immortality of the soul, etc.

General Metaphysics

This concerns the treatment of reality as complexes. Aristotle sees this as the first or fundamental philosophy while Martin Heidegger sees it as ontology. This classification of metaphysics is traceable to the works of Christian Wolff (1679- 1754). General metaphysics has to do with ontology where "being as being" constitutes the problem of metaphysics. Different schools of metaphysics have different perspectives of what being is and their thought currents inform us deeply on the horizon of the question of being. But first, let us consider being and its attributes since being is the main subject matter of metaphysics.

Being and its Attributes

Being as being may be defined as "what is," or as that which exists or simply as reality. The term being signifies a concept that has the widest extension and the least comprehension. Being is the first thing grasped by the human intellect, the first concept formed by the mind. If man knows anything at all, he knows being. Because being has the widest extension, our senses grasp the particulars, the individual things that exist in reality and our minds try to grasp the extension and the complexity of the whole.

For Marcel Onyeocha in his work: *Metaphysics: Cycle A- Theory*, "the concept of being is not only chronologically prior to all others; it is also analytically prior, in so far as every subsequent concept is some modifications of this first concept." For him, the recognition of the "thereness" of what is initially grasped in sense experience underlies the formation of the concept of what exists, what is there, what is present to the senses. Through this concept, the mind is enabled to embrace in a confused and universal manner whatever can be known in perception. The concept of being itself tells man the least about anything but it also tells him something of everything as desired. All terms arrived at by separation of being are therefore analogous in their major uses. Examples of these terms that are analogous are one or unity, goodness, beauty, truth, otherness, causality, etc.

Analogy of Being

First of all, analogy comes from the Greek "*ana*," (according to) and "*logos,*" ("ratio," "proportion"). It signifies a relation of similarity between two or more things, allowing the drawing of probable or necessary conclusions depending on the kind of relation in question. In ordinary every day speech, "analogy," may express almost any sort of likeness. Finding similarities in some respects we reason by analogy that there will be similarities in other respects. If the cases are not sufficiently similar to support the reasoning, we have a false analogy. This is because it is the business of analogy to illustrate or suggest, not demonstrate. A fallacy of false analogy is committed when one argues from the analogy to a conclusion claimed to follow necessarily. The fallacy is more pronounced where there are more differences in the cases compared. For teleologists and scholastics, analogy of being assumes a grade of excellence whereby we can argue from one case to another on differing levels of being (e.g., from the consciousness of a finite being to that of a perfect being). There are two types of analogies, (a) analogy of attribution and (b) analogy of proportionality.

Analogy of Attribution

This can be seen from the difference between primary and secondary or original and derivative meanings of terms. For instance, the term "health" applies intrinsically or fully to analogates such as man, animals and plants that have life. Here, health has its primary and original meaning. Example: Mr. Michael is a healthy man, and he has two healthy cats and three healthy trees in his compound.

On the other hand, health is applied extrinsically or derivatively to other analogates such as food, exercises and relationships that support life. Here, health takes on a secondary and a derivative meaning.

Examples: Running is a healthy exercise. Vegetable Salad is a healthy food.

Analogy of Proportionality

Analogy of proportionality can be seen in the sense of the proportion 2:4 and 4:8. There is a common quality which applies to each analogate proportionally. Similarly, when we say that "God is good," we are employing this form of analogy. We are saying that the goodness which exists in creatures pre-exists in God proportionally. This is regarded as the metaphysician proper analogy of proportionality.

Cajetan Thomas de Vio (1469-1534) championed this analogy of proportionality in his *Ontology of Substance*. He sees the existence of all things as participation in the pure actuality which is God.

We use the principle of analogy in fixing the appropriate import of our terms since there are certain "transcendental" terms which go beyond any genius and apply to everything, that is to say, they are attributes of everything. For instance, all beings are things with unity; hence they can be distinguished from what they are not. All beings are what they are, hence, in relation to knowledge, they are true. And all beings tend towards their ends or goals and so fit the Aristotelian and Thomas Aquinas' definition of goodness. Hence, all beings are good.

Transcendental Attributes of Being

The division of being into substance and accidents gives rise to words whose scope is less than that of being. For example, while every substance is being, not every being is a substance. There are other terms, however, whose range and scope are equal to those of being itself. Since what they mean transcends the division into categories, they are called transcendental attributes of being, or simply regarded as the transcendentals. They are properties that necessarily accompany being and thus are found in every being. Of these attributes, the most commonly discussed are unity or oneness or unique *(unum)*, truth *(verum)*, and goodness *(bonum)*. Some would also add beauty *(pulchrum)*, thing *(res)* and otherness *(aliquid)*. These properties are coexistent and coextensive with being; in them being manifests itself and reveals what it actually is. Just as being is never found without such properties, so these are inseparably bound up with one another in the sense that they include and interpenetrate each other. Consequently, W.A. Wallace says "according to the measure and manner in which a thing (or a person) possesses being, it partakes of unity, truth and goodness, and conversely, according to the measure and manner in which a thing (or person) shares in these properties, it possesses being."[4]

This ultimately implies that subsistent being is also subsistent "unity, truth and goodness." For him, "these attributes transcend all particularities in the order of being and are the most common determinants of all things."[5]

In elucidating these attributes of being, Catholic Encyclopedia asserts that "*Oneness* or *unity* is the attribute of a thing whereby it is undivided in itself and yet divided from others."[6] In other words, it is unique and as well separated and differentiated from other things. And it went further to say that "*Truth* is the attribute of a thing whereby it (the thing) has a relation to a knowing intellect and on this account is intelligible."[7] This means it is understandable and not obscure in nature. It is well known to all, far and wide. For W. Brugger and K. Baker, "*Goodness* is that whereby it (a thing) has a relation to an appetite and on this account is desirable and worth striving for."[8] For Aristotle, the good is that desired by all and it has happiness as an end. *Beauty* according to Thomas Aquinas is that which gives pleasure when it is seen while Albert the Great sees it as the splendor of form where transcendental qualities shine forth with luster and are perfect in themselves (not distorted) and must resound together harmoniously and shine forth brightly in their perfection. *Thing (res)* and *otherness (aliquid)* are the qualities whereby a thing is a substance different and separated from the rest of things.

When we join the transcendental attributes to the principles of analogy, we begin to be able to discern, within limits, God's nature and the nature of being. Most importantly, this goes to the heart and explains the very nature of the human being. These attributes define and give meaning to the human person in any state of life. Many are models in their endeavors because they have higher degree combination of these attributes. These attributes explain why some are great, others are not, some are wealthy, others are not, some are leaders and rulers, others are not, etc. For instance, the whole goal of high education and profession is to make one unique, to be set apart, and to be first among equals, etc. When you are unique in any chosen profession, you are intelligible too; and you will have high visibility in the profession.

Substance and Accidents in Things

The Substance theory, or substance-attribute theory, is an ontological theory about object-hood, stating that a substance is the thing-in-itself (to use Kant's terminology), and exists independent of any accidental property it may bear. Being is hence divided into substance and accidents. Substance is being in a primary sense; the being of accidents is derived from that of substance. In other words, accidents are not being by themselves but rather they are being by their relation to substance, and thus the being attributed to them is the being of substance. So, the meaning of being as applied to substance and to accidents is partly the same and partly different. Partly the same, because the being of substance is attributed to accident and partly different, because accidents do not have being in the primary sense verified of it in substance. This means that qualities like colors, tastes, heat, cold, sounds, odor, etc. are accidents. They do not exist independently rather they adhere to a substance like a body, a wall, a fruit; a dress, etc. This sustains their being.

Aristotle distinguishes a "primary" and a "secondary" meaning of substance. In the primary sense, a substance is an absolutely individual thing: this man, this dog, this apple, this rock. In the secondary sense, a substance is a class of things, such "man," "dog," "apple," and "rock" - one of the kinds of things that we find in nature and that we use in describing and classifying objects. Aristotle regards the changing characteristics of the substance as its attributes and they are universal in the sense that they can apply to indefinite number of particular things, e.g., redness, hotness, coldness of things, etc. The essential characteristics of substance include:

● It is always a subject and never a predicate, e.g., a leaf is a thing while green is a predicate.

● It has no contrary and admits of no degree, e.g., there is no contrary of man, and we cannot say Socrates is more man than Plato.

● It persists, it is identical, while accidents vary between contrary poles, e.g., the same man is now hot that was previously cold.

● Contrary qualities can be predicated to it, e.g., a man can be called black and another time white.

Aristotle distinguished three kinds of substance "one that is sensible" as:

● Eternal substance (e.g., the unmoved mover - God)

● Perishable substance (e.g., animals, plants, etc.)

● Immovable substance (e.g., stars, planets, etc.)

Matter and Form of Things (Hylemorphism)

Primary substances can be analyzed into two constituent factors, matter and form. Matter is the stuff of which the things consist, and this stuff may be the same kind as the stuff of which quite different things consist. Thus, gold is the stuff out of which rings, bracelets, etc., are made. According to Rader, this conception of matter is extended beyond any merely physical stuff. For example, psychological dispositions are the matter out of which a man's character is formed and various propositions are the matter out of which an argument is made.[9]

The form is the determination or organization given to the matter. Where there is matter there is form, and where there is form there is matter. What is form from one standpoint is matter from another standpoint. For example, one can think of homes as matter out of which a city is made, and of cities as matter that enters into the larger form of a nation. In the primary substance, the matter and form are thought of as combined to make an individual thing. Rader further stated that matter and form can also be conceived generally. For example, flesh and bones in general are the matter out of which human bodies in general are made.[10]

In summary, the fundamental tenet of this theory of Hylemorphism (from Greek words *"Hyle"* - matter and *"morphe"* - form) is that all natural bodies are composed of two incomplete substantial principles. One is the general principle common to all natural bodies indeterminate but determinable, called matter, while the other is the specifying principle which actualized and determines the matter, and it is called form. The union of both principles gives rise to a natural body as a unitary composite substance. The matter is passive while the form is dynamic and active as the essential factors in the constitution of things.

Potentiality and Actuality in Things

This is another way of describing a substance, that is, as something that is dynamic rather than static. Potency or potentiality is what may be while act or actuality is what is. Potentiality is related to matter and actuality is related to form. Matter has the potentiality of being shaped into certain form. For instance, iron ore has the potentiality of being shaped into different iron bars and sheets.

The Potency/Potency Principle

In Aristotle's Metaphysics, Book I entitled *A Philosophical Lexicon,* Chapter II; he distinguished between being-in-potency or being-in-capacity and being-in-act or being-in-perfection. According to him, the term potency can mean the following:

It is a principle of motion or change in something other than the thing changed. The principle enabling a thing to effect change or movement successfully - that is, according to intention. All conditions in virtue of which things are impassive generally or are unchangeable or cannot easily deteriorate.[11] In Latin, *"potentia"* means power. And as power, it has two main capabilities: first, it is the power of being acted upon, or of being changed by another. It is also the insusceptibility to change for the worse or to destruction by the agency of another thing.

Generally, potency may be divided into two, namely: objective potency and subjective potency. The objective potency is also called logical potency or mere possibility. It concerns something that is only a virtual reality like an internet friend. It can also be taken as a friend or something that exists only in the mind. It has no physical existence like the mortar and brick type of existence. In other words, objective potency is the capacity for existence, not in an existing (being) subject.

On the other hand, Subjective Potency refers to a being, a real principle of being. The subjective potency is divided into passive subjective potency and active subjective potency. The passive subjective potency is an aptitude or the capacity in an existing being for an Act, in order, to receive some determination or perfection. While the active subjective potency is the capacity in an existing being to perform some action or produce some effect. It is an operative potency, the real capacity or power for performing an operation such as the power to think or reason or will or work. Since pure potency is hard to hold in reality, we have mixed potency which is imperfect act because it is in potency to further Act.

The Act/Actuality Principle

Act, actuality or actuality principle is that into which potency is received or a source of actuality or perfection in an existing thing, i.e. that within a being which makes it actually this or that. In this light, the act is the goal of the potency - its perfection. Act is divided into pure and mixed act. Pure act admits of no potency, it is unlimited, perfect, unique or one. It possesses the plenitude (fullness or abundance) of all perfection. When anything if possible reaches a pure act, it means the thing has struck apotheosis. It has reached a divinization; a deification of essence. We have only one Pure Act, and this Pure Act is God. On the other hand, Mixed Act is limited by potency. It is composed of potency and Act. It is Act which is in potency to Act of another order. Things as we see them are mixed Act since they can be changed to other things.

The Five Causes of Things

Causation, or causality, is the capacity of one variable to influence another. The first variable may bring the second and the second the third, etc. For Aristotle, the word "cause" is that factor that makes a thing that which it is. This includes the why and the wherefore. We can enumerate about five causes:

• The material cause is that element out of which a thing is made, e.g., clay, wood, iron ore, etc.

• The formal cause is that mold into which the material is put, e.g., chair, pot, rings, etc.

• The efficient cause is the means by which the change is wrought, e.g., carpenter, goldsmith, or the Chef, etc.

• Instrumental cause: this is the implement used by the efficient cause, e.g., carpenter's hammer and tape, the Chef's pots and spoon, murder weapon like gun, knife, etc.

• The final cause is the end or purpose or intention for which the thing is made.

SCHOOLS OF METAPHYSICS

The primary concern of these schools of metaphysics is "what is the fundamental nature of man and the surrounding universe?" This question directs our mind to the metaphysics of the microcosm, that is, of the "I" or self which is consciousness as a small part of the whole scheme of things. This further connects with the metaphysics of the macrocosm, that is, of the great all-enveloping system of reality which can be called the universe of being. As a matter of fact, we shall not try to separate these two schemes of reality because they are not mutually exclusive.

Teleological School of Metaphysics

Many philosophers find the principal explanation of the nature and problem of existence in "teleology." Teleology comes from the Greek word, "telos" meaning end or goal. So, the school holds the view that reality is ordered and arranged according to goals, ends, purposes, and values. According to them, nothing is created or exists in vain. Consequently, these teleologists try to explain the past and the present in terms of the future. For them, "things occur to realize future ends."[12] Thus, a thing is good only and only if it is moving towards the purpose for which it is created. Aristotle is one of the leading members of this group, and they are known by the key concepts they analyzed and employed in their discourses and treatises.

Our analysis and interpretation of these concepts in chapter four constitute a penetrating insight into the nature and problem of reality. These concepts include being, substance and attributes, matter and form, potentiality and actuality, the four causes and motion, among many others.

The Materialists School of Metaphysics

The materialists are opposed to the teleologists in the sense that they try to explain the present and the future not in terms of purpose and goals but in terms of past and antecedent causes. The materialists conceive these causes to be material such as the movement of physical atoms. In the modern period, the materialists take the factors of production as among the material causes. This means land, labor, capital, information and entrepreneurship are the material causes of things.

On the Nature of Reality

The ancient materialists, Lucretius and Democritus expressed the view that things are made of atoms. However, their ideas about atoms have been rendered obsolete by modern science. But, the materialistic temper of Lucretius' philosophy as distinguished from the archaic details of his science remains as up-to-date as ever. Nothing in modern physics contradicts his vision of all things arising from and returning to a material base. This vision is equally shared by some modern philosophers like Santayana, Baruch Spinoza and Thomas Hobbes.

For Democritus, the only objective properties of things are size, shape, weight and motion. All other qualities such as sound, color, odor, taste and touch are sensations in us caused by the motion and arrangements of the atoms. This theory according to Rader was revived by Galileo and was reformulated by Hobbes, Locke, Newton and other influential modern thinkers. This theory has featured very prominently in modern theories of perception. For example, some modern naturalistic thinkers explain warmth as the reactions of our sense organs and nervous systems to molecular motions; sound as our reaction to air waves; color as our reaction to light and electromagnetic vibrations. Thus, the secondary qualities - colors, sounds, odors, and so on – exist as such, only for our minds. In the absence of our mental reaction, the universe is a pretty dull and abstract affair – a collection of soundless, colorless and odorless particles in various arrangements, drifting through space and time.[13]

Some modern thinkers like George Berkeley and David Hume have challenged the theory of Democritus and its modern counterparts that primary qualities are objective. According to them, primary qualities may be no less subjective than the secondary qualities. For them, if sound, colors, and tastes do not actually exist in things, and then primary qualities like shapes and motion exist because of subjective perception. But we know from experience that a moving vehicle is actually in motion. We do not have to stand before a moving train or vehicle to prove it.

On the Nature of Life and Mind

The materialists such as Democritus, Lucretius and Epicurus express the view that the human organism is made up of innumerable atoms and has vital characteristics which the atoms taken simply do not possess. Accordingly, just as the meaning of a sentence results from combination of meaningless letters, so life and mind result from the combinations of meetings and configuration of lifeless and mindless atoms. Applied to evolution, this theory means the recognition of diverse levels of complexity and organization, each with its emergent qualities, and the interpretation of these levels as successive stages in an evolutionary process. This position was propagated by Samuel Alexander (1859-1938). This materialistic view of the mind holds that the mind or consciousness arises out of matter and is a function of complex material bodies. For Alexander, out of dust man rises and to dust will he return. Vital process, including thoughts cannot survive the dissolution of the body any more than a football game can continue after the disbanding of the opposing teams.

The basic different between the materialist and the teleologist is seen when we put both in a house; the teleologist will be thinking about the functions and purpose of the house like shelter, privacy, security, comfort and happiness, the materialist will be looking at the physical blocks and other materials used to build the house and considering the basic stuff they made of like the cement, the sand, the stones, the wood, the tiles, the roofing sheets, etc.

Dualist School of Metaphysics

Dualism is a system of metaphysics which recognizes two distinct and irreducible kinds of being – the mind and matter. For them, man is a combination of mind and matter. The foremost protagonist of this school was Rene Descartes. He believed there are two spheres of reality, the mind and the material world. He tried to prove that certain and indubitable knowledge could be obtained about these two spheres.

On the Existence of the Ego - The Mind or the Self

Descartes was astonished by the uncertainties he discovered in the things he regarded as knowledge since childhood. He decided when he was intellectually matured to search for something he can know with certainty. He suspended all that he had taken as knowledge by casting doubt on all of them. Armed with his hyperbolic doubt or methodic doubt, he had the intention of setting aside all that in which the least doubt could be supposed to exist. In his words, "I shall ever follow in this road until I have met with something which is certain or at least, if I can do nothing else, until I have learned for certain that there is nothing in the world that is certain."[14]

Thus, Descartes, in the process of his search for at least one indubitable certainty rejected the senses and its information, and his fallacious memory. He sees the body, extension, figure and movement as figments of the mind. He thought of the source of his ability for passing this judgment on things, he considered God as the source but he waved this away since this ability may be found in him. This directly led Descartes to the fundamental question: What am I? It was in attempt to doubt the existence of self which is independent of other things that he became aware that he could not doubt that he exists. For in the very act of doubting things our physical existence is revealed.

However, Descartes hesitated to accept this new discovery because there may be in existence a powerful and deceitful demon that can use his ingenuity in deceiving him to affirm this existence of the self. After much meditations on this issue, he asserts convincingly: "if he deceives me, then again I undoubtedly exist; let him deceive me as much as he may, he will never make it that at the time of thinking that I am something, I am in fact nothing."[15] It was as a result of this conviction that Descartes affirmed the proposition: I am, I exist as necessarily true each time he pronounces it or mentally conceive it. Fredrick Copleson says "it is on this account that Descartes has given to philosophy and science a privileged truth which is immune from the corroding influence not only of the natural doubt which we may feel concerning judgments about material things but also of the hyperbolic doubt."[16] Having discovered that his existence is indubitable, he went forward to find out what he really is. After going through the litany of attributes he could predicate to the self, he found only thinking or thought as the only attribute that could not be separated from the self. He affirmed certainly *"Cogito Ergo Sum,"* "I think therefore, I exist." Descartes inferred from this that he is not more than a thing which thinks, in other words a mind or a soul. The question that arises at this juncture is: what is a thinking being? Descartes concludes that, "it is a thing that doubts, understands, affirms, denies, wills, abstains from willing, and that also can be aware of images and sensations"[17]

On the Existence of God

Descartes proves the existence of God in three forms: two of the proofs are from within his mind while the third proof is a restatement of Saint Anselm's ontological argument on God's existence. He started the first proof from the idea of God in us. We all have the idea of God in our mind. That is why everyone can talk about God. There is nobody without the idea of God. Perhaps, it is something that comes with the age of reasoning. For Descartes, this idea of God in us has a cause. On the cause of this idea, Descartes says that, "we should not have the idea of an infinite substance since we are finite if it has not proceeded from some substance which is variably infinite."[18] He therefore, believes that since the greater cannot proceed from the less, nothing less than God is adequate to explain this idea of God in our mind and in the world. This step involves the notion that the idea of a perfect being is in conception perfect and no imperfect being is capable of causing such an idea, hence it requires a perfect cause to produce it. Therefore, that infinite and perfect being, God exists.

In the second proof, Descartes used an argument by elimination – *argumentum eliminanda*. He started with the fact that "I think therefore I am." He argues that God is the cause not only of my idea of God but of me also. He said, "it is absurd for me to be the cause of myself because as he said: if I am the author of my being, I should doubt nothing, and I should have bestowed on myself all perfections of which I possessed any idea of and should thus be God."[19] Furthermore, Descartes argues that no other finite being, for example our parents, could be a sufficient cause of our existence, for if such a being existed, it in turn would have to be explained, as would any prior finite cause as well. Thus, we would have to trace the causal process back from stage to stage to the ultimate cause, an eternal and necessary being who requires no explanation beyond himself. Only such an infinite cause could be conceived as existing, not merely through my life but also through all the lives involved in the total succession of finite beings. It is only this kind of cause that can be adequate to maintain as well to originate the entire succession. Descartes argues that this ultimate cause cannot be multiple, since I conceive of God as absolutely one and the cause of this idea must be no less perfect than its effect, not falling short of the idea in its unity or in any other respect. Therefore, the only possibility that remains is that an infinite and monotheistic God is the cause. Therefore, God exists.

In the third proof, Descartes revived the ontological argument, which is an a priori argument which says syllogistically that 'the greatest conceivable being exists in reality; God is the greatest conceivable being, therefore, God exists in reality'. This is in line with Saint Anselm's view that God is a being, that which nothing greater can be conceived, and this Being must exist in understanding and in reality. This is because according to Hawkins, "to exist in reality as well as in the mind is greater perfection than merely to exist in the mind."[20] Descartes concludes from the fact that we cannot conceive of God without existence, it follows that existence is inseparable from Him and as such is one of God's attributes. He therefore concludes that God exists. Existence is the essence of God.

If existence is the essence of God then God exists everywhere including our minds. Even, the atheist has this idea of God in his mind before he can even think of doubting or rejecting God's existence. No one can doubt anything he or she does not have idea of. Hence, an idea must exist in our mind before we can doubt or believe its existence in reality. No one really desires or rejects what he has for he already has it. Thus, most atheists doubt in philosophy what they do not doubt in their minds.

On the Existence of the Material World

To complete the dualist tenet, Descartes asserts that the faculty of imagination is capable of persuading us through experience that material things exist. The fact we receive impressions which are sometimes against our will also make us believe that these impressions or ideas are conveyed to us by corporeal objects. Although we could doubt the cause or sources of these impressions but there are facts in our daily lives that really make us accept the existence of external objects; they include the following: we perceive that our body has different parts, and outside ourselves, we perceive the extension of things, figure and motion of bodies, and we also perceive in bodies other qualities like hardness, softness, heat, color and sound. These help us to distinguish the sky and the sea, the earth and other material things, and we are also able to exit from open doors but cannot exit from locked ones. These facts made Descartes to accept the existence of the external world. He affirms; "I believed myself to perceive objects quite different from my thought, bodies from which these ideas proceeded."[21] And he concludes by saying "I have a clear and distinct idea of myself in as much as I am only a thinking thing, and on the other hand, I possess a distinct idea of body, in as much as it is only extended and unthinking thing."[22] Descartes' proof of the existence of the material world is a reminder of something we all take for granted, that is, the existence of external world of physical things outside our minds, and the impact they have on our lives which may limit or assist us like when we use wooden materials to build a boat to help us cross a river, or construct a ladder enable us climb a wall or board a plane to reach distance places.

Idealist School of Metaphysics

Idealism as a system of metaphysics like the materialists denies the dualism of reality, but unlike the materialists, the idealist regards the mind as the basic constituent of reality. This school is well represented in the philosophy of Berkeley and Hegel. In the *Dialogues between Hylas and Philonous*, Berkeley presented Hylas as a Materialist while Philonous represented the Idealist, which he is. He as an idealist insisted that physical objects have no existence independent of the mind. The whole universe is made up of minds and nothing more.

According to Philonous in the Dialogues, "sensible things therefore, are nothing else but so many sensible qualities or combinations of sensible qualities in the mind."[23] And so for him colors, sounds, taste, in a word, all those termed secondary qualities have certainly no existence without the mind. On the primary qualities of objects such as extension, figure, solidity, gravity, motion and rest, the idealist also denied their existence independent of the mind. For the idealists *"esse est percipi"* which means "to exist is to be perceived." Berkeley went further to sum up his vision of reality as *"esse est percipiant percipere."* This means that "to be (or to exist) is to be perceived by a mind." A question that could be asked here is: if a person can exist independently of someone's idea of him, why cannot other things exist independently of our minds? According to Rader to argue that an apple must be in our minds because we are thinking of it is like arguing that a person must be in our minds because we are thinking of him. If we distinguish clearly between the act of thinking and the object of thought, the act of perceiving and the object perceived, there is no absurdity in supposing that things may exist even when they are unperceived or unthought-of.[24]

This fact did not occur to Berkeley or he refused to take it into account but he opines that mental perception is the result of the direct action of God on finite and independent spirits. The objects we perceive have their cause in God since they are not of our own making. Nature is the "visual language" through which He reveals His power to us and through which finite spirits, with the help of God's coordinating influence, communicate to one another. But God, although he acts upon us, is nonetheless distinct, and each one of us has his own individual identity. Thus, the universe is a pluralistic society of minds or spirits, the central position and coordinating role are assigned to God.[25]

This view marked out Berkeley as a subjective and pluralistic idealist different from Hegel who is regarded as an objective, absolute and monistic idealist. For Hegel as we discussed in his dialectical method in chapter three, the universe is an integrated system and all spirits are members of one another. According to Hegel, the whole of reality is a system in which each part is relational. And as a monistic idealist; Hegel rejects the dualism of Descartes where reality is divided into mind and matter. Hegel asserts that reality is one and absolute.

The Organicists School of Metaphysics

Organicism as system of metaphysics represents the view that there is no sharp and distinct leap from matter to mind, or from the inorganic to the organic. For them, reality is merely a greater and greater complication of organic structure. There is a complication of organic materials like proteins - amino acids and other materials to a level of consciousness. This school of thought is represented by the philosophy of Alfred North Whitehead. For him, the history of the universe as he envisages it is the evolution of organisms from the simple to the complex. According to him in his work, *Science and the Modern World,* the complication of reality ranges from electrons, atoms, molecules, cells, organs, plants, animals, man and human communities. Hence, these form a mounting series; the higher organisms embrace innumerable lower ones. For him, even matter at the lowest level is organic.[26]

This position of Whitehead was bought over by Lovejoy in his work the *Revolt against Dualism*. He affirms that reality should be better interpreted and understood in terms of form, process, emergence, and various levels of integration rather than in terms of a discrete mechanism or reductionism involving mind and matter.[27]

The Skeptics School of Metaphysics

In opposition to the above positive theories in metaphysics, skepticism contends that it is impossible to know reality. For them, the real nature of the external world and the nature of the human being cannot be grasped and be known. Immanuel Kant and David Hume stand out as the leading members of the school. Kant denied the possibility of metaphysics in his *Prolegomena to Future Metaphysics* and in his *Critique of Pure Reason*. He affirms that belief in God, freedom of the will and the immortality of the soul are articles of moral faith rather than doctrines that can be established by theoretical reason. Hume reduced human knowledge to perceptions and impressions.

Actually, we know that the proposition "knowledge of reality is impossible" is a kind of knowledge. During the time of Kant and Hume, metaphysics was reduced to the problem of knowledge. Hume said "when I enter most intimately into what I call myself, I always stumble on some particular perception. I never catch myself at any time without perception and can never observe anything but perception."[28] Hence, Hume even questions the possibility of self-knowledge as he held the view that what we call self is nothing but streams of perceptions. The quick successions of these streams of perceptions would not allow us to form a constant and reliable notion of self that could stand the test of time and space.

6

EPISTEMOLOGY
The Search for the Meaning of Truth

WHAT IS EPISTEMOLOGY?
Epistemology is a division of philosophy that deals with the theory of knowledge. Before we delve into the theory of knowledge, we must first and foremost ask, what is knowledge? The word "knowledge" in its philosophical expression is not as simple as it is in the popular usage of the word. Many philosophers were of the opinion that knowledge cannot be defined but can only be described. This is because many attempts to define it were almost parochial and usually spark off problems. Philosophers see knowledge from diverse perspectives. The different perspectives had undergone certain injections and ejections in the course of time. This is in line with the thought of C.N. Bittle that just because knowledge is a primary act of experience, the idea of knowledge eludes every effort to an exact definition.[1]

However, when we say we "know" something, what sort of claim are we making? It may imply acquaintance, to perceive, to recognize, to identify, and to recall. The popular usage of the word "know" implies that we are sure that what we are saying is true although what is discussed may be doubtful. For Richard Popkin and Avrum Stroll, there are still less positive usages of "know" as equivalent to "believe," and think. And as such when we say we known such and such is the case, we are not expressing complete assurance but only a conviction. Of course, the word "know" may be used to express nothing more than a hunch or a hope or pigheaded opinion.[2]

On the other hand to "know" as a philosophical expression is what Descartes would describe as something being clear and distinct, and this kind of knowledge should not be doubtful. For one to claim to have knowledge in this regard certain conditions must be fulfilled. According to D.W. Hamlyn, one condition is that what one claims to know must be the case, if it is an object that one claims to know, this object must exist and if what one claims to know is formable in a proposition, this proposition (or statement) must be true.[3]

THE NATURE OF THEORY OF KNOWLEDGE

In the rank and file of epistemology, it has as its subject matter the survey of the possibility of self-knowledge and the knowledge of other minds and the phenomenal world. So, Epistemology deals with whether we can know, how we can or come to know what we claim to know, and how valuable is our knowledge both educational and philosophical. For A.D.Woozley, "epistemology is interested in questions about what the mind works on, what its material is, what relation it has to its objects in the external world, to other persons' minds, and to the events of history."[4] So, the theory of knowledge can be said to be concerned with the justification of human knowledge. It is interested in the sources of knowledge, the status and the extent of our knowledge of the world, of ourselves and other people.

Every moment of his life, man is making relentless effort to know something and because of this fact epistemology extends its tentacles to the limits and the extent of human knowledge. In our life experiences, it is an existential fact that we accept the woman that fed us as our mother, and the man behind as our father, we accept doctor's prescription without hesitation, and we accept the competence of a cab driver or airplane pilot and the roadworthiness of the vehicle or the flightworthiness airplane without questions. We accept also the healthiness of the food we eat, and the water and wine we drink in restaurants, and the competence of the chefs that prepared them. These acceptances are based on belief or faith and not on certainty of knowledge.

Again as Titus Harold, Marilyn Smith and Richard Nolan pointed out that "as we look at objects, they appear to have some color - if we put on blue colored glasses, the world looks blue, if we put on red glasses, the world looks red, if we take anti-parasitic medication called Santonim or put it in our eyes everything looks yellow. Color appears to be either wholly or in part affected by the condition of our visual organs."[5] The question that arises is: are objects what they really appear to us to be? This uncertainty in the sense of sight is also applicable to other senses, namely: sense of sound, touch, smell and taste. It is because of the above fact that the epistemologists try to find a criterion for certainty the same way the logician analyses arguments which he knows are sound in order to find the source of their validity, so the epistemologists analyze what we already know about knowledge in order to discover the grounds for its trustworthiness.

At the level of the mind, we also discover that the mind is not infallible. Occasionally, we are baffled to discover that some things we have for a long time thought to be certain have often been proved dubious. A case in point was the disproving of the Dalton's Atomic Theory which holds that atoms are indestructible while atom is later discovered to have three other particles namely: electron, proton and neutron. Also, Einstein's special relativity theory rendered obsolete many previous ideas on the conversion of mass to energy and the relation between space and time. It is then the task of the epistemologist to find out whether all we take as knowledge are based on rational criterion and logical reasoning or are they the byproducts of faith and belief devoid of meaning. The goal of epistemology is to act as a kind of insurance policy against error. It highlights the risk of error we face when we use information from the various sources of knowledge.

The epistemologist works on concepts rather than facts. For instance, a psychologist deals with how people think and act, the epistemologist is interested in finding out what such psychological concepts such as thinking, feeling, perception, memory, stimulus, sensation and learning mean. The epistemologist makes effort to find out if the psychologist is applying these terms correctly. Again, while the educationist deals with the task of imparting and acquiring knowledge, the epistemologist deals with the fundamental meaning and sources of knowledge.[6]

THE SOURCES OF HUMAN KNOWLEDGE

A Latin adage holds that *"ex nihilo nihil fit"*- "out of nothing, nothing comes." If then human knowledge is something, the question that arises is how do we get the knowledge we have? Is there one source of knowledge? Or are there many sources? Are some more important than others? It has become a custom that we get satisfied with the things we think we know about the universe and we do not rack brains to ask how we obtain this knowledge. The question of the sources of our knowledge had been debated by eminent philosophers of different periods. Many sources have been recognized.

The Senses as a Source of Knowledge: Appeal to Sense Perception

Most philosophers hold that the primary sources of knowledge are the five senses of sight, smell, taste, hearing and touch. In our daily life, we see, hear, taste, smell, and feel objects around us. The sense organs make it possible for us to come in contact with these objects in the physical world. Thus, we are capable of distinguishing colors, tastes, forms, sounds and feel hardness, smoothness and roughness of surfaces and temperatures of various degrees.

We also have four internal senses: the common sense, the memory sense, imaginative and cogitative senses. These do not involve reason but are involved in the sensitive life of man. These phenomena of sensation are believed to be the sources of knowledge. Thomas Aquinas says we get in touch with the physical world through sensation. Hence, sensations are known to be sources of knowledge, and the lack of a certain sense means a lack of the science of those things that are perceived through the sense. Accordingly, a baby born blind and deaf can neither have the idea of colors nor sound.[7]

On the other hand, many philosophers hold that what is called knowledge cannot come from the senses because these senses are defective and always in flux. We know that the senses cannot give us precise knowledge. Galina Kirilencho and Lydia Korshunova acknowledged that "the senses are extremely keen yet they have limitations and cannot reveal to us all the properties of an object."[8]

With unaided eyes we cannot see things like atoms and molecules, bacteria and viruses; neither can we hear ultra sounds with our ears. From the above mentioned fact, it is required of us that as we bank on sense knowledge for our acquaintance with empirical things, it is also pertinent to exercise caution and be aware that we can be deceived in the area of sense data. All that glitters is not gold.

With the advancement in sciences and computer technology, the human senses have been aided significantly. Particularly, the invention of some scientific instrument such as microscope, telescope, binoculars and computers has improved human senses tremendously. But still the human senses and the scientific equipment cannot behold the substratum, the thing-in-itself that gives unity and form to a thing by holding the particles together in a definite shape. The knowledge we get from the senses or experience is called empirical knowledge. It is knowledge that is verified or confirmed by the senses. This is scientific knowledge. It is the model which the modern scientists use in their experiments and investigations. Scientific hypothesis are proved by observation or through experiment. This type of knowledge is particularly important to teachers and students. The teachers of science should make sure that their students are taught how to observe carefully, research meticulously and formulate hypotheses, and imbibe the attitude of scientific inquiry.

Thinking as a Source of Knowledge: The Appeal to Reason

Reason had been looked upon as the main fact that distinguishes man from other animals. Man is called a *Homo sapiens* because he is the only animal endowed with reason. Hence, man is a rational being, *homo rationales*. Reason is considered as the basis of any certain knowledge. For Woozley, man is thinking whenever he is conscious of anything, whether his consciousness takes the determinate forms of asserting, denying, questioning, doubting, remembering, imagining, day-dreaming, and whenever his mind is not blank.[9]

It is suitable to distinguish thinking from reasoning. All mental activity of man involves thinking but when thought is directed to an end, it becomes reasoning. In line with this, Irving Copi wrote that "all reasoning is thinking but not all thinking is reasoning."[10] This means that the rationality of man is more inherent in reasoning than in thinking. Thinking can be looked upon as an act of man while reasoning can be taken to be a human act. Reasoning reveals to us the important characteristics of things and the essence of things around us. We can see bodies fall but not the law of gravity. Laws are discovered through the reasoning process in the mind.

Rational knowledge is known to come from pure reasoning. The principle of rational knowledge is the type used in logic and mathematics. The truth in this type of knowledge is demonstrated by the exercise of abstract reasoning. An example of this reasoning is seen in the logical statement that says if "A" is greater than "B" and "B" is greater than "C" then "A" is greater than "C." Other examples include "if anything is A then it is A" and "anything must be either A or not A." Statements such as these are valid and independent of our feelings. They are universally valid. The weakness of this kind of knowledge is that it is abstract and formal - It does not take into account the actual state of the situation and the emotional needs of the people concerned.

Intuition as a Source of Knowledge: The Appeal to Insight

Intuition is called the natural light of reason. The word "intuition" is derived from the Latin *intuere* - which means to look at. According to Melvin Rader, "the looking, or directness of the insight, is its fundamental mark."[11] In intuitive knowledge as John Locke wrote, "the mind perceives the truth as the eye doth the light, only by being directed towards it."[12] Intuition can be defined as the direct apprehension that a proposition is true or that something is the case. So, from the above description, intuition can be regarded as knowledge which a person finds within himself. This kind of knowledge comes at the moment of insight. Insight is the sudden coming to consciousness of an idea or conclusion. This intuition or insight erupts suddenly to solve some problems which have been tasking the sub-conscious for days, months and sometimes for years. It comes as reward to the conscious for its efforts to solve problems. This moment of insight gives joy and pleasure to the individual because the psychic energy invested in the effort to solve problems is rewarded. It also gives the person a sense of the fullness of his mental power.

Intuition as a source of knowledge is significant especially in the scientific world. This is because most scientific discoveries and invention were products of intuition. "Eureka! I have found it." This remark was made by Faraday at that great moment of insight when he discovered electricity. This Eureka moment was repeated when Graham Bell discovered the principle of telephone. Eureka moments are found in all areas of life. It is especially unique in areas of great works of science and technology, great works of art, music and literature, etc. Thus, great works and innovation most often originate from intuition than sense perception. It must be noted also that intuition is common to all men. It knows no boundary in terms of race, color or creed.

Revelation as a Source of Knowledge: Appeal to Faith and Inspiration

The knowledge disclosed to man is known as revealed knowledge. At certain times in religious history, it is believed that God used angels as messengers to communicate to man, to reveal to man some hidden truths. At a point, God decided to use men as intermediaries to send messages to their fellow men, these men we call prophets, and at the fullness of time, Christians believe that God used his only begotten son - Jesus Christ to make possible the fullness of revelation. There is also Mohammed the great prophet and founder of Islam and the great Buddha, the Enlightened One and the head of Buddhism, etc. These men inspired by God wrote down certain truths or caused others to write them so that their followers and other people would come to know these truths. The Christians and Jews have such truths in the Bible. The Moslems (Islam) have theirs in the Koran. Hinduism, Buddhism and Confucianism have their inspired books. There are many other wisdom religions and faiths that lay claims to inspiration and revelation in their books. The important thing is the believers of each religion hold the content of their books as eternally true, otherwise God the author of these books would either be ignorant or deceitful, which he is not.

It is generally believed that God allowed men to use human language to record at the spur of the moment *(currente clamo or in affulatus)* these supernatural truths. Scripture scholars and theologians among these religious groups spend much time arguing about and interpreting the precise meaning of words and phrases contained in these sacred texts. Through these exegeses, the meaning of these texts hidden from non- theologians is better explained to the lay man in the relevant faith.

Authority as a Source of Knowledge: Appeal to Citation and Quotation

There are certain truths or knowledge we accept because of the authority of the person propagating that knowledge in a relevant field of human endeavor. As a result we have authorities in all fields of human endeavor; these are people who are experts and professionals in their particular field. They have adequate and proficient knowledge that could be a reference point. Authoritative knowledge is established when one accepts on somebody's authority that an idea is true or false or worthy of consideration. We accept our birthday as true based on the authority of our parents. We accept the doctor's prescription based on his authority in medicine. We also accept based on the authority of historians that Publius Cornelius ScipioAfricanus was the Roman general that led the Roman army in the Battle of Zama to defeat the Carthaginian military contingent led by the great commander Hannibal, and also destroyed the North African city of Carthage in 202 BC.[13] We feel that these facts do not need our verification because they are documented and taught by professional historians and are found also in relevant encyclopedias which are written and published by experts. The kind of knowledge we need determines which knowledge we could take for granted and the type we would verify. If for instance we want to know the law of relativity, we simply check the encyclopedia. But if we want to know the basis and the principle on which the law is built, we have to conduct the experiment in order to verify the truth of the law. It must also be acknowledged that dictionaries are works of authority. Definitions and meanings of words are sourced from them. Also works by great scholars and authors who are authorities in their field are basis of knowledge.

Hence, we cite them in our writings and quote them in our speeches until proved otherwise by other experts in the relevant field.

Memory as a Source of Knowledge

Memory is a source of knowledge in the sense that remembering is a cognitive act of mind which occurs now, but which has its objects as events or series of events belonging to the past. This means memory and remembering are interchangeable. Gilbert Ryle sees remembering as having learned and not forgotten, and on this account a reference to the past is a necessary part of the concept of knowledge. Throwing more light on what it means to remember, A.J. Ayer says to remember an event is to be disposed to state a fact about the past but not just any fact about the past, it must be a fact which oneself observed, either straight forwardly or as it were, at second hand.[14]

Norman Malcolm classifies memory into three types: a. factual memory, b. perceptual memory, and c. personal memory. For Malcolm, factual memory is just memory that such and such is, was or will be the case. Perceptual memory is the memory of something that involves seeing, hearing, tasting, touching, smelling, etc. It involves imagery. Personal memory depends on the person's previous perception or experience of the thing remembered.[15] The question that arises here is: in which sense can memory be regarded as a source of knowledge? According to Hamlyn's view, "I can gain new knowledge by using my memory either by making explicit to myself what I previously knew implicitly or by drawing further conclusions from the knowledge that I previously had."[16]

From the above we are made to understand that one can get new knowledge by reflecting on what one remembers. There are still strong controversies as to whether memory could be actually regarded as a source of knowledge or a case of making explicit what we have implicitly in the mind. Some scholars have seen knowledge as what we could remember after we have forgotten many other related issues. Even Plato regarded knowledge as recollection; that is, remembering innate ideas of the mind. These innate ideas existed with the mind in the world of form and hence are inborn ideas in the individual.

DIVISION OF KNOWLEDGE

Human knowledge can be divided into two kinds namely: theoretical and practical knowledge. This division is based on the purpose or end of human knowledge. Let us consider each separately.

Theoretical Knowledge

This is also called speculative knowledge. It is knowledge acquired for its own sake as a supreme natural good of human existence. This knowledge according to E.W. Carlo is "the natural movement of the intellect even before its cares to make or do anything."[17] It is also the first natural inclination with which the intellect seeks its object. In knowing, man possesses his objects of knowledge. In fact when a man knows, what he knows becomes his and his mind rests in the delight of its possession. So, theoretical or speculative knowledge is the natural movement of the mind seeking its objects and resting in the delight of its possession.

Practical Knowledge

This involves man using his intellect for a purpose outside its own inner, intrinsic constitution. In practical knowledge, human needs, necessities of life, the drive to solve problems, appetite and desires compel the intellect to move out of itself to accomplish things. For instance, moving vehicles were conceived by the intellect because of the need to cover a long distance at a short time. This problem compels the intellect to move out of itself to do something; build a structure, bicycle, a vehicle, a train, a plane, a ship, to accomplish and satisfy this human necessity and need. Practical knowledge therefore means knowing how to do something, how to build a car, how to build a house, how to cure diseases, how to teach, how to write, how to sing, how to play football, how to drive, how to swim, etc. When we know how to do these things, whether we actually do them or not, we already have a practical knowledge. In essence practical knowledge has to do with acquiring skills for job performance and for solving practical problems.

The Primacy of Theoretical Knowledge over Practical Knowledge

There is intense controversy on which of the two divisions of knowledge is more important. According to Carlos, the distinction between theoretical or speculative knowledge and practical knowledge is not based on the intention of the knower but on the direction of the knowledge itself. For him, "despite certain inadequacies, theoretical or speculative knowledge is the highest type of knowledge because it is the fulfillment of man's highest faculty, the intellect and its most basic appetite, the desire to know."[18]

This is in line with position of Aristotle in the first sentence of his

Metaphysics that "man by nature desires to know," that is to say man naturally wants to have knowledge for knowledge sake. This is good and necessary to keep the intellect active and prevent the brain falling into abeyance and deterioration. Intellectual exercises prevent and slow down diseases like dementia and Alzheimer's disease. So for Carlos and Aristotle, theoretical knowledge has preeminence over practical knowledge.

John Dewey sees fruitful inquiry and knowledge as essentially active and prospective rather than passive and retrospective. For him, intelligence develops within the spheres of action for the sake of possibilities not yet given. Intelligence as intelligence is inherently forward looking. A pragmatic intelligence is a creative intelligence not a routine mechanic. Intelligence is instrumental through action to the determination of the qualities of future experience.[19]

What Dewey is emphasizing is that knowledge or inquiry should turn away from illusory objects such as first and final causes and understand things in terms of their origin and functions. According to him, inquiry should be empirical in method and practical in motivation. He proposes to determine meanings and test beliefs by examining the consequences that flow from them. What can the idea or belief promise for the future? How can it help in resolving our perplexities? What predications are implied by the hypothesis and how could they be verified? Such questions apply even to propositions about the past, and even these propositions must be verified in terms of future consequences. This is because the past event has left effects, consequences that are present and that will continue in the future. Our belief about it, if genuine, must also modify action in some way and so have objective effects.[20] For Dewey, emphasis should always be on practical knowledge and acquisition of skills especially in our academic endeavor and educational enterprise. This type of knowledge involves and provides action. Hence, it produces results as consequences. It is the fulcrum of community development.

We could also see that John Dewey rejects in its entirety any type of knowledge or education which begins and ends with the intellect, solely concerned as in many countries with degrees and certificates, no skills, no practice and no production. He rejects this kind of education that involves learning without doing. This is the heart of Dewey's instrumentalism philosophy. We must conclude by saying that even though Dewey's assertions are insightful, it is not meant to abolish theoretical knowledge.

Theoretical and Practical knowledge work hand in hand and always go together. Hence, there is need to combine the two. That is to say, we cannot stop at the admiration of nature as it is the case in some disciplines; particularly in this age of practice and action, we should always try to do stuff and make things. We should imbibe Kant Synthetic a priori as a kind of mediation between theoretical and practical knowledge. A person that studies sociology, philosophy, psychology should at least be prepared to be a teacher, a writer, a social worker, a community organizer or an administrator as the practical component of his studies as Plato suggested in his philosopher – king module. While a person who studies medicine, engineering and architecture should also be taught courses that make people insightful as to make good decisions, pass valid and sound judgments especially on things pertaining to the needs and welfare of the society and individuals. The axiomatic statement that theory without practice is empty and practice without theory is dead emphasizes the need to combine theory and practice.

TRUTH AS THE GOAL OF EPISTEMOLOGY

What is truth? Before Pilate asked Jesus the question, many philosophers such as Socrates, the Sophists, Plato, Aristotle and some other western and eastern philosophers have discussed the problem of truth. Even after Pilate, philosophers are still posing the question in different fashions. Definitive answer for all times and for all people seems to be elusive. As a result, the claims to the possession of truth and the negation of these claims have become a central problem in our daily experience. This phenomenon has caused unfortunate situations in the human society, such as: strives, misunderstanding, literacy duels, and disintegration of cordial relationships. This is also responsible for most civil and international wars. The Iraqi war for instance was a result of claims and counter claims on whether Iraqi has weapons of mass destruction. So, international warfare has its root in the various claims to possession of truth by each of the warring sides.

In the political sphere, the claims to possession of truth seem even more evident. No one political party can stomach any allegation to the effect that it is not performing well. It would rather stigmatize such allegation as a mere attempt by detractors and political enemies to tarnish the image of the party and portray the party in bad light. "The truth will come to light" has become a popular adage of politicians and leaders. For instance, the terrorist attack at the United States Consulate in Benghazi, Libya has become a controversial political issue for Republicans and Democrats in the United States Congress. The Republicans are still waiting for the truth of what happened in spite of the pool of information from different panels of investigators on the issue.

In our daily transactions, truth is what everyone claims to have in our offices, market places, churches, industries, institutions like schools, hospitals and the courts, etc. In philosophy, the problem of knowledge also concerns the problem of certainty and truth. This is why Hamlyn says knowledge involves the truth of what is said to be known, hence a complete account of knowledge must involve an account of truth.[21] Etymologically, the word "truth" has the Greek equivalent *"al'etheia"* and the Latin *"veritas"* meaning discovered, perceived, visible and therefore, luminous. The Latin meaning involves ideas like beliefs, choice, thus derived, truth signifies the intellect's choice, its belief or again the thing chosen or believed. For L.M. Regis, the etymological definition of truth cannot serve as a basis for philosophical investigation of the notion, for words have a life of their own, and they are born and transformed in the course of time, and take on new meanings that become popular and then the common property of mankind.[22]

The Sophists asserted that truth is relative. Protagoras was one of the most important advocates of the school. As the protagonist of the school, he held that "man is the measure of all things." This means that truth depend on man's making. Gorgias adopted skeptical approach to truth and said that nothing exists and that if anything does exist, it is not known, if known, it cannot be communicated. Most modern philosophers have looked at truth from diverse perspectives. Husserl says truth signifies the "entity showing itself in its selfsameness". Heidegger sees it as "letting-be." For Kant, truth is the "coherence of thought with itself." Kierkegaard sees truth as "subjective." Dewey holds it "to be warranted assertibility." This means a true assertion is one that does the work it supposed to do. On the other hand, Russell says "for any successful theory of truth, the opposite falsehood must be admitted."[23] And Bittle writes that "truth and error reside formally in the judgment and not in the ideas taken alone."[24] The above statements tend to show us that truth can have various forms, namely: it can be empirical, experiential, ontological, verbal, moral or logical.

THEORIES OF TRUTH: SOLUTION TO THE PROBLEM OF TRUTH

Given that a statement is true, the following questions and problems at least can be raised. What do we mean that it is true? Are we attributing a property to the statement when we say that it is true, and if so what property? What are the necessary and sufficient conditions for its truth? The question of whether truth is a property has raised dust of disagreement among philosophers. Different theories of truth have arisen in an attempt to offer solution to the problem of truth. All currently influential accounts of the nature of truth agree that the meaning of "truth" and "falsehood" have an objective import, so that adequate account of them must include a reference to something independent of personal whims and individual act or thought. Philosophers sometimes differ over the sorts of "things" or "entities" they believe can be properly characterized as either true or false. Among the candidates for such characterization are propositions, statements, sentences, utterances, judgment, beliefs and ideas. But undoubtedly, the major difference among theories of truth lies in their conceptions of how a statement, if true must be related to whatever objectivity that determines its truth. In respect of this difference, three types of theories are commonly distinguished, and they are labeled as Correspondence Theory, Coherence Theory and Pragmatic or Instrumentalist Theories of Truth.

The Correspondence Theory

This maintains that truth depends on a relation between beliefs or piece of knowledge and a fact in the real world. For this school of thought, truth is the agreement between statement of facts and actual facts of the situation the judgment claims to describe. Truth and error reside formally in the judgment and not in the ideas taken alone. Truth, therefore, must be defined as the "conformity of judgment to reality or facts." Therefore, a statement is true if and only if it corresponds with facts. This means truth is fidelity to objective reality. This is widely accepted by the realists and it explains why the scholastics speak of truth as *"adequatio intellectus ad rem"* – the conformity of intellect to a thing. Here the thing or object is assigned an ontological existence. That is to say, truth is seen as conformity with "things on the ground."

Furthermore, some contemporary logical positivists who hold this view consider truth as "empirical verifiability." This means the conformity of an assertion to a matter of fact. For instance, if a professor tells the students it is raining heavily outside, the students can go outside to check if it is true. Likewise if the weatherman tells us there will be a tornado in New York City tomorrow, we have to wait for tomorrow to ascertain the truth value of the weather report.

These logical positivists also hold that a true judgment or statement is the one that attributes to the object or a thing the character it possesses otherwise the statement is false. For them, truth is independent of our beliefs and disbeliefs. Nevertheless; this theory witnessed some criticisms on various grounds. Firstly, the opponents of this theory maintain that the question of verification of truth is quite vague, and thereby repudiates the proponent's assertion that truth can be compared to and verified with reality. Secondly, this theory assumes that our sense data are clear and accurate as to represent reality as it is. We are aware of the fact that under many circumstances and in multifarious ways, we are disappointed by our senses, and so the critics concluded that it is foolish of us to talk about whether or not our judgment corresponds with things as they are in reality. They made it clear that there are many things we cannot subject to experimental verification, namely: such things as our knowledge of meaning (definitions), relations and values, logic and ethics and mathematics. Can we, then, hold them to be false? It is this irreconcilable predicament that gave birth to the coherence theory of truth.

The Coherence Theory

This theory was developed in the 19th century as a result of the influence of Hegel and the associated school of idealists. According to this theory, truth is not constituted by the relation between a judgment and something else, a fact or reality, but by the relations between judgments themselves. A good example of this is when lawyers quote Supreme Court decisions and verdicts to build support for their cases before a judge in a court of law. Many judges make their rulings conform to Supreme Court verdicts in similar cases. Under the coherence theory, for something to be true, it must be consistent in itself and with other true systems. The theory avoided the difficulty as to how we could know that judgments correspond to something which was not a judgment. For the Coherence theory, a judgment is true means that it fits into a coherent system with other judgments that are already accented as true. Since coherence admits of degrees, it follows from this theory that a judgment can be more or less true. Also, no judgment is absolutely true because we never attain a completely coherent system, but some judgments are truer than others, because they approach nearer the idea of truth. No wonder F.H. Bradley writes that "a judgment must always falsify reality because judgment implies partial and relative truth."[25] For him, therefore, every truth is not always *ad rem* – to the point. Every truth is partial since they cannot reflect the whole reality. This means no truth can tell us *hic et nunc* – here and now - the whole of reality.

Although this theory satisfied the purpose for which it was propounded at the specific time, nevertheless it has its own weaknesses. This is ostensibly manifested in its failure to distinguish between consistent truth and error because there are many false coherent systems. The premises of this theory are too rationalistic and intellectualistic, dealing only with logical relations among propositions, hence the theory fails to give or furnish an adequate test for the judgments of everyday experience. Some critics also point at the vagueness of the theory, especially the enlarged form of coherence which reveals the impossibility of one belief cohering with every other belief in the universe.

Furthermore, we do not see how coherence itself could be defined without already presupposing truth. To say "A" coheres with "B" is either to say that "A" is consistent with "B" or that ''A''necessarily follows from"B"or something more complex definable in terms of consistency or of "necessarily following from." But these notions already presuppose the notion of truth. To say "A" is consistent with "B" is to say that "A" and "B" may both be true. To say that "A" necessarily follows from "B" is to say that if "B" is true, "A" must be true. From the above propositional calculus or better logical calculus, it seems that anyone who defines truth in terms of coherence is defining truth in terms of itself and reasoning in a vicious circle proves nothing. It only assumes what is supposed to be proved. Finally, it is surely obvious that judgments are true not because of their relations to other judgments but because of their relation to something objective which is not itself a judgment. These conflicting issues created a way for another theory of truth.

Pragmatist/Instrumentalist Theory

The instrumentalist sees ideas and beliefs as instruments that function as guides of actions, and their validity or truth value is determined by the success of the action. Truth has been defined by pragmatists as standing for beliefs or ideas that "work." In other words, the test for truth is on "utility" and satisfactory consequences or results. The theory rejects metaphysical substances, essences and ultimate realities because they are out of reach. Truth is rather something that happens to a judgment, belief or idea. This is made clear in the words of William James that "what makes a thing true is its value, or the benefits one can derive from it. True ideas therefore are those we can validate, corroborate and verify, while false ideas are the reverse."[26] Inferring from the above view, it is clear that for the pragmatists truth depends on workability and satisfactory consequences. This view hinges on the fact that we cannot attain absolute truth and therefore we must be concerned with what works.

This pragmatic theory is known to have some adverse implications such as: if abortion is satisfactory to the performer then it is good. If rice millers and corn millers starve the poor through artificial scarcity and high prices to get high profit which is utility to them then their actions are good. If pharmaceutical companies profiteer from essential drugs and indigent patients die as a result then their profit is utility to them and therefore it is good. This means that truth depends on the individual whims as long as he or she has a reason for whatever is done. Again, if a powerful country like the United States, with the greatest fighting force ever known to man, sees going to war against a weaker country like Iraq as something that has utility and satisfaction and can work, then it is good or proper for them to do so. This is a case of might is right and as well as true. As a result of the above insights, the critics say that it is quite conceivable that a belief might work well and yet be false. There are also many judgments that cannot be pragmatically verified. Some value and moral prescriptions cannot be pragmatically checked and verified but we still need them.

Because of the pitfall in each of the theories; there is need to take the theories complementarily. One has to be eclectic in the application of the theories. For such combined effort therefore, we define truth as the faithful adherence of your judgments and ideas to the fact of experience or to the world as it is. But since we cannot always compare judgments with actual situation we test them by consistency with other judgments that we believe are valid and true or test them with useful and practical consequence.

7

ETHICS
The Morality of Human Actions

It is good and pertinent to note that there is no period in history that escaped ethical problems. We have many of them at present, and all of them would not likely go away in the future. The history of human morality can be classified into two major periods, namely: the Age of Customs and the Age of Conscience. During the Age of Customs, cannibalism in some cultures, human sacrifice, abortion, incest taboo, polygamy, prostitution, child marriages and child labor were major concerns and they are still ethical problems today. At this stage of morality, customs, traditions and culture dictate what is right or wrong in a particular society, and they have different forms of social controls.

At our present level of morality, the Age of Conscience, ethical problems still pervade all the areas of human endeavor including engineering especially genetic engineering, agriculture, science and technology, economy, politics, religion, medicine, local and international affairs, to mention but a few. Specifically, the problems of corporal punishment, capital punishment, euthanasia or mercy - killing, letting - die, murder, genocide, mass murder, abortion, suicide, bestiality, pornography, rape, sexual abuse, torture, physical violence, terrorism, business and medical malpractices have become a reoccurring decimal in any moral discourse of our time. Because of this, diversified meanings have been given to what ethics really is, but at the end, they all point to human action in the society.

Thus, the question of how I ought to act and my moral obligation to others are perennial ethical problems. These are bound to remain with the individual conscience and the human society. Likewise many ethical principles have been formulated, and they may remain constant but their applications in solving ethical problems might vary slightly over time and space.

ETHICS AS THE SCIENCE OF MORALITY

Ethics or Moral Philosophy is a science which concerns human conduct as to whether it is good or bad, right or wrong. In general, ethics is often defined as the normative science of human conduct. Ethics is normative because it evaluates human actions. To say that Ethics is a normative science is to say that it is also a critical science. It critically examines moral standards, principles, ideals and concepts. It is also prescriptive in nature in the sense that it attaches value to human actions. It is called a science because it is a systematic inquiry to discover principles and laws for evaluating and understanding the morality of human behavior.

The Human Act

Austin Fagothey in his epic work, *"Right and Reason: Ethics in Theory and Practice"* says that "human act is one which man is master of, one which is consciously controlled and deliberately willed; so that the agent is held responsible for it."[1] This is to say that human acts are deliberate acts of freewill and one which man is morally responsible. Such acts can be good or bad, right or wrong. The above views have outlined the type of human conduct Ethics deals with, namely: that which involves moral evaluation and judgments. They also have shown that it deals with the conduct of mature and normal human beings. This means it excludes the behavior of infants or little children who lack self-awareness. It also excludes the actions of lunatics or behaviors that are unconscious or done as a result of reflex actions. There is no gain-saying that the action of animals like dogs, sheep, goats, cats, horses, and other wild animals are excluded from the spectrum of ethics. Their actions are based on instincts and as such are not a product of knowledge, free will and voluntariness. Hence, they lack behavior and character and so they are not moral actions.

It should be noted that the acts of man are convertible to human acts depending on the agent's advertence, that is, his awareness, attention and consent. The acts of man are some of those acts he has in common with things, animals and plants. Such acts include when man is under the laws of physics, e.g., the law of gravity. He can fall from a tree or building against his wish just as thing would fall. Man also digests food and grows just like animals and plants. He sneezes and sweats, he feels cold and heat and he can be ill just like any other animal and he dies as well like other living things. These are acts of man because they do not proceed from the intellect and the will. Man is only master of those acts that he has previous knowledge of. These are voluntary acts that proceed from the will with the knowledge of the purpose of the act. Succinctly, Thomas Higgins in his great work "Man as Man" says that "human act is a free deliberate act which man is fully a master of. The act of man which man is not the master is called the act of man as man. In this respect, his act differs from that of other visible created things."[2]

And in summary, Paul Glenn says a human act is an act which proceeds from the deliberate will of man. The term "human act" means any sort of activity internal or external, bodily or spiritual performed by a human being.

The Constituent of HumanAct

It has been acknowledged that for an act to be human, it should consist of the followings: knowledge, freedom and voluntariness. And the degree of presence or absence of these make-ups tends to affect the human act and modify it. Their presence increases responsibility while absence reduces responsibility of the individual concerned.

Knowledge as Constituent of HumanAct

Obviously, we know that the human intellect is imbued with the power of reason. This is why man is regarded as a Homo sapiens – a being that reasons and have knowledge as opposed to other animals that make use of instincts. The absence of this intellectual knowledge brings ignorance. The intellect needs knowledge and uses it to deliberate on any act it wants to present to the will for choice and action. With knowledge the intellect analyses the act as to what it is in itself and the purpose of the act. The intellect assesses the act as to whether it is good or bad, right or wrong, true or false, necessary or unnecessary, lawful or unlawfully, pleasant or painful, doable or undoable, means or ends, dangerous or safe, sad or happy, etc.

Voluntariness as Constituent of Human Act

This concerns the motion or action of the will. Man is regarded as a *Homo Volens* – a willing being. To say that every human act must be voluntary is to say that it must be a willed act; it originates or proceeds from the will of man. There are many forms of voluntariness of human act, namely: Perfect voluntariness; Imperfect voluntariness, Simple and conditional voluntariness, Direct and indirect voluntariness, Positive and negative voluntariness, Actual voluntariness, Virtual voluntariness, Habitual voluntariness and Interpretative voluntariness.

Perfect Voluntariness

This is the case where the performer of an act knows the act very well and has intention to perform the act without hesitation. When the person performs the act, the act is said to be fully or perfectly voluntary.

Imperfect Voluntariness

This is the case where the performer of an act does not have perfect knowledge of the act or the intention for carrying out the act is not clear or well-conceived. So, in imperfect voluntariness the intellect presents to the will an improperly conceived object for action.

Simple and Conditional Voluntariness

A human act is said to be under simple voluntariness when and where the performer of the act, performs it whether he likes or not. The conditional voluntariness is the case where the moral agent performs a human act under duress, that is, under coercion, and constraint. The performer would have done differently in the case if given the chance to choose. Here, the action is done with remorse, disdain and hatred.

Direct and Indirect Voluntariness

In direct voluntariness, the human act is willed by the performer. In indirect voluntariness, on the other hand, the human act is the foreseen outcome of another act willed directly.

Positive and Negative Voluntariness

We talk of positive voluntariness in any human act actually done. It exists only in actions that have been performed. Negative voluntariness on the other hand exists or is found in acts that are aborted, that is, acts the performer changed his mind and refrained or neglected putting into actuality.

Actual Voluntariness

This is present in an act the performer willed and instantly carried out, *hic et nunc* (i.e., here and now).

Virtual Voluntariness

This is present in a human act done as a result of a former actual intention which may no longer be there at the performance of the action.

Habitual Voluntariness

This is present in human action that is done in conformity with but not as a result of former intention even if the intention is now forgotten.

Interpretative Voluntariness

This is predicated to a human act by the judgment of prudence and common sense. This means the voluntariness is supposed to be there if opportunity or the ability is given.

Freedom as a Constituent of HumanAct

There is freedom in a human act if the performer of the act has a choice to act or not to act. If he is capable of making choices, he chooses between alternative actions. E.M. Kirkpatrick defines this freedom as "the power of free choice."[3] For A. Appardoria, "it involves the faculty of willing and the power of doing what has been willed without interference from any other source or from without."[4] Supporting this view, J. Donceel sees freedom as "the facility that involves the power of self-realization which characterizes the person and enables him to respond to his vocation and to achieve his destiny."[5]

There are many kinds of freedom that come into the making of human acts, namely:

Physical Freedom

This emphasizes the absence of physical constraints and impediments to the performance of an act. So, when a man is released from the prison, he is said to have recovered his physical freedom. He can move from one place to another without hindrance, coercion or restraint.

Psychological Freedom

This is also called freedom of deliberate choice. It is the exemption from the impulses of other human faculties or psychic pressures on the will to make it act in a determined way, and their stultifying effects on the human creative and imaginative powers. This kind of freedom is rooted in the mind; it is the freedom of deliberate choice. It is that capacity which a man has to choose to do or not to do a given thing, to perform or not to perform a determinate action when all the conditions for acting are present. It has to do with having an absolute control over a situation. It is also absolute domination, a complete self-control as well as complete control of one's actions and all that concerns oneself.

Economic Freedom

This has to do with the financial security and the opportunity to find a reasonable significance in the earning of one's daily bread, made possible through reasonable hours of labor, adequate wages and to self-government in industry. Succinctly put, it is freedom from economic impoverishment. Positively, it means economic self-reliance and self-sufficiency.

Moral Freedom

This is the absence of moral pressures, force or restraint of an obligation of a law, of threats or of rewards. Here, the individual acts as seems good to him.

Political Freedom

This is the right of every citizen to share in the government of the state. It concerns the right to vote and be voted for. It also involves the absence of political marginalization of any kind or disenfranchisement.

Civil Freedom (Liberty)

This is usually seen under the different names of social, civil, constitutional or private liberties and it refers to the sum total of rights recognized by law and secured by the coercive agency of the state. This freedom belongs to the people by mere fact that they are human beings, existing in a society. Thus, in the words of Laski, "it has to do with the rights and privileges which the State allows and protects for its citizen."[6] Thus for B.F. Nwankwo, civil liberty is the "basic conditions of happiness which an individual must enjoy in order to have a satisfactory social life."[7] These rights include the following:

Social Rights - These are:

Right of education, Freedom of association, Freedom of religion/conscience, Freedom from discrimination on the basis of sex, race or religion; Right to life

Economic Rights - These are:

Right to own property;

Right to pursue any business allowed by law;

Freedom from the compulsory acquisition of one's property, except with adequate compensation; and

Freedom to work and earn salary

Political Rights - These are:

Right to vote; Right to be voted for (i.e. to stand for election);

Freedom to be appointed and to hold any political or public office,

Right to form a political association or a political party as may be directed by law.

Legal Rights - These are:

Freedom of access to the law courts;

Freedom from subjection to torture or other inhuman or degrading treatment;

Freedom from deprivation of personal liberty except in accordance with the law;
Respect for private and family life and for private correspondence.

Classification of Human Act

The human act may be classified into two major divisions, namely: Acts with Complete or Adequate Cause, and Acts that are related to Reason.

Acts with Complete or Adequate Cause

A human act can be said to have complete or adequate cause if it is (a) Elicited or Free Acts and (b) Commanded Acts

Elicited Acts (i.e. Free Acts)

Elicited or Free acts have the following characteristics:

- Wish – this is the simple love of anything. This is the first tendency of the will towards anything.

- Intention – this is the purposive tendency of the will towards a thing regarded as realizable.

- Consent – this is the acceptance by the will of the means necessary to carry out the intention.

- Election – this is the selection by the will of the appropriate means to be used in carrying out an intention

- Use – this is the employment of the will of the powers (of the body or mind or both) to carry out intention by the means selected.

- Fruition – it is the enjoyment of a thing willed and done.

Commanded Acts

The commanded acts should have the following characteristics: They should be internal acts of the mind. This is to say that they must be acts done by internal mental powers under the command of the will, e.g., effort to control oneself from certain emotions like anger; fear or efforts to remember something. They can be external acts affected by bodily powers under the command of the will, e.g., speaking, writing, reading, eating, swimming, jumping, driving, etc. It could be mixed acts which involve the employment of bodily powers and mental powers, e.g., studying which involves the eyes and the mind. When the external act of seeing is affected by bodily powers it becomes the act of looking. So, the act of looking is commanded act of the will. Thus, we say if you see for instance an obscene image you have not sinned (i.e., it is not immoral) but if you see and look you have sinned (i.e., it is immoral). This applies to other senses and faculties like hearing, listening, thinking, reasoning, etc.

Acts that are related to Reason

In relation to reason, human act can be:

- Good – when they are in harmony with the dictates of right reason

- Evil – when they are in opposition to the dictates of reason

- Indifferent – when they stand in no positive relation to the dictates of reason: But this is only in theory or in the mind but in practice, the circumstance, the end or the intention of the performer can give it a moral value that is either good or evil. For instance, sex in theory is an indifferent act but in practice it is good in marriage but outside marriage, it is evil in some cases, namely: legitimate rape, statuary rape, incest taboo, pedophilia, prostitution, bestiality and adultery.

The Object of Human Act

Moral philosophers assert that every human act must have an object. This means that when the will moves, it moves towards something. According to Higgins, "as you cannot know without knowing something, so you cannot will without tending to some object."[8] The objects of the will are of two kinds:

- Direct object of the will: This is an intrinsic act that ends with the will, e.g., hate or love for somebody. This includes objects involving external activity placed at the will's command, e.g., eating, walking, singing, writing, reading, etc.

- Indirect object of the will: This is an effect which is not intended but is foreseen. It is one of the consequences of the intended object of the will. Vehicular accident can be unintended but foreseen result of driving under influence of alcohol or drugs - DUI.

Modifiers of Human Act

These are things that affect the constituents of the human act. The essential constituents of human act as we have already noted include knowledge, voluntariness and freedom. When these constituents are affected directly or indirectly, they make the act less human, that is to say, they lessen the moral quality of the human act. Some of the things that can modify human act include ignorance, passion, coercion and habit. Let us consider each of them.

Ignorance

This is the absence of intellectual knowledge in a man. Ignorance is negative when it is a negation of knowledge, that is, the person does not have the knowledge because the area concerned is not his field of expertise. But ignorance is a privation when it is the absence of knowledge that ought to be present. This ignorance can be about an object, e.g., ignorance in matters of law, facts or penalty. Ignorance could also be in the subject, that is, a person. It is regarded as vincible ignorance if it can be dispelled by little effort of the person like making a phone call to clarify information, cross-checking a calculation or spelling, examining available facts and evidence before going to the press. This person is regarded as having culpable or blamable ignorance or willful ignorance because he resisted illumination or did not crosscheck facts. Then, there is invincible ignorance which cannot be removed by little effort and as a result of this, the person is not culpable. For instance, the failure of a non-pilot to land Boeing 777 when the actual pilots had heart attack could be attributed to invincible ignorance. Or the failure of an adult to swim when pushed into a deep river can also be the result of invincible ignorance.

Passion

These are bodily appetites or tendencies, e.g., love, hate, joy, grief, desire, aversion, hope, despair, anger, courage, fear, etc. These can affect the moral quality of human act in a positive or negative way.

Violence or Coercion

This is external force applied by another agent for the purpose of compelling a person to act against his will. Violence, it must be noted cannot reach the will directly. This means that violence can cause a willed act but it does not determine the action. It takes a will to determine an action. However, violence and coercion can affect human act adversely and that is why people disown statements made under coercion.

Habit

It is a routine of behavior that is repeated regularly and tends to occur unconsciously. This is born out of frequent repeated act. It also affects the moral quality of a human act in a positive or negative way.

The Morality of Human Act

Human acts have two aspects, the physical and the moral aspect. Having treated in detail the physical, let us turn to the moral side of human act. At this juncture, we ask the question: what is morality? For Fagothey, morality is "the quality in human acts by which we call them right or wrong, good or bad."[9] For some moral philosophers, morality has to do with certain qualities in human act that lead man towards his end, happiness. This end towards which man's actions drive to is regarded as an absolute value. Higgins regarded this absolute value as supreme enduring value whose presence spells total success and happiness and whose absence spells total failure.[10]

Morality is the goodness and badness of an action. Some thinkers have considered that any action is morally good if it brings pleasure to the individual agent, bad, if it brings pain to the agent. For clearer understanding, one may like to know; what is good? For Aristotle, "the good is the cultivation and fulfillment of man's faculties especially reason."[11] For Cicero, and Bates, "the good is the life in harmony with the nature of man and his environment."[12]

For now, what we could get from the two views above is that the value good or bad is an aspect of being. If anything lacks what belongs to its fullness of being, we would say that it is not good, not in absolute but only in a relative sense. If a human action lacks anything of the fullness of being due to human action to that extent it lacks good and deserves the name evil. Again, we could say that an action has its full quality of human action and is morally good when it strives for an object which man should or ought to seek. And when an action seeks an object which is contrary to the nature or form of man, the action is considered evil. So, for the object of an action to be good, it must be in harmony with reason or rationality.

Sources of Morality

Here we ask; how does human action become morally good or bad in concrete terms? The elements of human action that give it moral value include:

The Object of the Act

This considers the act in-itself. This is the first principle of morality and is also the foundation of morality. The nature of the acts has to tell us whether the act is moral or not. There are acts that are intrinsically evil such as stealing, torture and bestiality, and under no circumstances can they lose their evil quality.

The Circumstance of the Act: Circumstances of the human act is the moral condition of the act. However, it does not cause the act to be the kind of act that it is. The circumstances can be that of time, place, and other moral conditions.

The End or Intention of the Agent

What a person has in mind, that is his intention, is also a source of morality to an act. The intention can be good or bad. The intention of the agent can only turn an act that is good in-itself to be morally evil. It cannot turn morally evil act to be good act. Stealing with intention to give to the church or the poor can never make stealing a morally good act.

The Circumstance of the Intention or End

The circumstances or the conditions that brought about a particular intention of a person, or the things or ends that made him to consider performing an act help to determine the morality of the act. The circumstances can turn a good act into evil act but they can never turn an evil act into a morally good act. A single mother engaging in bestiality for a fee with the intention to send her children to school does not make bestiality a morally good act.

Agents for Determining Moral Standards

Based on the above morality of human acts and the sources of morality, one can see that it is difficult to fix a point or find a fixed point as a guide for concrete action for people living in a particular society. This necessitates the coming into being of agents that determine moral standards. Thinkers and scholars have proposed many agents that could act as moral standards in a human society. They include social customs, the law, revelation, right reason, universalizability, pleasure, intuition, conscience, etc.

Social Customs as Moral Standard

By social customs we mean societal norms, mores, cultural laws or rules and regulations, tradition and social rituals. Every human society has customs that evolve over time. Most often they are enforced by the society through social controls such as opprobrium and ostracism. Harman sees social customs as a way of checking the moral standard of any society. However, we must acknowledge as he did that at times an approved social practice may only have come to be an approved mistake. This is especially the case when a social practice runs contrary to statuary provisions or contravenes state laws or international law. The case of cannibalism in New Guinea, caste system in India and Africa and the killing of twins, women circumcision, child marriage and child labor in some primitive cultures could be among such approved mistakes.

Law as the Basic Moral Standard

Law comes from the Latin word "*Legare*" meaning "to bend." 'Some thinkers and scholars have seen law in diverse perspectives as a rule of action, a rule of direction or a settled principle of action, etc. Law can be seen as the body of rules, regulations or constitution set up for guidance. It could be regarded as external principles or yardstick or standard to which our acts must conform to be moral. It helps one to find out whether his conduct is moral or not. Thomas Aquinas gave a comprehensive definition of law when he said that law is "an ordinance of reason for the common good, promulgated by him who has the care of the community."[13]

For Kant, it is this law that accounts for ought in our actions, imposes an obligation and a categorical imperative.

Division of Law

There are two divisions of law, namely: the physical law and the moral law.

Physical Law – This is the law that imposes a physical necessity and directs non-free beings to uniform action towards their ends by an inner necessity of their nature. Some of these laws include the laws of physics, chemistry and biology which apply to all bodies.

Moral Laws – These are laws that impose moral necessity and direct free beings to act towards their ends by imposing obligation on their free will. This is what law is in the strictest sense of the word.

Kinds of Law

Law can be differentiated into three kinds, eternal, natural and positive.

Eternal Law

This is the law as it exists in the mind of God directing all creatures unto the purpose and end of the universe. This is the plan of God's wisdom, and as a result the government of all things exists in His mind in the eternal now. For St. Augustine, eternal law is "the law by which it is just that all things be most perfectly in order." He went further to say that, "it is the divine reason or the will of God commanding that the natural order of things be preserved and forbidding that it be disturbed."[14]

On the same line of thought, Aquinas says that eternal law is the exemplar of divine wisdom as directing all actions and movements. This means that eternal laws encompass both the physical and moral laws. It can be said that this eternal law operates in man at least we know that everybody has reason, and as such has an idea of what is good and what is bad. Hence, everybody desires what is good. For Aristotle, the good is that desired by everybody. The moral law is expressed in our conscience.

Everybody also has conscience which has been defined as the God in us; the little voice of wisdom in us urging us do something or not to do something, and at the same time giving us mental qualms, sense of guilt and sense of shame, and making us remorseful when we go contrary to its dictates. The physical aspect of the eternal law guides the body metabolism and the systems of the body like injection, digestion, absorption, nutrition, reproduction, blood circulation, excretion, ejection, etc.

Natural Law

Cicero says that natural law is right reason. For Aquinas, it is the rational creature's participation in the eternal law. Natural law is a law discovered by reason, and it directs us to real goods without which we cannot be happy, and forbids those apparent goods which destroy happiness. From it the first principles of moral law and human rights emerged. Examples include all the fundamental human rights like; the right to life, freedom of movement, freedom of speech, freedom of association plus other inalienable rights and freedoms.

Positive Law

This is human law as made by the state and other associations. These are derived from the natural law in the sense that they are ordinances of reason and it is binding on the consciousness of subjects and as such forms a moral standard for the state or association.

Revelation as a Moral Standard

Revelation is a way whereby God manifests truth to man. This revelation could be natural or supernatural. Natural revelation is associated with the things of nature. When we look at the external and internal structures of plants and animals we see a kind of design not created by us, and this tells us something of a perfect designer in existence. The motion we see in our environment also reveals to us the idea of the existence of an unmoved mover and uncaused cause. These natural revelations have from all ages inspired natural religion in some societies and at the same time it sets moral standard for the people. African traditional religion and some oriental religions are such religions borne out of natural revelation.

Supernatural revelation involves direct revelation from God to man. Angels and prophets could be intermediary in the process. Hence, it has to do with faith, belief, inspiration and religion. We know already that inspired words and writing as contained in the Holy Books such as the Bible and Koran have for ages formed the moral standard for action of the Christian and Islamic believers.

Right Reason as a Moral Standard

Right reason is the faculty in us for differentiating right from wrong, good from bad. Many scholars have advocated the primacy of reason over law since law is one of the products of reason. The Stoics maintained that reason is our guide in morals, that the good life alone is a reasonable life and anything else is folly. The right reason shows the good life to be life in conformity with nature, both universal nature and human nature.

However, it is pertinent to distinguish three uses of reasons:

Right Reason – this is reason which is rationally exercised, that is, one which is consistent with self and faithful to its own law and function.

Wrong Reason or Contradictory Reason – this is reason that contradicts itself, enthralled or captivated by a law foreign to it. Here, the Freudian Id, that is, the irrational self and the superego which is the society take over the ego – the rational self of the individual and dictate for it. Wrong reason is often the reason used to steal or commit murder.

Practical reason – this is reason not in its function of contemplating the truth but of directing action, providing or presenting the good to the will for its acceptance.

Universalizability as a Moral Standard

This holds that an action or a principle is morally justifiable in so far as it is universalizable, that is, it is applicable to all similar and relational situations. According to R. M. Hare, "the most important truths about moral judgments are: firstly, that they are a kind of prescriptive judgment, secondly, that they are chiefly distinguished from other prescriptive judgment by being universal."[15] Certain acts like stealing, murder and cheating are universally unacceptable. They are wrong everywhere. We cannot legalize and universalize an act like stealing because there will be unfavorable outcomes and the world will be worst for it and invariably will become a horrible place to live in. In terms of moral principles, the golden rule "do unto others the way you will like to be done unto" can be universalized with favorable results.

Forms of Universalizability

There are three forms of universalizability.

Descriptive Universalizability

It holds that the application of any moral predicate to any object or subject is by implication applicable to any other object or subject like that in the relevant respects. For example, keeping a promise is universally acceptable in relevant respects. It is a duty and is good too to keep your promise always but in some respects the consequences of keeping a promise will outweigh the duty to do that. Sometimes failing to keep a promise saves life. For instance, King Harold could have extracted a promise from the biblical three wise men to come to him with information about where the Messiah king was borne. But the wise men went home without reporting to King Harold because they knew the consequences of reporting back to Harold would be grave.

This principle is also applicable to the duty to tell the truth. It is universally accepted that it is good to tell the truth. But this holds in relevant respect as some people (like judges in the courts, the policemen on duty, parents, etc.) have right to the truth while some others do not. A child who wants to know how much the father makes in a month may not have the right to the truth as the mother might have. Likewise a terrorist and a hijacker who want to know how many Americans and Jews are in a plane definitely have no right to the truth. A criminal who wants to know where in the house you kept your $1.2 million Dollars cash definitely have no right to the truth. Truth is most often denied to whosoever lacks the right to it in the relevant respect. The right to the truth is most often is earned; some earn it by position or relation like parents while others earn it by law like the police and judges in the court. There is also the biblical account where Abraham denied the Egyptians the truth about Sarah, his wife he was travelling with. Instead of telling them Sarah is his wife, in Genesis 20:2 Abraham said "She is my sister." He lied basically for the reason that he wanted to secure and save his own life from the Egyptians who would have killed him in order to take away his extremely beautiful wife.

Consequential or Evaluative Universalizability

This is different from the descriptive universalizability in the sense that it refers to all circumstances rather than relevant or relational respects. Kant acknowledged this type of universalizability when he said that for any moral proposition to be true it must be that it is not tied to any particular condition, including the identity of the person making the moral deliberation. In the view of Kant, in his work, *Grounding for the Metaphysics of Morals*, "a moral proposition must have universality which is to say that it must be disconnected from the particular physical details surrounding the proposition and could be applied to any rational being."[16] For example, stealing is wrong in all circumstances even in the case where an employee steals from a rich employer who owes him arrears of salary for many months or in the case of Robin Hood who steals from the rich to give to the poor. It is also wrong to steal from the government to give to the church. Thus, stealing is wrong intrinsically and in all circumstances. There will be serious consequences universally if stealing is to be allowed in some respects.

Social Universalizability

This differs from descriptive universalizability in the sense that when one speaker applies a moral predicate to any object or subject in one respect, it is expected that other speakers would use it in the same respect.

Finally, universalizability can be used in different modes, namely:

- E-type or looser type used in a particular situation or region

- U-type or stricter type used in all situations or in all regions or ages.

Pleasure as a Moral Standard

Man by nature is at the pursuit of good life. This implies that man is in the pursuit of pleasure which as it were one of the most essential ingredients that makes life interesting. There are two kinds of pleasure.

Bodily Pleasure

This is the whole range of sensations, of feelings that man gets through the stimulation of bodily organs especially the erogenous organs and the nerve endings. This is most often realized in eating and drinking and in some physical and sexual activities.

Intellective Pleasure

This is a kind of pleasure generated by the intellect. It concerns the enjoyable and pleasant experiences that any person enjoys, likes and finds satisfactory as opposed painful and unpleasant experiences of life. This kind of pleasure could come from intellectual activities like reading a good book, scientific research, writing a book, directing or watching a movie, or producing an art work, talking with a family member or best friend, traveling to different lands to see people and cultures or see wonderful natural features.

Positive/Dynamic Pleasure

This involves one going for those things that would give him pleasure and tries to judge things and situations in the light of whether they will increase or reduce pleasure.

Negative/Passive Pleasure

This involves one avoiding those things that would give him pain and tries to assess things and situations in that perspective.

Intuition as a Moral Standard

This holds that man can have a direct knowledge of morality without any appeal to reason. This means that one does not need to study ethics to pass moral judgment on human acts just as the aesthetic sense makes us to know that something is beautiful without any appeal to the intellect. So, intuition involves an immediate grasp of the moral worth of an action. For Bergson, "intuition is a synthetic faculty and its function is to grasp the wholeness and concrete individuality of things."[17] Everybody knows that murder is wrong but to be at the scene of gruesome murder brings out the intuitive perspective that murder is evil.

Conscience as the Ultimate Moral Standard

Conscience is regarded as the inner voice. It is often called the God in us. It is summed up as the power of evaluating moral judgment, making evaluative moral judgment of oneself or actions totally independent of what others may think or do. For Martin Heidegger, it is a call to authenticity – a kind of calling by the self, addressed to the self, who needs to hear the call and need it in order to be the person that the self can be but is not yet. A person feels remorse whenever he goes contrary to the dictates of the conscience. It is the source of the sense of guilt and sense of shame. Guilt feelings flood the mind when we fail to obey the dictates of the conscience.

Kinds of Conscience

Strict or Lax Conscience

This is seen in the attitude of one in making moral judgment; whether he considers or overlooks certain moral principles or values. A strict conscience is severe in discipline, stringent in requirement and inflexibly maintains or adheres to moral principles. People with strict conscience take into consideration relevant moral laws before performing an act. On the other hand, a lax conscience lacks rigor, strictness or firmness in sticking to moral principles. It is rather loose and slack when it comes to following a given moral law. People with lax conscience perform the act before they think about the moral rules and obligation involved, and whether their actions are right or wrong.

Scrupulous or Perplexed Conscience

A strict conscience can be scrupulous or perplexed in the process of making moral judgment. A scrupulous conscience is painstaking and exact in following a moral law. It is meticulous and principled in acting according to a given moral law. Individuals with scrupulous conscience spend so much time in the assessment of moral laws and obligation surrounding a particular law to the extent that when they act it may be too late in the day. On the other hand, a perplexed conscience is confused and puzzled and as such doubtful in the process of making moral assessment for action. Persons with perplexed conscience do not act at all. They often adhere to the thumb rule that says "when you are in doubt do not act."

Certain or Doubtful Conscience

This is seen in one's ability to form moral judgment which has high probability or without the least prudential certainty. A certain conscience is one that acts with certainty. It is sure of itself. A doubtful conscience is one that is always entangled in doubt. This doubt has a crippling or stupefying effect on the will to act.

Correct or Erroneous Conscience

This depends on the resultant effect of an already formed and executed conscience, and on whether it corresponds to the general standard. If the conscience conforms to general standard and the result is good it is regarded as correct conscience. If it does not conform to generally accepted norms and the result is bad it is regarded as erroneous conscience. Erroneous conscience also depends on the ability of the person to correct the error. If the person cannot correct the error the conscience is completely erroneous.

Schools of Morality

From the above agents that determine moral standard, many schools of morality have emerged and we shall mention some of them briefly.

They include:

The Rational School of Ethics: Morality based on Reason

This school asserts that for any action to be moral it must not be contrary to reason. It must conform to reason and rationality. Aristotle was one of the greatest protagonists of the school. For him, "the good is the cultivation and fulfillment of man's faculties especially the reason."[18] So, a good human act is one that conforms to reason. Aristotle went further to establish that happiness is the end of every human action. In his view, if the good is what all men in the last resort aim at, then it must be happiness. This is because happiness is everything it needs to be, and it has anything it needs to have. Happiness is the best, the noblest, the most delightful thing in the world and it meets all those qualities which are separately enumerated in the inscription upon the temple of Delos: Justice is loveliest, health is best and sweetest to obtain is heart's desire."[19]

Aristotle concluded that all these qualities are in the activities of the virtuous soul, and it is these, or the best of them, which we say constitute happiness. Thus, happiness is the ultimate good and the reason for our actions.

We have to mention at this juncture that the school is very much at home with the cardinal virtues of prudence, justice, temperance and fortitude or courage, as these are components of right reason and happiness.

Prudence – this is the habit whereby the mind is skilled in recognizing reasonable things to do in all areas of human conduct. This helps a man to control his pride with caution, care, good judgment and wisdom. It makes a man to accept his dislikes or get involve in acts of self-denials and self-sacrifice.

Justice – this habit disposes a man's will to respect the good of his fellow men and act reasonably towards them. It means being fair and impartial to others in our actions. It involves treating people equally in relevant respects.

Temperance – this is the habit whereby human concupiscible appetite is moderated by reason. This habit helps a man to control excessive sexual desires. The man that has a good habit of temperance would not be involved in rape or bestiality.

Fortitude or Courage – this is the habit found in human irascible appetite. It restrains a man from acting unreasonably in the face of difficulty or danger. It helps a man to control his anger or hot temper. If a man has a good habit of courage he would not be easily provoked to fear or anger which leads to other vices. He would not quit a good course in the face of difficulties.

The Natural Law School of Ethics: Morality based on Nature

This school of morality was made strong by Marcus Tullius Cicero (106-43 BC) through his powerful intellectual orations and writings as a statesman, philosopher and a man of letters, in last the days of the Roman Republic. For Cicero, out of all the material of the philosophers' discussions, surely there comes nothing more valuable than the full realization that we are born for justice, and that right is based not upon man's opinion but upon Nature. According to him, reason is that which is implanted in us by nature and for those creatures who have received the gift of reason from nature have also received right reason, and therefore, they have also received the gift of law, which is right reason applied to command and prohibition. And if they have received law, they have received justice also.[20]

Rader acknowledged the existence of this school of morality and summed up their ethical philosophy in three interrelated headings:

• The concept of a cosmic order as the ground of objective moral laws: nature is divine reason infused through the cosmos and human reason is the divine element in man. By reason, man can discover the fundamental laws of the universe and can direct his conduct in conformity with these laws and in harmony with the divine order of the cosmos.

• The idea of law of nature: this is based on the conception of natural harmony which is grounded in innermost nature of man, society and the universe. It is independent of convention, legislation and all other institutional devices. It is both a law of nature and a moral law. It is universal, irrevocable and inalienable. Far from being an arbitrary construction based on human wish or decree, it provides the ultimate standard of right conduct whether of individuals or of states.

- The doctrine of the natural kinship of all human beings: all men by nature are kin and equal and as a result there should be natural brotherhood and universal fellowship as opposed to allegiance to local state, race, or tribe or color.[21]

The Egoist School of Ethics: Morality based on Self- preservation

Thomas Hobbes was one of the modern adherents of this school in his life and works. In his epic work, the Leviathan, [22] he tried to show that man by nature is egoistic. The term Egoism is derived from the Latin word "Ego" meaning "I" or "Self." For Kirkpatrick, Egoism is a doctrine that we have proof of nothing but our own existence. So, an egoist is one who thinks and speaks too much of himself or of things as they affect him. This school of morality maintains that the criterion for judging an action right or wrong is the amount of good or bad it produces for the agent of the action. As a result, the egoist has only one moral obligation, to produce for himself the greatest balance of good over evil. For this school, our judgments of what is good or bad should be based on what is to our own advantage. A member judges other person's actions according to how they favor him. This school includes the hedonists, the Cyrenaic and epicureans.

Forms of Egoism

There are two forms:

Ethical Egoism

This is the view that each individual should seek as an end only his own welfare. As a kind of intuition, it holds that the individual's welfare is the only thing that is ultimately valuable and good for him. Therefore, the perfect duty of each man is to maximize his own respective good and by all means preserve and perpetuate his being.

Psychological Egoism

This holds that the determining, though perhaps concealed motive of every voluntary action is a desire for one's own welfare. This means we ought to seek our own interest because it is natural to do so. Again, self-preservation is a natural tendency of everything in existence, and is often taken as the first law of nature for all things. We will always meet certain degree of resistance when we try to cut down a tree or break a stone or kill an animal.

The Intuitionist School of Morality: Morality based on Insight

This school of morality holds that there is direct and immediate perception of the rightness or wrongness of human conduct without any consideration of the value of their consequences. Members of this school believe that in addition to the senses and introspection, human beings possess a further faculty, which discloses to them certain objective existing qualities or relations.

Forms of Intuitionism
There are three:
Perceptual Intuitionism

This holds that only judgments relating to the rightness or wrongness of particular acts are intuitive:

Dogmatic Intuitionism
This holds that some general material propositions relating to the rightness or wrongness of acts may be intuited, e.g., obedience is better than sacrifice.

Philosophical Intuitionism

This holds that only certain general propositions about what is right or wrong are intuitive, and they are few and formal. In recent times, philosophical intuitionism has taken various forms, as follows: Aesthetic intuitionism which holds that moral values are grasped by immediate insight. Axiological intuitionism is of the view that only moral values of an act are grasped through immediate insight. Phenomenological intuitionism contends that certain properties of moral phenomenon are known through insight. Deontological intuitionism asserts that duty or right is known through insight, while Utilitarian intuitionism opines that utility and happiness in a moral act are known through insight.

Phenomenological School of Ethics: Morality based on Individual Experience

This school of morality holds that there are certain natural and moral properties of action or state of affairs that can be observed by one or the other of the physical senses. This school is very much interested in the individual moral experience than on how men ought to act. So, for them, the rightness or wrongness of action depends on the examination of individual moral consciousness and judgment.

Sometimes and for many people experiences in life tend to become sign posts as well as guiding principles for day to day living. Many of us believe that experience is the best teacher. If a man is robbed of his car and a huge amount of money on a lonely road by a fake vehicle accident victim lying on the road, it is unlikely the same person will stop to assist in some supposedly genuine accidents under similar circumstances. If he didn't stop to help, it is likely he has been influenced by the previous moral phenomenon, and has acted based on the experience. Also, some people who have been duped in the process of giving to charity may likely doubts genuine cases of charitable appeal. To understand some moral actions of a person you may have to examine his moral consciousness and judgment to see if they have influence from the past or present phenomenal situation.

The Teleological Schools of Ethics: Morality based on Consequences and Utility

The teleological school of morality holds that in order to assess the morality of an act it is always necessary to examine the consequences of the action. If the consequences are good then the act is right but if the consequences are bad then the action is wrong. For many utilitarian thinkers, if an action gives pleasure or brings happiness for the greatest number then the action is right but if it gives pain then it is wrong.

The Utilitarian School of Ethics: Morality based Pleasure

This is one of the teleological schools of Ethics. The school emphasizes morality based on utility or consequences. Here, Utility means usefulness or pleasure. This school was propagated by scholars like: Bentham, Mill, More, and H. Sedgwick. For Bentham, Nature has placed mankind under the governance of two sovereign masters: pain and pleasure. It is for them alone to point out what we ought to do as well as to determine what we shall not do. According to him, the standard of right and wrong, and the chain of causes and effects are fastened to their throne. They govern us in all we do, in all we say, in all we think: every effort we can make to throw off our subjection, will serve but to demonstrate and confirm it. In other words, a man may pretend not be influenced by pain and pleasure; but in reality he has remained subject to it all the while. Later on, this school of morality substituted the pain and pleasure principle with the principle of greatest happiness for the greatest number, or greatest felicity principle which asserts "the greatest happiness of all whose interest is in question, as being the right and proper, and the only right and proper and universally desirable."[23] From this perspective, utilitarianism seeks pleasure or happiness of the entire human race or the greatest number of people.

Forms of Utilitarianism

There are two forms:

Extreme or Act Utilitarianism

This seeks for an act that has the greatest utility. The extreme utilitarian judges the rightness of any human action in terms of the consequences of the individual acts. The right act is that which brings the best results in the particular circumstances. It is extreme because it believes that if breaking a rule or law does produce the best possible consequences, then the rule or law ought to be broken. Extreme utilitarianism appears to be anti-legislation and opposed to authority. Thus, it favors law breakers and can inspire criminal activities like faking and adulteration, cheating and malpractice; drug trafficking, prostitution and gambling where individuals may perceive breaking the law as offering more monetary benefit and pleasure than keeping the law.

Restricted or Rule Utilitarianism

This seeks for a rule that without exception may be allowed and must have the greatest utility. So for them, acts are to be tested by rules and rules by consequences. The only exceptions are when rules conflicts or when the particular act falls under no rules. A rule utilitarian believes in the primacy of law over reason forgetting that laws and rules are products of reason.

In summary, utilitarian school of morality sees consequences as the test of right and wrong. An action is right if it brings the best result. And the best result is the greatest happiness for the greatest number. Happiness means here the surplus of pleasure over pain. However, utilitarian principle did not consider there are actions that are painful but still beneficial like caring for the sick, self-denials, self-sacrifice, philanthropy and some hard labors, researches and studies.

Deontological School of Ethics: Morality based on Duty or Right

Deontology is from a Greek word *"deon"* meaning duty. The school emphasizes duty for duty sake. They adhere to the following maxims "let us do right even if the heavens will fall." "Let us tell the truth even if the heavens will fall." "Let us keep our promise even if the heavens will fall." The teleologists disagree with the above expressions of duty for duty sake and its maxims. For the teleologists if doing right; keeping our promise, and telling the truth will make the heavens to fall then we should refrain from them for if the heavens fall it will be catastrophic and painful for all.

Kant is the forerunner and protagonist of the deontology school. He refutes the above teleological views. For him, rightness of an action depends on right incentives and right maxim. The right incentive for Kant is the respect and reverence for moral law. A moral act must be done for duty's sake with good will. This means obeying the moral laws is a call of duty for every man. Disobeying the moral law is an attempt to cut the fiber that holds the human society together. Things like obedience to the laws of a country, paying taxes, jury obligations, witness in court, and selective service in the armed forces are moral duties for citizens of a country. Kant believes all our moral actions should be guided by a right maxim. For right maxim, Kant presented his principles of categorical imperative. The different formulations include:

• Act that you treat humanity, whether in your own person or in that of another always as an end never as a means only.

• One should act as though one were through his ends a law making member of the kingdom of ends.

• Act so that the maxim of your will can always at the same time be valid as a principle making universal law.

Contingency School of Ethics/Situation Ethics: Morality based on Circumstances

Contingency school of morality also called situation ethics is an ethical framework that helps one in very difficult moral situation to strike a balance between absolutism of the state/law and the absolutism of reason/individual conscience. It involves a delicate act of balancing to meet appropriate standard of morality in difficult circumstances. The contingency school of morality is an attempt to integrate the various schools of moral thought. Its development was stimulated by moralists who tried to apply the principles of major moral schools to real life situations but found out those principles which were highly effective in one situation would not work in other situations. They sought for the explanation for these moral experiences. They examined teleological and deontological principles. Why does a principle work brilliantly in one situation and fail woefully in another?

The contingency school answers the question by saying that results differ because situations differ. Results vary because the circumstances matter when we talk of human action. Hence, we have to consider the circumstances in assessing human conduct. That one principle works in one situation does not necessarily mean it will work in another. Thus, this calls for the integration and balancing of these principles to get the desired result or meet the best moral standard.

For instance, even though it is a moral duty for us to tell the truth always, but no rational person tells the truth in every situation especially if we consider that the consequences of telling the truth could the cause the loss of life of beloved ones or innocent people or undermine the security of our beloved country. In some situations, we do not tell the truth to people who do not have right to it. In such cases we have no choice than to deny them the truth, and we often say "we don't know" or "we don't remember."

The Skeptics School of Ethics: Morality based on Limited Doubt

For the skeptics, there is no absolute law, and there is no absolute standard for anything. Likewise, there is no absolute standard of morality. Everything is relative including morality. As man is the measure of all things. At the same time, he is not an absolute being.

Sometimes what is abhorred in one place is tolerated in another. Polygamy is accepted in some African communities while in the Western world it is unacceptable. Child marriage is accepted in some Islamic cultures and religions while it is regarded as child abuse in the Western world. Likewise guy marriage is legal in some countries and illegal in others. In the United States it is lawful in some states but in others it is not yet permitted.

Thus, for the skeptics where lies the boundary between right and wrong, good and bad becomes a question of debate. The side with stronger argument carries the day but may not win in the future. If morality is to be based on the outcome of debate, it will lack universal character and as such limited skepticism becomes a guide. Under these doubtful circumstances the skeptics will claim they are still evolving in a particular moral matter. They often suspend judgment and adopt a wait and see attitude towards such moral issues until the call for decision by public opinion becomes overwhelming on them. This could force them to take a stand either for or against the moral issue. A good example is President Obama's evolution or transition from indifference to guy's rights to a front runner in the defense of guy's rights in the world.

The Experimentalist School of Ethics: Morality based on Experiment

Morality based on experiment was advocated by John Dewey. The main emphasis of this school is on valuation rather than values of human actions. They are not only interested in whether an action is right or wrong, but more importantly they want to know the process used to determine the rightness or wrongness of the action. For them, in testing actions, we must see ends and means as "continuous" – the ends as means to future satisfactions, and the means as not merely instrumentally but intrinsically valuable or not valuable. For Dewey, in accessing a moral situation, what is needed is to find the right course of action, the right good. Hence, inquiry is exacted: observation of the detailed makeup of the situation, analysis into its diverse factors, clarification of what is obscure, discounting the more insistent and vivid tracts, tracing the consequences of the various modes of the action that suggest themselves, regarding the decision reached as hypothetical and tentative until the anticipated or supposed consequences which led to its adoption have been squared with actual consequences.[24] According to Rader, the heart of Dewey's ethical philosophy is the attempt to link science, technology and morals which have been described by critics as strong in method but weak in vision.[25]

From the above views of Dewey, we can say that his experimental morality is keenly used by many psychoanalysts to carry out mental and moral evaluation of rehab patients who could be murder suspects, substance abuse individuals, domestic violence suspects or victims of child labor and child abuse, sex molestation victims, victims of sex addiction, victims of torture and other degrading situations. The method appears to be working as we see persons including celebrities check in for rehab for certain awful behavior, and they experience some favorable results for the decision. At least we often see a kind of normalcy in the life of the individuals who went through the process.

This type of moral valuation helps to determine whether a crime suspect is suitable for trial in the court of law. It also helps in the rehabilitation of the victims and reintegration into the human society. This moral evaluation is also used in the screening of applicants for important positions and for the selection of candidates for elective positions in government. As a result of the current successes in this method, rehabilitation is now often recommended for people who inflicted or suffered psychiatric injuries. These injuries often affect the human action and behavior of the individual if left untreated.

Systems School of Ethics: Morality based on Globalization

This can be regarded as the Ethics of Globalization. This school of morality sees the world as a system made up of units and subunits. Most often what affects one of the units or subunits may affect the whole system. The systemic ethics believes that the whole is greater than the sum of its parts. This means that what we can accomplish working together is more than what could be accomplished if each man would work separately. Each man has strengths but when they pull their strengths together, they produce something more than the individuals could if they work alone. When people work together as a system, the outcome is usually synergistic. The school also holds that the chain is as strong as its weakest link. There would be justice, freedom or peace in the world if everyone works together for this purpose.

With the coming of globalization the world has become global village and the system is contracting and has become so small that an action in any part of the world is felt globally. Injustice done in Iraqi is seen as injustice to the whole of humanity. A denial of freedom in Syria is seen as a reduction of freedom of the whole world.

Financial corruption that brought about economic meltdown in United States of America was felt all over the world. Hence, action taken in Washington is most often felt around the world. It is often said that when Washington sneezes, the whole world catches cold. Washington is also affected by crisis in any part of the world. Politicians use them either to influence those in government or change public opinion about those in government. In some cases, the arms industry and aid organizations are influenced too.

In a globalized world, before an individual or groups posit an action they will not only ask themselves how their action will be seen by their immediate community but also they will think of how their action will be seen around the world. This also applies to actions of states and their government. As a result state sovereignty is becoming diluted while the sovereignty of international community and world bodies like Security

Council of the United Nations and the International Court of Justice is being upgraded and upheld.

The problem that arises is: when the United Nations and the World Court are unable to execute their judgment because of lack of consensus or parochial interest of a few member nations, who is authorize to act to save the world system from catastrophe? We can go back to the principle of divine rights of a king. From the ancient period to the present, God has always selected to one or two nations to lead the world by way of moral strength and military might. Egypt, Greece, Rome, Germany, Britain, Japan, China, Russia, United States and a few Eastern Empires like Persia, Babylon and Turkey had once played the role. At present, the *P5+1*, that is, the Five Permanent Members of the United Nations Security Council plus Germany are playing the role. But when they unable to do that for any reason, the principle of *"primes inter pares,"* the first among equals, allows the United States no doubt to play the role. They did it in Europe in World War 11; they did it in Bosnia, Iraqi, Libya and Syria. Whenever, they fail to do it there is always a human catastrophe like in Rwanda and Biafra. In a post-American world, another leading country will likely take up the responsibility. Fareed Zariah reviewed the prospects of this fact in his two epic works, *The Future of Freedom, and the Post American World* and examined the possibility of China or any of the BRIC countries (Brazil, Russia, India and China) playing this leadership role in the world. However, not everyone agrees with this divine right of a king principle, both foes and friends of the king. Some would see it as attempt to buttress a decadent principle but the fact remains this principle actually reflects reality that stares us on the face every now and then in crisis or peace. It is a *law sui generis,* that is, a law of a special kind which is quite different from might is right some suppose it to be.

8

AESTHETICS
The Criteria for Value Selection

Axiology etymologically is derived from the Greek word *"axios"* meaning worth or worthy, value or standard. So, axiology is the science of values. Ethics and Aesthetics are the two branches of axiology. While ethics is concerned with moral values and standards, aesthetics is concerned with artistic values and with the nature of beauty.

The term aesthetics comes from the Greek word meaning "to sense or perceive." Aesthetics is also called Philosophy of Art. And as a philosophy, it tries to make clear the laws and principles of beauty. It is a systematic attempt to investigate and analyze the nature of art so as to understand not only its essence but also to clarify and make explicit the categories and assumptions of artists. Art is a human activity through which one may by means of certain external signs hand on to others feelings he has presently or has lived through so that others are infected by these feelings and can also experience them. From these definitions, we see that to define and understand the nature of art, we have to examine the feelings we draw from the work of art, the environment of the work of art and the artist. These variables as well as the contemplator of an art work are important in our knowledge of what values are expressed or ascribed to a work of art.

It is noteworthy that man as a person or subject can confer value on a thing (object). This is seen in every aspect of human life including economics, religion, politics, culture etc. Since things do not appeal to us in the same way, some appeals may supply a need or satisfy a desire while some may arouse an interest or motivate some deeds or draw an approval, and we begin to value such appeals.

Thus, there are subjective and objective values, the changing and non-changing values. Subjective values are formulated by the individual while objective values exist irrespective of the individual choice. Some reggae music collections may appeal to an African differently from how they appeal to some Europeans. While classical music collections may appeal differently to an Irish man from how they appeal to a Chinese man. Art differs from science; while science deals with facts which can be verified and can be quantified, Art deal with values which are not easily verified or quantified. It involves cultural and emotional values which are not part of the subject matter of science.

Kinds of Value

There are diverse classifications of values. Here, we shall consider two of them:

Subjective Values

Values that involve expressions of sentiments or emotions of liking or disliking are regarded as subjective values. This brings to mind the school of thought that asserts that values are matters of the mind and not of objects out there in the physical world. For instance, George Santayana opines that "there is no value apart from some appreciation of it."[1] Likewise, D.P. Parker reaffirms the above position when he expressed the view that values belong wholly to the inner world, to the world of the mind. The satisfaction of desire is the real value; the thing that serves it is only an instrument. A value is always an experience, never a thing or object. According to Parker, "things are valuable but they are not values. We project value into the external world, attributing it to the things that serve our desires."[2] This subjectivist school of thought on values insists that values vary because they are subjective. The interpretation of valuable objects varies from one individual to other and from place to place. The perception of a thing of beauty also varies from one person to another, from one group of people to another and from one culture to another.

For Titus Harold, Marilyn Smith and Richard Nolan, values "are in some sense subjective in that they depend upon a relationship between an observer and that which is being evaluated."[3] Going further on this, Melvin Rader asserts that 'values are not passively "given" without intelligent effort, but are actively constructed.'[4] This means that values are more than subjective appreciation; they have intellectual overtone; a relation to the intellect and reason. This intellectual orientation is often objective and certain to the extent it can be grasped by anyone who has reached the age of reason and intelligence.

Objective Values

The objectivist school of thought holds that values are strictly seen here in the physical world. For them, values exist independent of the mind or a perceiver. So, the role of the mind or the perceiver of value is to describe them when they appeal to his aesthetic sense. The proponents of this thought current assert that we should differentiate the act of judging and the thing judged. In their view expressed in Harold, Smith and Nolan "if I judge a landscape (or a work of art or designs, or a woman, etc.) to be beautiful, it is not my judgment that is beautiful but the colors, shapes and curves before me. There is a quality present in the beautiful landscape or woman that is independent of my judgment."[5] And this quality resides with the object not in my eyes or mind of the perceiver. Philosophers like Plato, Aristotle, Thomas Aquinas and some modern realists and idealists believe that values in some sense have objective existence. For Plato, values belong to the world of ideas: the realm of the universals and the world of form, and as such have objective existence and are real. Consequently, values like happiness, joy, beauty can be described in a similar or the same way by all normal persons who have reached the age of reason. Also individuals or groups that deviate from what is held to be good standard usually get unfavorable criticism from the generality of the human race. In most serious negative deviations, the culprit may face social opprobrium; ostracism, excommunication, banishment or imprisonment and sometimes even execution.

Nature of Aesthetic Values

Aesthetic values are values that appeal to us and we admire and appreciate them. They can be objective or subjective values. The sense organs, e.g., the eyes, the ears, tongue, skin, nose, etc., with the corresponding senses of sight, hearing, taste, touch, smell, memory and imagination are necessary for one to have genuine aesthetic value. Reason plays a special role in enhancing the appreciation of aesthetic value. Right training also contributes and makes possible the perception or discovery of aesthetic values in a person or in an object.

Aesthetic values go with value judgment. Value judgment is about whether an object of art is beautiful as evaluated or not. Hence, we can say that value judgment is right if the value is as good as judged or wrong if it is not as good as assessed. Value judgment contributes in appraising the worth of the object of value like a work of art. This is different from factual judgment which is often descriptive statement of empirical qualities of the object of value or the relations it has with other things.

Selection of Aesthetic Values

Aesthetic values just as other values, be it the moral, religious, intellectual, scientific or economic, go through a selection process. Likewise, principles used in the selection or choice of these values can be used in the selection of aesthetic values. Harold et al enumerated a number of principles that are generally accepted in intellectual circles as a guide to value selection. They include the ones below:

Intrinsic values are to be preferred to those that are extrinsic. Something is intrinsically valuable (good-in-itself) when it is valued for its own sake and not for its capacity to yield something else while something is extrinsically valuable (good for something else) when it is a means to the attainment of other things. For instance, self-fulfillment, good health, good will and good name are values that are intrinsic and are preferred to silver and gold which are extrinsic values. However, there are other things that have both intrinsic and extrinsic value (e.g., education) and so they are valued for themselves and for what they may bring or they may be valued now intrinsically and later extrinsically.

Values that are productive and relatively permanent are to be preferred to those that are less productive and less permanent. Economic values are used up in life activities and so are less permanent while social, intellectual, aesthetic and religious values tend to be intrinsic and relatively permanent. We ought to select our values on the basis of self-chosen ends or ideals.[5] Values that are geared towards self-chosen ends lead to self- realization and self-fulfillment.

John Dewey's Thoughts on Value Selection

John Dewey's contribution to the selection of value both moral and aesthetic is insightful. In his thought, Dewey shifts emphasis from value to valuation for the purposes of selection. No one has insisted more strenuously than Dewey upon scientific study of the actual needs of human beings and the concrete experimental means of satisfying these needs.[6] John Dewey says "not all who say ideals; ideals shall enter into the kingdom of the ideal, but those who know and respect the roads that conduct to the kingdom."[7] Dewey's bid or effort to explore the roads rather than to describe the destination is anchored on the fact that he does not believe in a fixed destination but rather in a never ending and exploratory journey. Since conditions are constantly changing, rules cannot be made or goals ascertained in advance. "Living well is an experiment, and there should be flexible reappraisal and reorientation as the experiment progresses"[8] Thus, nobody should be assessed based only on the worst moment of their life because he or she also had best moments in the past and could still have another best in the future.

Analyzing this process of valuation that leads to value selection, Dewey says it is stimulated by tension, conflict, unsatisfactoriness (or dissatisfaction), and a successful valuation points to ways of resolving the tensions and releasing the pent-up energies. Dewey, as a pragmatist, conceived inquiry as the instrumentalist tool for controlling experience. And this inquiry helps to distinguish values for selection, such as what is merely "liked" and what is genuinely "likeable," merely "desired," and really "desirable," merely "admired," and truly "admirable," merely "satisfying" and dependably "satisfactory."[9] For Dewey, only the later values are to be selected in the sense that they have been validated by inquiry, experiment and experience.

9

BRANCHES OF PHILOSOPHY
Thoughts on Society, Law, Religion, Science and History

Philosophy is one of the sciences that have many branches. Philosophy does some jobs for other sciences because of the nature and importance of philosophical methods. These methods could be used to clarify concepts and words used by other sciences. Again, many of these sciences grew out of Philosophy, as a result, we have philosophy of this and philosophy of that. The major ones include:

Social and Political Philosophy

Philosophy of Law

Philosophy of Religion

Philosophy of Anthropology

Philosophy of Science

Philosophy of History

We shall take a purview of each of them to bring out their subject matter.

SOCIAL AND POLITICAL PHILOSOPHY

Man by nature lives in a society and relates with fellow human beings.

As a result, man is regarded as a social being – *ens socialis*. His being social enhances his happiness and well-being in the society. Man is also a political animal. He makes effort to maintain order and control within the society where he lives, in order to realize some ends, such as: good life, ownership of property, liberty and happiness.

In his work, *Problems of Political Philosophy,* D.D. Raphael acknowledged that social and political philosophy is a branch of philosophy. According to him, it is "an application of philosophical thinking to ideas about the society and the state."[1] Thus, we can say that social and political philosophy studies the political and social theories postulated by great thinkers in different ages on how man can realize and enjoy life, liberty and the pursuit of happiness. Furthermore, it evaluates ideal forms of social life and group behavior, how men or group ought to behave in pursuit of common goals or ideals in life. It concentrates also on how people ought to be governed, and examines ideal forms of government.

Some scholars see social and political philosophy as that branch of philosophy that deals with practical social and political situation. S.I. Benn expresses the view that political and social philosophy flourishes when the state is sick, its practitioners believing themselves qualified to prescribe solutions and claiming objective validity for the reasons with which they support their prescriptions. This is in line with William Reese's views that Social and Political Philosophy centers on the problems of the society and of the state considering not only how these entities are but how they ought to be ordered.

Schools of Thought in Political and Social Philosophy

From the various definitions and meaning of social and political philosophy, we could see that there are diverse perspectives on the subject matter. We shall consider three dominant schools of thought:

The Logical Positivist School

Logical positivism is a thought current that emerged from Vienna Circle intellectuals. For this school of thought, social and political philosophy should concern itself with analysis and clarification of social and political concepts. This school came into being as an attempt to formulate a set of normative political principles, and to explain the political order using these principles. For them, man should develop and use concepts which are logically related to one another, such as justice, equality, freedom, law and rights.

The logical positivist school believes that task of a political philosopher is to closely scrutinize these concepts and offer analysis of their meaning, logical functions and relationships. Furthermore, some members of the school exclude the normative component of political theory on the grounds that normative discourse is emotive or non-cognitive. They contended that normative statements are neither true nor false because they are neither analytic nor empirical statements. William Blackstone shared this view that normative statements do not meet the verification criterion of meaning and hence should be avoided in any socio-political discourse.[2]

Nevertheless, value judgments as normative statements which often go with "ought" or "should" play important role in human society by reason of the fact that they tend to influence and guide behavior in the society. They help to instruct, build character, and as such, they are useful for training, directing and controlling people in any socio-political setting.

Behaviorist School of Thought

This school of thought says that social and political philosophy should be empirical. As a result, they see the discipline as an empirical behavioral account of the political life of man. This means therefore that the function of social and political philosophy should be to form hypotheses and theoretical framework to support political norms and institutions. This is to free the subject matter from values that are not factual and empirical, and also to free it from values that are not supported by theories and laws. This is in order to make possible the prediction of social and political behavior of a given society or state them with the techniques of the empirical sciences.

Normative School of Thought

This school of thought sees social and political philosophy as concerned with the formulation of social and political norms and goals plus rational defense of these norms and goals. The normative school asserts that the primary concern of social and political philosophy should be the prescription of standards and provision of guidelines for justification of the aims and principles of a political entity. It is to provide guidelines for resolution of conflicts that arise in the course of governing the state and society.

From the above schools, we acknowledged that scholars have not agreed on one thing about the subject matter of political and social philosophy. There is a necessity for the three schools to come together for a holistic view and treatment of the subject matter of social and political philosophy. This is supported by the position of Blackstone when he opines that political and social philosophy cannot be purely empirical nor can it be purely analytical or conceptual. It must also be normative. Without its concern for norms it cannot perform its principal and classical function – the rational justification of the aims and purposes of political society and provision of guidelines for the rational resolution of political conflicts on all levels. The empirical and conceptual elements are necessary but in the last analysis they are subsidiary to the normative task.

The Task of Political and Social Philosophy

The principal questions, which should be the task of political and social philosophers to answer include:

- Why should man live in society and have government?

- What is the basis of political obligation?

- What should be the goals of any political society?

- What is the nature of a good social order?

- What is the right social action?

- Is state an organism?

- Big government and small government which one serves best the interest of the people?

- Are the actions of government to be justified with reference to the ends of the individual or of society?

- Does history has a pattern that can be known and predicted?

- What form of government is the best in getting the goals of the society and the state?

- The middle class majority or the top rich minority who should the government consider more in its policy? For example: who should have more tax cut; the rich who are the business owners and employers of labor or the employees who constitute the mass middle class and the bulk of tax payers?

- Where do sovereignty and political power belong: to the people or to the elected government?

- What is the limit of the government authority?

- Can civil disobedience and revolution be justifiable?

- How can laws become unjust?

- What are the limits of people's rights?

These questions are just some of the many that could be raised and they are replete with notions of political and social philosophy, and to a great extent they involve questions of ethics, epistemology or metaphysics that philosophers are best qualified to answer and proffer solutions. And this is why social and political philosophy is a very important branch of philosophy. However, it is not within the scope of this work to deal with these issues because of the verse nature of the issues. But the principles that provide answers to them are not lacking in this work.

PHILOSOPHY OF LAW

Thomas Aquinas' definition of law is one of the definitions of law which have survived the test of time. According to Aquinas, "law is an ordinance of reason for the common good, promulgated by him who has the care of the community." He went further to say that "it is a rule and measure of acts, by which man is induced to act or is restrained from acting."[3] The state and its laws provide security to the people and because of that they receive obedience from the people. This is a social contract that came into being in the formation of the state and the government, and it imposes obligations on the state and the citizens.

Etymologically, Law (*Lex* in Latin) comes from the Latin word "*Legare*" meaning "to bind." Therefore, for H. J. Paton, a law is "an objective principle valid for every rational being and it is a principle on which he ought to act."[4] This also means that law guides actions of those who live in the state.

In Philosophy, there are different conceptions of law. When philosophy takes on law, it sees law largely in the form of jurisprudence. An appropriate review of the schools of jurisprudence would give us a purview of what the philosophy of law is all about. But first, a concise meaning of jurisprudence is pertinent and necessary.

Meaning of Jurisprudence

Etymologically, the word jurisprudence comes from the Latin word "*Jurisprudentia*" meaning either "a knowledge of law" or "skill in law." The term has also been used as an exposition of any particular branch of law such as equity jurisprudence. In a much wider sense, the concept of jurisprudence is used to connote and describe the relations and connections of law with other body of knowledge, such as medical jurisprudence, architectural jurisprudence, business and economic jurisprudence, etc.

The use of the term jurisprudence is still current in the intellectual circles, but no longer enjoys high visibility and popularity in countries practicing the common law system. In England for instance, jurisprudence as a concept was used through the early period of common law. With the development of the English law consequent on the decline of the Roman Empire and the Roman law, the term jurisprudence was submerged and was not commonly used.

In his discourse on jurisprudence, Bentham made a distinction between the examination of law as it is and the examination of law as it ought to be. While Bentham was interested in the formal notions of law instead of the substantive aspect, J.L. Austin, a professor of law, went further, and was concerned with "the formal analysis of the structure of substantive law and its concepts."[5] So, with Austin, jurisprudence came to be understood as the formal analysis of the structure of substantive law and its concepts. Many other conceptions have been seen in the history of law, social and political philosophy, and these have given rise to the existence of some schools of jurisprudence, such as the Natural law school, the Logical Positivist School, the Historical school, the Sociological school and the Realist school. We shall consider each of the schools briefly to find out their viewpoints that could answer some of the questions which agitate our minds sometimes about the state and the law.

The Natural Law School of Jurisprudence

The natural law school as we have earlier seen was propagated by thinkers like Plato, Aristotle, the Stoics, Cicero, Aquinas, Hobbes and Locke, etc. They assert as Cicero would put it, that true law is right reason in agreement with nature. It is of universal application, unchanging and everlasting. For them, natural law is eternal, immutable and unchanging. It is the source of all other laws in the society and any law that runs contrary to it becomes automatically null and void.

Critics of the natural law school say that the "Achilles heels," that is, the weak point in the position of the school is their contention that natural law is immutable and unchanging. Opponents saw this view as running contrary to the nature of the society which has shown itself to be dynamic and developmental. Nothing seems to remain the same over the years, the laws inclusive.

However, the position of the natural school cannot be entirely be thrown overboard since natural law is the basis for the fundamental human rights, the inalienable rights of the human person as a being created by God and that lives in the society. The right to life, freedom, ownership of property and pursuit of happiness drive their legitimacy not only from the constitution but mainly from the conception of natural law. The notion that all human beings are created equal and endowed with the capacity to reason and feel and have a language is also derived from the notion of natural law as it is expressed in the human being.

The Logical Positivist School of Jurisprudence

We know from the history of western philosophy that logical positivism was propagated by professional philosophers of the Vienna Circle with members such as Rudolf Carnap and A.J. Ayer as the forerunners. In jurisprudence, they argued that the natural law school runs contrary to the realities of law especially the modern laws and their conventions. According to them, the natural law school pronouncements cannot survive the test of scientific philosophy of the modern era. For the positivist school of jurisprudence, "law is a command."[6]

For J. K. Austin, an analytical philosopher and an adherent of the logical positivist school, law is an expression of desire that others behave in a particular way backed by the power and will to enforce that expression in event of disobedience. He reminds us that law as command must have the following qualities:

It must be a command possessing an imperative character (i.e., imposing an obligation on a free will and some ought in the mind). Such commands must be binding on all. Such commands must be backed by the ability and willingness to employ sanctions. Such commands must emanate from the sovereign or a sovereign body.[7]

As an analytic philosopher, Austin divided law into:

- Law properly so-called; and

- Law improperly so-called

Law properly so-called

This is what he called "general command" addressed to the community at large. This is law made by superior authorities (i.e. positive law). This type of law carried both moral and prudential obligation. Prudential obligation has to do with the threat or use of force to obtain and ensure compliance. Such laws made by the state are the subject matter of jurisprudence. Although laws made by the master for the servants, and the rules of associations like a club or institutions are commands and therefore laws properly so-called but they are not positive laws rather they are positive morality.

Law improperly so-called

This is subdivided into laws set by God – divine law, and laws set by men. For Austin, Laws improperly so-called are not backed by any visible sovereign power and are not general commands. Laws of fashion and international laws are under law improperly so-called. These laws may carry moral obligation but they do not have prudential obligation. They may impose moral obligation in as much as they are reasonable laws and are for the common good and order of the society. But they are laws improperly so-called because they do not impose prudential obligation which is the awareness and fear in the individual that punishment may be imposed or is actually imposed if one goes contrary to the law.

Law improperly so-called can be turned into law properly so-called by making them an act of the parliament or a constitutional provision. Fundamental human rights and inalienable rights became enforceable through acts of the parliament and constitutional provisions. Some articles of the Ten Commandments (e.g., Thou shall not steal and thou shall not commit murder) are in the criminal code and thus are law properly so-called. In some countries, the Seventh commandment, thou shall not commit adultery has entered the criminal code and thus becomes law properly so-called in these countries while in others it is still belongs to law improperly so-called.

Under the present structure and modus operandi of globalization, international laws are becoming laws properly so-called as the United Nations Security Council now uses military force for peace enforcement and economic sanctions as punishment in cases involving crimes against humanity or a breach of international treaty. Recent cases include the Libyan intervention which led to the assassination of Muammar Gaddafi, and the sanctions against Iran for their development of nuclear weapons and the sanctions by European Union and United States against Russia for breach of international treaty in the annexation of Crimea from sovereign Ukraine.

Historical School of Jurisprudence

The Historical School of law came into existence as a result of historical circumstances and events of significant nature such as the fall of the Roman Empire, and the decay of the Roman law and Canon law, the French Revolution and the fall of Napoleon, the Russian Revolution, and the rise to power of Great Britain and Germany in Europe, the rise of Japan and China as Asia and Pacific powers. At present, it has been reinforced by the disintegration of the Soviet Union (described by President Vladimir Putin as the worst event of the Twentieth Century) and the emergence of United States of America as the sole super power of the world. These epochal events threw questions as well as doubts on the natural law theory and gave impetus and credence to the Historical School of jurisprudence. According to Friedrich Carl von Savigny, a 19th century jurist and a prominent member of the historical school, law is not something that should be made arbitrarily by a law maker, but a product of internal, silently operating forces. It is deeply rooted in the past of a nation, and its sources were popular faith, customs and the common consciousness of the people. Like the language, the constitution and the manner of a people, laws are determined above all by the peculiar character of a nation, by its national spirit. He maintains that certain traditions and customs grow up and by their continuous exercise evolve into legal rules.

Thus for Savigny, only by a careful study of the traditions and customs can the true content of law be found. Law, like language, is a product, not of an arbitrary and deliberate will but of a slow, gradual and organic growth. Law has no separate existence but simply a function of the whole life of a nation. Law, Savigny concludes "grows with the growth and strengthens with the strength of the people, and finally goes away as the nation loses its individuality or sovereignty."[8] This is why failed states are lawless states. So, the spirit of the people of a particular society becomes manifest in their customary rules. Law therefore is the product of this unconscious growth and a reflection of the inner life of the people. Customs do precede legislation and are superior to it, and legislation should always conform to the popular consciousness otherwise it will face noncompliance and civil disobedience.

The Sociological School of Jurisprudence

This school holds that jurisprudence as a science of law is a comparative anatomy of developed system of law that is concerned with the legal order and social control of people living in a particular society. It involves the examination of the legal ordering of human relations in a politically organized society with the means of legal institutions and the law. Andre-Jean Arnaud et al estimated jurisprudence from sociology of law perspective. For them, it is a systematic, theoretically grounded, empirical study of law as a set of social practices or as aspect of social experience that has become sources of consensus, coercion and social control. Following the same line of thought, Ben Atkinson Wortley conceives it as the use of social scientific methods to study law, legal institutions and social behavior.

From the above views, it is clear this school of thought sees the essence of law in any human society as socialcontrol which guides relationships among institutions and the people to bring about the right social order in the society. It is this right social order that keeps the society together, sustains it and prevents it from falling apart. Law as being synonymous with right social order dies if the right social order evaporates like in cases of failed states like Somalia and some parts of Syria, Libya, Yamen and Iraqi controlled by Islamic extremists.

The Realist School of Jurisprudence

This school came into existence as a reaction to the positions of the historical and sociological schools. The forerunner of the Realist School was Judge Oliver Wendell Holmes (1841-1935). He espouses the view that if one wishes to know what law is, one should view it through the eyes of a bad man who is only concerned with what will happen to him if he does not do certain things like paying his taxes, obeying traffic laws, paying his child support, and staying away from drugs and armed robbery. If the bad man commits any criminal offence, he will be arrested, taken to court and the court could put him in prison for the good of the society. The court could also under the benefit of doubt tell the man, "Go home and sin no more." "Stay away from crime." So, the realist school sees law from its socially desirable consequences.

Furthermore, according to M.H. Fisch, this school sees the law as an instrument of government manifested through the wishes of the courts. The members of the school contended that law is the expression of the will of the state but this expression is not in the state but it is realized through the medium of the courts.[9]

On the sovereignty of the law, the realists assert that it lies with the sovereignty of the judges. The function of law depends on the bias and subjective inclinations and interpretations of the judges. The judges give interpretation as to what the course of law should be and how it is to be followed. As it were, the primary function of the law is to settle disputes in accordance with the subjective denotation of most judges.

Law simply exists to actualize the wishes of those sitting on the benches. Law therefore reflects the subjective inclination and meaning given to it by the judges. The realist school emphasized that what is actually law is what the court decides. So, the letters of the constitution or the criminal code is not in real sense the law, it is the whips and caprices of the judges, so to speak that is law. And as such, it is difficult sometimes to say which side the judges will rule in a case before the court.

Another exponent of the realist school, J.C. Gray (1839- 1915) distinguished between law and the sources of law. He declares that law is what the judges decide. Other things are only sources of law until interpreted by a court. The courts put life into the dead words of the statue. So, the spirit of the law is not in the letters of the law that make up the constitution, the criminal code and civil code but the spirit of the law resides with the courts and it is reflected in the verdicts and sentences of the judges. This spirit lives on to become Lodes stars that guide and direct future court verdicts. They illustrated their position by saying that the reason why statues and precedents (e.g., Supreme Court verdicts) are followed is because they are laws already.

Nature and Scope of the Philosophy of Law

We have seen from the above schools the nature of philosophy of law and that the scope is wide. The scope is wide in the sense that it encompasses the philosophical, the sociological, historical as well as the analytic components of legal theory. So, jurisprudence includes the rules of external conduct, all kinds of general speculations about law and its functions, the value of law and the relations which law has with other social institutions.

PHILOSOPHY OF RELIGION

This is the branch of philosophy in which all the divisions of philosophy are on duty to play a role. It employs epistemology as it examines the logical grounds of religious beliefs. It involves metaphysics in its interpretation of the nature of the universe. It is also concerned with values and as a result it involves axiology. Axiology as theory of value deals with ethics and aesthetics.

The word "Religion" comes from the Latin word *"Religare"* meaning to bind, to link back. It means therefore to bind back to what is supposedly broken. Actually, it means man getting connected back to God, the creator after a presumably loss of contact. In philosophy of religion, we shall examine some schools of thought such as skeptic's school, the school of theism and the humanist school.

The Skeptic School of Thought

Skepticism in religious matter has grown so much in our contemporary period. Modern man suffers from metaphysical anemia because of overdose of science. Some countries are now scientific giants but metaphysical infants. The full impacts of the seventeenth century scientific revolution, the physics and astronomy of Galileo and Newton destroyed the old confidence that the world is a friendly place governed by a beloved spiritual force. The positivists and phenomenologist explicitly deny the principle of metaphysical causality. For them, it is not possible for the human mind to know anything about God, and therefore it cannot demonstrate the existence of God. Some philosophers have been predicated with the word "Atheist" because of their views about the existence of God. Such philosophers include Immanuel Kant, Nietzsche, David Hume, Baruch Spinoza, Goethe, etc.

In Kant's work, *Critique of Pure Reason*, he made statements and took postures that suggest doubts in the existence of God. In his other work, *Prolegomena of Future Metaphysis,* Kant out rightly denied the possibility of metaphysis. He denied the possibility of the human mind attaining or having knowledge of transcendental ideas. According to Kant, the idea of God, the idea of soul and its immortality are among the transcendental ideas and they belong to noumenal world (i.e., Kant's metaphysical world). For Kant this kind of ideas are outside and beyond the capacity of the two main sources of knowledge in the physical world, namely: experience and reason. Hence, God and the soul are beyond human knowledge.[10] In Kant's opinion the ideas of God and human soul are not within the categories of human understanding. That is to say even if they exist, we cannot know anything about them. And as such we cannot understand them.

David Hume, in his writings on philosophy of religion also took a skeptical stand in many instances. In his work, *Dialogues Concerning Natural Religion,* he took a swipe on the existence of God and argued that God is not a necessary Being. For him, "nothing is demonstrable unless the contrary implies a contradiction. Nothing that is distinctly conceivable implies a contradiction. Whatever we conceive as existence, we can also conceive as nonexistent."[11] Hume concludes "there is no being, therefore, whose nonexistence implies a contradiction if necessity thus applies to logically necessitated propositions and not to things, nothing, not even God is a necessary being."[12] Hume rejects the proof of existence of God based on design. He doesn't think that all complex structures we see in plants, animals and the universe in general require a necessary being for their explanation.

Also, David Hume by denying the principle of causation, he also denies all proofs of the existence of God. The idea that God is the unmoved mover and the uncaused cause of things does not make sense to him. He sees causation as mere succession, that is, a number of things sharing a specified characteristic and following one after the other in close proximity. So, wherever people talk of causation, Hume says in his work, *Treatises on Human Nature*, that he sees only contiguity and succession of ideas.

W.P. Montague in his work, *Belief Unbound* refers to the problem of evil to refute the belief in a perfect and omnipotent God. According to the argument, "if there is evil in the world it means that either God could not overcome it in which sense He is not omnipotent or He allows it in which sense He is not perfect in goodness. But since there is evil in existence, he concludes that God is not omnipotent."[13] We know that one of the serious arguments that took a serious swipe on the existence of God and tries to render the existence of God probable is the one based on the existence of evil and suffering in the world vis-à-vis the existence of the

God of Love. It is to refute this argument that Theodicy (i.e. the defense of the existence of God against the problem of evil in the world) came into being.

For theodicy, the traditional attributes of God which include Omni benevolence, omnipotence and omniscience can still coexist with evil and suffering in the world if we consider the existence of man's free will. The history of theodicy has scholars like St Augustine of Hippo, St Thomas Aquinas, St Irenaeus, Gottfried Leibniz, and Alvin Plantinga. All tried to reconcile the existence of God and evil in the world as something not logically impossible. John Hick in his work, *Evil and the God of Love* gave an account of these attempts to bring closure to the mind bugging questions about suffering in the world.

Finally, B. Pascal in his *"Wager,"* says that human reason in judgment is incapable of either proving or disproving the existence of God; he regarded the question whether God exists or not as a great gamble. Pascal reasoned that even if the probability of winning eternal happiness by leading a religious life is small, nevertheless, since the gain may be infinite and the possible loss no more than finite, it is a good gambling venture to lead such a life and to incline to whatever belief that may be necessary as its bases.[14] Of course, the loss of beatific vision, infinite happiness and bliss is far greater than the gains of finite pleasure and joys of this world.

William James in his work, *The Will to Believe,* shares the view of Pascal's Wager and asserts that whichever way a person may argue on whether God exists or not, some risk is involved. For him, by believing, one runs the risk of falling into error; by disbelieving, or non-believing, one runs the risk of losing the benefit of the truth. For example, if you should believe in God and God does not exist, you would fall into error. But if you should not believe in God and God does exist, you would lose the benefit of a salutary truth. James concluded that sometimes, it is better to believe in the hope of gaining the truth than to disbelieve in the hope of avoiding error.[15]

We must note that it may be improper to call some philosophers atheists strictly because they did not express absolute skepticism about the existence of God. There are other instances in their lives and works where they expressed the necessity for the belief in God at least from moral behavior point of view, as we noted in Kant, Pascal, Montague and even

Hume. Some of them acknowledged and lived in their day to day lives what they refused to profess with their mouth, that is, the existence of God.

The School of Theism

Theism is the belief in the existence of God. Rader defines God as a being who is personal, supreme and good. For the theist, the key to understanding reality lies in God and his design. This belief does not exclude several positions that we have already examined since a theist can be a teleologist, a dualist or an idealist, but he cannot be a complete materialist or an absolute skeptic.

For the theist, God is personal in the sense that he is a conscious mind or spirit. But He is much larger than the human mind and spirit. God is also supreme in that he is omnipotent, that is, immensely great and all-powerful. The theist also regards God as good in the perspective that he is perfect as man is imperfect. The question faced by theism as a school of philosophy of religion is: whether the conception of God as we have seen could withstand the test of reason?

Many arguments have been forwarded by theists to show that the belief in God is mature and defensible. They include Ontological arguments, Cosmological proof and Teleological arguments. We shall consider each of them briefly.

The Ontological Argument

The word "ontological" means pertaining to the nature of being. The protagonist of the ontological argument and proof of the existence of God was St. Anselm of Canterbury, and he stated the views clearly in his work, *Proslogion*. His proof of God's existence is an a priori argument that is based on reason alone devoid of experience. He defines God as the greatest conceivable being. In other words, a being than which nothing greater can be conceived. According to him, "this being must not only exist in the understanding (the mind), it exists also in reality. And it assuredly exists so truly that it cannot be conceived not to exist."[16] This proof of God's existence has been criticized by Gaunilo, a Monk and was rejected by Thomas Aquinas. It was revived by Descartes as we have seen in Descartes proofs of God's existence in an earlier chapter.

The argument was restated by Spinoza and Leibniz but seriously criticized by Locke, Hume and Kant. The ontological argument still provides for many people food for thought up till today.

According to Gaunilo, to accept Anselm's argument means that we can also accept the existence of a perfect island. For him, if God is thought of as perfect, existence is necessary to perfection, therefore, God exists. He says this type of reasoning is fallacious because it could be used to prove the existence of many other things like a perfect island. Anselm did not accept this criticism for he said that "an island is finite in nature and cannot be conceived to be perfect in the sense in which God could be."[17]

Aquinas rejected the ontological argument on the ground that we could only know God relatively. His existence is not self- evident to us. We cannot leap from our imperfect idea of God to the conclusion that an absolutely perfect being exists. So, what Aquinas is saying is that man as a finite being has only an inadequate and indirect knowledge of God. And because of the infirmity or imperfection of our understanding, we cannot discern God as He is in Himself, but only by the effects that He produces. If we could know God's essence absolutely, we would surely see that His essence involves His existence.[18]

The Cosmological Proof

The cosmological arguments are based on the fact that the insufficiency of nature requires the sufficiency of God to explain it. For instance, for us to explain change or motion in the world, it requires the existence of the unchanged changer or unmoved mover for the explanation. Likewise, "cause" required an uncaused cause for complete explanation. At the same time, a contingent being like man requires the existence of a necessary being for his explanation.[19] Aquinas was the major proponent of the cosmological arguments. His five ways of demonstrating God's existence are fully discussed in this work. Hume was one of the strong critics of the proof. Hume doubts the principle of causation as a true fact and reflection of reality. Instead of causation, he sees succession of sense impressions, and the existence of God cannot be derived from them.

The Teleological Argument

This is argument from design.[20] The proponents of this line of reasoning include Plato, in his Laws, St.Augustine, St.Thomas Aquinas, Locke and Rousseau. The argument from design is based on the fact there is order in the world, there is purpose in the world and there is a sign of perfect intelligence behind the nature of things and the designs in them. This wonderful natural order requires God as its source. For instance, if astronauts land on Mars or the NASA Curiosity Rover on Mars sees something like a strange wrist watch, astronauts are likely to conclude that extraterrestrial intelligence lives in Mars or have visited it. The watch would not be there by a stroke of chance. Likewise, if we observe the metamorphosis of a butter-fly with a microscope we could see the evidence of an intelligent designer as it unfolds.

This argument was criticized by Kant. In Rader, Kant says, the design argument can only prove the existence of a kind of architect but it cannot prove a creator who makes the world out of nothing.[21] As a result, John Stuart Mill and William James preferred to believe in a finite God struggling against evil but not wholly able to eliminate it. They preferred this rather than accept completely the Darwinian hypothesis of natural selection as sufficient to explain the higher levels of evolution.

The School of Humanism

The word humanism comes from the Latin word *humanitas* which means people who show benevolence toward their fellow humans and the values got from humane learning. But if we look at it from the Italian word *"umanisti"* it means "humanists." It was a term given in the 15th century to teachers and scholars of classical Greek and Latin literatures. Humanism as a thought current started around 14th century as kind of affirmative action and advocacy by some concerned civil and religious authorities, book collectors, writers and teachers who wanted a reform in the scholastic education system of the time which was monopolized by abstract Aristotelian philosophy and logic. They wanted something that would solve human existential problems, something closer to human life. At the same time, according to Craig W. Kallendorf in his work, *Introduction to Humanist Educational Treatises*, there was agitation for the establishment of broad system of education that will go beyond mere school for doctors, lawyers, and theologians to involve mass literacy and enlightenment. The aim is to produce a society where everybody can read, write and speak with knowledge, eloquence and clarity and hence be able to contribute in community development. As the humanist movement gathers momentum, it spreads like wild fire and assumes many trends. It became a medium for mass expression of long suppressed feelings. Some of the emotions were borne as the result of what some people then saw as the greatest event in history, that is, the fall of the Roman Empire and the suppression of learning by the Turks invasion of Europe which threw the whole Western Europe into the Dark Ages. Thereafter, these emotions were kept in check by the dogmatism and authoritarianism of the ecclesiastical and civil authorities of the medieval period. The humanist movement brought in the fire of revival in all sectors of life, the religious, social, scientific and economic sectors, and as such, we can talk of different kinds of humanism. We have Renaissance Humanism, Modern Humanism, Secular Humanism and Religious Humanism.

Renaissance Humanism

Renaissance as the name implies is the period in history that started with the revival of learning after the dark ages. It is a period of reawakening in the people's consciousness that as humans we have ability to determine for ourselves what is true and what is false. Renaissance humanists carried out a kind of advocacy that urged people and communities to resist dogmatism, indoctrination, and superstitious beliefs from any quarter. For them, as humans we have the right to express our opinions and live our lives without any coercion from any religious or civil authority. Renaissance humanism flourished in the Italian cities such Naples, Venice, Florence and Rome.

A strand of this humanism was anti religion particularly leaders of Christianity, the official religion of the Roman Empire, for their perceived role in weakening the Roman Empire and her military power and responsibilities. According to them, the literary misinterpretation of the Christian teachings on forgiveness, nonretaliation, love of enemies, and the golden rule which says 'do onto others the way you like to be done unto' contributed in weakening the Roman army. Rather, these humanists imbibed the dictates of Machiavellian principles in his epic work, The Prince, which rejected the above Christian principles on the ground that they are not for a Prince who is a world power and wants to retain and maintain power. For Machiavelli, the prince should be a lion and fox at the same time, a lion to be able to scare away the wolves and a fox to be able to detect traps. And the prince should value dictatorship and the respect that goes with it more than to love or be loved which are often not sustainable.

Modern Humanism

This has been described as a naturalistic philosophy that rejects all supernaturalism and relies primarily upon reason and science, democracy and human compassion. It centers on the western cultural humanism which derives its strength from the rational and empirical tradition that started in ancient Greece and Rome, and evolved throughout European history to become the basic part of western approach to science, political theory, ethics and law. It also has a philosophy that has its bases on human needs and interest as opposed to doctrinal and ideological interests.

Secular Humanism

This kind of humanism is known to have arisen from the ashes of French revolution. It quickly spread to Germany under the auspices of left Hegelians. Here, humanism was seen as philosophy that espouses humanity without reference to the divine. Scholars like Karl Marx, Ludwig Feuerbach and Fredrick Nietzsche helped to propagate and develop this non-theistic movement. This school of thought is seen as an attempt to offer an alternative to theism – the belief in God. According to Ludwig Feuerbach, a powerful proponent of this school, the aim of humanism is to change the friends of God into friends of man, believers into thinkers, worshippers into workers, candidates for the other world into students of this world, Christians; who on their own confession are half- animal and half-angel, into man, whole man[22]

In his work, *The Essence of Christianity,* Feuerbach argues that he is nothing but a natural philosopher in the domain of mind, and the natural philosopher can do nothing without instruments, without material means.

For him therefore, the principle of humanism is not the substance of Spinoza, not the ego of Fichte, not the Absolute Identity of Schelling, not the Absolute Mind of Hegel, in short, not abstract, merely conceptual being, but a real being, the true *Ens realissimum* - man, its principle, therefore is in the highest degree positive and real.[23]

The secular humanists carried out intense attacks on religion; they intended to destroy religion in order to build up their position. Feuerbach asserts for instance that "speculations that move out of the senses, the positive and real make religion say only what it has itself thought and expressed far better than religion. They assign a meaning to religion without any reference to actual meaning of religion." Feuerbach went further "It is not I, but religion that worships man, although religion, or rather theology denies this; this is not I, an insignificant individual, but religion itself that says: God is man, man is God; it is not I, but religion that denies the God who is not man, but only an *ens rationalis* – since it makes God become man, and then constitutes this God, not distinguished from man, having a human form, human feelings and human thoughts, the object of worship and veneration."[24] He concludes that religion is the dream of the human mind, and God is the heart and soul of man, the manifested inward nature, the expressed self of a man, religion the solemn unveiling of a man's hidden treasures, the revolution of his intimate thoughts, the open confession of his live secrets.

We can see from the above that secular humanism was a life stance. For Fred Edwards in his work, *What is Humanism?*, Secular humanism is a worldview which embraces human reason, metaphysical naturalism, altruistic morality and distributive justice, and consciously rejects supernatural claims, theistic faith and religiosity, pseudoscience and superstitions. Nietzsche sees the goal of this humanism as the enthronement of the real man, the overman which he calls the superman. It is in this pursuit and quest for actualization of the idea of a superman that Nietzsche intoned the *Requiem aeternam deo* implying that "God is dead."[25]

He believes that for the superman to be then God must give way. The ship of life must have only one captain. Nietzsche believes that secularization was a great turning point in human history, and that this fact occasioned by the advancement in science and technology in the world brings to life a new freedom and scope. For him, the "death of God" would be a prelude to the rebirth of man.

This rebirth of man is aptly captured in the submission by Harvey Cox that it is "the loosing of the world from religious and quasi-religious understanding of itself."[26] This involves the dispelling of all closed worldviews, the breaking up of all supernatural myths, dogmas and sacred symbols. It represents what another observer has called the "*defatalization of history*," the discovery by man that he has been left with the world on his hands, that he can no longer blame the gods, fortune or fate for what he does with it. So, secularization is man turning his attention away from the worlds beyond and toward this world and this time. It is what Dietrich Bonheoffer in 1944 called "man's coming of age."[27] and for the International Humanist and Ethical Union (IHEU) it is man becoming "a happy human."

At present, there are still humanist movements which recognize nature as self-existing and disassociate themselves from any religious beliefs and faith inclinations. In fact, American Humanist Association has as its motto "Good without a God"[28] and opines that ethical values are derived from human needs. Their aims and aspirations are expressed in the Humanist Manifesto of 1933, 1973 and 2003. They only accept functional definition of religion as an activity that serves the social and personal needs of the individuals in their cultural festivals, moral education, and marriage ceremonies.

Religious Humanism

This is a mixture of humanist ethical philosophy, culture, religious rituals and beliefs that recognize human needs, interest, abilities, free spirit and free thoughts. This strand of humanism developed as a result of the coming into being of liberal religious organizations which adopts more democratic ideals like freedom and human rights among their humanistic goals, and at the same urging others to pursue virtuous and prudent acts for human welfare.

Thus, we have Christian humanism which advocated for self-fulfillment of man within the framework of Christian principles like "love thy neighbor like yourself." We also have the positive humanism of Martin Buber. In Buber, "rather than the superman supplanting the idea of God, God rather becomes the meeting point of I – thou relationship. The real fulfillment of community requires allegiance to God. This is theistic humanism."[29] This is often regarded as the philosophy of religion of the contemporary period.

PHILOSOPHICAL ANTHROPOLOGY

Anthropology is the study of the origin, development and nature of the human species. It is also the science of man especially of the beginnings, development, customs and beliefs of mankind. The word "Anthropology" is derived from the Greek terms "*Anthropoi*" (human beings) and "*Logos*" (words) and this means "the study of humanity."[30] Anthropology seeks to develop increasingly profound and useful knowledge about the human condition through the systematic analysis and comparison of all that can be discovered about humanity. The five major branches of anthropology are: Biological anthropology, Cultural anthropology, Archaeological anthropology, Linguistic anthropology, and Philosophical anthropology. A little explanation of each branch is insightful.

Biological Anthropology

This is also called physical anthropology. It uses the techniques of the biological sciences in the study of fossil and living human beings.

Cultural/Social Anthropology

This is also called Ethnological anthropology. It is the use of techniques of historical research, observation and interview in the study of recent and living peoples and cultures.

Archaeological Anthropology

It is the use of techniques of excavation and historical research to study dead and living peoples.

Linguistic Anthropology

This is the use of the techniques of historical research, observation and interview in the study of the languages of different peoples and cultures.

Philosophical Anthropology

This is that branch of philosophy that examines philosophically man's essential make up. Through the influence of Max Scheler, philosophical anthropology has gained prominence in recent years. In this discipline, the essential elements of man studied include: his person, language, origin of his life, culture, knowledge, work, auto-transcendence, death and immortality of the soul, etc. There are many schools of thought involved in this examination. They include the existentialists, structuralists, Marxists, Thomists, evolutionists, spiritualists, atheists and Christians. We shall look succinctly at some of these tenets and see the core of their views.

The Evolutionist School of Thought

This school is led by an English evolutionist, Thomas Henry Huxley also known as Darwin's bulldog for being among the first adherents to Darwin theory of evolution based on natural selection. For him, the interest of the school is to determine what place man occupies in nature and his relation with the universe of things. He asserted that questions needed to unravel the mystery called man include: from where is our race? What are the limits of our power on nature and of the power of nature on us? What is the end toward which we are moving? We must point out that these questions are beyond the scope of this chapter as they needed a comprehensive discussion for justice to be done to them. They are provided here as food for thought. But brief answers to the questions are not lacking in this work.

The Phenomenologist School of Thought

One of the protagonists of this school is Max Scheler. For him, all the fundamental problems of philosophy could be reduced in a certain sense to the question: What is man and what metaphysical position does he occupy in the totality of being, of the world and of God? For the phenomenologist, there is need to bracket all things that are not essentially of man.

The Existentialist School of Thought

Martin Heidegger, one of the greatest exponent of existentialism said that no epoch has ever had so numerous and varied notions of man as ours. For him, these various notions made the real meaning of what man is to be lost in the debris of past speculations. He called for a fresh asking of the question of the being of man – with existence as the most essential quality. He sees man as a bundle of possibilities. Man is still an uncompleted project open to a lot of variables. Man's future is indeterminate because he will keep changing by taking on new capabilities.

The Marxists School of Thought

A popular Marxist, Dieter Uller said that to question oneself on man; on his present and future position in the world is part of the central problems of philosophy. The Marxist sees man as a social being (*ens socialis*) and his world is economic in the sense that his development depends on how he uses the factors of production, land, labor, capital, entrepreneurship and information. Any great human achievement is a mix of these factors.

PHILOSOPHY OF SCIENCE

This is another branch of philosophy which has become very important since the scientific revolution of the 17th century. Philosophy of science is the philosophical study of the nature of science and the concepts it uses. It is a philosophical reflection and analysis of the fundamental assumptions, principles, theories, methods and concepts of science. In philosophy of science, we could see some of the things we cannot see in any physical science text especially the limitations of scientific methods, and the problem of induction as lacking rational justification in its predictive power.

The Scope of Philosophy of Science

Philosophy of science covers a wide range of issues on philosophy and science. Philosophy of science attempts to answer such question as: What is science? What is the nature of scientific knowledge? How does it differ from other forms of knowledge? How do we arrive at a scientific truth? What are the aims and objectives of science?

Philosophy of science defines science variously as: Body of knowledge that deals with the various aspects of material reality, their properties, functions and the changes they undergo. It also sees science as a method of acquiring knowledge that is empirical and formal. As empirical method, it involves observation, experimentation procedures, and use of instruments and formulation of theories. And as a formal method it uses inductive and deductive procedures to formulate concepts, rules and theories which could be expressed in quantitative and statistical forms. It even sees science as the various instrument used by man to effect physical transformation of the world, and also as an institution that undertakes the training of scientists, conducting of researches, the development of knowledge and products.

Branches of Science

Science could be broadly divided into four groups according to the method used and the subject matter:

Formal Sciences: These sciences use concepts, rules and theories systematically to arrive at their conclusions. These sciences include mathematics, logic, geometry, statistics, etc.

Empirical Sciences: These sciences use experimentation and observation to reach their conclusions. The empirical sciences include physics, chemistry, biology, etc.

Social Sciences: These are sciences that conduct systematic study of the human society and its institutions. Examples are economics, government, sociology, anthropology, philosophy, psychology, etc.

Human Sciences: These are branches of learning that concern human culture. Some of them include languages, music, drama, poetry, art and history, etc. Some classifications have philosophy under humanities.

General Scientific Principles

Science has generally accepted the following principles and works with them in all its departments. Some of the major principles include:

The Law of the Uniformity of Nature

This asserts that nature acts uniformly. This implies there is order in the works of nature. For instance, we have uniform motion, gravity, speed of light and sound.

The Law of Universal Motion

It has been accepted by science that motion is an objective reality and that it is universal. This includes the fact that anything that moves is moved by something. Again, bodies remain in a state of rest or inertia or constant motion until they are acted upon by another force.

The Law of Universal Causation

Science has accepted also that causality is real. So for it, anything that happens is caused by something. There is nothing that happens without something prompting it. Science often juxtaposes causes and the effect.

The Law of Planetary Motion

This holds that the sun is the center of the solar system and other planetary bodies revolves and moves around it. Consequently, the heliocentric view replaced the geocentric view.

The Law of Gravitation

This is the force that operates within the earth that attracts anything within a certain range in the earth's atmosphere. It allows bodies to fall to the earth at a speed of 9.8 m/s.

The Law of Natural Selection

This is the brain child of Charles Darwin. This holds that perfect forms of species are gradually approximated through sensible changes. The weaker forms give way to stronger forms of species. So, in all living forms, a specific type is presently directing the earlier stages of growth to the realization of its own perfection. This principle runs within the theory of organic evolution.

Scientific Theories

A theory explains how things are related or their common properties. It is an outcome of systematic research or investigation about certain phenomenon. Some of scientific theories considered in the philosophy of science are: atomic theory, theory of evolution, theory of relativity, quantum theory, nuclear theory, theory of optics, wave theory, big bang theory, corpuscular theory, theory of conservation of mass, etc.

Scientific Methods

There is no universal agreement, even among scientists on what scientific method is. The reason for this is not far-fetched. It is a self-evident truism that science evolved from common sense and transition from one level to the other is gradual and continuous. In Titus Harold, Marilyn Smith and Richard Nolan, Bryant Conant asserts that careful examination of the sciences, such as physics, astronomy and psychology, fails to reveal any single method in use. Sciences like astronomy proceeds by means of observation and mathematical calculations from these observations. According to him, other sciences like physics and chemistry emphasize controlled experimentation. In some other sciences trial and error, statistics and sampling are used. He concludes that we need "to speak about scientific methods rather than the scientific method."[31] We can estimate and enumerate a number of methods used in science like: Observational method, Experimental method, Statistical method and Sampling method.

Generally, these methods reach some of their conclusions through analysis and inferences. The inferences could be induction or deduction.

The Steps to Scientific Research and Knowledge

The above scientific methods are interrelated and can supplement one another. It is difficult to physically make a distinct separation of them. Scientific method is a collective term designating and denoting the numerous process and steps by which the various sciences are built up.

There are about six steps in the process of scientific research, namely: identifying and stating a problem, collection of data or fact-gathering, conjecture, hypotheses formulation and testing, proof substantiation and theory construction. The knowledge that proceeds from this process is systematic and is endowed with universality and objectivity.

Limitations of Scientific Methods

Scientific methods have been shown to have certain limitations. Harold, Smith and Nolan enumerated some of them as:

- In scientific research, we can find only that which our methods and instruments are capable of finding.

- Scientific classification gives valuable information but no single classification includes everything in the subject being classified.

- The whole may have qualities absent in the parts,

- There may be many interpretations of a thing, a person or an event, each of which is true as far as it goes.

- When we consider anything that is in a process of development, we find the later stages as real as their earlier stages, and probably more informative as to the nature of the process.

- The sciences are dependent upon man's sense organs and upon his general intellectual equipment, which are imperfect.

- The sciences cannot prescribe values.

It is because of the above limitations that Karl Popper sees the whole scientific endeavor as tentative proposal of hypotheses or conjectures which aim to describe some part of the world or solve some problems, followed by the vigorous attempt to falsify them with experimentation.[32]

The History and Aims of Science

Science could have started with the emergence of man as *homo sapiens*, but remains rudimentary for centuries. So, the history of science can be

classified as: the sciences of the ancient periods, the medieval and renaissance science, Modern science and Contemporary science.
The aims of science during this long history include:

- To provide a reliable explanation, prediction and control of the world;

- To provide systematic, objective and reliable knowledge of the world;

- To provide mechanisms and instruments to improve man's performance in the world of objects and phenomena

PHILOSOPHY OF HISTORY

Philosophy of history is a philosophical study and understanding of history. It is a philosophical consideration, a reflection and analysis of the fundamental assumptions and conceptions of history. History itself is regarded as the branch of knowledge dealing with past events of a country, continent or the world, and they can be political, economic, social, religious events, etc.

Divisions of History

History is divided into periods and the major periods include: the ancient period, medieval period, renaissance period, modern period and the contemporary period. Let us consider briefly each of them.

Ancient Period: This period cut across the BC's–that is before the Birth of Christ to A.D. 476, when the Western Roman Empire fell as a result of the Goths invasions. The ancient period contains the cradle of civilizations in the ancient world such as those of Egypt (2000 BC), Mesopotamia about (1800- 1600 BC), Greece (624 BC) and Rome (50 BC) to mention but a few.

Medieval Period: This period lasted from 476 to 1453. It ended with the fall of Constantinople which was defeated and conquered by the Turks. This period contains the Dark Ages when there was a clamp down on learning in philosophy and science (AD 400-1200) and then the Age of Arabian influence also called Scholasticism (Ad 1200-1500). This was the glorious period of Islam and it flourished in places in the Eastern World such as Baghdad, Mecca and other Arabian trade centers.

Renaissance Period: Renaissance is a French word that means "rebirth." This period lasted from the 14th century to the 17th century. The Renaissance is a cultural movement that took off in Italy and spread to the whole of western world. It is a period in history that marked the reawakening in learning especially philosophy and science. The rebirth of learning brought high level of enlightenment to the people. It involved an intensive interest and consideration of the intellectual heritage and patrimony bequeathed to the world by the ancient world especially the Greeks, the Egyptian and the Islamic bloc. The invention of printing machines and advances in printing made possible the faster development and spread of classical knowledge and wisdom. Publication of works became a serious enterprise that flourished during the Renaissance and gave rise to rapid spread of ideas in Europe and America.

Modem Period: This lasted from the 17th century to the 19th century. It contains the rise of modem science and the industrial revolution. Popular individuals that contributed to the making of this period include Johannes Kepler (1571-1630), Galileo (1564-1642), Isaac Newton (1642-1727), Francis Bacon (1561-1626), etc. It must be noted here that the Ptolemaic and Copernican systems perfected in the works and thoughts of Isaac Newton formed the spring board of the contemporary period of history.

Contemporary Period: It started from the 19th to the present 21st century. This is a history of advancement in science and technology. The 20th century was a period when the Newtonian physics gave way to Albert Einstein's Theory of Relativity. The Relativity theory demonstrates that time and space, which in classical physics were thought of as objective properties or postulates, were rather dependent on the motion of an observer. Time, or our sense of time in this theory is some calibrated duration or clock in our mind (brain) which gave readings that vary proportionally according to one's speed (in our case, according to the speed of the earth). The motion of an observer determines the "chunk" of space that such an observer can perceive, and it is such that time and space co-vary; thus giving the idea of space – time in which time can be calculated as units of space. The contemporary period has made great advances in the application of quantum and nuclear theories, the computer and information technology.

CONCEPTIONS OF THE NATURE OF HISTORY

The Cyclic Conception of History

The early Greek thought perceived history to be cyclic in nature. For the early Greek thought it was unnecessary to ask the following questions: is man really free? Can men really make decisions of their own free will? These questions were not keen problems in Greek antiquity because of the following reasons:

Greek thought considers all things subject to fate and human conducts, they believed, were controlled by stars, which were in turn controlled by the gods. For them, men are not masters of their fate. They maintained that man, being part of nature is subject to the general laws which govern nature. The laws of motion and the law of gravity for instance. Finally, they asserted man is subject to the cyclic movement of history in which everything is regularly repeated within a period of time. So, the early Greek thought believed in the immutability and regularity of events in which human actions were based on fate and destiny, and as such man's free actions were swallowed by the importunate determinism and necessary causality.

Theocentric Conception of History

In the medieval and patristic Christian thought, the nature of history became theocentric. The role of fate in history gave way to a provident loving God. Consequently, nature and history itself no longer stand above man but are put in the service of man. Man is a free being. At this turning point in human history, the liberty or freedom of man is seen as a relationship with God. Man became the maker of history.

Clement of Alexandria often gave theological justification that man is free and is the maker of history, calling on the authority of the scriptures, he said, "we know from the scripture that man received from God the capacity to choose or to reject something." Again, appealing to the absurd consequences if liberty were denied (*argumentum ex absurdis*) he points out that praises (eulogy), reproaches and punishments would not be just if there were no freedom of choice among men.

Thomas Aquinas follows the *ex absurdis* of Clement of Alexandria, adding that the deterministic opinion of man and history is a strange thought because not only that it is contrary to faith but it also upsets all principles of morals. He argues further that it is not possible that stars control our will because that would mean that man's faculty for election is useless while "to no being is a faculty given in vain."[33] Aquinas has made profound argument for the existence of liberty based on the metaphysical notion of necessity. According to him, human election (which enables man to make history) is not necessary since that is not necessary which may or may not be. Human election is rather indifferent in the sense that reason is liable due to its limitations to present an evil as good to the will for choice. He maintained that it is perfect good – happiness that cannot be learnt by reason as an evil or defect. The subject of choice is not the end but the means to this perfect good and as such cannot be necessary. If choice is not necessary then it is free. Aquinas is saying that the existence of varieties or alternative course of action and things to choose makes choice possible. The alternatives could be the good or the bad. This is why history teams with good and bad events, most of them being the products of men's choice.

We must acknowledge here with Harold, Smith and Nolan that man is conscious of history and has a cumulative cultural tradition. He looks into the past and makes plans for the future. Man participates in the making of history by his decisions, whether these are responsible and intelligent or irresponsible and impulsive. Man can influence and make history, today he can even blot out history.[34]

Materialist's Concept of History

The materialist's conception of history is often called historical materialism. The Marxists are the proponents of this view. The leader of the school, Karl Marx transformed Hegel's dialectics and applied it to the development of human society. Historical materialism respects science and asserts the view that the sense perception of science provides our real knowledge of the world. It went further to emphasize a historical development in which matter in the form of economic organization of the society has gone through the following stages, namely: the stage of primitive communism, the tribal stage, the feudal stage, the capitalist stage, and the stage of scientific socialism. So, for Marx history could be divided into six stages, namely; the stage primitive communism, the tribal stage, the feudal stage, the capitalist stage, and the stage of scientific socialism and the Stage of Pure Communism.

These stages emerged through dialectical movement of thesis, antithesis and synthesis. The final stage which is called the pure communism is regarded by Marx as the most perfect stage of history and society. It is the final transition to a classless society. According to Marx, economic forces or means of production are the bases and determinants of all changes in society. Actually, for Marx, the word society is an ideological expression, for the division of labor, forms of property ownership or productive relations. Some scholars hold that historians have not discovered any dialectical necessity operating in the history of human societies. And that Marx's concept of dialectics including the historical aspects offered no objective standard by which to assess and judge events that happen in the society and in history.

Mechanistic Interpretation of History

This is the conception of history by the empirical and natural sciences. Some scholars have proposed that since mechanism as a theory and method has produced great results in the natural sciences; why then they queried should mechanism not be used to account for most situations and events of history? Other scientists asked; if mechanical causation could be used to explain the phenomenon of life, history as part of this phenomenon could also be explained the same way.

Thomas Hobbes (1586-1679) was one of those who attempted to explain conscious life as sensations that are movement in the brain and nervous system. By the 20th century, various physiologists, biologists and psychologists were employing physical and mechanistic explanations in their interpretations of all living creatures including man. A man's thought was regarded as movement and as such could be explained without appeal to any non-physical principles. The behavior of man and his actions in history could be explained through and based on stipulations in physics and chemistry.

The implications of this kind of view include among other things the denial of the moral responsibility of man's actions in history. And again, there is no justification for a universe with purpose toward which history is moving to and there is no place for belief in omnipotent and all loving God to which man is accountable to for his action in history.

10

HUMAN THOUGHT PATTERNS
Naturalism, Materialism and Supernaturalism

Naturalism as a System of Thought

The term "naturalism" etymologically is derived from the Latin word, *"Natura"* meaning nature. Nature by definition means the whole universe and every created thing. It includes the whole forces controlling the phenomena of the physical world. In philosophy, the term nature has come to assume a number of meanings. For W.E. Hocking, nature as it is used in philosophy is not only the "nature" of forest, mountain, and wildlife. It also has to do with astronomy in its vast reaches of space and time, and of physics and chemistry as well in their atomic and subatomic analyses. In this perspective, the term "nature" is also not set in contrast to man, his works and his culture - but includes them in a single undivided system of phenomena.[1]

Naturalism in popular parlance is an adoration of nature in religion or adherence to nature in literature and art; seeing, drawing and painting things in a way true and respectful to nature. On the other hand, Naturalism as a school of thought in philosophy is "a theory that accepts "nature" as the sum total of reality."[2] Thus, the theory denies that any event or object has a supernatural significance.

The General Elements of Naturalism

The doctrine of naturalism was first given elaborate account by ancient philosophers, namely: Democritus, Epicurus and Lucretius. Naturalism especially the metaphysical and scientific forms espoused by Lucretius in his epic work, *On the Nature of Things* are known to be composed of the following elements:

• Everything is made of invisible particles called atoms; and these elementary particles of matter; the seeds of the things are eternal. As the foundational particles of bodies of matter, everything is formed from them and when bodies dissolve they return back to atoms. The atoms are redistributed again to form different kinds of things. This process leads to a ceaseless mutation of forms composed of indestructible substances. The elementary particles are infinite in number but limited in shape and size, and all particles are in constant motion in an infinite void. They clash with one another and form new bodies according to a code of attraction and repulsion, addition and subtraction, division and multiplication over an infinite and everlasting time.

• Space and time are unbounded. There are no fixed points, no beginning, middle, or end, no limits. There is a void in things which allows movement of particles through different bodies. The universe has no creator or designer. There is no end for which everything is moving toward. There is no purpose for existence either. There are only compositions and disintegrations according to chance. The pattern of order and disorder in the world are not a product of divine scheme. Everything comes into being as result of a swerve; a slight deflection of particles traveling in a straight line leading to collisions, formations and disintegrations. This swerve is the source of free wills because if all motions are for long predetermined, there will be no room for any free will. Cause will follow cause and we will have only causal series. So, through swerve nature ceaselessly experiments. There is no single moment of origin, and there is no location, no cardinal point or mythic scene of creation. All living being evolve through the evolutionary process which involves trial and error from simple to complex forms. All organs of living beings adapt to the environment to perform specific function (On the contrary, for Aristotle, what initiates their movement fixes their functions and aims). Living things which are unable to adapt their organs and adjust to the environment die off. While those that adapt and reproduce survive. There was life before us there will be life after us, and certainly a different form of life.

• The universe was not created for or about humans, and so humans are not unique. They are composed of the same material particles which other things including non-living things are composed of, and have the same characteristics with other living things. And certainly the human species will not last forever. Human society began not in a Golden Age of tranquility and plenty, but in a primitive battle for survival in all facets of human endeavors and the environment i.e. in a state of nature. The ability to form bonds and live in communities is guided by customs developed gradually over time. Alongside this is the development of other things like: family, language, work, culture, religion, education, state, and government.

• The soul is nothing but lighter particles of matter, and hence it is also mutable. It dies when the body disintegrates. There is no afterlife, no punishment, and no rewards. There are no angels, demons, or ghosts, and death is nothing to us. Hence, all organized religions are superstitious delusions and are invariably products of rooted longings, desires, dreams, imaginations, fantasies, fears and ignorance. Any religion is cruel if it inflicts anxiety among the adherents with fearful and dreadful eschatological events.

• The highest goal of human life is the enhancement of pleasure and reduction of pain. The greatest obstacle to pleasure is not pain; it is the inordinate desires and morbid fears in the individual which lead to suffering.[3]

Kinds of Naturalism

There are different kinds of naturalism, namely: Ancient Naturalism, Scientific Naturalism, Metaphysical Naturalism, Methodological Naturalism and Theistic Naturalism.

Ancient Naturalism

Early naturalistic philosophers were observers of nature. They wondered at the basic constituents of reality. The foremost naturalist was Thales (600

BC) of Miletus in Ionia who was regarded as the father of science. He saw water as the basic stuff of which all elements of nature are made of. After him, Anaximander (600 BC) from Miletus surmised and suggested that boundless is the primary element of reality. According to him, this is because boundless is the neutral element that forms the basic material stuff known by the senses and observation. For him, "all the elements we know are in conflict with each other and if any of them were the original stuff, it would conquer and submerge the others." He concluded that the primary element of nature, boundless is therefore a neutral element, different from all the elements we know; and it is infinite, eternal and indeterminate.

Anaximenes (494 BC) of Miletus followed the footsteps of his contemporaries and proposed that the basic stuff of nature is Air. For him, just as the air we breathe in hold our being together, so also the air in the cosmos makes and sustains it through condensation and rarefaction processes. The Pythagoreans made a departure and showed a little independence from the previous thought currents by positioning "number" as the best thing that could explain the observable things of nature. They conceived all observable things of nature as being made up of points and units. And infinite number of points makes up lines and distances.

Apart from physical things of nature, the early naturalistic philosophers also perceived laws operating in nature. Heraclitus accepted change as the law of nature and the condition of all things. According to him, all things of nature are in a state of flux. Nothing is permanent, constant or stable except change. However, the views of Heraclitus were rejected by another observer of nature; Parmenides, who asserted that being is one and unchanging. For him, there is no becoming, nothing comes into being and nothing goes out being, being simply is and does not change. According to him, change is illusion of the senses.

It was Empedocles who became eclectic in his study of nature. He put together most of the previous positions and adopted four elements: earth, air, fire and water as the basic constituents of things of nature. This is because for him, these four elements are unique in most material things of nature. Later on, Democritus turned this naturalism to materialism. He became the first materialist and the forerunner of modern materialism with his atomic conception of all things of nature.

Scientific Naturalism

This is a scientific account of the world in terms of causes and natural forces. It rejects all spiritual, supernatural or teleological explanation of the universe. It also projects a meta-ethics which holds that moral properties are reducible to natural ones or that ethical judgments are derivable from non-ethical ones. It also asserts that all religious truths are derived from nature and natural causes and not from revelation. So, scientific naturalism asserts that only natural laws and forces as opposed to supernatural or spiritual ones operate in the world. Hence, nothing exists apart from the physical world of matter.

Methodological Scientific Naturalism

This is an extension of scientific naturalism and a trend some scientists have imposed on themselves. One of the protagonists of this trend is Robert T. Pennock, and he "is concerned not with what exists in reality but with methods that we use to know what actually exist naturally."[4] So, methodological scientific naturalism has to do strictly with the idea that all scientific endeavors - all hypotheses and events - are to be explained and tested by natural causes and events. This trend ignores and overlooks any discussion of the supernatural and spiritual beings like God and soul. It disregards the notion that nature was created by Supreme Being – God. It urges scientists to concern themselves with only scientific methods of learning about nature and ask them not address anything like God, Soul, spirit, ghost, angels, heaven, hell, religion, faith, etc. in all their scientific endeavors.

The significance of methodological naturalism is vividly portrayed in the popular ruling by Judge John E. Jones on Kitmiller v. Dover Area District on whether intelligent design is science. According to the judge, expert testimony reveals that since the scientific revolution of the 16th century and 17th century, science has been limited to the search for natural causes to explain natural phenomena. While supernatural explanations may be important and have merit, they are not part of science. Methodological naturalism is thus "a self-imposed convention of science."[5] It is a ground rule that requires scientists to seek explanations in the world around us based upon what we observe, test, replicate and verify. So, the judge sees the methodological naturalism as a ground rule of science since scientific method has long confine itself to the explanations of nature without assuming the existence of the supernatural and it has no dogmatic stance in any of its findings. Every stipulation of science, every discovery and invention are seen as tentative, nothing is final, and everything is updated gradually and steadily.

Metaphysical Naturalism

This is an absolute position that nothing else exists except material principles. Rather than being scientific, it is philosophical in stance; it holds that "nature is best accounted for by reference to material principles."[6] These principles include: mass, force, energy and other physical and chemical properties accepted by the intellectual community. It also maintains that God and soul and their manifestations like spirits and ghosts have no real existence. And the universe itself cannot be explained teleologically. No purpose or end can be design from the operation of the universe different from what we can observe. Matter is seen and elevated to the position of the ultimate reality.

Theistic Naturalism

This is the view that nature or being is essentially rational. This school of thought is a kind of antithesis to both scientific and metaphysical naturalism. It criticizes and rejects their nontheistic views of nature. It upholds emergent evolution similar to the notion of seminal reason of St Augustine which holds that God created the initial stuff and gave it potentiality to develop to other things. This is to say that the process of creation is a continuum and remains emergent. And all is evolving gradually in an orderly fashion, in a sequence and to that extent it is considered purposeful and rational.

Materialism as a System of Thought

The term materialism comes from the word "material" meaning that of which something is or can be made or with which something is done. Ordinarily, materialism means the tendency to value too much material things such as wealth, riches, bodily comforts, pleasures, and value too little the spiritual, artistic and intellectual things. As a theory, materialism holds that only material things exist and are real.

According to Harold, Smith and Nolan, the theory holds that extended, self-existent atoms of matter in motion are the constituent elements of the universe, and that mind and consciousness - including all psychic processes – are mere modes of such matter and are reducible to the physical elements. This means that the universe can be fully interpreted and understood by naturalism.

Materialism, however, is a narrow or more limited form of naturalism. In the extreme sense of materialism even the mind and consciousness are modes of matter which are also reducible to physical elements and processes. And as such mind and consciousness like other forms of matter could be the subject matter of the physical sciences. Consequently, for the materialists, it is nonsense to talk of ultimate reality different from the extended and self-existent atoms of matter.

Modem materialism emerged from the ancient naturalism of Democritus, Epicurus and Lucretius. Marx who was one of the protagonists of materialism wrote his doctoral thesis on the materialism of Lucretius. According to Charles S. Steely, modem materialism holds that universe is an unlimited material entity; that the universe, including all matter and energy (motion or force), has always existed and will always exist; that the world is a hard, tangible, material, objective reality that man can know. It holds that "matter existed before mind…, the material world is primary and thoughts about this world are secondary."[7]

TYPES OF MATERIALISM

There are two types of materialism. They are mechanistic materialism and dialectical materialism.

Mechanistic Materialism

This holds that the universe and things within it could be explained by the laws governing matter and motion as described in the principles of physical sciences such as in chemistry and physics. Among these principles is the principle of causation which outlines that all events and conditions are necessary consequences of previous events and conditions. Consequently, the higher forms of organic matter are more complex than the inorganic lower forms of matter which are regarded as prior in causal relations. Because of this causal relation, it is taken that processes in organic and inorganic matter are determinable and predictable especially if facts about their previous conditions are known.[8]

The forerunner of materialism or better the first materialist was Democritus. His quantitative atomism emphasized that the universe is merely atoms in motion. For him, even mental processes and psychic activities are merely motion of fine, highly mobile atoms. This position of Democritus has a mechanistic undertone. His system of thought is regarded as the first systematic presentation of mechanism and his later disciples such as Epicurus and Lucretius elaborated similar views. According to George Santayana in his work, *The Three Philosophical Poets,* "Democritus made a notable advance over the systems that selected one obvious substance, like water, or collected all the obvious as substances, as Anaxagoras did, and tried to make the world out of them."[9] Democritus thought that the substance of everything ought not to have any of the qualities present in some things and absent in others; it ought to have only the qualities present in all things. It should be merely matter. For Democritus, materiality consists of extension, figure and solidity; in the thinnest ether, if we looked sharp enough, we should find nothing, but particles possessing these properties. All other qualities of things were only imputed to them by a convention of the mind.

Going further on the mechanistic materialism of Democritus, Santayana saw the mind as a born mythologist that projects its feelings into their causes. Light, color, taste, warmth, beauty, excellence, were such imputed and conventional qualities; only space and matter were real. Summarizing the whole system of thought of Democritus, George Santayana asserted that "Democritus gave mechanism to motion, atomism to structure and materialism to substance."[10] The two major disciples of Democritus: Epicurus and Lucretius popularized these tripod views before they were suppressed during the medieval period. They emerged again during the renaissance and modern period. Lucretius epic work, "*On the Nature of Things*" made a significant impact on human intellectual tradition. Some of the ideas in the work are still worthy of note today. With the demise of the medieval period and the dark ages, the coming of the renaissance brought about the revival of learning in philosophy and sciences, mechanistic materialism came to live again and took a center stage during the enlightenment.

The development of the mathematical sciences and the objective experimental methods of the natural sciences in the modern period around 15th century gave mechanistic materialism another thrust. Among those who gave rhythm to modem mechanistic materialism were Descartes and Thomas Hobbes (1588–1679). Descartes applied mechanical concepts to physical universe only and unlike the core materialists, he accepted the existence of non-physical entities. Descartes said regarding physics, "I should believe myself to know nothing of it if I were able to say only how things may be without demonstrating that they cannot be otherwise; for having reduced physics to the laws of mathematics it is possible to do this, and I believe that I can do it in all that little I believe myself to know."[11] It must be mentioned that in this endeavor, Descartes found out that deduction of physics from mathematics and metaphysics, it appears, applies only to general principles. In a more special research, he discovered that brute fact eludes determination by pure deductive reasoning. And from experience, he discovered and recommended that we need to fall back to empirical method for observations and experiment.[12] This is to say that Descartes believed that general principles of natural science could be demonstrated a priori while experience could serve a valuable function as an additional check and confirmation.

Thomas Hobbes on the other hand, went further and attempted to raise the science of his day to a philosophy by presenting a thorough going mechanistic materialism. In the words of Hobbes, nature, the art whereby God has made and governs the world is the art of man, as in many other things. For what is the heart, but a spring; and the nerves, but so many wheels, giving motion to the whole body, such as was intended by the "artificer."[13] As a result of the mechanistic way of interpreting life and other things, 17th to 19th century became filled with this scientific spirit. Many disciplines (e.g., physiology, anatomy, biology, psychology and sociology) started moving towards this direction using scientific methods with diverse results.

One of the outcomes of the approach for the mechanists was that all changes in the world, from those involving the atom to those involving man were accepted to be strictly determined. This spirit also produced great results in science and technology which operate on causal series espoused by the principles of the natural Sciences.

Dialectical Materialism (Economic Determinism)

This is a scientific world outlook, a component of Marxist – Leninist world view on the universal method of knowing the laws governing the development of nature, society and thought. Marxism is a philosophy created by Karl Marx (1818– 1883) and Fredrick Engels (1820–1895). The most important precondition for the development of Marxist theory was German classical philosophy which at that time represented the best of philosophical thinking, particularly Hegel's dialectics and Feuerbach's materialism. Marx reinterpreted Hegel's dialectics and applied it to social phenomena. He then fused it with the materialism of Feuerbach to give birth to dialectical materialism.

Harold, Smith and Nolan have rightly pointed out that dialectical materialism grew out of the intense social struggles that arose as a result of the industrial revolution when the worker is separated from the fruit of his labor and was poorly rewarded for it. Dialectical materialism places emphasis on historical development of human society in which matter in the form of factors of production and economic organization of society is regarded as basic. As such, it is also known as historical materialism or economic determinism. Dialectical materialism as a system of thought believes so much in determinism and projects natural sciences as the accurate method for enhancing knowledge of the world of matter. However, it insists that politics and history teach more about man and his society. According to Marx, matter as manifested in nature appears in the economic organization of society and modes of production, and determines the nature of development of the social and political institutions of society. Through these then it goes on to influence or determine the ethical, religious and philosophical worldview of that society.

The dialectical materialists assert that matter is prior to mind as the mechanistic materialist do. This is a clear departure from Hegel's dialectics which confers on the mind a superior and prior position than to matter. According to Kirilenko and Korshunova, "the creation of dialectical materialism paved the way to a consistent materialist interpretation of nature, society and man himself in their historical evolution."[14] The above materialists view is opposed to that of many idealist view of history. The idealists regarded history as a gradual embodiment of man's idea, wishes and will. For instance, Hegel held the universe to be an unfolding process of thought in a continual process of development. This gave rise the process of nature and human history, and the development of organizations and institutions of the society.

However, for the dialectical materialist matter in the form of material forces are the societal determinants. They determine evolutionary development, as well as all other phenomena; inorganic, organic and all human endeavors such as the economic, religious, social and political. Succinctly put, for the dialectical materialist, there was a time when no life existed in the universe except matter. Hence, everything including man had a natural origin and development from inorganic matter. The physical manifestation and realization of dialectical materialism in the human society is called historical materialism. Historical materialism "as a component of Marxism holds that man alone can alter the conditions of his life and make his own history."[15] For it, there is no force outside this universe that gives power to the weak. Rather, through the struggles of life such as class conflicts and antagonisms, productive forces and labor relations every man realizes himself, and consequently the best form of the society emerges and realizes itself.

It is a fact the materialists failed to give the mind its rightful place in history. They failed to understand that wherever we are today we were brought there by our mind. The mind, also known as, the organizer or entrepreneur brings together the factors of production; the material forces of Marx. Just as a school that has everything including books, classrooms and all other material infrastructure cannot function without the administrators.

Supernaturalism as a System of Thought

Supernaturalism holds a dualistic world view. There are two sides of reality, namely: the natural and the supernatural. According to this tenet, there is some power or being above and beyond all natural things we see in the universe. This power or being is taken to be the source of eternal laws and of natural laws which operate in natural things. Natural law is the unwritten law which in its most common precept is fundamentally the same for all things. Hence, natural law operates in and runs every created thing.

Supernaturalism presupposes the existence of a supreme being God and it takes natural law as an aspect of eternal law and as such one of the determinants of moral standard. Members of the school see natural law as part of eternal law conferring inalienable rights to the human person which we also call the fundamental human rights like right to life and personal liberty and ownership of property. Supernaturalism holds that for its effectiveness, natural law must be issued from the divine legislator and be received by all who are to be governed by it. As a result, beings operate through their own internal and intrinsic principles. This shows that God does not move his creatures toward their destined ends by means of some external force. Natural laws are said to be natural on the following counts:

• It is law made by reason so much as discovered by reason; all men thus naturally know the most universal precepts expressed in natural law. Consequently, natural law is clearly understood as a fundamental or an underlying principle for directing human conduct.

• For supernaturalism, the natural law is simply nature moving us to those real goods without which we cannot be happy, forbidding those apparent good which destroys happiness. The particular content of natural law flows directly from human nature, and ultimately from the divine nature of which ours is a reflection. Its obligatory character, they say comes from the divine will of God that is imparted to nature.

This tenet emphasized that the promulgation of natural law has two aspects:

• God on his part gives us the light of reason which is endowed with the power of correctly formulating the necessary rules of conduct;

• Man makes use of reason to set up a moral code for himself including a system of criminal and civil laws and principles of conduct.

Thomas Aquinas, one of the foremost scholars of supernaturalisms identified this inclination from which men may learn natural law and appealed to synderesis as a kind of sympathetic understanding found in men, a disposition (habit) of the practical intellect inclining them to the good and murmuring against evil. He defined natural law as the rational creature's participation of the eternal law.

St. Augustine as a member of the school of supernaturalism has emphasized on eternal law from which the natural law is derived. According to Augustine, eternal law is that law by which it is just that all things be most perfectly in order, and also as the divine reason or the will of God commanding that the natural order of things be preserved and forbidding that it be disturbed. This is to say that it is the exemplar of divine wisdom as directing all actions and movements. Since the eternal law includes both the physical laws and moral laws, it is taken then that God rules the world by law.

It is the fundamental basis of all other laws that everything is subject to the divine intellect and the prime mover. The eternal law cannot operate in man as a blind impulse as it would on irrational beings. We have an innate appetite for the good and happiness. So, eternal law functions rationally through our intellect which is endowed with the power to judge what is orderly and must be done, what is disorderly and must be left undone. Eternal law prescribes a course of conduct for man while man has the physical freedom to act otherwise. And because eternal law exists and operates in man, it is called natural law. They are the means to the maintenance of universal order. So for the supernaturalists, eternal law is law as it exists in the mind of God and natural law is eternal law as it is expressed in natural things.

Marcus Tullius Cicero as a proponent of the theory of natural law and the tradition of supernaturalism had a great regard for human reason and its abilities. He sees natural law as right reason. For him and for many of his followers right reason should have primacy over law. This is because law proceeds from right reason and with right reason one is capable of striking a delicate balance between the absolutism of the individual freedom, and the absolutism of the state authority and law.

Cicero's emphasis on right reason and liberty marked a turning point in Roman intellectual tradition and literary history. His thought current underscores a period in history when men's thoughts and actions are no longer believed to be dictated and controlled by the gods. Man now have the power of free thought and has become a free thinker and believes in the primacy of reason over law. It was a period which the

French novelist Gustave Flaubert described as just when the gods had ceased to be, and Christ had not yet come, a unique moment in history, between Cicero and Marcus Aurelius, when man stood alone. Standing alone, as Flaubert puts it; they found themselves in the peculiar position of choosing among sharply divergent visions of the nature of things and competing strategies for living.[16]

Furthermore, Cicero believed in the concept of cosmic order as the ground of objective moral law. This followed from his metaphysical stoic background which conceives nature as rational and divine. For this stoic tradition "nature" is the divine reason infused through the cosmos - the inner essence and animating force of all things and human reason is the divine element in man. By means of reason, man can discover the fundamental laws of the universe and direct his conduct in conformity with these laws. To live according to nature is to develop one's essential faculties and at the same time, to be in harmony with the divine order in the cosmos. Following from this cosmic harmony, Cicero arrives at natural law and sees it grounded in the innermost nature of man, society, and the universe and is independent of convention, legislation and all other institutional devices. It is a law of nature that is moral, universal, irrevocable, and Man is obliged to obey it only by his reason and conscience, but it is not automatically compulsory. For instance, this "natural law" that underlines the doctrine of brotherhood and equality of men and inclines us to live in peace and friendship with our fellow men is frequently violated in all cases of racism and hate crimes. Equality here means that all men have similar psychological composition, all can think, feel, imagine and know, and therefore should be regarded and treated with dignity and respect that befit a human being.

One of the monumental implications of this position of Cicero is that the highest allegiance is not given to the local state but to the universal fellowship. All men, as children of nature and God are bound in conscience by the same laws and belong in the sense to the same "commonwealth." Those who share law must also share justice and those who share these are to be regarded as members of the same commonwealth. Even though, everyone belongs to one local state or the other, and is allegiance to it, ethically this allegiance should be subordinate to the wider allegiance to nature and humanity.[17] This means for instance, in the course of duty one is asked by state authority to detonate an Atom bomb that will wipe one third of humanity or an entire nation, the person is obliged by right reason and natural law to refuse to do so even under the threats of execution or imprisonment. With this, it is no longer tenable for a defendant to claim innocence by saying 'I acted under authority or I was obeying authority when I committed this genocide; a hate crime and a crime against humanity.'

Consequently, if the laws of a state do not conform to the laws of nature and God, they do not deserve to be called laws than the dictates of some hoodlums. Here is the ultimate source of the revolutionary doctrine that men owe a higher allegiance to nature and to nature's God than to any temporal ruler and have the inalienable right to civil disobedience and revolt against an unjust and tyrannical state and obnoxious dictator whether in a military regime or in a democracy.

11

SCHOOLS OF PHILOSOPHY
Empiricism and Rationalism

Empiricism as a System of Thought
This is a system of philosophy which holds that knowledge is acquired mainly from experience while other things like reason and intuition are mere auxiliaries. It has high regard for the method of hypothesis and observation as the principal foundation of knowledge. The main protagonists of this tenet are John Locke, George Berkeley and David Hume. The empiricists did not deny the role of the mind in knowledge but were of the view that thinking would not add anything new and substantial to knowledge. Reason reflects only on what is given to the mind through the senses. They further hold that error and uncertainty in knowledge are the results of the operation of the mind since what is given in perception is objective and cannot be erroneous.

For Titus Harold, Marilyn Smith and Richard Nolan, the empiricist tenet poses a question; "how do we know that water can freeze or that it can revive drooping plants? We may say that we know by means of our sense organs from our own past experience."[1] So, for Empiricism, the things we see, hear, touch, smell and taste – that is our concrete experience – constitutes the realm of knowledge. Thus, Empiricism stresses man's power of perception, observation or what the senses receive from the environment as the basis of human knowledge. Knowledge is obtained by forming ideas in accordance with observed facts.

Succinctly put, this school of philosophy holds that we know what we have found out from our senses. Furthermore, D.W. Hamlyn tells us more about empiricism. According to him, the central point in empiricism is the idea that perception is at some point indubitable.[2] It is free from the possibility of error because error has no place in what is given. Error is due to imagination or the frailty of human judgment.

On the origin of knowledge, the empiricists were against the view that knowledge is gotten from innate ideas. They argued as Aristotle did, that "there is nothing in the intellect that was not first in the senses."[3] *Nihil est in intellectu quod non prius fuerit in sensu.*

John Locke, who was the foremost critic of the innatism, took the criterion of innate ideas to task and argued that universal concept (e.g., the laws of contradiction, identity and excluded middle) if existed, would be no proof of innateness, unless it could be shown that these cases could not have arisen in any other way. It must be the necessary commitment of all innate truths, should such exist. Any exceptions to the alleged universality of concept amount, therefore, to a strict demonstration of the falsity of the theory. Locke went further to "assert that experience assures us that such exceptions exist, since your children and idiots and savages have no knowledge of the principles for which this origin is claimed."[4] Thus, Locke advocated the notion that at birth the intellect is a tabula rasa, that is, a blank sheet on which the senses write on. He argues that if we have innate ideas, we will be conscious of having them, for it is a fact that children and the uneducated are not conscious of having innate ideas. They acquire knowledge during the course of their life time as no man can have knowledge of what he is not conscious of. Locke therefore rejected universal concept as a ground for accepting the existence of innate ideas.

Contrary to the doctrine of innatism, Locke holds that ideas stand for whatsoever is the object of the understanding when a man thinks. He went further to say that ideas are used to express whatever is meant by phantasm, notion, species or whatever it is which the mind can be employed about in thinking.[5] So for Locke, idea is the object of thinking, and all ideas come from sensation or reflection. Simple ideas have their origin and source in sensations. They result from the senses being conversant with particular objects. The senses usually convey to the mind several distinct perceptions of things according to those various ways those objects do affect them. This is how we come by those simple ideas we have of yellow, white, heat, cold, soft, hard, bitter and sweet, etc. And there are still others which we call sensible qualities which the senses also convey to the mind.

Apart from the above simple ideas, Locke recognized the existence of complex ideas. For Locke, complex ideas are "ideas that could come from reflections which are the operations of our minds."[6] These reflections could also be described as the perception of the operations of the mind within us as it employs the ideas it has got from the senses. And from this, other ideas would emerge which could not have come from outside things. These complex ideas include that of perception, thinking, doubting, believing, reasoning, knowing, willing and other different actions of our own minds which we receive into our understanding as distinct ideas. Succinctly put, Locke is saying that external objects through the senses furnish the mind with the ideas of sensible qualities while through reflections the mind furnishes the understanding with ideas of its own operations. We can also see that Locke has fallen into the phenomenalist prejudice that "man does not know things directly but grasps only the impressions these objects make upon him." These impressions come in form of simple and complex ideas of both sensation and reflection. Locke asserts that ideas belong to the mind while qualities are of the body. And quality is the power to produce an idea in the mind. For him, we have both primary and secondary qualities. Primary qualities include that of solidity, extension, figure, mobility while secondary qualities include color, taste, smell, sound, etc.

FORMS OF EMPIRICISM

Empiricism may take a number of forms, namely: weak empiricism, radical empiricism and scientific empiricism.

Weak Empiricism or Narrow Sensationalism

This school of thought asserts that knowledge is essentially sensation, and that there is no other knowledge apart from what we get from the senses. For these weak empiricists, one can get knowledge by deducing from experienced objects. Locke for instance tried to prove God's existence based on experience. He thinks there is no other way to prove the God's existence than to deduce it from experiences of the world.

Radical Empiricism

This is a more recent empiricism. It has abandoned a large proportion of the ideas in the weak empiricist theory of knowledge. Pragmatism, as a form of radical empiricism views the mind as active in selecting and molding experiences in accordance with the interests and purposes of man. It emphasizes the changing world of experience. We shall see the position of the pragmatists as a school of philosophy later on.

Scientific Empiricism

This concerns modem science and its empirical tradition. Modem science is especially interested in particular facts and their relations with other facts. It is therefore empirical in practice and outlook. Empirical scientists are interested in controlled observations and experiments, not merely in general sense perceptions and experiences, and they strive to keep irrelevant factors from disturbing the examination of some special problem or event. Items or variables can be changed or manipulated, and the effects can be recorded. Furthermore, the scientific empiricists believe that "if the conditions are controlled, the experiment can be repeated by other observers; thus more accurate and objective information can be obtained."[8] Special instruments can be used to aid observation, help eliminate errors, and measure results. The conclusions, however, are always tentative and are set forth in the form of hypotheses, theories or possibly laws, which after further observation and research may need to be modified or changed. We must say that even though the process and procedure for building up scientific knowledge is slow and laborious, it however enables us and enhances our capability to exercise considerable control over our world. And it is of constant service in our daily lives. Most often, they can also invalidate our ordinary mental and physical concepts of the world.

From scientific empiricism, other forms of empirical traditions such as positivism, logical atomism and analytic philosophy have emerged. These groups regarded as meaningless anything that cannot be subjected to the verifiability principle. Anything that cannot be empirically verified is declared nonsense or utmost a useful nonsense. We must not forget to mention that Berkeley and Hume created their own empirical doctrine. Berkeley rejected the existence of material substances while Hume denied the existence of a mental substance (ego) and also the concept of causality. Following this tradition, Locke denied the existence of innate ideas.

Consequently, one can say that one of the consequences of empiricism, as a school of philosophy is that it leads to skepticism. For many empiricists only particular sensations exist, this means that one is only left with plurality of sense data (ideas). The problem is then how to justify our many beliefs which we cannot sense nor abandon. Bertrand Russell on this basis says that even though only sense data exist, it is still convenient to hold our beliefs. Again, it is the opinion of Marcia that "the chief defect of empiricism is that it ends in mechanism, in considering only the quantitative aspect of matter, which is subject to the laws of motion."[9] They ignored the fact that without their minds they cannot discuss matter, and there will be nothing like self-consciousness and the awareness of other things.

Rationalism as a System of Thought

This system of philosophy considers thought or reasoning as the central factor in knowledge. Rationalism is taken to be one of the most powerful thought current in modem philosophy. It holds that genuine knowledge is got from reason. They take the method of mathematics as their model. So, this system of thought emerged in 17th century Europe as continental rationalism. The pioneers of this school of philosophy were Descartes, Spinoza and Leibniz. These men were not the first rationalists; there are some philosophers both in the ancient, medieval and modern periods that could be regarded as rationalists in the fundamental sense of the word. They include philosophers such as Plato, Aristotle, Thomas Aquinas, Augustine, Anselm to mention but a few. We are not referring to these fundamental rationalists here as part of this school of philosophy. Every school of philosophy that springs up does so for different reasons; it could be any of the following reasons: to protect the existing system; or to reject it. It could be also to solve a particular contemporary problem or issues.

Thus, the 17th century brand of Rationalism, came into existence partly because the rationalists were dissatisfied with the explanation given by previous schools of philosophy, they were dissatisfied with the method which the philosophers used too. Rene Descartes for instance, wanted a method of philosophy that will exhibit the exactness of mathematics. Partly also the 17th century rationalists were unhappy with the empirical brand of philosophy which they claimed was an uncertain subject and untrustworthy in the search for truth as its method rely solely on fluctuating sense impressions. And human knowledge cannot be based on a chaotic bunch or chaotic amalgam of fluctuating sense impressions as man has higher values. So, reason among other things plays an organizing role in the acquisition of knowledge.

The Position of the Rationalists on Knowledge and its Source

Rationalisms as school of thought asserts that reason alone can give knowledge about the world. For them, all real knowledge comes from reason. The rationalists were interested in the rational capacity of the human mind. They were of the opinion that the senses are not authentic source of knowledge since the senses are defective, and what is gotten through them is only a raw data which cannot give us any reliable knowledge without undergoing processing by the mind. If the sense experience is the sole source of knowledge, then it implies that animals and birds will be scientists, intelligent and rational. They concluded that knowledge is possible due to the activity of human reason, which is capable of penetrating the essence of things.

Furthermore, the rationalists assert that one needs not appeal to any supernatural source in order to have knowledge of the real world. Consequently, faith and beliefs have no place in rationalism. The only source of truth is reason. Anything not in harmony and accord with reason could not be regarded or tagged rational. The rationalists accepted innate ideas as one of the foundations of certain knowledge. They see knowledge as the unfolding of the mind's innate powers in such a way that from one or some evident principles all knowledge can be derived without involving or relying on experience. In virtue of this, Leibniz contra posed the image of a would be statue to that of a tabula rasa opinionated by the empiricists. He supplemented the dictum of the empiricist which states that "there is nothing in the intellect that is not first in the senses," with the phrase "except the intellect itself."[10]*Nihilest in intellictu quod non prius fuerit in sensu, excipe nini ipse intellectus.*

Leibniz emphasized that the soul comprises being, substance, unity, identity, cause, perception, reason, and many other notions which the senses cannot give.[11] Speaking in favor of this position of the rationalists, Robert McRae says that the tabula rasa conception of the mind which Locke espoused allows, of course, that all knowledge exist potentially in the mind, for the blank sheet of paper or wax tablet has the capacity or faculty for receiving any figures whatever which will be imprinted or impressed on it in fullness of time. But such potentiality Locke considered hardly worth mentioning.[12]

Following on the heels of innate ideas, the rationalists acknowledged the existence of certain evident principles like the principle of contradiction, the principle of sufficient reason and moral truth, the principle of excluded middle, the principle of causality, the principle of identity, etc. It is through the means of these principles that one comes to know every finite thing. The rationalists went further to affirm that the existence of a supreme reality can be demonstrated through the aid of reason alone.

FORMS OF RATIONALISM

There are different shades and kinds of rationalism. We have the following:

The Classical Rationalism

The classical rationalism is often known as traditional rationalism. It is represented by Plato, Aristotle, Saint Augustine, Saint Anselm, Thomas Aquinas, etc. They used reason and believed reason as a source of knowledge.

Weak Rationalism

This type of rationalism affirms that reason is one of the sources of knowledge. Reason introduces and makes possible the knowledge of the universal laws of thought and the physical laws. It also brings about the knowledge of the law of causality and moral conduct. The weakness in this rationalist theory of knowledge lies in their belief that reason is not the only source of truth. As the main current in rationalism, they insist the following principles can only be known through reason:

The principle of identity says that "if P is true, then P is true" (all A is A).

The principle of non-contradiction, e.g., "not both P is true and P is false."

The principle of excluded middle, "P is either true or false," either A or not A.[13]

From the above principles we derive other examples like: Two things each equal to a third thing, are equal to each other; if equals are added to equals the sums are equal; a thing cannot both be (exist) and not be (not exist) at the same time.

For the rationalists, the senses by themselves cannot give us coherent and universally valid judgments. The sensations and experiences which we gain through the senses are just raw material of knowledge. These must be organized by the mind into a meaningful system by comparing ideas with ideas before they become knowledge.

Extreme Rationalism

Extreme rationalists make the claim that we are capable of arriving at irrefutable knowledge independent of sense experience. These extreme rationalists claim that reason provides genuine knowledge, truths (laws) about the world and not merely laws of thought. The issue of a priori knowledge independent of experience (a posteriori) is still debatable in philosophical circles.

Kant used his synthetic a priori propositions to mediate between empiricism and rationalism, and show at the same time that "there is a type of knowledge that depends both on the senses and the mind. This synthetic a priori knowledge combines or cut across experience and reason, and as such it is a product of the two." This mediation is important because sense experience may be necessary to draw out or to make clear the above general principles. This means that we have to experience lines and angles before we think of building geometric systems.

12

SCHOOLS OF PHILOSOPHY
Idealism and Realism

Idealism as a System of Thought

This system of philosophy made its presence felt mostly during the latter half of the 19th century but the tradition could be traced back to the ancient period of Western philosophy. Plato had idealist lining in his thought especially his world of forms and universals. His world of ideas is basically an idealist philosophy on the origin of universal concepts. He also attempted to establish an ideal state through his work, *The Republic*. We can say that Plato gave impetus to modern idealism. He can be regarded as the forerunner of modern idealism.

Understanding Idealism as a Concept

Idealism as a concept is one of the most interesting but difficult to understand. It is difficult because most often it ends in the metaphysics of man and God. But it is fascinating that it stretches the human thinking and understanding, and makes one to think out of the box. It gives something different from empiricism and rationalism.

Generally, there are three conceptions of an idealist: popular and positive; negative; and philosophical conceptions. The popular and positive conception of an idealist concerns one who accepts and lives by lofty moral, aesthetic and religious standard or one who is able to visualize and advocates some plans or programs that do not yet exist. Every social reformer is an idealist in this sense because he is supporting something that has not yet come into existence. "Those who work for permanent peace or for the elimination of poverty may be called idealists in this sense."[1] But some realist thinkers assert that poverty can only be alleviated and cannot be eradicated. And that peace can only be kept and maintained but it can never be permanent.

However, for Titus Harold, Marilyn Smith and Richard Nolan, the negative conception of an idealist "concerns a person who stands for goals that other people generally believe to be quite unattainable or who ignores the facts and practical conditions of a situation."[2] They are most often fanatics and adherents of false beliefs, and they most often resist illumination to change in their thoughts and ways.

On the philosophical sense, the word idealism comes from the word idea rather than ideal. So, the term "idea-ism" straightens the meaning than the term idealism. The Idealists, philosophically assert that reality consists of ideas, thoughts or minds or selves rather than of material objects and forces. On the same note, Melvin Rader says that "idealism (idea- ism, with, the "I" inserted for the sake of euphony) may strike beginning students as exceedingly odd; but it is quite possible that the universe is very odd, and the arguments for idealism are strong.[3]

Russell threw light on what idealism is all about and said that it is the doctrine that whatever exists, or at any rate whatever can be known to exist, must be in some sense mental. This is to say that physical objects have no existence independent of thought. The whole universe is made up of minds and the immaterial objects of minds and nothing more.

Furthermore, Russell says that those who are unaccustomed to philosophical speculation may be inclined to dismiss such a doctrine as obviously absurd. In his view, "there is no doubt that common sense regards tables and chairs and the sun and moon and material objects generally as something radically different from minds and the contents of minds, and as having an existence which might continue if minds ceased."[4] We think of matter as having existed long before there were any minds, and it is hard to think of it as a mere product of mental activity, Russell asserts that whether true or false, idealism is not to be dismissed as obviously absurd.

Idealism as system of thought holds that mind is prior to matter. While the materialists defend the position that matter is real and mind is an accompanying phenomenon, idealism on the other hand contends that the mind is real and matter is in a sense a by-product. Idealism is a denial that the world is basically a great machine to be interpreted as matter, mechanism or energy alone. So for the idealist, mechanism does not produce minds rather minds produce mechanism.

As a worldview and metaphysics, idealism builds upon the view or belief that the basic reality is made up or is closely related to mind, ideas, thoughts or selves. The world has a meaning apart from its surface appearance. The world, the universe or reality could be understood and interpreted by a study of the laws of thought and of consciousness and not exclusively by the methods of the empirical sciences such as physics and chemistry.

Types of Idealism

Idealism is known to appear in various forms. We have among others, the following forms:

Subjective or Pluralistic Idealism

This type of idealism is also called mentalism, phenomenalism or immaterialism. This is the most controversial form of idealism. Subjective idealism contends that all that exist in the universe and in reality are minds or spirits, and the perceptions and ideas they have. According to these idealists, the physical or material things which we could see and touch such as houses, mountains, rivers, trees, lands and animals exist only in the mind that perceives them solely as ideas and nothing more. Hence, the knowledge you have of these things is nothing but the ideas in your mind you have of them. For Herold, Smith and Nolan, "the subjective idealist does not deny the existence, in some sense, of what we call the "real" world; the question at issue is not its existence but how it is to be interpreted."[5] The idealists contend that "the external world exists in our minds as idea and that is our knowledge of them. And ideas cannot exist independent of the knower."[6]

The foremost proponent of subjective idealism was George Berkeley (1685-1753). He tried to prove through his arguments that secondary qualities such as taste, color, smell, etc. have no existence without the mind. He went further to prove with his arguments that primary qualities of things such as extension, figure, solidity, gravity, motion and rest have no existence independent of a perceiver.[7]

In his *Three Dialogues between Hylas and Philonous,* Berkeley gave an example to buttress his position. According to him, "if we approach to or recede from an object, the visible extension varies, being at one distance ten or a hundred times greater than at another."[8] For instance, from the 2013 NASA unmanned space craft orbiting planet Jupiter, the Earth appears in the size of a tennis ball. It could be assumed on this basis that the size of an object depends on the distance from which it is being looked at. It is this fact that made Berkeley to conclude that extension is not inherent in an object. For Berkeley, if extension is once acknowledged to have no existence without the mind, the same must necessarily be granted of motion, solidity and gravity since they all evidently suppose extension. This means that when secondary and primary qualities are denied of things what is left is the fluctuating idea we have of them. Berkeley's subjective idealism summed up reality in his dictum *"esse est percipi percipere,"* To exist is to be perceived by a perceiver or a mind. He argued persistently that "things" are mere collections of "ideas" and that ideas cannot exist unless they are perceived. But one may ask a question here; but if a person can exist independently of someone's idea of him, why cannot a thing exist independently?

For Rader, to argue that an apple must be in our minds because we are thinking of it is like arguing that a person must be in our minds because we are thinking of him. If we distinguish clearly between the act of thinking and the object of thought, the act of perceiving and the object perceived, there is no absurdity in supposing that things may exist even when they are unperceived or unthought-of.

However, we must concede that the plausibility of Berkeley's contention depends upon his constant use of the word idea. We can think of "idea" as something in the mind, and therefore as incapable of existing apart from the mind. Hence, if we are told that apple consists entirely of "idea," it is natural for us to suppose that the apple can exist only in some mind. Bertrand Russell also agreed that to understand Berkeley's argument, it is necessary to understand his use of the word "idea." He gives the name idea to anything which is immediately known, as for example, sense-data are known. This or that particular color which we see is an idea; so is a voice which we hear, and so on. Russell went further to say that the term (idea) is not wholly confined to sense data. There will also be things remembered or imagined for with such things also we have immediate acquaintance at the moment of remembering or imagining. All such immediate data Russell calls "idea."[10] This means that "idea" for Berkeley means immediate object of thought or experience including both imaginative and perceptual experience.

However, it is possible despite the above conception of an idea that an object known as a set of ideas may continue to exist when the thought of it ceases. So, when we speak of bearing a person in our minds, that a thought of him is in our minds does not mean that the person is in our mind. When a man says that some business he had to arrange went clean out of his mind, he does not mean to imply that the business itself was ever in his mind, but only that a thought of the business was formerly in his mind, but afterwards ceased to be in his mind.[11]

Berkeley, having denied through his arguments that things can exist independent of the mind or spirit, went further to assert that there must be some other mind where they exist. For him, the sensible world really exists so sure because there is an infinite omnipresent spirit - God, who contains and supports it. In his words, "it is evident that the things I perceive are my own ideas, and that no idea can exist unless it be in a mind. Nor is it less plain that these ideas or things I perceived either themselves or their archetypes exist independently of my mind; since I know myself not to be their author, it being out of my power to determine at pleasure what particular ideas I shall be affected with upon opening my eyes or ears. They must therefore exist in some other mind whose will it is they should be exhibited to me". Berkeley concluded that there is a mind which affects us every moment with all the sensible impressions we perceive. And from the variety, order and manner of these, he takes the Author of them to be wise, powerful and good, and beyond comprehension.[12] It appears here that Berkeley's argument was actually intended to be a demonstration of God's existence based on impressions or ideas of things we have in the mind. For he thinks it is the way things are designed to be not by us but by omnipotent and omnipresent creator – God.

Thus, the only way to understand Berkeley argument is that sensory and mental perceptions are the result of the direct action of God on finite and independent spirits. The objects we perceive have their cause in God since they are not of our own making. Nature is the "visual language" through which God reveals His power to us" and through which finite spirits with the help of God's coordinating influence communicate with one another. But God, although He acts upon us, is nonetheless distinct, and each one of us has his own individual identity. Thus, the universe or reality is a pluralistic society of minds, or spirits, and the central position and coordinating role is performed by God, the Infinite Omnipresent Spirit or Mind.

Objective or Absolute Idealism

The objective idealists hold that the universe is one all-embracing entity and that its basic and essential nature is mind or spirit, and consequently it is an organic whole. The mind tries to discover what is in the order of the world. Plato (427-347), the forerunner of objective idealism asserts that behind the physical world of individual things that we see there is the world of form, the world of ideas or the world of universals. The first world is the world of sense perceptions, the world of change where we can see, feel, taste, smell individual things. This world is characterized by concrete things, temporal things and perishable things. It is the unreal world because it is illusory and deceptive in nature. Succinctly put, it is a world of fleeting appearances.

The second world is the world of form, that is, the world of supersensible, of concepts, ideas, universals, and essences. For Plato, ideas are the original transcendent pattern and perceptions, and individual things are mere copies or shadows of these ideas. The world of ideas is known to man through his reason while the material world is perceived through the senses. As such, the two worlds converge in man. Thus, man becomes a convergent point, and as such a unifying point of the two worlds.

Hegel (1770-1831) gave idealism a modem overtone and its absolute nature. For him, all parts of the universe are included in one all-embracing entity, and he attributed this unity to the idea and purpose of the Absolute Mind. As a result, Hegel sees thought or mind as the essence of the universe, and nature as the whole of mind objectified. Hegel went further to contend that the universe is an expanding and unfolding process of thought. Nature is the Absolute Reason expressing itself in outward form. He concludes that the laws of thought are also the laws of reality.

The above view of Hegel projects the idea of a monistic reality as opposed to the pluralistic one of Berkeley. It also portrays the idea of a dynamic universe of reality in contrast to fixed or static universe of reality. In such a thought current, distinctions and differences belong to the phenomenal world and are relative to the observer; they do not affect the unity of the one purposive intelligence. For Herold, Smith and Nolan, "when we think of the total world order as embracing the inorganic, the organic, and the spiritual levels of existence in one all-inclusive order, we speak of the absolute or the absolute spirit or God."[13]

Thus, with this emphasis upon comprehensive unity, the absolute idealist sees the whole of reality as an entity with a system in which the parts (or sub-units) are relational. The absolute idealist rejects any dualistic system of metaphysics like that of Descartes which would sharply divide reality into mind and matter.

Hegel in his work, *The Spirit of Modern Philosophy,* espouses this Hegelian system that consists of the logic, the philosophy of nature, and the philosophy of spirit. He contends that the dynamic nature of reality is manifested in history and nature as the dialectic movement of thesis, antithesis and synthesis. Thus, according to Rader "this contradiction and its resolution in the realm of thought are paralleled by a similar movement in nature and human affairs." Here, too, there are antithetical tendencies, each bent upon destroying its opposite, and producing a kind of crisis by its inordinate one-sidedness. The clash of these tendencies exposes the logical ridiculousness of each factor taken in isolation and thus releases corrective forces which restore the balance. In this way, the whole process leads on to more coherent and comprehensive states of equilibrium.[14] This dynamism does not stop there; it continues ad infinitum as an inherent nature of reality. And as a force of nature, it can be harnessed by those who have knowledge of its workings to achieve their own motives. It works like tapping energy from nature using a hydro dam, a wind vane, solar panels or capturing or hijacking an asteroid and using it as a vehicle for transportation in deep space travel.

Realism as a System of Thought

The term realism draws its meaning from the concepts: real and reality. The word "real" means the actual or the existing. It refers to things or events that exist in their own right, as opposed to that which is imaginary or merely in our thought. To be real is to exist in fact, not imagined or supposed, not made up or artificial. So, the real is what is. By extension, reality is the quality of being real; real existence; that which underlines appearance.

The term realism in the ordinary usage means the showing of real life and facts in a true way, omitting nothing that is ugly or painful, and idealizing nothing. It is also a behavior based on facing facts and disregarding sentiment and convention. For Herold, Smith and Nolan, "in a popular sense, realism may mean devotion to fact, to what is the case, as opposed to what is wished, hoped or desired."[15]

In the philosophical context, realism is a school of philosophy which emerged in beginning of the 20th century, in countries like Britain and the United States. It is a reaction against the 19th century Idealism of Western Philosophy. The main contention of the realists is "that matter has real existence apart from our mental perception of it."[16] This is direct opposite to the idealist's assertion that to exist is to be perceived by a mind or a perceiver, which may imply the nonexistence of material things if there is no mind to perceive them. For the realist if man becomes extinct today, the mountains and the oceans will still exist.

Thus, the realists strictly maintained that the objects of our senses are real in their own right. Men, trees, mountains, stones and rivers existed independent of their being known or perceived by the mind. Following the above assertions, realism propagates that the universe and all that it contains are empirical, and practical realities exist out there, and the best way to live is to accept this realization and come to best possible terms with them.

Despite the position of the realists on objective or factual existence of matter, they did not deny the existence of the mind and ideas. Rather they tried to distinguish matter from the mind and its ideas. According to a prominent modern realist, Murray, "we cannot get away from the primary fact that there is a distinction between things and ideas."[17] For ordinary common sense, an idea is the idea of something; a thought in our minds which represents the thing that it is the idea of. In that case the thing is the reality while the idea is merely "how the thing appears to us;" that is, our mental picture of the thing.

Murray went further to suggest that our thought must adapt itself to things if it is to be proper thought, that is to say, if our idea is to be true. If the idea does not correspond with the thing of which it is the idea, then the idea is false and useless. According to him, a thing does not accommodate and adapt itself to our idea of it. We have to change our ideas and keep on changing them till we get them right. He concludes that this common-sense way of thinking is essentially realist. And it is realist because it makes "the thing" and not the "the idea" the measure of validity, the center of significance, and it makes the thing real and the idea the true or false appearance of the thing.[18] We understood from Murray that there exists a great temptation to think and regard ideas as more real than things because we see man as a thinking being but practical realities and demands of everyday life prove otherwise. For instance, having naked fire on our hands will be more real than the idea of fire in our mind, at least the consequences make the difference clear.

Forms of Realism

Realism as a thought current exists in various shades and forms. These include classical realism, scientific realism and critical realism.

Classical Realism

This system of thought is well represented by Aristotle than by Plato. While Plato believed that the universal ideas in the world of form are more real than individual things in physical world, Aristotle accepted that physical things are real and factual, and ideas or form as also real. For Aristotle the two realms are real and inseparable, and both could undergo development as they have potentialities.

Scientific Realism

This kind of realism tends towards mechanism and materialism. This position is well represented by the organicism of Alfred Whitehead in his work, *Science and the Modern World*. Whitehead put forward the idea of organicism which states that there is a concrete unity of reality. The universe and its characteristics influence the intrinsic character of its parts. The history of the universe, he opines is the evolution of organisms from the simple to the complex. Electrons, atoms, molecules, cells, plants, animals, men and human communities form a monumental series, the higher organisms embracing innumerable lower ones. Even matter at its lowest level is "organic."[19] Actually, we know from the analysis of compounds found in nature that the organic and inorganic mater has certain commonalities and that consciousness is the only missing link.

Whitehead went further to assert that all things are interrelated; even the entire universe is an organic system, an "interlocked community" of events. For him, every event has contemporaries. This means that an event mirrors within itself the modes of its contemporaries as a display of immediate achievement. An event has a past. This means that an event mirrors within itself the modes of its predecessors, as memories which are fused into its own content. An event has a future. This means that an event mirrors within itself such aspects as the throws back onto the present, or in other words, as the present has determined concerning the future. Thus an event has anticipation. This means that past events cause present events, and present events have consequences that are futuristic.[20]

Summing up his realist position, Whitehead says that in taking account of each other, the organisms function and the events occur in a concrete world of qualities, where color, sound, beauty and selectivity are objective factors throughout nature. Whitehead rejects the dualism not of the organic and inorganic but the primary and secondary qualities and of mind and body. For him, nature should be interpreted in terms of form, process, emergence, and various levels of integration rather than in terms of a discrete mechanism or reductionism.

Commenting on this Whitehead's view, Gotshalk says that the view is now so prevalent as to indicate a basic transition in science and philosophy. In its stress upon creative synthesis and interrelatedness, it is an expression of "the interconnection principle, now write large over the face of the globe" - globalization as it is now called. For Gotshalk, Whitehead gave reasons for accepting that the things we experience are to be distinguished clearly and distinctly from our knowledge of them, and at the same time he made a case for realism which he said is adapted to the requirements of science as well as to the concrete experiences of mankind. As a result of his realistic stance, Whitehead makes the following affirmation that we live "within a world of colors, sounds, and other sense - objects."[21] The world is not within us nor does it depend on our sense perception.

Critical Realism

This form of realism was the position of a group of professional philosophers who wanted to reactivate and buttress the common sense view of the real and objective world. They are regarded as the neo-realists or new realists. These professional philosophers rejected subjectivism, monism, absolutism and all mystical teachings about the universe, and assert that the knowledge of an object does not change the object known. For the neo-realists, our sense experience and awareness are selective, not constitutive. This means that we give attention to some things rather than others. We do not affect or shape objects by experiencing or sensing them.

The critical realists assert that the existence of objects is independent of our knowledge but they refused to accept the position that objects are apprehended immediately and directly by the observer. For the critical realists, physical objects are not actually or directly present in the mind. It is only the sense data that are actually present to the mind.[22] This implies that we can only be directly conscious of sense data and these sense data put us in fairly direct contact with objects and reveal what they are to show us the nature of the external world.

13

SCHOOLS OF PHILOSOPHY
Existentialism and Marxism

Existentialism as a System of Thought
Existentialism is a technical philosophical position which came to its full development in the 20th Century, and it is still in vogue in this 21st century. Members of this system of philosophy include Soren Kierkegaard, Gabriel Marcel, Karl Jaspers, Martin Heidegger and Jean-Paul Sartre. Existentialism is a revolt against the methods and outlooks of traditional western philosophy which appears to be engrossed with things that are not relevant to immediate human existence. Existentialism is a world view that lays emphasis on concrete human existence. It is interested in the distinctive qualities of individual persons rather than abstract nature of man and the world. The existentialists assert the primacy and priority of existence over essence. They are indebted to life philosophy, and are in certain ways an expansion of the latter especially in its actuality, its analysis of time and its criticism of rationalism and natural science.

All existentialists discussed the typically metaphysical problem of being but most often man and the problems of existence take a center stage in these discussions. They made efforts to use their knowledge of metaphysics to explain basic problems of human existence rather than dwelling on abstract concepts of being and substance. Nevertheless, some of the existentialists such as Heidegger displayed a profound acquaintance of the great ancient and medieval metaphysicians and made effort to reconstruct traditional metaphysics.

Common Features of Existentialism

Existentialism is a literary as well as a saphilosophical movement that is opposed to the dehumanizing and depersonalizing forces at work in modern and contemporary societies. The philosophy is concerned with concrete and every day human experience rather than any abstract or specialized areas of knowledge. Existentialism is thus, a philosophy that confronts the human situation in its totality, ask questions about these basic conditions of human existence and at the same time show how man can establish his own meaning out of these conditions. It seeks to provide solution to the fundamental problems of life and existence.

In short, the mission statement of the existentialists is to recover man, the individual self or the thinker that is lost in abstract universals or in a universal ego and the speculative world views of men like Plato and Hegel. Its method is to begin with this human existence as a fact without any already-made pre-conceptions about the essence of man. There is no pre-fabricated human nature that freezes human possibilities into a pre-ordained mold. On the contrary, man exists first and makes himself what he is out of the conditions of birth, society and environment which he is thrown into without consultation and choice. Nobody chooses to be a male or female, white or black race, to be born in a rich family or poor family, etc. "Existence precedes essence" is the formula and assertion of the existentialists. Existentialism is opposed to schematic and abstract answers about human facts, about the concrete individual situated in a definite place and time. Man is a historical being that is to say that he is unique among other animals. And he would not be understood apart from his history.

The commonest characteristic among various existentialist philosophers is the fact that they all arise from the so called existential experience which assumed a different form in each of the existential philosophers. Kierkegaard combined his theory of dread with a theory concerning the utter loneliness of man in his relationship with God and the tragic destiny of man who constantly fights for survival and at the same time he is irrevocably propelled towards death.

This existential experience is expressed by Jaspers, for instance, in his awareness of the brittleness of being; something or somebody is here today, tomorrow he is no more and when he is taken out of sight, he is quickly out of mind. It is expressed by Heidegger through his conception of experiencing "propulsion towards death," and by Sartre in the general "nausea" of bad faith in human relations. The existentialists do not conceal the fact that their philosophies originate in such experiences. They take so-called existence as the supreme object of inquiry, but the meaning which they attach to the word is extremely difficult to determine. However, in some cases, it signifies a peculiarly human mode of being. It is a protest as it were in the name of individuality against the concepts of "reason" and "nature" that were so strongly emphasized during the 18th century Enlightenment.

For Walter Kaufmann, existentialism is a refusal to belong to any school of thought, the repudiation of the adequacy of any body of beliefs whatever, and especially of systems of belief. For him, it is a marked dissatisfaction with the traditional philosophy as superficial, academic, and remote from life - that is the heart of existentialism.[1] In the same line of thought, Herold, Smith and Nolan see Existentialism as a revolt against the impersonal nature of the modern industrial or technological age and against the mass movements of our time. Industrial society and capitalism as the existentialists see them tend to subordinate the individual to the machine. Man is in danger of becoming a tool, a robot, a computer, an object. Scientism recognizes only the external behaviors of man and interprets them as a mere part of a physical process.

Existentialism is also "a protest against totalitarian movements, whether fascists, communists, or whatever, which tend to crush or submerge the individual in the collective mass."[2] This means existentialism is against the dehumanizing forces of the contemporary world. In some existentialist's writings and teachings, man is often known as or replaced by "otherness," *Dasein* or *being-in-the- world*, "existence," "ego," "being-for oneself." And he is unique in possessing existence, or more precisely, man does not possess, but he is his existence. If man has an essence, either this essence is his existence or it is the consequence of it. Human existence is conceived as freely creating itself, it becomes; it is a projection; with each instant, it is more or less than it is. The existentialists often support this thesis by stating that existence is the same as temporality.

Existentialism speaks against any objectification of the human person. For them, any man must be treated as a subject always, never as an object or a means. This subjectivity is understood in a creative sense; man creates himself freely, and he is his freedom. For the existentialists, man is not shut up within himself. On the contrary, man is an incomplete and open reality – a continuum. However, his nature pins him tightly and unnecessarily to the world and to the other man in particular. This double dependence is seen in many existentialist ideas in such a way that human existence seems to be inserted into the world so that man at all times not only faces a determinate situation but also he is his own situation. On the other hand, they assert that there is a special connection between man and the world that gives existence its meaningful and peculiar quality. This connection is expressed in Heidegger's "togetherness," Jasper's "communication," Marcel's "thou," Okolo's "being-with the community" and Buber's I-Thou relationship.

Consequently, existentialism according to Paul Tillich is the attempt of man to describe his existence and his conflicts, the origin of these conflicts and the anticipation of overcoming them. So, wherever man's predicament is described either theologically or philosophically, either poetically or artistically, there we have existentialist elements.[3] All existentialists repudiate the distinction between subject and object, thereby discounting the value of intellectual knowledge for philosophical purposes. According to them, true knowledge is not achieved by understanding but through experiencing reality; this experience primarily concerns the dread with which man becomes aware of his finitude and frailty in that position of being thrust into the world without the knowledge of when and how, and at the same time propelled towards suffering and death. This means we cannot completely understand a person's suffering until we experience it.

Existentialists' Ideas

The existential ideas of Heidegger are remarkable, those of Sartre are mind blowing and those of Nietzsche are well expressed in this work; but here we shall consider that of the Danish Protestant thinker Soren Kierkegaard (1813-1855) who is regarded as the forerunner of existentialists' ideas. He made a fierce attack upon the Hegelian system on account of its "publicity" and "objectivity." He denies the possibility of mediation, that is, the possibility of merging the opposition between thesis and antithesis in an all-embracing rational synthesis.

So, Kierkegaard is not concerned with the issue of "being" in general, but with the individual existence. For him, the individual is one who thinks, knows, talks, and at the same time feels happy, angry, sad, thirsty and hungry. The individual can have fear, dread, and can be sick and can die. "The fundamental drive or urge in the individual is to exist and to be recognized as an individual." If man is so recognized, he may gain a sense of meaning and significance in life. The most meaningful point of reference to any person is his own immediate consciousness, which cannot be seen in systems or abstractions. Abstract thinking tends to be impersonal and lead away from the concrete human being and the human situation. Being or reality is existence that is found most in the "I" rather than the "it."

For Kierkegaard, the center of thought and meaning is the existing individual thinker. According to him, the man who pretends that his view of life is determined by sheer reason or what others thought is both tiresome and unperceptive; he fails to grasp the elementary fact that he is not a pure thinker, but an existing individual.[4] Kierkegaard shows much concern to the life of existing individual as opposed to the crowd which is most often anonymous and sometimes misleading. This is because individual loses himself and life opportunities when he hides in a crowd whether as a student in school or in any other organization. It is always important and self-defining to stand out in any organization one works or studies. In the work, *The Point of View,* Kierkegaard asserts that the crowd, including the press, is untruth because they are abstractions and have no hands. But each individual ordinarily has two hands; and he is the communicator of the truth. And again, the communication of truth can only be addressed to the individual, for the truth consists precisely in that conception of life which is expressed by the individual. He goes further to say that the truth can either be communicated or be received as it were under God's eyes, not without God's help, not without God's being involved as the middle term, He himself being the Truth. It can therefore only be communicated by and received by "the individual," which as a matter of fact can be every living man. The abstract, the fantastical, the impersonal, and the crowd - the public - exclude God as the middle term and thereby exclude also the truth.

On the question of what truth actually is for him, Kierkegaard asserts God is the truth and the middle term which renders every other relationship intelligible. According to him, to honor every man, absolutely every man is the truth, and this is what it is to fear God and love one's "neighbor." But from an Ethical-religious point of view, to recognize the "crowd" as the court of last resort is to deny God, and it cannot exactly mean to love the "neighbor." And the "neighbor" is the absolutely true expression for human equality. In any case where everyone was in truth to love his neighbor as himself a complete human equality would be attained.[5] Thus, there is no nobility in being superior to your fellow man, your neighbor but nobility lies in being superior to your former self.

As a result of his belief in the individual, Kierkegaard sees truth as subjectivity. According to him, truth should be defined as an objective uncertainty held fast in an appropriation process of the most passionate inwardness. This is the highest truth attainable by an existing individual. Kierkegaard as a personal thinker has a mission; in his own words is: "to seek for truth which is for me, to find the idea for which I can live and die."[6]

Kierkegaard, according to Bretall, is opposed to the stereotypes of mass society and the abstractness of philosophical systems. He detested the anonymity of "the crowd" and "every kind of dehumanizing collectivism." To exist as an individual means to suffer, to struggle, to develop, to be open to new possibilities, to be incomplete and inconsistent - while a system by its very nature is closed, static, dead, complete. A logical system is impossible. In the view of Kierkegaard, life is lived forward and understood backward. If we were ever to understand it completely, we would have to be already dead, without a future and with no untried and novel possibilities before us.

Three Stages of Life

Kierkegaard was conscious that an existential system could not be formulated. His aim was not to create a philosophical system but rather by speaking as it were to himself he would speak to others with a view to drawing attention to the concrete conditions and possibilities of human existence. For him, there are three stage of life of an individual. The movement from one "stage" to another is accomplished by choice, in the instant, not by learning and understanding.

The Aesthetic Stage

This describes a personal phase of cynical observation of life, indifference and nonchalant attitude to things that matter. The absence of self-commitment to any worthy course is universalized to be the aesthetic stage of life. He does not mean really the life of the artist or art-lover. Rather, it means the attitude of those who have no direction and continuity in their lives. This lack of continuity is due to lack of fixed and observed moral standards and principles. Kierkegaard calls it the Don Juan Stage, which is a stage of life full of phantasmagoria. This stage includes much more than the life of mere sensuality and over indulgence to things of the mundane. It includes the attitude of those who hate fixed lines and definite contours, who wish to taste all experiences, to put on all characters, who strives after a "false infinity." The aesthetic man refuses to recognize and to choose himself, to commit himself to anything which binds him down and gives him shape. Anything that ensures definiteness to his life, such morality and religion, he rejects.

The Ethical Stage

Above the aesthetic stage is the moral or ethical stage. The shapeless "individualism" of the first stage is renounced in favor of the subordination to the universal moral law with its claims on all. In this stage, typified by the life of Socrates, we have the reign of the universal moral law. But though the law is affirmed absolutely, and through it the individual gives determination to his life thus becoming more of an individual than the aesthetic man. He obeys the moral laws as much as possible in his relation with other people. He obeys the laws of the state and performs his civic and family duties. He respects the freedom and rights of others and accepts all constituted authority. He does these things because he sees them as moral and prudential obligations.

The Religious Stage

The religious stage is considered from the stand point of faith. The fact here is that individual does not subordinate himself simply to an impersonal universal law but stands in an immediate relation, affirmed by faith, to the supreme subject, the personal absolute God. He realizes what he is a finite individual before God. The individual recognizes that he is imperfect, he has weaknesses, and that at times he can be sick and needs to be healthy, he has needs and at times needs a helping hand and that one day he will die and needs to rest in peace. He can thus be said to choose himself in the deepest sense. According to Kierkegaard, the individual in affirmation of this relationship to God transcends the universal moral law. He likes to use the Bible account of Abraham's willingness to sacrifice his son Isaac as an illustration. Abraham's action (the attempt to sacrifice his son Isaac to God) which is against the universal moral law but in faith he recognized that the absolute relationship of the individual to God transcends the universal. It is through the affirmation, in fact, of his relationship to God that the human being becomes the individual in the highest possible degree, for the relationship of finite person to infinite and personal - absolute transcends the universal and is appropriated in the pure inwardness with passionate interest.

Thus, Kierkegaard contends that at this stage of life the proofs of God's existence are irrelevant and undesirable. The individual is left with the leap of faith; the passionate appropriation by the individual of an "objective uncertainty." For him, the truth which matters is my truth, the truth which I have chosen to live, rather than the public property truth achieved as a conclusion of logical argument.[7] This means for him truth is subjective, a resource of the individual's data base.

Furthermore, Kierkegaard asserts that the totality of this existential choice goes with "dread" or "anxiety." This dread or anxiety is expressed in the individual as a "sympathetic antipathy" and "antipathetic sympathy." And its nature may be seen most clearly in the case of a man faced with the choice for or against God. God is transcendent, invisible and unprovable. To choose oneself before God, not to commit oneself to faith, appears to be equivalent to losing oneself; throwing oneself into the abyss. This invokes the feeling of dread or anxiety.

On the other hand, if a man risks all and leaps, he finds himself, he chooses his true self, which is both finite and infinite. He who has no God is alienated from himself. He is "in despair." He who makes the leap of faith "recovers" himself, his true self, after the dispersion of the aesthetic level. Faced with the leap, therefore, man is simultaneously attracted and repelled. He is like a man standing on the edge of a precipice and simultaneously attracted and repelled by the yawning chasm below him. He would experience a "sympathetic antipathy" and an "antipathetic sympathy." This also invokes the feeling of anxiety or dread. Thus, the whole of existential choice involves dread or anxiety as one faces objective uncertainty. This happens because when we make a choice, our choice will turn around and make us for good or for bad as the case may be.

Marxism as a System of Thought

It is important to note that communism would not probably have come into existence as a system of government in Soviet Union, North Korea, and China if Marx had not laid its foundations in his philosophy. The above countries and some others in Eastern Europe and Africa imbibed the ideas expressed in the philosophy and put them into action. Here, we are out to articulate some of Marx ideas that went viral and became revolutionary after his time. Marx adopted the eclectic method in the making of his philosophy, in the sense that he borrowed from many sources. Marx met Hegel's dialectics at the University of Berlin Germany. He got his philosophical assumptions and apparatus in Hegel and Feuerbach. Marx's historical dialectics (conflicts of classes) came from Saint Simon while his labor theory of value was derived from John Locke and his knowledge of revolutionary movements he got from his association with Engels. What was original in Marx was that out of these sources he distilled a unified scheme of thought, which he fashioned into a powerful instrument of social analysis and social revolution.

The 19th and 20th Centuries witnessed series of crises of unparalleled scope and intensity; these include the two world wars, a very severe economic depression, revolutionary movements of tremendous magnitude and fury, dehumanizing slavery and colonialism. There were also different forms of imperialism, the threat of global militarization with the attendant armament and threat of nuclear holocaust. Social and political philosophers reacted with varying degrees of concern. It is on record that the existentialists and Marxists were most responsive to the suffering of the individual and the society. The responsiveness of Marxism to human suffering makes it one of the most dominant schools of thought in the past two centuries.

Marx after the Hegelian Influence

Marx was studying law, history and philosophy at the universities of Bonn, Berlin and Jena when he was hit and deeply touched by the Hegelian philosophy whose influence was at its zenith at the time. Marx was never the same again. His doctoral thesis reflected on the philosophies of Democritus, Epicurus and Lucretius which have emphases on materialism. What began to feature in the mind of Marx after the Hegelian influence includes:

• The notion that there is only one absolute reality and this can be discovered as embodiment of rationality in the world.

• The recognition that history is a process of development and change from less to more perfect forms in all of reality including physical nature, social and political life and human thought.

• The assumption that the thoughts and behavior of men at any given time and place is caused by the operation in them of an identical spirit or mind, that is, the spirit of a particular time or epoch.

The Influence of Feuerbach's Materialism on Marx

The writings of Ludwig Feuerbach made Marx to drop certain philosophy of Hegel and reinterpreted some others in his own way. Feuerbach is known to have seriously criticized the philosophy of Hegel. He rejected the foundation of Hegel's idealism. Marx's encounter with Feuerbach's thought made him see more useful assumptions that Hegel's idealism provided for explaining the human thought and behavior. Hegel regarded the thought and behavior of an epoch as the working in men of a particular spirit or mind. Feuerbach on the contrary contends that the generating influence of men's thoughts and behavior was the sum total of the material circumstances of any historical time. This contention of Feuerbach inverted and turned around Hegel's notion of the primacy of spirit and idea, substituting it with the primacy of the material order.

In his work, *Essence of Christianity,* Feuerbach argued that "man and not God is the basic reality." According to him "when the idea of God is analyzed, we found that apart from human feelings and wants, there is no idea of God." He went further to say that "the so called knowledge of God is man's knowledge about himself. God therefore is man. The spirit or the ideas of God are reflections of the modes of man's existence. God is the product of man's thought."[8]

The resulting materialism from the above inversion of Hegelian philosophy struck Marx's mind with the power of an atomic bomb. From that point Marx's thinking and reasoning went nuclear, he shifted from God to man as the focal point of historic development. Instead of the spirit struggling to realize itself in history as Hegel said, for Marx it was man struggling to realize himself in history. Man has alienated himself, and so history has to do with man's struggle to overcome self-alienation. Marx consequently said "if this is the condition of man, then the world should be changed in order to facilitate man's self-realization."[9] This is why Marx said philosophers have interpreted and explained the world differently; the point now is to change it. Marx grounded his thought in two notions: Hegel's dialectic view of history; and Feuerbach emphasis on the primacy of the material order. These two conceptions Marx fused together, and these enabled him to carry out a thorough and down-to-earth socio-political analysis, followed with practical program of action. Marx's later encounter with Saint Simon's account of class conflict helped to broaden his focus on the classes as the bearers of material and economic order - which has much to do with the factors of production. While Marx's relationship with Engels, the son of a textile manufacturer brought him into contact with the emergent working class movement, and the implications of those movements for political economy of the time were very fascinating to Marx.

The Core of Marx's Philosophy

First and foremost, we must note that the core of Marxist system of thought consists in the analysis of the following paradigms:

- The Major Epoch of History

- The causal power of material order

- The source and role of ideas

The Marxists used the above facts to prove their basic doctrine that:

- The existence of classes is only bound up with particular historic phases in development of the factors of production.

- Class struggle necessarily leads to dictatorship of the proletariat – the mass working class.

- The dictatorship of the proletariat itself constitutes the transition to the abolition of all classes and to a classless society.

Here, we shall undertake brief consideration of the above historical paradigms in the development of the society.

The Five Epochs

Marx's treatment of history, generally known as historical materialism holds that history can be divided into five major stages: the stage of primitive communism, the tribal stage; the feudal stage; the capitalist stage; and the stage of scientific socialism and communism. In our treatment of these stages, we will concern ourselves primarily with the dialectical principle, its movement and the factors that brought about the transition from one stage to another.

Primitive Communism

This first stage of history is characterized by shared property. No man lays claim on anything except personal possessions like clothes and weapons of war. The idea of individual ownership of property has not taken root. Property belongs to the community as a whole. Labor involves hunting and gathering of fruits and the laborer owned all the product of his labor. There was absence of capital and land owning classes. For effective and efficient hunting and security people lived in communities. With increase in population, different tribes that have some commonalities emerged. The communalism of these egalitarian hunter-gatherer communities in the tribes became the basis of production. Then, the primitive form of hunting gave way to primitive form of agriculture and cattle rearing following the domestication of animals.

Tribal Stage

This stage of historical dialectics marked the beginning of class society. Private property and class distinction appeared here. At the tribal stage of production, the production methods were still very primitive, and the primary producers at this stage were the slaves who were individually owned and controlled. This state of affairs constituted the thesis. However, the state of affairs did not favor the slaves, and so there was discontent among the slaves. This led to frequent violent disobedience and revolt by the slaves against the landowners and this constituted the antithesis. As a result, many of the tribes merged to form larger communities for efficient and effective management and control of the factors of production. Thus, the idea of statehood emerged here. The state developed as tool used by slaves owners to control slaves. The slaves were used in the cultivation of land to offset seasonal scarcity, wants or demand. Democracy and private ownership of slaves started. This is the synthesis. Then, as the population grew, some individuals became more prominent and wanted to exert more personal control over others, the system could no longer suffice, and this development became the antithesis. This led to the formation of a feudal stage, a state of affairs where the feudal lord was owner of all the lands within his domain, and laborers worked for him. These laborers were his serfs. The serfs became the primary producers.

The Feudal Stage

The synthesis of the tribal stage gave rise to the feudal stage and this constituted another thesis. As the lords exercised their powers over the serfs, it was not to hold *ad infinitum,* the serfs decided to abandon their lords and left for the small towns which were newly founded in Europe and America. The new towns sprang up here and there because of rapid development of machines and factories. In the towns, the serfs started off with their own skills (if they had acquired any) or become apprentice to those who established before them. Thus, while in the county, there was hierarchy of feudal lords, nobles and serfs. In the towns, another hierarchy grew up of the guild and guild-masters. This became the antithesis to the feudal stage.

This conflict of thesis and antithesis could be read in the social revolutions of 15th to 18th centuries; the French Revolution of 1789, the English Civil War, etc. The feudal lords tried to frustrate the development of towns and the migration of the serfs to the new towns. The feudal lords were dealt with in the conflicts that arose between them and the town officers to make way for the growth of productive forces in the new towns. Aided by the discovery of steam engine and industrial manufacturers, the towns merged with the feudal system in a synthesis and big markets for goods and services emerged. As a result, the towns developed into the next stage of production and society; the capitalist stage.

The Capitalist Stage

The capitalist stage became the new thesis having emerged from the feudal stage. The capitalist stage according to Marx is characterized among other things by free competition, individual planning, large capital and big industries. In this stage also, we have the two classes – the capitalists or business owners which Marx called the bourgeoisie, and the workers which he called the proletariats. The capitalists (most often the upper class) own the means of production while the workers were the primary producers. The bourgeoisie or capitalists were faced with opposition and competition from other foreign bourgeoisie over exploitation of old instruments of production. And because of over production, and unfavorable working conditions, the proletariats became opposed to the bourgeoisie and as such were antithetical to it. The workers' conflict with the capitalist or bourgeoisie started with an individual conflict with a capitalist, and then followed with workers of the company, then other companies and then National Movement of Trade Unions and then international movement. As capitalism develops, despite its numerous potentialities, it is still subject to the law of dialectics. It employs the workers, and is sustained by the workers, and at the same time it continuously impoverishes the working class. By so doing, capitalism necessarily creates and develops its antithesis.

The proletariat - the mass of working class, at the option of its own extinction, strives for self-preservation and rises in protest against the bourgeoisie – the capitalists and overthrows it. But then, unlike in former conflict what results now is a classless society, not a society of classes which involves the domination of one class by another. How does this happen? According to Marx, the proletariat – the working class by its universal nature destroys the state as the state destroys the bourgeoisie and also destroys itself as a class bearer. What ensues therefore is a classless and just society. This is the stage of scientific socialism of Marx.

The Stage of Scientific Socialism

Socialism is regarded as the first phase of communism. This is what comes into being with the fall of capitalism in the society. For Marx, this change and transition of the society that gave rise to scientific socialism is determined by economic forces and means of production of that society. In his words, society is an ideological expression for the division of labor, forms of property ownership or productive relations. At the final stage, due to the enormous powers of big industries, there will be abundant and enough means of livelihood, and even more to spare such that there is no more need for division of labor or the existence of classes. The state which is the machinery for the oppression of one class by the other becomes superfluous and withers away. For Marx, history will end with the emergence of stateless and pure communism which also marks the end of all class conflicts and struggles. This principle of dialectical movement or cause will disappear, classless society will emerge. Everything – forces or interests in the human society will be in equilibrium. The classless society will run on the principle of "from everyone according to his abilities and to everybody according to his needs."[10] The result will be an association in which the free development of each is the condition for the free development of all.

The Sub-Structure: The Material Order

For Marx, materialism means the sum total of the natural environment which includes all inorganic nature, the organic world, social life and human consciousness. He defined matter as objective reality that exists outside the human mind. For him, there is no single form of matter in all things. There is diversity in material world. However, he denied the notion of any spiritual reality existing outside the human mind like God. According to Marx, the human mind is an organic matter that has developed to the point in which the cerebral cortex of the organ is capable of the intricate process of reflex action called human thought. Marx concludes that the material order is prior to the mental activity. The mind or mental activity is a byproduct of matter. The earliest of life were without mental activity until man's ancestor developed the use of limbs and tools. The use of tools later points to the factors of production and the relation of production in the human society on one hand and the status of property or its ownership on the other hand.

The Superstructure: The Origin and Role of Ideas

For Marx, ideas are the reflections of basic material reality of a historic period. For this reason, ideas came after the material order has affected man's mind. Here, Marx talks of the relationship between man's conscious life and his material environment. He asserts that it is not the consciousness of man that determine his social being but on the contrary the social being determines his consciousness. This is say that where a man is; where he lives, and what he does like his work determines is consciousness. This is to say, if we raise our children in small communities that have sporting infrastructure for tennis, football, soccer, baseball and golf, the tendency that they will be well rooted in one or more of these sports will be very high.

Thus for Marx, the source of ideas is rooted in the material order. Ideas of justice, goodness, religion, salvation he maintains are various modes of rationalizing the existing material order. The conflict of ideas within a society at a given time is due to the dynamic nature of the economic order. The dialectical principle which is the struggle of opposites has its ideological aspect and material aspect. The interest of the classes differs therefore as their ideas are opposed. For Marx, the ideas of the ruling class are in every age the ruling ideas. That is to say the class which is the dominant material force in any society is at the same time its dominant intellectual force and authority. The class which has the means of material production at its disposal has control at the same time over the means of mental production, so that in consequence the ideas of those who lack the means of mental production are in general, subject to it.[11] The mental production includes the ownership of educational institutions, mass media like television and radio stations, books, magazines and newspaper publishers, and telecommunication and information technology networks, etc.

Self -Alienation and the Quest for Authentic Existence

Marx held the view that it is in the nature of human beings to cooperate in a process of collective and freely chosen labor. He believes that human beings come to self-realization and self- fulfillment in the process of transforming the world in their own image through their labor. But most often workers donot achieve self-actualization because workers are separated from the product of their labor. It is the belief of Marx that people are alienated when they are separated from the products of their labor and from the labor process itself. This occurs when workers have no control over the circumstances in which they engage in productive activity and they are treated as something that can be used and disposed of at will.

The effect of self-alienation is that one is separated from one's essential humanity to the extent that one is unable to live a fully human life. What Marx is saying is that most often workers do their jobs under sub human conditions and are not rewarded appropriately in terms of the fruits of their labor. In this kind of situation the human being is depersonalized, he is no longer a person, and he is no longer a subject but an object. He is enclosed, subjugated, misappropriated and dispossessed of his energy, efforts and knowledge. He is treated like a machine or a service dog. Sometimes he is seen as just a number and as such a statistical variable in production reports.

For Marx, self-alienation exists in all societies where there is a division between those who own and control the means of production and those who do not. But it is in the capitalist societies of Europe and America according to Marx that self-alienation assumes an alarming proportion a consequence of the industrial revolution. This is because capitalism is characterized by a fundamental conflict between the bourgeoisies that is the owners of factors of production (like land, capital, entrepreneurship and information) and on the other hand, the proletariat, the mass majority of the population who are the middle and lower class workers who have only their labor power to boast of or bargain with.

The proletariat suffers self-alienation because they are not favored in the collective bargaining that often takes place between them and the employers of labor. In most cases they are compelled to sell their manpower under unfavorable circumstances beyond their control. These circumstances include obnoxious employment policies, inhuman management controls and supervisions, intolerable labor process and conditions of service, and sub human working conditions. All these are meant to maximize production output and profit for the factory owners.

In any work environment where the worker suffers self- alienation, according to Marx, "the worker does not fulfill himself in his work but denies himself; he has a feeling of misery rather than well-being, does not develop freely his mental and physical energies but is physically exhausted and mentally debased."[12] The worker feel himself at home only during leisure time, whereas at work he feels homeless. His work is not voluntary but forced labor. His work is not a satisfaction of a need, but only a means for satisfying other needs.

Marx sees light at the end of the tunnel for the mass of workers, the working class. In his mind Marx thinks that every suffering carries the seed of its own refusal, the refusal to suffer and every problem contains the seed of its solution. So for Marx, the proletariat, the working classes are the bearers of the emancipatory potential of mankind. They are the seeds of development and progress in any human society. And for Marx, "capitalism is not indestructible; indeed it is riddled with contradictions which at the end will result to its downfall; and it is the proletariat that will make this to happen."[13]

However, Marx was not pleased that the proletariat, the working classes are not yet conscious of the enormous power they wield. The working classes are not yet a class-for-itself, that is, a class aware of its own reality and situation; a class aware of its historic destiny as a revolutionary force. Rather the working class is still a class-in-itself for the fact that it is still enclosed by the Bourgeoisie class and their capitalist ideology, tax system, communication system, their educational system, their mass media which are instruments of persuasion, propaganda, brain - washing and mass control.

For Marx, it is in the destiny of the working classes to free themselves from this strangle hold and emerge in a shining armor to abolish all class distinctions and then institute a new form of society based collective and fair ownership of the factors of production. And under this rule, self-alienation will be abolished. Marx was unable to put a date or time frame when this will happen neither was he able to predict the place where his prophecy will come to realization. Instead, Marx felt that the overthrow of capitalism and bourgeoisie class would not come through peaceful means or through negotiations or collective bargaining but only through the use of force and civil disobedience.

Thus in the Communist Manifesto, Marx and Engel made a call for arms from the working class and openly declare that their ends can be attained only by the forcible overthrow of all existing social conditions. They asserted "Let the ruling classes tremble at the communist (i.e. working class or middle class) revolution. The proletarians have nothing to lose but their chains. They have a world to win. Workers of countries unite!"[14]

Let us say at this point that Marx set out to buy freedom for man, and as a means to this end he took over Hegel's dialectics. The effect and result of this take-over and the eventual application have not been wholly positive and contributory to the achievement of the set objectives. By imposing the dialectics as an inviolable fate, Marx philosophy snowballed to determinism. The wellbeing of man no longer resides in man's intelligence or will, but in economic forces. Marx imposed a hard determinism on man and consequently deprived man completely of the freedom and authentic existence which he initially sought to win for him. He denied them the participation in a free market economy and private property that has become the engine of development and progress for many people in the Western world.

The effect of this determinism and the lack of free market economy could be seen in the attitude of treating men like machines which must conform to scientific laws. There is also total rejection of nonviolent protest and resistance from the masses who are oppressed and subjugated under this obnoxious and unfavorable socio-political and economic climate. These led inevitably to such things as the absolute dictatorship of Stalin in the former Soviet Union. The inordinate application of his thoughts accounts for the low level of civil liberty, poor socio-economic and political development in some socialist countries like North Korea and Cuba. However, the ingenuity of his philosophy and its applications and efficacy are not in doubt. The growth of China as the number two economy in the world after the United States of America could be traced to Marx's development philosophy that the leaders borrowed from Soviet Union and have modified it by substituting some of the irrational restraints and constraints with rational ones and mixed market economy is becoming the fulcrum of Cheese development philosophy.

14

SCHOOLS OF PHILOSOPHY
Pragmatism and Logical Positivism

Pragmatism as a System of Thought
Etymologically, the term pragmatism is derived from a Greek word *"pragma"* meaning action. Before Charles Sanders Peirce used the term, he had projected the content in a review of Fraser's edition of Berkeley's Works. In that review, Peirce suggested a rule for avoiding the deceits of language. He asked: do things fulfill the same function practically? Then let them be signified by the same word. Do they not? Then let them be distinguished. So, he uses pragmatism to indicate "practice" or something being "practical," experiential, empirical or as it were a hands-on. This helps to differentiate words or concepts that are practical or action oriented from those that are not. It also separates those words or concepts that involve actual doing or use of something from those that mere theory and ideas.

Later, Peirce introduced the concept into modern philosophy to designate "the method of ascertaining the meaning of hard words and abstract conceptions." He used it first in 1878 in his article *"How to Make Our Ideas Clear"* in the *Popular Science Monthly* for January of that year. Peirce pointed out in the article that our beliefs are really rules for actions. They act as a guide as to how we act and behave in practical situations. For him, to develop a thought's meaning, we need only determine what conduct it is for us, its sole significance. William James referred to Peirce as maintaining that "the tangible fact at the root of all our thought distinctions, however subtle, is that there is no one of them so fine as to consist in anything but a possibility of practice."[1] This means the essence of every thought is to foreshadow and anticipate action. Peirce went further to say that to attain perfect clearness in our thoughts of an object, then, we need only consider what conceivable effects of a practical kind the object may involve, what sensations we are to expect from it, and what reactions we must prepare for. Our conception of these effects whether immediate or remote is for us the whole of our conception of the object, so far as, that conception has positive significance at all.[2] For Jeremy Stangroom and Marcus Garvey, what is being claimed here is that we get clarity about the content of a thought or concept by discerning, under a multitude of different conditions, its various real-world instantiations. Or to put it in another way, clarity comes by working through the experimental consequences of the content of a thought or concept.[3]

After the introduction of the term pragmatism to modem thought by Peirce, the word was not accorded the recognition it deserved by scholars until James resurrected the term from a twenty-year slumber. In a lecture before Professor George Holmes Howison's Philosophical Unwind at the University of California Berkeley, James brought up pragmatism and made a special application of it to religion. Consequently, the word pragmatism spread like wild fire in the Western world, and the term fairly spots the pages of the philosophical journals and applies itself conveniently to a number of tendencies that have lacked a collective name, and to a great extent it has come to stay.[4]

The Nature of Pragmatism

Pragmatism is essentially an American philosophical movement that has come to prominence during the last one hundred years. Its popularity started with a lecture as we mentioned earlier entitled *"Philosophical Conceptions and Practical Results"* delivered by James in the University of California. In the lecture, James acknowledged and hailed Peirce as the founder and originator of pragmatism. So, it is a philosophy that strongly reflects some of the characteristics of American life. Likewise, John Smith in his work, *The Spirit of American Philosophy* sees pragmatism as something that grew out of American life and experience; it was not in the main an academic movement, and its chief expositors were marked by independence of judgment.

In the view of Herold, Smith and Nolan, pragmatism seeks to mediate between the empirical and idealist traditions and to combine what is most significant in each of them. Pragmatism is an attitude, "a method and a philosophy that uses the practical consequences of ideas and beliefs as a standard for determining their value and truth."[5] Some members of the school see pragmatism in different perspectives.

For James, who was the chief protagonist of pragmatism, it is an attitude of looking away from first things, principles, categories and supposed necessities and of looking toward last things, fruits, consequences and facts. Pragmatism as a method, James says, is primarily a method of settling metaphysical disputes that otherwise might be indeterminable. Is the world one or many? Is the world fated or free? Is the world material or spiritual? These are notions which may or may not hold good of the world; and disputes over such notion are unending. The pragmatic method in such cases is to try to interpret each notion by tracing its respective practical consequences. What difference would it practically make to anyone if this notion rather than that notion were true? If no practical difference whatever can be traced, then the alternatives mean practically the same thing and all dispute is idle. James maintains that whenever a dispute is serious, we ought to be able to show, some practical difference that must follow from one side or the other being right.

Pragmatism as an attitude in philosophy places emphasis on method than on a systematic philosophical doctrine. It represents perfectly familiar attitude both in a more radical and in a less objectionable form than it has ever yet assumed. Pragmatism as a method of experimental inquiry extends into all realms of human experience. However, a pragmatist turns his back resolutely and once for all upon a lot of unusual habits dear to professional philosophers. He turns away from abstractions and insufficiency, from verbal solutions, from bad a priori reasons, from fixed principles, closed systems and pretended absolutes and origins. He turns towards concreteness and adequacy, towards fact, towards action, towards utility and towards powers and results. That renders the empiricist temper regnant and the rationalist temper sincerely given up. It means also the open air and possibilities of nature, as against dogma, artificiality, and the pretense of finality in truth. It is clear that pragmatism uses the modern scientific method as the basis of philosophy. Its affinity is with the sciences, especially the biological and social sciences, and it aims to utilize the scientific spirit and scientific knowledge to deal with all human problems including those of ethics and religion. Ever at this, pragmatism does not stand for any specific results.

For James, it is a method only but the general triumph of that method would mean an enormous change in the temperament of philosophy. Ultra-rationalistic philosophers would be frozen out of science and metaphysics would undergo a metamorphosis and become more useful to man. Also, the pragmatists are critical of the older systems of philosophy such as the various forms of materialism, idealism and realism which have seen reality as an enigma whose key must be sought in the shape of some illuminating or power-bringing word, such as: God, matter, reason, absolute, energy. These words are in principle the answers to any problem, and to possess them is after a fashion to possess the universe itself. You can rest when you have them. You are at the end of your metaphysical quest. But if you follow the pragmatic method, you cannot look on any such word as closing your quest. You must bring out of each word its practical cash-value, set it at work within the stream of your experience. When this is done, these terms will appear not only as a program for more work, but more particularly as an indication of the ways in which existing realities may be changed. At the same time, theories thus become instruments, not answers to enigmas, in which we can rest. This means that pragmatism unties all our theories, gets them into practice and sets each one at work.

We must also note the pragmatism is not antagonistic to every system of philosophy. It agrees with nominalism in always appealing to particulars rather than to universals, with utilitarianism in emphasizing practical aspects; with positivism in its disdain for verbal solutions, useless questions and metaphysical abstractions. There is nothing new in the pragmatic method; Socrates was an adept at it. Aristotle used it methodically; John Locke, George Berkeley and David Hume made contributions to truth by its means. According to Melvin Rader, the term "pragmatic" and "pragmatism" were suggested to Peirce by his study of Kant. In *The Metaphysics of Morals,* Kant distinguished between "pragmatic" and "practical." The former term, deriving from the Greek *pragma* (things done), applies to the rules of art or technique based upon experience; the later term applies to moral rules which Kant regarded as a priori. Hence Peirce, wishing to emphasize an experimental and non a priori type of reasoning, chose the word 'pragmatic' to designate his way of clarifying meanings.

Thus, pragmatism in its nature is at home with anti-intellectualist tendencies that make no pretension. We shall conclude this section by stating an analogy of the nature of pragmatism as the Italian Pragmatist Papine sees it. According to him, pragmatism lies in the midst of our theories, like a corridor in a hotel. Innumerable chambers open out to it. In one you may find a writing on atheistic volume; in the next someone on his knees praying for faith and strength; in a third a chemist investigating a body's properties. In a fourth, a system of idealistic metaphysics is excogitated; in a fifth, the impossibility of metaphysics is being shown. But all own the corridor, and all must pass through it if they want a practicable way of getting into or out of their respective rooms.[6]

Pragmatism as a Solution to the Problem of Truth

Pragmatism has come to be used in a wide sense as a theory of truth. Having discussed this under theory of knowledge, much detail is unnecessary here. Many adherents of pragmatism rejected the correspondence and coherence theories of truth. For them, truth cannot be correspondence with reality nor can it be formal and rationalistic. They maintain also that we cannot know "substances," "essences" and ultimate realities. Consequently, they reject absolutism, authoritarianism, intellectualism and rationalism in dealing with the problem of truth.

For the pragmatist, the test of truth is utility, workability or satisfactory results. They assert that there is no such thing as static or absolute truth. They assert that truth is something that happens to a judgment or an idea. For James, the dictionary conception of truth as a property of some of our ideas in which their "agreement" with reality is truth while their disagreement with reality is falsity, is acceptable to the intellectualists and to the pragmatists. According to him, quarrels only arise when what is meant by the term "agreement" and what is meant by the term "reality" is asked. In answering this question, the pragmatist is more analytic and painstaking while the intellectualists are more offhand and unreflective. The popular notion is that a true idea must copy its reality. The pragmatist on the other hand, asks its usual question: Grant an idea or belief to be true, it asks what concrete difference will its being true make in anyone's actual life? How will the truth be realized? What experiences will be different from those which would obtain if the belief were false? What in short is the truth's cash - value in experiential terms? For James, the moment the pragmatist asks this question, it sees the answer: "True ideas are those that we can assimilate, validate, corroborate and verify. False ideas are those that we cannot."[7] This is the practical difference it makes to us as to have true ideas; that therefore, is the meaning of truth. Thus for the pragmatist, truth is always impact bound.

James went further to defend the above thesis, saying that the truth of an idea is not a stagnant property inherent in it. Truth happens to an idea. It becomes true, is made true by events. Its verity is in fact an event, a process: the process namely of its verifying itself, its verification. Its validity is the process of its validation. But what do the words verification and validation mean in pragmatism? They again signify certain practical consequences of the verified and validated idea.[8]

Furthermore, explaining in pragmatic terms the definition of truth as agreement with reality, James says to "agree" as the pragmatists see it in the widest sense with a reality only means to be guided either straight up to it or into its surrounding, or to be put into such working touch with it as to handle either it or something connected with it better than if we disagreed; better either intellectually or practically! Agreement therefore means essentially an affair of leading – a leading that is useful because it is into quarters that contain objects that are important. So, true ideas lead us into useful verbal and conceptual quarters as well as directly up to useful sensible termini. They lead to consistency, stability and flowing human intercourse. They lead away from eccentricity and isolation, from foiled and barren thinking. In the end and eventually, all true processes must lead to the face of directly verifying sensible experiences somewhere which somebody's ideas have copied.[9]

Succinctly put, James' position is that true ideas are useful ideas. For Stangroom and Garvey, an idea of X is only a useful idea if it helps us to deal with X should X exist. James applied the pragmatic notion of truth as utility and usefulness to the existence of God and he asserts the view that the existence of God cannot be proved based on empirical evidence but on the ground of a belief which improves life most, the belief in God wins, just because it leads one to better attitude towards the future and put some much needed meaning into a life.[10]

William James conception of truth still raises some concerns because there still false systems or beliefs that still improves the life of the believers. But his application of pragmatism to the proof of existence of God is remarkable as well as useful.

The Instrumentalism of Dewey

John Dewey was remarkable for sustaining the pragmatic system of thought. He applied their principles to all phases of life and thought. Instead of pragmatism, he called his brand of it instrumentalism. No matter the differences he had with James' ideas, he agreed with James in his forward-looking and empirical temper, his attitude of looking toward last things, fruits, consequences and facts. Dewey rejected a dualism of nature and experience. For him, the stuff of the world is natural events such as we directly experience. Dewey's thought current could be described as experimental naturalism. For him, things should be understood in terms of their origins and functions, and inquiry should be empirical in method and practical in motivation. Dewey regards fruitful inquiry as essentially active and prospective rather than passive and retrospective.

Dewey in his work, *Creative Intelligence,* maintains that intelligence develops within the sphere of action for the sake of possibilities not yet given; intelligence as intelligence is inherently forward looking. He asserts, "A pragmatic intelligence is a creative intelligence, not a routine mechanic. Intelligence is instrumental through action to the determination of the qualities of future experience."[11] This means for Dewey, a true intelligence is a productive intelligence. A true knowledge is a productive knowledge. Likewise, a real idea is a productive idea.

Thus, to ascertain true knowledge and true ideas, Dewey was in favor of determining the consequences that follow from them. This is to ask the questions against any knowledge or idea: what can the knowledge or idea or belief promise for the future? How can it help us in resolving our perplexities and problems? What predictions are implied by the hypothesis involved and how they can be verified? For Dewey, such questions apply even to propositions or discussions about the past, and even these propositions must be verified in terms of future consequences. He maintained in his work, *The Influence of Darwin on Philosophy and Other Essays* that "the past has left effects, consequences that are present and that will continue in the future. Our belief about it, if genuine, must also modify action in some way and have objective effects. If these two sets of effects interlock harmoniously then the judgment is true."[12] This means that if theory and practice work out well, the result is always good and the ideas are true.

Dewey regarded this emphasis on consequences as the essential characteristic of pragmatism. The term 'pragmatic,' he asserts "means only the rule of referring all thinking, all reflective considerations, to consequences for final meaning and test."[13] It is on this basis that Dewey resent any system of education that involves learning without doing as is the case with the system of education in many countries which lays emphasis and relies solely on the possession of certificates and degrees without practice, all theory and no action, and therefore of no consequences, no results, uncreative and uninventive.

THE ANALYTICAL SCHOOL AND LOGICAL POSITIVITISM

The Analytic School of Thought

Analytic philosophy embraces a set of philosophical activities or doctrines, some of which differ remarkably from each other. In spite of many divergences, a common outlook runs through all of these views. The common outlook might briefly be described as the belief that philosophy when properly performed consists, at least in part, in an activity called "analysis." Within the analytic school, the core agreement among them is the acceptance that many philosophical problems are mainly a problem of conceptual confusion; that such confusion is due, at least in part, to the misuse of language; that a process of linguistic clarification is therefore, at some stage, requisite to the ultimate solution of these problems.

"Analysis" is the term commonly assigned to the various forms which the process of clarification may take. Philosophers associated with this system include: Alfred Whitehead, Thomas More, Gottlob Frege, Gilbert Ryle, T.L. Austin, Bertrand Russell, Ludwig Wittgenstein and others. Since language is the chief tool of the philosopher and the medium through which he finds expression, he is sensitive to its ambiguities and defects, and makes sympathetic efforts to clarify and improve it. The last two centuries produced the crop of philosophers enumerated above, who ignited the interest in the problems of language and communication and the function of signs and symbols. The interest ignited or rekindled, according to Herold, Smith and Nolan has led to the development of semantics, or the study of the meaning and the function of words and the relations between words and things. It has led to the development of the schools of linguistic or philosophical analysis, and symbolic logic. It has also led to a renewal of attention to details of grammar and syntax.[14]

They went further to say that philosophers of the Ancient World and Middle Ages were concerned mainly with a reality that transcended that of the temporal world. Their search was for "being." The philosophers from the Renaissance – the Enlightenment Period to the nineteenth century looked inward; they were interested mainly in the self, idea in the mind, and the problem of knowledge. While these earlier interest have not disappeared from philosophy, some philosophers restrict their attention to linguistic analysis and the details and theory of discourse. Words, definitions, propositions, hypotheses, axioms and the principles of verification are now increasingly regarded as central topics of philosophical investigations.

Detailed review of the nature of language is beyond the scope of this work; however, we must note that language is made up of names or symbols. A name is the symbol that stands for the thing named, which is called the referent or the object. It can also stand for a quality or a relation expressed in words or symbols spoken or written. For ages, languages have served several functions ranging from cognitive function, emotive function, and imperative function to ceremonial function – as a form of social rituals, e.g., greetings and conversations. Thus, Harold, Smith and Nolan insist that there is need to distinguish clearly between statements that point out or describe actual things in the world of physical things, and the way these things are related, and statements that have no referent in the external world. That is to say that we may use language to talk about objects (i.e., object language) or to talk about language or a word (i.e., Meta language).[15]

There is a controversy over the possibility of private versus public language. Wittgenstein, in his work, *Philosophical Investigations* has a famous argument against the possibility of a purely private language (i.e. private to one person), which highlights the fact that such a language would have no publicly established rules for its use. Language, he argues requires rules, following a rule is a social practice, and therefore, one cannot follow a rule "privately." Following the empirical tradition of Locke and Hume which emphasized that knowledge comes from the senses, analytic philosophers such as the early Wittgenstein in his *Tractatus Logico - Philosophicus* emphasized what might be called object - designation theory of meaning. This asserts that to understand a sentence with factual import one must know what each word in the sentence refers to. A sentence is not only meaningful but true if its words match up with the corresponding objects; and the sentence is so constructed that it represents, by analogy of structure, the actual relationship of objects. In the same line of thought, Ryle went further to add that a true sentence is like a map and when tested by observation or experiment, if it has no anchorage in fact; it is nothing but disguised gibberish.

However, Wittgenstein did not agree with the logical positivists that metaphysical statements are wholly nonsensical. According to Wittgenstein, there are metaphysical insights that cannot be stated in language, but if they could be, they would be true insights and not mere muddles or expressions of feelings.[16] Nevertheless, the logical positivists regarded Wittgenstein as a valiant ally as well as an active partner in dismissing most of the traditional problems of philosophy as nonsensical. Their opinions about Wittgenstein may not be unconnected with the anti-metaphysical stance of Wittgenstein's *Philosophical Investigations* which sees metaphysics as a kind of false puzzlement, a matter of "pictures" which holds the person "captive." This is so, in spite of the fact that he acknowledged in the work, that there are different conceptions of meaning and many ways of making sense. According to Wittgenstein, there are countless different kinds of use of what we call "symbol," "words," "sentences," and if these expressions turn out to be apt tools, they are meaningful. For Rader, this theory that "the meaning is the use" implies that useless discourse is gibberish.[17]

Austin was a famous analytic philosopher who advocated for the use of ordinary language in philosophy. He is opposed to the search for an ideal or special language for philosophy or other sciences. For J.L. Austin, our common stock of words embodies all the distinctions men have found worthy drawing and the connections they have found worth making, in the life times of many generations: these surely are likely to be more numerous, more sound, since they have stood up to the long test of the survival of the fittest, and more subtle at least in all ordinary and reasonably practical matters, than any that you or I are likely to think up in our arm-chairs on an afternoon - the most favored alternative method.[18]

In a sharp opposition to the views of Austin, Bertrand Russell criticized what he called "the cult of ordinary language." According to Russell, the language of daily life, with words used in their ordinary meanings, cannot suffice for philosophy. He asserts that the use of ordinary language for philosophy makes philosophy trivial by encouraging endless dispute over "what silly people mean when they say silly things." It also excuses "ignorance of mathematics, physics and neurology in those who have had only a classical education" and it makes almost inevitable the perpetuation among philosophers the middle - headedness they have taken over from common sense."[19] But we know from experience that the problem of language will always remain with humanity, and hence analysis will always be relevant for those who are confused by one language or the other. To invent a special language for the sciences will lead to "*multiplicanda explicanda,*" a multiplication of explanations and a duplication of language problems.

Logical Positivism as a System of Thought

The term positivism was first used by Henri de Saint - Simon to designate scientific method and its extension to philosophy. It was adopted by Auguste Comte to designate a great philosophical movement which in the second half of the 19th century and the first decade of the 20th century was powerful in all the countries of the Western World.

General Characteristics

It maintains a number of notions including the following:

• Science is the only valid knowledge and facts are the only possible objects of knowledge;

• Philosophy does not possess a method different from science;

- The task of philosophy is to find the general principles common to all the sciences and to use these principles as guide to human conduct and as a basis of social organization.

Consequently, positivism denies the existence of intelligent forces or substances that go beyond facts and the laws ascertained by science. It opposes any kind of metaphysics and in general, any procedure of investigation that is not reducible to scientific method.

Principal Sources of Positivism

The principal philosophical sources of positivism are the works of Francis Bacon, the English Empiricist, and the Philosopher of Enlightenment. But the cultural climate that made it possible was that of the 18th century industrial revolution and the grand wave of optimism that arose as a result of the first success of industrial technology. Positivism turned this climate into a philosophical program - that is, a universal project for human life. It exalted science without concerning itself (as in contemporary positivism) with the condition and the limits of the validity of science, and it claimed that not only ethics and politics but also religion can become scientific disciplines. In one direction, this led to an attempt to establish a positive religion as the true religion in place of traditional theological religion.

Kinds of Positivism

There are three fundamental kinds of positivism:

Social Positivism
This is well represented in the practical-political character of S. Mill and Comte.

Evolutionary Positivism

This is theoretical in character. It shares with social positivism the general idea of progress but whereas social positivism deduces human progress and development from the consideration of society and history, evolutionary positivism deduces them from the fields of physics and biology. Herbert Spencer was one of the advocates of evolutionary positivism. His materialistic metaphysics is often associated with evolutionary positivism.

Empirical-Critical Positivism

Contemporary forms of positivism (logical positivism and neo positivism) are directly connected with Empirical – critical positivism. The theme of positivism re-emerged after the First World War in the movement of Neo-positivism which the Vienna Circle propagated. Logical positivism is more radical than Comte's social positivism. Comte discussed the influence of distrust of all metaphysics, the cult of experience, the belief in the moral efficacy of science, the hierarchy of the sciences, the notions of progress and evolution, the natural subordination of the individual to the society, the creation of a new science of sociology, the establishment of morals on the basis of human solidarity and the law of three stages - theological stage, metaphysical stage and positive stage. But the neo-positivists were far from the historical perspective of the law of thethree stages.

For the neo-positivists, the positive is that which is verifiable and is susceptible to enumeration in a coherent way by language. They conceive of the function of philosophy as the clarification of meanings rather than the discovery of truths. Moritz Schlick, founder of the Vienna Circle of logical positivists stated that "by means of philosophy, statements are explained, by means of science, they are verified." The latter is concerned with the truth of statements, the former with what they actually mean.[20] Wittgenstein maintained the same view in his *Tractatus* as he affirmed that philosophy does not result in philosophical propositions but rather in the clarification of propositions. For him, there are no philosophical doctrines or theories, only a philosophical clarification of the propositions that men use in science or other pursuits. The job of philosophy is to clear up the puzzles of misunderstanding. As a result, he asks the question: what is your aim in philosophy? He answered: to show the fly the way out of the fly-bottle.[21]

The logical positivists, Rudolf Carnap, and A.J. Ayer enunciated a theory of verification and meaning that provided a foundation for the subjectivist ethical conclusions. For them, for a statement to have cognitive truth or meaning, it must be either analytic or empirically testable. If the statement is analytic, it can be confirmed or disconfirmed by the test of logical consistency, and it then has logical meaning. Examples would be the propositions of pure mathematics and formal logic. If the statement is empirical, it is verifiable by observation and it then has factual meaning. To understand factual statement for them is to know how to obtain evidence for or against it. For Ayer, when there is no conceivable way to find such evidence, the statement is factually meaningless.[22]

From the above views we can sum up the main positions of the neo-positivists as follows:

• Philosophy is the logical analysis of the concepts and sentences of the sciences.

• To understand thoughts, one must examine language, since it is in language that thought finds its expression, and only a universal and logically perfect language is the language of the sciences or the language of any knowledge.

• Natural or ordinary language often "misleads us both by its vocabulary and by its syntax." Hence, it must be reduced to or translated into an artificial or ideal language that is purely formal.

• The main task of philosophy is to reform language by making its grammatical and syntactical forms to conform to their actual logical function.

• Any metaphysics based upon the existence of non-empirical entities or the belief in internal relations (e.g., idealism) is rejected. Relations are external. The world is a plurality of externally related sensible or logical entities. In the opinion of Schlick, "metaphysics is a sickness of language which creates pseudo problems."[23] Definitions must be operational.

Thus, the neo positivists' fundamental dictum is that things which cannot be measured have no meaning. We should not end this section without remarking that the history of philosophy is replete with great philosophers who were speculative rather than analytic or critical. So, the clarion call by the analytic philosophers especially the logical positivists for philosophy to be restricted to clarification of meaning represents a decisive turning point.

However, analytic philosophers have often been attacked for being too restrictive. A known critic of analytic philosophers even came from the camp of the logical positivists, Friedrich Waismann, one of the founding members of Logical Positivists of the Vienna Circle, attacked his fellow members as being myopic of what philosophy is all about. According to him, philosophy is not a matter of "clarifying thoughts" not of current use of language, not any other of these damned things. What is it? Philosophy is many things, and there is no formula to cover them all. But if I were asked to express in one single word what is its most essential feature, I would unhesitatingly say vision. It has always been felt that philosophy should reveal to us what is hidden.[24]

In spite of the above position of the positivist, C.D. Broad still recognizes the legitimacy of speculative philosophy, and pointed out as we said earlier that its object is to take over the results of the various sciences, to add to them, the results of the religious and ethical experiences of mankind, and then to reflect upon the whole. The hope is that by this means, we may be able to reach some general conclusions as to our position and prospects in it. Broad noted also that philosophy unifies the results of other disciplines because they tend to be parochial in their subject matter. For instance, the empirical sciences (except psychology) deal with objects and their changes, and leave out of the account as far as possible the mind which observes them. Psychology, on the other hand, deals with minds and their processes, and leaves out of account as far as possible the objects that we get to know by means of them. A man who confines himself to either of these subjects is likely therefore to get a very one-sided view of the world.

Furthermore, the pure natural scientist may forget that minds exist and that if it were not for them, he could neither know nor act on physical objects. The pure psychologist is inclined to forget that the main business of minds is to know and act upon objects; that they are most intimately connected with certain portions of matter; and that they have apparently arisen gradually in a world which at one time is nothing but matter. Materialism is the characteristic speculative philosophy of the pure natural scientist, and subjective idealism that of the pure psychologist. To the scientist, subjective idealism seems a fairy tale, and to the psychologist materialism seems sheer lunacy. Both are right in the criticisms, but neither sees the weakness of his own position. The truth is that both doctrines commit the fallacy of oversimplification, and we can hardly avoid falling into some form of this unless at some time we make a resolute attempt to think synoptically of all facts. Our results may be trivial but the process will at least remind us of extreme complexity of the world and teach us to reject any cheap and easy philosophical theory, such as popular materialism or populartheology.[25]

15

LOGIC
The Instrument of Philosophy

Laws of Thought: The Basis of Human Reasoning

Many philosophers agree that the human mind runs and operates essentially on the laws of thought. These laws of thought are the basic axioms which underlie all human reasoning process and discourse. They direct, organize and govern the entire sphere of the mental and conceptual order. Some philosophers claim these laws are innate ideas every human is borne with. While some other philosophers insist the laws are activated by experience. Hence, they attribute them to experience as opposed to something innate or inborne in the mind. These laws of thought include the following:

The Law of Identity

This is called the first law of thought. This law guides and directs the identification processes of the mind. One is able based on this law to identify and recognize any person or thing one has seen before. At a very early age a child can recognize the parents. The important thing is that if the mind loses this category of thought and understanding as result of some diseases like dementia, Alzheimer, psychosis, schizophrenia, brain damage and some serious psychosomatic problems like drug addiction, the mind will no longer be able to identify things consistently. Memory loss will become the order of the day. The Law of identity can be stated as follows: If P is true, then P is true. The following are stylistic variants of the law: If any statement is true, then it is true. If anything is A then it is A. If two things are identical to a third thing, then they are identical to each other. Nothing is bigger than itself. If X and Y are identical, then every property of X is a property of Y, and vice versa. Nothing stands to the left of itself. Everything differs from something.

The Law of Non Contradiction

This law enables the mind to make consistent judgments. It enables the mind to recognize lies and deceits in statements. This law exists in the mind of everyone who has reached the age of reason but in its absence the mind is unable to make consistent judgment. This law is stated as follows: Not both P is true and P is false. The following are stylistic variants of the law: Nothing can be both A and not A. No statement can be both true and false. The same attribute cannot belong to a thing and not belong to the same. Contradictory statements are not at the same time true. It is impossible for the same thing both to be (exist) and not to be (not exist) at the same time. Contradictory judgments cannot both be true.

The Law of Excluded Middle

This law guides the mind in making a distinction between one thing and the other within the horizon of the question of being. A thing is unique because it is differentiated from others. There is no middle course; it is either one or others. The Law states that for any statement, either it or its negation is true. The following are stylistic variants of the law: P is either true or false. Anything must be either A or not A. Of two contradictory judgments, one must be true and the other false. Between two contradictory things there is no middle term, e.g., white or not white, being or non-being, existence or non-existence, etc.

We must note that the principle of excluded middle does not involve contrary terms which express the widest possible difference among classes belonging to the same genus such as white-black, beautiful-ugly, sane-madness, bitter-sweet, love- hatred, joy-sadness, etc. This is because these contrary terms have middle positions. It only involves contradiction in the following instances: white or not white, sweet or not sweet, good or not good, bad or not bad etc. Here, there is no mean between the terms.

These laws of thought are universal in the sense that they are known to exist in every human mind that is sound and have reached the age of maturity and reasoning. The mind has many other profound principles or innate ways of operating. For some philosophers, they are laws of thinking – directives without which meaningful discourse cannot occur and no genuine knowledge gained. The laws of thought guide the basic operations of the mind. These operations of the mind include: simple apprehension, judgment, and reasoning or inference.

Simply Apprehension

Apprehension is the grasping of ideas. It means the understanding of something which could be quick or slow. So, in the simple apprehension of the mind, the intellect perceived a thing or an idea or concept without judgment. For J.J. Sanguineti, it is "the comprehension of the minimum units of thought, such as, the notions of rock or blue."[1] The act of simple apprehension by the human mind could be said to be simpler and more immediate intellectual vision which is normally expressed through words or terms of language. We can regard these as the product of the first encounter of the mind with sense impressions and ideas.

Judgment

Another level in the operations of the mind is judgment. It could be regarded as a higher level since in it the mind affirms or denies something. Judgment has been defined in this context by Aquinas "as the act of the intellect by which it composes and divides by affirming or denying."[2] G.H. Joyce was apt when he sees it "as the act of the intellect by which the mind affirms or denies the attribute of a subject." It is in the act of judgment that propositions are constructed in the intellect. This is why the act of denying or affirming is done with propositions or statements.

Reasoning or Inference

For Sanguineti, "reasoning is the movement of thought through which, from the comparison between some judgments, a new judgment is reached."[3] This is the third level in the operation of the mind. It is in this act of reasoning or inference that the mind moves from the known to the unknown.

THE DYNAMICS OF LOGIC

Logic may be defined as that division of philosophy which reflects upon the nature of thinking itself. It attempts to answer such questions as: What is correct reasoning? What distinguishes a good argument from a bad one? Are there any method to detect fallacies in reasoning and if so what are they? Logic is perhaps the most fundamental division of philosophy. All divisions and branches of philosophy employ thinking; whether this thinking is correct or not, will depend upon whether it accords with the laws of logic. When logic is seen as dealing with the nature of thinking, it is not intended to imply that logic is a branch of psychology. Logic has no interest in some types of thinking, such as: learning, remembering, day-dreaming, supposing, etc. It only deals with the type of thinking called "reasoning." Thus, we can agree with Irving Copi that "all reasoning is thinking but not all thinking is reasoning."[4] Thus, one may "think" of a number between one and ten, as in a parlor game, without doing any "reasoning" about it. There are many mental processes or kinds of thoughts that are different from reasoning. One may remember something or imagine it or regret it, without doing any reasoning about it. Or one may allow his thoughts "drift along" in a daydream.

The logician is not in the least concerned with the dark ways by which the mind arrives at its conclusions during the actual process of reasoning. He is concerned only with the correctness of the completed process. His question is always: does the conclusion reached follow from the premises used or is it assumed? If the premises provide adequate grounds for accepting the conclusion, and if asserting the premises to be true warrants asserting the conclusion to be true then the reasoning is correct, otherwise it is incorrect. So, the distinction between correct and incorrect reasoning is the central problem which logic deals with. The psychologist is concerned with the mental processes of the thinker, the logician's interest is in the reasoning itself; he is not concerned with why people think in certain ways but with formulation of rules that will enable us to test whether a particular reasoning is coherent and consistent.

The characteristics of reasoning include the fact that we produce reason as evidence for certain conclusion we wish to establish. Reasoning is closely connected with inference. The reasons we provide allow us to infer a certain conclusion. The inference could be either deduction or induction.

In another perspective, Stephen Layman sees logic "as the study of methods for evaluating whether the premises of an argument adequately support (or provide good evidence for) its conclusion."[5] This means that Logic is the study of the principles and techniques of distinguishing good arguments from bad arguments. This is the same as saying that logic is the study of the methods and principles used to distinguish good (correct) reasoning from bad (incorrect) reasoning. Most often than not, our reasoning are expressed in sentences. A sentence has been defined in a number of ways by grammarians. They include: A sentence is a word or a group of words that contains a verb and makes sense. A sentence is a group of words which forms a complete thought and expresses one main idea. The idea expressed may be in form of a statement, question or command. A sentence is the largest grammatical unit, consisting of phrases and/or clauses used to express a statement, question, command and emotion.

It must be noted at this juncture that Logic, as a science of good reasoning, does not deal or concern itself with all kinds of sentences. So, it is good and pertinent to distinguish the different kinds of sentences in order to set apart the type of sentence that Logic deals with.

KINDS OF SENTENCES

Interrogative Sentence

This is a sentence that asks a question. It is also simply called a question. Logic does not concern itself with questions that appear in discussions. Questions do not give facts and so are not true or false.

Example: What is your name?

Imperative Sentence

This is a sentence that expresses or gives a command, request or an advice. It is simply called a command. Logic is also not interested in sentences that give command whether in a speech or a write-up because they do not state facts or make claims that can be true or false.

Examples: Don't cheat your friend; be honest and hardworking.

Exclamatory Sentence

This is a sentence that expresses some strong and sudden feeling. It could be feeling of joy, happiness, fear, anxiety and surprise, etc. It is simply called an exclamation and it ends with exclamation mark (!)

Logic is not interested in exclamatory sentences.

Examples: What a bright summer day! Oh my gracious God!

Optative Sentence

This is a sentence that expresses a wish, desire or prayer.

Examples: I wish you success in your exams (a wish); May our friendship last forever (a desire); Thy will be done (a prayer).

Logic is not concerned with optative sentences because they are neither true nor false. Their truth value is indeterminate.

Assertive or declarative Sentence

This is a sentence that asserts or states a fact. It is also called a statement or a proposition. This is the type of sentence that Logic deals with. In Logic, they are used to form arguments, where they make up the premises and the conclusions. In Logic, a statement or a proposition is a sentence that is either true or false.

Examples: All flowers are plants. All men are mortal. Dogs are Mammals. Atlanta is in Georgia.

TYPES OF PROPOSITIONS

Specifically, logic works with the following kinds of propositions: Categorical; Hypothetical, Conditional; Disjunctive; Conjunctive; Negative.

Categorical Propositions

Categorical propositions are unique type of propositions or statements in logic. A categorical proposition is a statement that asserts a relationship between two sets, categories, terms or classes. The relationship they assert can be that of inclusion or exclusion.

FORMS OF CATEGORICAL PROPOSITIONS

There are four standard forms of categorical propositions:

Universal Affirmative Propositions

These propositions assert that all numbers of one class are included within another class.

Example: All artists are good painters.

This is expressed in standard form as: All S are P. Where: S= Subject, and P=Predicate

Universal Negative Propositions

These are propositions that assert that all members of a class are excluded from another class.

Example: No artists are good painters.

This is expressed in standard form as: No S are P

Particular Affirmative Propositions

These propositions assert that at least one member of a class is a member of another class.

Example: Some artists are good painters.

The standard form is: Some S are P

Particular Negative Propositions

These propositions assert that at least one member of a class is excluded from another class.

Some Artists are not good Painters.

The standard form of this proposition is: Some S are not P

In the standard form, we represented the subject term with "S" and the predicate term with "P." Logic presents the standard forms of the four categorical propositions collectively as: A, E, I, and O propositions; where:

A: All S are P; E: No S are P; I: Some S are P; O: Some S are not P

The letters A, E, I, O, are used to represent the four different categorical propositions in logic for easy understanding. And they feature prominently in arguments as premises and conclusions. Categorical propositions are simply true or false.

The Elements of Categorical Proposition

The main elements of a categorical proposition include: the quantifiers, the copula and the terms. The quantifiers are most often seen at the beginning of any categorical proposition. Words that are used as quantifiers include: "all," "no," "some," "none." These quantifiers are used to show the coverage or the extent members of a class are covered in the subject term. The Copula is the verb that links the subject to the predicate of a categorical proposition. Most often they are parts of the verb "to be" or "to have." The terms of a categorical proposition are two, namely: the subject term and predicate term. The subject term is the first class term or the thing being talked about in proposition. The predicate term is the second class term of a categorical proposition and it is that which is asserted of the subject. The predicate tells us something about the subject.

Logic 343

The Distribution of Terms in Categorical Propositions

A term in a categorical proposition is said to be distributed if the term covers all members of a class referred in the term while a term is undistributed if only some members of the class are referred in the term. Let us take a look at each of the categorical propositions and see whether their terms are distributed or undistributed.

In "A" proposition such as "All men are mortal," the subject term "men" is certainly distributed because the term refers to all in the class of men without exception. However, the predicate term "mortal" is not distributed because the term does not refer to all mortal beings.

In the "E" proposition such as "no cat can fly," the subject term "cat" is distributed because all class of cats are excluded from the class of flying things. The predicate term "fly" is distributed because it refers to the class of all flying things.

In "I" proposition such as "some lawyers are senators," both the subject term "lawyers" and the predicate term "senators" are undistributed. This is because only some lawyers and some senators are referred to.

In the "O" proposition like "some leaders are not wise," the subject term "leaders" is not distributed while the predicate term is distributed. The predicate term "wise" is certainly distributed because it refers to all class of wise beings.

Hypothetical or Conditional Propositions

These are hypothetical or conditional statements. They have the structure of "if --- then ---" assertions.
The symbol for hypothetical proposition is a horse shoe (>)
Examples: If it rains then the ground will be wet. (If R > W) If John goes to school then he will be educated. (If S > E)
This type of proposition is false if its antecedent is true and the consequent is false; otherwise it is true.

Disjunctive Propositions

These are statements that contain "either ... or... " structure. The symbol for a disjunctive proposition is a Vee (v)

Examples: Either it is night or it is day (N v D). Either it is good or it is bad (G v B). Either Mary goes to school or she stays at home (S v H).

In Logic, a disjunctive proposition is false if both its disjuncts are false; otherwise it is true.

Conjunctive Propositions

These are statements that have two conjuncts. These conjuncts express two ideas. The symbol for conjunction is a dot (•)

Example: Mr. Bush and Mr. Clinton were former Presidents of United States (B•C).

A conjunctive proposition is true if both its conjuncts are true; otherwise, it is false.

Negative Propositions

Propositions or statements can be negative. The symbol for a negation is a minus sign (-)

Example: If it is true that Bill Clinton was a former President of the United States (C). Then the negation: Bill Clinton was not a former President of the United States (-C) is false. A negation has the opposite truth value of the statement negated.

ARGUMENTS

An argument is a set of statements, one of which is called the conclusion is affirmed on the basis of the others which are called the premises. A statement as contained in the definition means a proposition that is either true or false. From the above definition also, the premises of an argument are the statements on the basis of which the conclusion is affirmed or denied. By implication, the conclusion of the argument is the statement that is affirmed or denied on the basis of the premises. This also means it can be true or false just as premises as propositions can be true or false. Arguments are used in verbal or written discourse to discover and state the truth and to persuade others to believe the conclusion. However, it must be noted that arguments can be sound or unsound. A sound argument is that which provides good reasons for believing that the conclusion is true, while unsound argument fails to support the conclusion adequately with good reasons. Arguments are formally said to be valid or invalid, and these are quite different from their being sound or unsound.

Types of Argument

There are two types of arguments in logic, namely: Deduction and Induction.

Deductive Argument

Although every argument involves the claim that its premises provide some grounds for the truth of its conclusions, only a deductive argument involves the claim that its premises provide conclusive grounds. Deductive arguments move from general statements to particular conclusion. In this, we draw conclusion from one or more premises. In the assessment of deductive arguments, the technical terms "valid" and "invalid" are used in place of "correct" and "incorrect." A valid argument has this essential feature: It is impossible for its conclusion to be false while its premises are true. On the other hand, an invalid argument is one such that it is possible for its conclusion to be false while its premises are true.

Specifically, deductive arguments are valid under the following forms:

It is possible to have a valid deductive argument, all of whose premises and conclusion are in fact true, for example: all mammals are mortal; all cats are mammals; therefore, all cats are mortals.

A valid argument can also have false premises and a true conclusion for instance: all Mexicans are Americans; Bill Clinton is a Mexican; therefore, Bill Clinton is an American.

It is also possible to have a valid argument with false premises and a false conclusion, for instance: all Italians are Asians; all Asians are Chinese; therefore, all Italians are Chinese.

It must be noted that it is not possible to have a valid argument with true premises and a false conclusion. Deductive arguments are invalid under the following forms:

It is possible to have an invalid argument with true premises and a true conclusion, for instance: all British are Europeans; all English are Europeans; therefore all English are British.

Again, it is possible to have an invalid argument with at least one false premise and a false conclusion; for example: If Murdoch is the owner of Wall Street Journal then he is a renowned publisher; Murdoch is not the owner of Wall Street Journal; therefore, he is not a renowned publisher.

It is also possible to have an invalid argument with true premises and a false conclusion, for instance: If Mandela was a former President, then he is well known in South African; he was a former president; therefore he was not well known in SouthAfrican. The guide that helps in determining the validity or invalidity of any deductive argument is that if an argument is certified valid, any other argument having that form will be valid. Likewise, if an argument is certified invalid, any other argument having the same form will be invalid. In essence, it means that it is the form of an argument that determines its validity or invalidity. Validity is not determined by the truth value of the propositions that make up the argument.

Deductively Sound and Unsound Argument

For Layman, "validity matters because true premises by themselves do not make good arguments."[6] But we obviously want our arguments to have true premises. A deductively sound argument has two essential features: it is valid, and all its premises are true. A deductively sound argument cannot have a false conclusion. Because a sound argument is valid and has only true premises, it must have a true conclusion.

Examples:

All men are mortal. Socrates is a man. So, Socrates is mortal.

A deductively unsound argument falls into one of the following three categories:

It is valid but has at least one false premise;

It is invalid but all its premises are true;

It is invalid and has at least one false premise.

These categories mean that a deductively unsound argument is one that is invalid or has at least one false premise.

Example:

All reptiles are animals. Some small elephants are not animals. So, some small elephants are not reptiles.

Inductive Argument

This type of argument moves from particular statement to general conclusion. It proceeds from the known to the unknown. An inductive argument involves the claim, not that its premises give conclusive grounds for the truth of its conclusion, but only that they provide some grounds for it. Inductive arguments are neither "valid" nor "invalid" in the sense in which those terms are applied to deductive argument. Inductive arguments concern tests for strength and weakness, and as such may be evaluated as strong or weak according to the degree of likelihood or probability which their premises confer upon their conclusions. One of the essential features of a strong inductive argument is: it is unlikely (though possible) that its conclusion is false while its premises are true. On the other hand, for a weak inductive argument, it is not likely that its premises are true while its conclusion is true.

There are some factors that can make inductive arguments strong. They include the following:

Appeal to Authority

An inductive argument can be made strong by appealing to legitimate authorities in the field in question. We appeal to authority by quoting them or making reference to their expert or professional opinion on a fact.

Example:

X is a reliable authority on Y. X seriously supports Y.

Therefore Y

Appeal to Analogy

This is an inductive argument that reaches a conclusion through analogy. The argument can be made strong by giving a comparative analysis of instances that are similar to the fact in question. It is usually said if it looks like duck, swims like a duck and quacks like duck, then it is probably a duck.

Example:

B behaves like C in certain conditions, B has property A; So, C has property A also.

Appeal to Enumeration

This involves the use of frequency distribution of past event to predict the probability of occurrence of the event in the future. By giving a series of instances of a fact we make inductive argument strong.

Example: Brazilian National Football team defeated the English National Football team all the time they met in their matches in 1970, 1974, 1980, 1985, 1990, 1995, 2000, 2004, 2008, 2012. So, the Brazilian team will likely defeat English team in 2016. This also involves the use of sampling method to predict an event or estimate population characteristics.

Inductively Sound and Unsound Arguments

An inductively sound argument is one that is strong, and all its premises are true.

Example:

The sun has risen from the east and has set in the west for more one million years. So, the sun will rise from the east and set in the west tomorrow.

An inductively unsound argument is one that is either weak or strong with at least one false premise. An example of an inductively unsound argument that is weak and with at least one false premise is:

More than 50 percent of Americans are older than 90 years. President Obama is an American. Therefore, President Obama is older than 90 years.

An example of an inductively unsound argument that is strong and with at least one false premise is:

In 2001 there were weapons of mass destruction in: Liberia, Israel, Syria, North Korea, Pakistan, India and Iran. Therefore, in 2001 there are weapons of mass destruction in Iraq.

It is unsound because we know that Liberia does not have weapons of mass destruction but it is strong because Iraqi is related in some ways to those of them that have weapons of mass destruction.

ARGUMENT FORMS

Argument form is the pattern of reasoning in an argument. Knowing the form is necessary for understanding and inferring the validity and invalidity of an argument. We must remember that the validity of an argument is guaranteed by its form and does not depend on its content. And what makes the arguments "formal" is that they have certain fixed patterns or structures.

Examples of Valid Argument Forms

Any argument that has the following form is valid.

All A are B; All B are C; Therefore, All A are C.

All A are B; Some C are B; Therefore, some C are not A.

All A are B; All C are B; Therefore, all A are C.

All A are B; Some B are not C; Therefore, Some C are not A.

No A are B; All B are C; Therefore, No A are C.

The letters or alphabets in the above argument forms represent "terms," "categories" or "classes" of things, plants, animals, ideas or statements. Hence, they could appropriately be substituted with suitable terms. For instance, the alphabets in the first example under the argument forms could be replaced with the suitable terms: Thus

All A are B, All B are C. Therefore, all A are C
All English are British. All British are Europeans. Therefore, all English are Europeans.

SYLLOGISM

Syllogism comes from a Greek word meaning "to reason together" or to put statements together with a pattern of reasoning. So, wherever there are propositions in which the first and second propositions are premises and the reason for the third proposition which is the conclusion is taken or follows from the two premises, we say the argument is syllogistic.

Examples:

All those who studied in Oxford are intelligent. Ben studied in Oxford. So, Ben is an intelligent man.

Forms of Syllogism

There are different forms of syllogism in logic. We shall consider briefly some of them.

Categorical Syllogism

This is an argument that has three propositions, two of which are premises while the third proposition is the conclusion. The inference in a categorical syllogism is mediate, in the sense that there is only one premise between the first premise and the conclusion.

Example:

All men are rational. Clinton is a man. Clinton is rational.

Division of Terms in Categorical Syllogism

Terms are mainly divided into three, namely: the major term, the minor term and middle term. A categorical syllogism contains three premises as in the above example, the first premise is the major premise, the second is the minor premise and the third is the conclusion. The major term is the predicate of the conclusion and it appears in the major premise, e.g., "rational" in the above argument. The minor term is the subject of the conclusion and it appears in the minor premise, e.g. "Clinton" in the above categorical syllogism. The middle term is the term that appears both in the major premise and minor premise, e.g., "man" in the above argument.

The General Rules for Determining the Validity of Categorical Syllogisms

These are rules that can assist one in verifying whether a categorical syllogism is valid or invalid. They include:

• Every valid categorical syllogism must contain only three categorical propositions.

• Every valid categorical syllogism must contain three terms each of which occurs only twice (but not in the same proposition) and must bear the same meaning throughout the course of the argument.

• If a term is distributed in the conclusion, then it must be distributed in the premise. This means the term must have the same extension both in the premise and in the conclusion. The middle term must be distributed at least once in the premises.

• If the conclusion of a valid categorical syllogism is negative, then one and only one premise must be negative.

• If both the premises are affirmative, then the conclusion must be affirmative. Every valid categorical syllogism must have at least an affirmative premise (A or I proposition)

• Every valid categorical Syllogism with a particular premise (I or O proposition) must have a particular conclusion.

• Every valid categorical syllogism must have a universal premise (A or E proposition) No conclusion can be drawn from two particular premises.

• In any case where the Venn diagram is used to determine the validity of a categorical syllogism which contains a universal premise and a particular premise, the extension of the universal premise must be inserted first regardless of their order in the premise.

Hypothetical Syllogism

This is an argument that involves only hypothetical or conditional statements. It has the "If... then..." statements.

Example:

If A, then B; If B, then C; If A, then C.
The above example can simply be read as follows: If there is A, then there is B, If there is B, then there is C; Therefore, If there is A, then there is C

Disjunctive Syllogism

This is an argument that contains "either ... or" statements.

Example:
Either A or B; Not A; Therefore, B.
Under the disjunctive syllogism, we have the inclusive sense in which "either ... or" means "both." Then there is also the exclusive sense in which "either ... or" means "not both."

OTHER FORMS OF INFERENCES

In logic, there are other valid forms of inferences. They include the following:

Modus Ponens

This means "a way of affirming" in an argument. It is a rule of inference in propositional logic that if a conditional statement (if p then q) is accepted and the antecedent (p) holds then the consequent (q) may be inferred. Note, here the consequent of the first premise is affirmed, one of the key premises is a conditional, and the conclusion cannot be false while its premises are true. The form runs like this:

If A, then B. There is A. Therefore, B.

Example:

If it rains then the ground will be wet. It rains. Therefore, the ground is wet.

Modus Tollens

This means "a way of denying" in an argument. It is a rule of inference in propositional logic that "if the conditional statement (if p then q) is accepted, and the consequent does not hold (–q) then the negation of the antecedent (–p) can be inferred. Note: the consequent of the first premise is denied. The argument form is:

If A, then B
Not B
Therefore, not A

Example:

If you go to school then you will be educated. You are not educated; Therefore, you did not go to school

Constructive Dilemma

This is an argument based on necessity. Here, the reasoning follows necessarily. It is a valid rule of inference in propositional logic that states if (p) implies (q) and (r) implies (s) and either (p) or (r) is true, then (q) or (s) has to be true. In other words, if two conditionals are true and at least one of their antecedents is, then at least one of their consequent must be. This is seen in a situation where one reasons or argues with two opposing assertions. Note: this argument form combines conditional statement with disjunctive statements. In the argument, the first two premises are conditional statements, the third premise is the disjunction of the antecedents of the conditional statements in the first premise and second premise, the conclusion is the disjunction of the consequents of the two conditional statements in the first premise.
The argument goes like this: If A, then C; If B, then D; Either A or B
Therefore, either C or D

The form is presented this way: If (P>q) • (R>S)
P v R
Therefore, q v S

Example 1:

Consider this example taken from the Theodicy of William Pepperell Montague (1873-1953) in his work, *"Belief Unbound,"* which deals on the problem of evil vis-à- vis the existence of a good God.

If God cannot prevent suffering, then God is not omnipotent. If God does not want to prevent suffering, then God is not perfectly good. But either God cannot prevent suffering or God does not want to prevent suffering. Therefore, either God is not perfectly good or God is not omnipotent.[7]

Scholars hold that the above argument even through valid in its form, may not actually be sound reasoning. The statements that make it up may not be true since God's idea of what is good, what is evil and what is suffering may differ from man's conceptions of these concepts. If any of the statements is found to be false, then the argument is not sound in spite of its validity.

Example 2

If you go to school then you will be educated; If you stay at home, then you will be illiterate; Either you go to school or you stay at home. Therefore, either you are educated or you are illiterate.

Destructive Dilemma

This is also an argument based on necessity. It is a valid form of reasoning in propositional logic and it states that if (p) implies (q) and (r) implies (s) and either (q) is false or (s) is false then either
(p) or (r) must be false. In other words, if two conditionals are true, but one of their consequents is false, then one of their antecedents has to be false. Note: this form of argument combines the conditional statements with disjunctive statements. The first of these arguments is a conjunction of two conditional statements. The second premise consists of a disjunction of the negation of the consequents of the first premise. And the conclusion is made up of the disjunction of the negations of the antecedents of the two conditional statements in the first premise.

The form of the arguments is: If (P>q) • (R >S)
-q v –S
Therefore, -P v –R

Example:

If I learn a trade (p) then I can make money (q) and if I remain at home idle (R), then I will be poor (S)
Either I do not make money or I will not be poor; Therefore, either I do not learn a trade or I will not remain at home idle.

The reasoning in destructive dilemma appears awkward but it is still a valid form of reasoning in logic.

INVALID FORMS OF ARGUMENTS

There are many forms which the above arguments can take and they become invalid. Consider the following instances:

Denying the Antecedent

In conditional argument if the antecedent is denied, it renders the argument invalid.

Example:

If A, then B,
Not A,
Therefore, not B

Affirming the Consequent

In conditional argument forms when the consequent is affirmed, the argument is rendered invalid.

Example:

If A, then B,

There is B,
Therefore, A

THE RULES OF LOGIC

Thus, in both propositional logic and predicate logic when the rules of Logic are contravened an argument is rendered invalid. Some of these rules we have already considered above, while many of these rules are beyond the scope of this work. There are two divisions of the rules of Logic. We have the inferential or implicational rules and the replacement or equivalent rules. The inferential rules include the following:

Modus Ponens (MP) Rule; Modus Tollens (MT) Rule; Hypothetical Syllogism (HS) Rule; Disjunctive Syllogism (DS) Rule; Constructive Dilemma (CD) Rule; Destructive Dilemma (DD) Rule; Simplification (SIMPLI) Rule; Conjunction (CONJ) Rule; Addition (ADD) Rule.[8]

There are also equivalence rules that must be followed for arguments to be valid. They are also called replacement rules. They include:

Double Negation (DN) Rule; De Morgan's Theorem (DMT); Rule of Commutation (COM); Association (ASS) Rule; Distribution (DIST) Rule; Reductio Ad Absurdum(RAA); Rule of Tautology (TAUT) or Redundancy (RE) Rule; Transportation (TRANS) Rule; Material Implication (MI) Rule; Exportation (EXP) Rule; Assumption (ASSUME); Conditional Proof (CP) [9]

These rules have been treated fully in my other work entitled, *Dynamics of Logic and Scientific Reasoning*. Again, proving validity using things like Square of Opposition, Venn Diagram, Truth Tables, and Conditional Proofs, etc. is beyond the scope of this work. However, we shall treat in the next chapter, some of the fallacies that result from contravening some of the above rules of logic.

16

FALLACIES IN LOGIC
The Errors of the Human Mind

The word fallacy has been given different meanings by different authorities. Some refer to fallacies as typical mistakes which we make in the use of everyday language. Still, some refer to them as false statements, erroneous beliefs or mental confusion. Many fallacies appear persuasive and may lead some people to false conclusion. Essentially, fallacies are violation of logical principles (rules) disguised under a show of validity.

For Sydney Herbert Mellon, there are some principles governing the formation of concept of judgment and of inference. According to him, a fallacy is a violation of some rules or regulative principles of logical thought.[1] Fallacies are therefore classified according to the logical principles violated in a given argument. In his view, it is only when an argument did not fall in line with the principles or rules which govern the method through which a judgment is made that it could be said to be fallacious. It therefore implies that when a conclusion of an argument is not in line with the given premises, the truth or falsity of such premises notwithstanding, such argument according to Mellon is a fallacious argument.

To Roland Munson, the word "fallacy" simply refers to any kind of argument that rests on mistake. He writes that, "All arguments that are invalid or that have premises that do not adequately support their conclusion are fallacies."[2] There are so many ways in which an argument can go wrong, that is, there are innumerable kinds of bad arguments. But some occur more frequently than the others; some are more tempting to believe. Munson toed the same line with Mellon by holding that a fallacy is committed when the conclusion of an argument did not follow from given premises. Both thinkers therefore agree that an invalid argument is a fallacious argument.

In a write up on fallacies, Daniel Okezie asserts that the fallacy of any argument does not mean its falsity; rather it depicts the inconsistency of the premises of such argument.[3] Other definitions of fallacies which one could find interesting include that by Robert Baum. For him, fallacy is a synonym for bad argument. He went further to say that "although some arguments are blatantly fallacious, many are more deceptive and can be difficult to recognize."[4] As a result, fallacies are used knowingly or unknowingly by writers, advertisers, politicians, lawyers, administrators, preachers, and all those whose goal is to persuade an audience to accept their conclusion which can be recognized as such with little or no reliance on the method of formal logic.

For Kahane Howard, fallacious arguments are arguments that are not cogent, which means arguments that are either not valid, contains unwarranted premises or ignores known or available relevant information.[5] Consider this example: Anyone who shakes hands with the Pope will have good luck. Teddy shook hands with the Pope. Therefore, Teddy will have good luck. According to Howard, such arguments though valid, has unwarranted premises. It is fallacious because it fails to use all relevant information. The Pope in the argument can be any pope like that of a secret cult in Mexico and not the Roman Catholic Pope in Vatican City. Consider another example: Any good President gets a second term. George Bush got a second term. Therefore, George Bush was a good President.

Here, the argument like the previous is valid but fallacious. This is based on the fact that it omitted relevant information which is that many presidents have got a second term by rigging elections or buying up votes with money or using the power incumbency to carry out dubious manipulation of election process and results. Accordingly, Howard holds that fallacies can be classified according to what makes such argument fallacious (logical factors) or according to what leads us to commit such fallacies (psychological factors). If we classify according to logical factors, we get three broad fallacy classes; where invalid inference, unwarranted premises and suppressed evidence were used as the criteria for labeling an argument fallacious. Argument can also be classified as fallacious base on the psychological factors that led us to accept bad argument. They include: Strong desire to believe certain ideas leading to self-deception and wishful thinking; Strong emotion (in particular conflicting emotions) or emotional confusion; Limitations on our reasoning ability or rational limitation.

The first of these psychological classes are made up of many species of defense mechanism that we use in everyday discussions. The second of the classes includes strong negative emotions like fear, hatred, anger, lust or positive emotions like love, joy, confidence and pleasure. But the third class which is rational limitation can properly be divided into three species, namely *"complexity,"* where the mind is unable to handle a mass of information or to grasp relevant information, and *"similarity,"* where we become confused by the similarity of a fallacious reasoning process to a legitimate one; and *"false principle,"* where we accept as genuine a fallacious principle of reasoning.

Finally, Robert Rafalko asserts that fallacy is an "error in reasoning."[6] Hence, he divided fallacy into formal and informal fallacies. And it is under this broad division we shall consider the different types of fallacies.

Classification of Fallacies

In the broad sense, fallacies in Logic are divided into two major classifications, the formal and informal fallacies.

FORMAL FALLACIES
Formal fallacies are committed when an argument that appears plausible actually violates a formal rule of inference. They occur as a result of errors or mistakes in the process of drawing inference in logic. They are known as deductive fallacies because they result from different kinds of invalid argument forms.

Formal fallacies include:

Fallacy of Special Pleading

The fallacy of special pleading is a distinctive type of formal inconsistency that occurs if and when two statements, mutually contradictory are advanced by the speaker or writer. It therefore occurs whenever one argues for a special exemption from inconsistency on the basis of one's own interest or advantage. It is a kind of appeal to superstition. Though logical contradiction baffle people, many people sometimes are fooled into believing such statements to be plausible. Politicians and lawyers mostly apply this argument technique.

Example:

Perhaps we believe that "a stitch in time saves nine" and we use such proverb whenever we want to do a job right on the spot. Other times, we may feel a bit like procrastinating, then we may involve another proverb "haste make waste" or the Latin proverb *"festina lente"* meaning "make haste slowly." Note that there is nothing formally inconsistent about the three proverbs, but using one to do whatever it is you want to do now and the other to put off anything you want to leave off until tomorrow, may constitute a case of special pleading. Special pleading is therefore "an inconsistency of special interest." One adopts a principle of action and follows through on it when it suits him and falls down on the job when it does not suit him.

Fallacy of Affirming the Consequent

The fallacy of affirming the consequent occurs whenever an argument takes the following form; given any two desirable statements (P and Q), the fallacy of affirming the consequent occurs, if we assert that:

If P then Q; There is Q; Therefore, P
Consider for example this line of thought: (P) If it rains then the ground will be wet (Q). The ground is wet (Q). Therefore, it rained (P)

To argue that whenever the ground is wet it means it has rained is to reason fallaciously. This is because there are other factors that could make the ground wet like snow, heavy dew and water sprinklers. On the other hand, whenever it rains the ground must be wet. It is unheard of that it rained and the ground was never wet.

Fallacy of Denying theAntecedent

This fallacy as we noted in the last chapter, is committed if one asserts that:
If P then Q; Not P; Therefore Q (or not Q)
Consider this reasoning pattern: If you are a banker, then you must be dressing well. You are obviously not a banker. Therefore, you are sure not to be dressing well.

Fallacy of Unequal Negation

Unequal negation is the third way syllogism can exhibit faulty reasoning. It violates the rule that states that the number of negative premises must be equal to the number of negative statements in the conclusion.

Example:

No snow is hot. No rice is snow. So, no rice is hot.
The above argument violates the rule that both premises in an argument cannot be negative. Because of this, the conclusion of the above argument is absurd.

Fallacy of Affirming a Disjunct

This fallacy is committed when given two discrete statements (p or q) one goes ahead to affirm a disjunct as follows: Either p or q Therefore, P This fallacy is called "the fallacy of the Christmas tree light." Anyone who has ever tried testing Christmas tree lights wired in series will know why the above argument is fallacious. When such lights are in series, if anyone of them is burned out, none of the bulbs will light. Suppose you suspect that it is the red bulb at the string, you test the bulb and it is burned out. You might be making a serious mistake if you went ahead and strung the wires over the tree, because there is a very good chance that at least one other has burned out. The argument form goes like this: "Either the red (R) or the green (G) or the black (B) or the yellow (Y) bulbs burned out." You know after testing that R is burned out. It is fallacious however to conclude that no other bulb is defective. Or that any other bulb is. Thus either "R" or "G" or "B" or "Y" is burned out, "R" is burned out, but no other conclusion necessarily follows.

Fallacy of Mal-distributed Middle

This fallacy is also called fallacy of excluded middle or undistributed middle. This fallacy violates the rule that the middle term in a valid categorical syllogism must be distributed at least once in the premises. It must not appear in the conclusion. Usually, the middle term is distributed in the major premise in order to be included in the minor premise.

Example:

Some scientists are Germans. Willy is a scientist. Therefore, Willy is a German.
Note that the middle term "scientists" is not distributed in the major premise and so the argument is invalid. It should be "all scientists" if not it is fallacious.

Fallacy of Improper Conversion

The fallacy of improper conversion is committed when a proposition is converted without due consideration of the possible exceptions in the subject matter of the statement. Bear in mind that the rule of conversion ensures that only E and I propositions are to be converted. One can commit the fallacy of improper conversion if one tries to convert A and O propositions. The proposition that is converted is called the convertend while the result is known as the converse.

Examples:

All bankers are rich men - convertend. All rich men are bankers - converse. All wise men are educated men - convertend. All educated men are wise men - converse.

Fallacy of Fourth Term

This fallacy involves a violation of the structure of which categorical syllogism is made of. Usually, a categorical syllogism contains three terms: the major term; minor term; and middle term. The three terms appear twice in the two premises and the conclusion. This fallacy often occurs when one suddenly introduces a fourth term into an argument in order to change the topic of discussion or divert attention from an issue in the argument.

Example:

All men are mortal. Samson is a man. Therefore, Samson is strong.
The four terms in the above argument are "men," "mortal," "Samson" and "strong." Note that only "men" and "Samson" occurred twice while the terms "mortal" and "strong" occurred once with the term "strong" as the fourth term. This is a distortion in the formal structure of categorical syllogism.

The Existential Fallacy

This fallacy violates one of the rules of logical reasoning which states that a conclusion with I or O propositions should not be drawn from premises with only A or E universal propositions. As we stated earlier in this work, categorical syllogism with particular premises (I or O) should have a particular conclusion.

Example:

All trees are plants.
All plants are living things.
So, some trees are living things.

Fallacy of Illicit Major Term

It is a rule in logic that a major term in a valid categorical syllogism must be distributed in a premise if it is distributed in the conclusion. Any reasoning that goes contrary to this rule commits the fallacy of illicitness.

Example:

All artists are painters.
All artists are successful men.
So, no successful men are painters.
In above argument, "painters" which is the major term in the argument is distributed in the conclusion but it is not distributed in the premise.

Fallacy of Illicit Minor Term

This fallacy is committed when a minor term in a categorical syllogism is distributed in the conclusion but not distributed in the premise. Any argument or reasoning that goes contrary to this rule commits the fallacy of illicitness.

Example:

All senators are wise. Some lawyers are senators. Therefore, no lawyers are wise.
In the above argument, the minor term is lawyers. It is distributed in the conclusion but it is not distributed in premise.

Fallacy of Excluded Premise

It is also formal rule in logic that two premises of a categorical syllogism should not all be negative propositions. In other words, the two premises should not all be E or O propositions. Consequently, any categorical syllogism that has two negative premises commits a fallacy of excluded premise.

Example:

No teachers are poor men.
Some poor men are not business men. Therefore, no teachers are businessmen.

FALLACIES INVOLVING IMPROPER INFERENCES

A number of fallacies result from wrong conclusion. They include:

The Fallacy of drawing Affirmative Conclusion from Negative Premises

It is an error in formal reasoning to infer affirmative conclusions (A or I) where we have negative premise(s). The rule is: if the conclusion is affirmative (A or I) the argument must have two affirmative premises (A or I).

Example:

All lawyers are liars. Some senators are not lawyers. Therefore, some senators are liars.

The Fallacy of drawing Negative Conclusion from Affirmative Premises

This fallacy is committed when a negative conclusion (E or O) is drawn from affirmative premises (A or I). This fallacy violates the rule which says that "if the conclusion is negative, one and only one premise must be negative."

Example:

All teachers are traders. Some teachers are tourists. Therefore, some traders are not tourists.

Fallacy of Drawing Conclusion from two Particular Premises

This fallacy is committed when two particular premises are used to draw a conclusion in a syllogistic argument.

Example:

Some teachers are traders. Some traders are painters. Therefore, all teachers are painters.

Fallacies that violate the Law of Contradiction

The law of contradiction states that contradictory judgments cannot both be true. Thus, if statements are made to the effect that something is the case and at the same time deny that the same thing is the case, a fallacy has occurred. For example, "John is a man," "John is not a man" cannot both be true.

Fallacy of Accident Correlation

This fallacy is committed when we wrongly take correlational causes as relational causes. This happens when one picks out one cause among other possible causes as the cause of an event. For example, if we say that the environment is responsible for the juvenile delinquency in youths and at the same we ignore the problem of genetics, nurture and other variables that are correlational or that can be associated with juvenile delinquency.

INFORMAL FALLACIES

Informal fallacies are those committed as a result of attempts to divert the attention of the audience in a subtle manner from the subject matter of the argument. This diversion of attention from the subject matter is possible due to one psychological lapse or the other. It may be due to the fact that the arguer is either careless or not sufficiently careful in focusing attention on the relationship between the premises and the conclusion of the argument. Informal fallacies are divided into:

Fallacies of Relevance (Material Fallacies)

Fallacies of Ambiguity (Linguistic Fallacies)

Let us consider each of them in detail with their types.

FALLACIES OF RELEVANCE (MATERIAL FALLACIES)

Fallacies of relevance refer to fallacies that are committed when a conclusion in an argument is not relevant to or did not follow from the premises of the argument. In otherwords, the fallacy have irrelevant conclusion when related to their premises. The premises of such fallacies are usually not sufficiently relevant to logically imply their conclusion. Some logicians refer to them as fallacies of irrelevance. Sometimes in arguments, the arguer gets carried away and may reach a conclusion establishing something other than what he set out to establish in such arguments. Sometimes, the irrelevant nature of such argument may be so glaring that anybody can notice it. At times, the irrelevance may be subtle that unless one is trained in the field of logic, he may not be able to detect such fallacies in arguments. These fallacies can be used purposely by the presenter to deceive the audience. We shall consider the subdivision of this fallacy below.

Fallacy of Argumentum Ad Hominem (Argument Directed to the Man)

The fallacy of argumentum ad hominem occurs in an argument when we focus attention not on the real issue or subject matter under discussion but on the person, that is, our opponent in the argument or discussion. In this way, we might persuade the audience to accept our opinion or position in the argument by trying to discredit our opponent, who holds a contrary position, through remarks directed at his person rather than the issue of discussion. Aspersions are cast on the person for holding an opinion or expressing a view. There are two kinds of this fallacy:

Fallacy of Abusive Argumentum Ad Hominem

This is a direct attack on the person of the opponent. This is a situation where we try to discredit the position of an opponent by directly attacking his person. This is usually achieved by painting a negative picture of the person. When we include negative or abusive comments about a person as an extra premise, and hope that such extra premise will turn away the person from his position or persuade him to accept our position. This means in such arguments, instead of trying to disprove the truth of what is asserted in our opponent's position; we question or attack the integrity of person who made the assertion as an attempt to discourage him from expressing the view in question or for the audience to see him in a bad light.

Example:

Obasanjo's government in Nigeria was corrupt and untrustworthy because he was an ex-convict. And the above argument deviated from the line of argument because, instead of giving cogent reasons why Obasanjo's government was corrupt and untrustworthy, Obasanjo's personal life was rather attacked by his opponent; hence the arguer falls into the fallacy of argumentum ad hominem (abusive). The reason is that it may be true that Obasanjo was an ex-convict, but this does not have anything to do with the corruption and trustworthiness of his government. We must note that the personal character of a man is logically irrelevant to the truth or falsehood of what he says or the correctness or incorrectness of his argument. To argue that a book, a proposal or an assertion is bad or false because it is written by a communist (or by an atheist or by a Muslim or by a hippie or by a whore) is to argue fallaciously and to be guilty of committing an argumentum ad hominem. We know that the most wicked or immoral or irreligious of all men sometimes tell the truth or argue correctly. And the best of humans sometimes lie – "even angels do eat beans at times."

Fallacy of Circumstantial Argumentum Ad Hominem

This fallacy is committed in an argument, when we appeal to an opponent's special circumstance while trying to defend a position. The opponent's special circumstance could be religious, political, social, economic, health and so on. In other words, one may ignore the question of whether his own contention is true or false, and seek instead to prove that his opponent ought to accept it because of the opponent's special circumstances. Thus, if one's opponent is a clergyman, one may argue that a certain contention must be accepted because its denial is incompatible with the scriptures.

Example 1:

Mr. Michael: I support the idea that a man whose wife is confirmed HIV positive should use condoms not as a contraceptive but as a means to prevent being HIV positive and to prevent his death.

Mr. Sunday: Your argument is interesting, but I am surprised that this position is taken by a staunch and devout Catholic-Christian like you!

In the above argument, one can notice that Mr. Sunday attempts to make Mr. Michael drop his strong argument on the AIDS prevention on the basis of Catholic doctrine against contraceptives as unnatural way of family planning.

Example 2:

Mrs. Jones: I do not support any increase in the minimum wage of workers by federal and state governments without measures to curb inflation and increase production output in the manufacturing and agricultural sectors to strengthen the value of the dollar.

Mrs. Pauline: Your argument is interesting but I'm surprised that this position is taken by a poorly paid worker like you!

Also, we have to note that the reference made to the economic status of Mrs. Jones by Mrs. Pauline in the above argument is irrelevant. But Mrs. Jones might be wrongly persuaded psychologically to drop his position in the argument. Consequently Mrs. Pauline has used the fallacy of argumentation ad hominem (Circumstantial) to make Mrs. Jones drop her position.

Fallacy of Argumentum Ad Populum (Appeal to Popular Sentiment)

This fallacy occurs when one makes an appeal to popular sentiment in the way that is irrelevant to the issue being discussed. Here, the popular sentiment is used to arouse the emotions and enthusiasms of the multitude of listeners, rather than appealing to relevant and reasonable facts. This is often the method of some politicians, propagandists, advertisers and pastors, etc. Faced at times with the task of mobilizing public interest for or against a particular course, the propagandist will avoid the laborious process of collecting and presenting evidence and rational argument by using the short-cut methods of the *argumentum ad populum*. Where there is proposal for a change of political order and governmental leadership, and if he is against it, he is suspicious of "sinister innovations" or "hidden agenda," and he praises the wisdom of the "existing order" or "continuity and experience." But if he is for it, he will be for "progress" and "a new world order," or "new breed politicians" and he will be opposed to antiquated and anachronistic leadership or wicked conservatism or recycling of old politicians and sees it as sawing the sawdust which is already sawed, a journey in futility and a road to nowhere. Here, we see the use of insidious terms with no rational attempt made to argue for them or to justify their application.

Example:

African-American Presidency: An African-American presidential candidate of the Republican Party, in one of his political campaigns to win his people's vote, asked his people to vote for him on the grounds that he is their son and that his victory will be the victory of his people and the race. In the above argument, the African-American politician, instead of making his distinctive qualities clear to his people, he appeals to racial prejudice and through this sentiment, tries to make them realize that he is their son, and therefore they should vote for him. In the process, he neglects other relevant factors which could earn him their votes. Some politicians have also used religion in this way, too.

Fallacy of Argumentum Ad Baculum (Appeal to Force or Threat)

This fallacy is committed when one appeals to force or the threat of force to cause acceptance of a conclusion. In other words, the person uses intimidation and coercion as a way to force his opponent to accept a position without properly addressing the issue or fact of the matter. It is usually resorted to only when evidence or rational arguments have failed to achieve the desired purpose. Here, the arguer avoids a relevant logical relationship between the premise of an argument and its conclusion by introducing an element of threat in an extra premise in the argument.

The *argumentum ad baculum* is epitomized in the saying "might makes right." The use and threat of "strong-arm" methods to instill fear and coerce political opponents provide contemporary examples of this fallacy. The lobbyist uses the *argumentum ad baculum* when he reminds a representative in the congress that he (lobbyist) is a political Godfather and a molder of public opinion, and as such represents so many thousands of voters in the representative's constituency or so many potential contributors to campaign funds, and that he could deny the congressman access to these important people.

Example:

The labor unions often threaten that they will use all in their power including numerical strength and money to recall a governor or a congressman who opposes collective bargaining. Here, instead of giving the merits of collective bargaining and why a governor and the congressmen should not annul collective bargaining in the state, the unions use threat of sack to make the governors and congressmen think twice about it. Here, the labor union is using the fallacy of *argumentum ad baculum* to achieve its motives or preserve an interest.

Fallacy of Argumentum Ad Verecundiam (Appeal to Authority)

This fallacy is committed when one makes an appeal to wrong experts or inappropriate authorities in a field as the major reason why a position should be accepted or rejected. By this, the arguer appeals to the feeling of respect people have for the famous to win assent to a conclusion. An appeal to authority is fallacious when the person appealed to is not truly an authority on the subject under consideration. This is an illicit appeal to authority or pseudo authority. An appeal to authority is not fallacious if the reference is to an admitted authority in the social field of his competence where he is also an expert. If students are disputing over some questions of physics and appeal to the testimony of Albert Einstein on the matter, that testimony is very relevant. Although it does not prove the point, it certainly tends to support it. But when an authority appealed to for testimony is outside the field under consideration, the appeal falls into this fallacy. There are two ways we may appeal to authority fallaciously:

when the person considered is not an authority; when the person has some, but not sufficient knowledge to serve as an authority, an expert or a professional on the matter under discussion.

Example:

Robert Rafalko: Wole Soyinka's remark that Indian and African Literature pursue the same moral goals of communal spirit and brotherhood settles this debate on the moral relationship between Indian and African Literature.[7] In view of the fact that Soyinka is the African winner of the Nobel Laureate for Literature, he is considered an expert or professional in the field of literature. But the above example could be a fallacy because of two major reasons:

If Soyinka has not studied Indian Literature; If Soyinka has not studied the ethical dimension of African Literature. Within the confines of these two reasons, Soyinka could be a false authority, his expertise in literature notwithstanding.

Fallacy of Argumentum Ad Misericordiam (Appeal to Pity)

This is committed when pity is appealed to for the sake of getting a conclusion accepted. The sympathy of the listeners is appealed to in the way that is irrelevant to the issue. The appeal is more concerned with sentiment and emotions rather than reason. Mostly used in courts, a lawyer may argue that a convict should be pardoned because he is the bread-winner of a family with ten children. This is fallacious.

Example:

Your lordship, sending my client to prison will not help anybody, neither the state nor this honorable court would benefit, rather his family will be subjected to untold hardship and avoidable difficulty if he is sent to prison. He would say, "your Lordship, remember it is not fair to extend the punishment of my client to his family, particularly his three month old twins and other eight children. This fallacy might sometimes be used with ludicrous effect as in the case of the young boy who was tried for a particularly brutal crime, the murder of his father and mother with an axe. Confronted with overwhelming proof of his guilt, "he pleaded for leniency on the grounds that he is an orphan."[8] However, this fallacy is generally used by defense counsels to make the judge passionately write judgment in their favor or at least to reduce the sentence given to their clients. This is to say that this fallacy could be used to elicit a feeling of sympathy from the judge and make him disregard relevant issues in reaching his judgment, instead of dispassionately considering the issues.

Fallacy of Argumentum Ad Ignorantiam (Appeal to Ignorance)

This fallacy results when one argues that the absence of evidence for a conclusion counts as reason to believe the truth of the conclusion. This fallacy shifts the responsibility or burden of proof or providing evidence from those affirming the case to those who remain to be convinced of the correctness of the case.

Example:

There is no evidence that HIV is transmitted through mosquito bites. So, mosquitoes do not transmit HIV. In the above argument, the arguer asserts that HIV is not transmitted through mosquito bites on the basis that it has not been proved. Although this mode of argument is fallacious in most contexts, it should be pointed out that in the court of law, it is generally accepted that an accused is presumed innocent until proven guilty. Hence, the judge could legitimately and appropriately acquit the accused as not guilty on the grounds that the prosecution counsel has failed to provide evidence to show that the accused is guilty as charged. Even at this special legal principle, it is still consistent to say that the *argumentum ad ignorantiam* is fallacious in all contexts. It exists in two forms; the first pattern states that there is no proof that "P" is true. Therefore "P" is false, or in the second form, there is no proof that "P" is false therefore "P" is true.

Appeal to Tradition Fallacy

This fallacy is committed when we appeal to customs and tradition to think for the fact that something, such as, a law, fashion or habit has last so long that it is therefore good or right. We assume it has survived the test of time hence it should be upheld. We all know that some accepted customs and traditions in some places have turned out after many centuries to be accepted mistakes. For example, the killing of twins in some African cultures and cannibalism in Papua New Guinea were accepted norms for some centuries. If we argue that this law, dogma or custom has been there for centuries therefore it is right without providing relevant reasons why the law is right, we have committed a fallacy.

Appeal to Novelty Fallacy

This fallacy is committed when we accept something as good just because it is new and we reject another because it is old. This is based on erroneous belief that everything that is new is desirable and better than the old ones. For some, any new Apple cellphone or Samsung cellphone is good and desirable and preferable to old models. Actually, we know that some old cellphones are better than new ones in certain respects like durability and reliability. But of course, we know that in terms of wines, old wines are sometimes preferable to new ones. The point is we have to give some reasons for accepting new things as better and not to consider things better just because they are new versions. Many in our generation are obsessed with things that are new while few prefer the old-school model.

Fallacy of Ignorantio Elenchi (Irrelevant Conclusion)

This fallacy is committed when the premises of an argument are addressed to the wrong conclusion. Premises, as we know are supposed to provide some justification for the conclusion. For this to be possible, the subject matter of the premises must be reflected in the subject matter of the conclusion. In certain cases, however, the conclusion may be different from what the premises lead to. This results to fallacy of *ignorantio elenchi*.

Example:

The Golden Rule is basic to every system of ethics ever devised; everyone accepts it in some form or other. Therefore, the Golden Rule is an undeniably sound moral principle. Notice that the premises do not validly lead to the conclusion. Even though the premises have the Golden Rule as subject matter, none of them says anything to suggest that it is a sound moral principle.

Tu Quoque Fallacy

This fallacy is committed in an argument when the arguer, in an attempt to give a reply to a charge put against her, put the same charge against the opponent. This fallacy is mostly committed by young people in a family dispute.

Example:

Mary: "Mr. Tony called me a thief." John: Why? Mary: "Because Mr. Tony is a thief."
Note that in the above argument, Mary ended up putting against Mr. Tony, the same charge he made against her.

Fallacy of Complex Question

This fallacy occurs in an argument when from a complex question an implied but not obviously stated conclusion is inferred. It consists in demanding a plain answer "yes" or "No" to a question which really is an assumption. Hence one commits the fallacy of complex question if one asks two or more question in a fashion that makes it appear that only one question has been asked, or when the question is asked in such a way that the answer is presupposed in the question.

Example:

Mr. Green: "James, have you stopped your intemperate habits?" James: "Yes sir." Mr. Green: "James, have you stopped beating up your mother?" James: "Yes sir."
In the above examples, if James had even answered "no" to the questions above they will still imply the same thing.
Complex questions are common devices used by lawyers who try to force

the defendant to admit something not explicitly stated. A complex question is a question that requires either "yes" or "no" for an answer.

Fallacy of Non Sequitur

Non sequitur is a Latin phrase that means "it does not follow." This fallacy is committed when a conclusion of an argument is granted on the grounds of relevance but insufficient evidence. At most, the conclusion bears no relationship with the premises. This means the drawn conclusion did not follow from the premises.

Fallacy of False Cause
(*Non causa pro causa, Post Hoc Ergo Proter Hoc*)

Generally, a false cause fallacy occurs whenever one argues for a particular causal connection on the basis of insufficient evidence or when other explanations are plausible that fit the facts. In other words, the fallacy is committed when one possible cause of a phenomenon is assumed to be the cause although reasons are not given for excluding other possible causes. It occurs when one hastily takes one event or set of circumstances as the cause of another events or set of circumstances. Often the mistake is made for effect or self- serving purposes.

Example 1:

Most students in Harvard University are all children of the rich and most influential men in the country. Therefore, admission into Harvard is based on one's parental influence in the society.

In the above argument, the arguer is trying to hold that Harvard University admits only candidates whose parents are influential. But the fact is that Harvard University admits students based on the merit, hence anybody who gained admission into Harvard University must have passed his high school diploma very well and met the cutoff points. This fallacy appears in other forms.

Example 2:

Since sex education has become common and female circumcision uncommon in Africa, we've had a marked increase in promiscuity among girls. So, sex education and the prohibition of female circumcision have caused promiscuity among girls. The above argument fails to acknowledge many other weighty causal factors for promiscuity among girls, and again it fails to show the alleged link or association between sex educations or the prohibition of female circumcision with promiscuity.

The form of the above false or questionable Cause fallacy is: A occurred, then B occurred. Therefore, A caused B.

When B is undesirable, this pattern is often extended to the reverse: Avoiding A will pervent B. This fallacy is seen in many cases of wrong diagnosis and medical malpractice.

The two types of this fallacy are considered below:

Fallacy of Non Causa Pro Causa

This literally means "no cause for cause." For instance, the idea of this fallacy is that if B follows A, whether once or several times, A comes to be regarded as the cause of B. The fact that I see you first in the morning and later things did not work out smoothly during the rest of the day for me does not mean that you carry "bad luck" around. But yet this is a common superstition among some people. Again, the fact that an eclipse of the sun cleared after the whole community in a primitive society beat drums and made a whole lot of noise does not mean that it was the noise that caused the sun to resurface.

Fallacy of Post Hoc Ergo Proter Hoc

This is simply called *Post Hoc* Fallacy. The fallacy of *Post Hoc Ergo Proter Hoc* is translated as "this before that, therefore this because of that." One can quite innocently fall into this fallacy of false cause not because the attribution of a cause in the case follows from pet theories or disfavored sources, but because one simply observed a temporal connection between two events and then falsely assumes that the earlier event is the cause of the later. For instance, that your bad uncle drove your car and your car started having an engine problem does not mean he caused the engine problem.

Surely, if there were a set of criteria for causation, one such criterion would be the temporal priority. For instance, Cause A comes before Effect B in time. But there would have to be other criteria as well. One of them that have found favors among past philosophers and scientists includes spatial proximity. For instance Cause A is close to Effect B, so, 'A' is the cause of 'B'. It is not sufficient to assume that since an event immediately preceded another in time, the former was the cause of the later, when the criterion of spatial proximity or constant conjunction is violated or not considered. Thus, the fallacy involves reaching a conclusion based solely on the order of events, instead of considering other factors that could rule out the connection or the association. This fallacy is usually a tempting mistake because temporal sequence appears to be integral to causality. All post hoc fallacies are species of the false cause fallacy, but not all false cause fallacies are post hoc. When the criteria of spatial proximity or constant conjunction (e.g., "Cause A" is close to "Effect B," so, "A" is the cause of "B") are violated, these are instances of the more general false cause fallacy. A vehicle that is not at the scene of an accident cannot be the cause of the accident.

Straw Man Fallacy

This fallacy occurs when the arguer attacks a misrepresentation of the opponent's view. The idea here is to describe something that sounds like the opponent's view which is easier to knock down and demolish, and then refute it with some rational arguments. Sometimes, the audience may not know that the view being demolished by the arguer has been misrepresented. The result of the argument appears thus:

Premise: A misrepresentation of the view is false. Therefore, the view is false.
Politicians involved in bitter politics often involve themselves in this fallacy. They are often unfair and uncharitable in interpreting the views of their opponents. They hardly read them accurately.

Example 1:

Consider the case when Republican Vice Presidential candidate Sarah Palin in 2008 asserted that the Patient Protection and Affordable Care Act, also called "Obamacare," would create a "death panel"[9] of bureaucrats who would decide whether Americans – such as her elderly parents or children with Down Syndrome - were worthy of medical care. But Palin's view was debunked by experts and was referred to as the "death panel" myth. Palin's position was actually a misrepresentation of the healthcare law and was regarded as false in its entirety.

Example 2:

According to Bertrand Russell in the work "Has Religion made useful contribution to civilization?" He stated "my own view on religion is that of Lucretius. I regard it as a disease born of fear and a source of untold misery to the human race. I cannot, however, deny that it has some contributions to civilization. It helped in the early days to fix the calendar, and it caused Egyptian priests to chronicle eclipse with such care that in time they became able to predict them. These two services I am prepared to acknowledge, but I do not know anyothers."[10]

Note that Russell took up the weakest contributions of religion to civilization, overlooking its great contributions to mankind so that it would be easier for him to give it a debilitating attack. So, in Straw man fallacy, a weak or oversimplified or implausible characterization of an opponent's point of view is attacked in place of the real and probably more formidable argument. Sometimes, a persuasive (i.e., biased) definition or statement at the beginning of a speech is used to set up a straw man fallacy.

Fallacy of Petitio Principii (Begging the Question)

An argument is said to fall into the fallacy of begging the question when such argument has its conclusion as one of the premises of the argument. So, an argument begs the question when it assumes the point to be proved. This may result to arguing in a circle. When one begs the question, the soundness of the argument is always in doubt.

Example:

God exists because the Bible says so. But how do I know that what the Bible says is true? It is true because it is God's word. Or better it appears like this:

i. The Bible is God's word.
ii. So, What the Bible says is true. (From i) iii.The Bible says that God exists.
iv. So, God exists. (From ii and iii)

Fallacy of Argumentum Ad Dictum Simpliciter (Hasty Generalization/Converse Accident)

This fallacy is committed when one applies rules that are valid for accidental or specific cases to a general situation. It consists in assuming that what holds true in some particular respect or under a particular respect or under some special circumstances will hold true without any restriction as a general rule. This is also referred as fallacy of dramatic instance which is tendency to overgeneralize in matters of fact where we use one or two instances or samples to draw conclusion about the entire population. This amounts to oversimplification of the issue concerned.

Example:

Professor Philip Emeagwali of Nigeria was voted as one of the most valuable scientists of the 20th century and was touted by some as the man who invented the Internet. He emulated the bees on honeycomb construction to develop 65,000 processors in his 1989 project in the United States. His machine performed computations at 3.1 billion calculations per second and was assumed by many as the world fastest computer.[11] Therefore; all Nigerian scientists are very good.

We note from the above inductive argument that the premises are not only doubtful; the sample size is too small to warrant the conclusion. Again, the unsound argument is inconsistent with the low state of science and technology development in Nigeria.

Fallacy of Accident

The fallacy of accident is committed in an argument when general rules are applied to particular cases, where its application is clearly wrong, unacceptable and misleading. The fact remains that there are exceptions to general rules and where such exceptions exist; they must be understood as such. It is when we fail to recognize the exception and insist on the general rule that the fallacy of accident is committed.

Example:

The failure to prove something true does not make it false. The failure to prove a person guilty does not prove him innocent. In the above statements, the general principles are correct but they can be wrongly applied to a case in special circumstance, like in the legal presumption that a person is innocent until proved guilty.

Fallacy of Slippery Slope

This fallacy occurs when the arguer claims that a chain reaction will occur but there is insufficient evidence that one or more events in the chain will cause the others. In other words, one unjustifiably concludes a kind of "chain reaction" of cause or reason which if it is allowed to continue leads irrevocably to disaster.

Example:

If young people are allowed to drink beer, it will surely lead them down the road to hard liquor, then marijuana and cocaine and "before you know it" they will be addicted to heroin and methamphetamine! Again, consider an excuse given by some men and women who committed adultery: One thing led to another, we had some alcohol, and then some marijuana then we became drunk and had sex. The problem in the fallacy is the assumption that A, B and C necessarily lead to D. Even though, these things may have association, there is no necessary connection or direct causal relations between them.

Black-or-White Fallacy (Fallacy of False Alternatives)

This is committed when we falsely assumed in an argument that only two alternative positions are possible with regard to a certain issue. We ignore the possibility of a third alternative to the two already allowed.

Example:

We commit this fallacy when we argue that "anybody who is not part of the solution is part of the problem." Or "If you are not for our union then you are against it." "If you are not for us, you are against us." The arguments above assume wrongly that every person must be either for or against the union, whereas a third position is possible; the people who are not interested in the union. President Putin of Russia accused the United States of committing this fallacy always in international relations especially during President George W. Bush's war against terrorism after the September 11, 2001 attack, in which for Bush if you are not for War against Terrorism then you are against the United States. Consequently, Bush used it to determine those who are friends of the United States and those who are not.

Fallacy of Retrospective Determinism

This fallacy is committed when we argue that things could not have worked out or happened any other way than the way they happened. This is usually a deterministic stance referring more to the past instead of the future. This argument assumes that what happened in the past are unavoidable and that it is the way things ought to be. This means that we should learn to live with past events and their consequences, we should not worry about them. This is an attempt to evade responsibility for what happened in the past such as our past misdeeds, as they are what they are, they are beyond our control. This fallacious argument incapacitates one from taking corrective or preventive action in respect of future events. This is because the argument suggests that the future holds events pleasant and unpleasant which are unavoidable because they are determined by forces beyond our control. Hence, any attempt to change them will not have any effect.

Fallacy of False Dilemma

The fallacy occurs when a person poses a restrictive set of undesirable alternatives, when other legitimate alternatives may be possible. Here, one attempts to bring a premature end to a debate by declaring a dilemma when none exists. Other alternatives may be possible or other courses of action can be pursued.

Example:

Jane: I do not like the northern and the western candidates for the 2016 elections. So, I will not vote in the 2016 elections. In the above argument, Jane argues in a way to preclude consideration of candidates from other geo-political zone as third alternative like candidates from the eastern and southern zones.

Fallacy of False Analogy

This fallacy is committed when we draw a conclusion on the basis of a false or questionable comparison without offering sufficient evidence for the truth of the comparison. Consider this: A has properties X, Y and Z; B has properties X, Y and Z; A has the additional property Q. Therefore, B has the additional property Q. In the above argument, there is no additional justification given to prove that B has property Q as A has.

Genetic Fallacy

This fallacy is committed when in an argument we canvass for the rejection, dismissal or non-acceptance of a view, belief, claim or position because of the origin of the view or claim, etc. This is a fallacy because the truth value of any claim or view is independent of the origin. Just like asking, "Can anything good come from Nazareth?" There are people who would reject a book because it is written by a gay person, an African or Indian, a white person or black person.

Fallacy of Inconsistency

This fallacy is committed when in an argument we use some contradictory statements in the premises and the conclusion. Inconsistencies result when we argue from contradictory statements or when we end our argument with contradictory conclusion. Two contradictory statements are inconsistent with each other and cannot both be true at the same time. However, one can change his position over time without being accused of contradiction. One can evolve from one position to another. One can be against gay marriage this year but the next two years he becomes a supporter of gay marriage may be on the ground of human rights and civil liberty or a change in the definition of marriage from a union of a man and a woman to a union of two consenting adults. He will be accused of being inconsistent if he fails to give good reasons for the change of position.

Fallacy of Provincialism or Territorialism

This fallacy is committed when we accept a position or proposal because of the professional group the presenter comes from, or the territory of the arguer. If we accept a proposal presented by a computer engineer from Silicon Valley just because he is from Silicon Valley without caring to find out the authenticity of what is in the paper he presented then we have fallen into this fallacy. Furthermore, a politician who asserts without sufficient reasons that the police are more racist than politicians commits this fallacy. The politician is defending the group he belongs blindly or falsely.

Red Herring Fallacy

We commit this fallacy when we introduce logical red herring in an argument to divert attention of the listeners or readers from the real issue at stake. Red Herring is an irrelevant topic used by someone who does not want to discuss an unpleasant topic or talk about a private matter which is the bone of contention the audience wants to hear about. For instance, Ms. Hillary Clinton avoided question and answer from the press on whether she wiped her server clean of emails to obstruct investigation on Benghazi attack and the existence of classified information on private server by talking to the press on irrelevant topics they are not there for.

Colloquial Fallacy

We commit this fallacy when we rely on old sayings as excuse for our actions. A colloquial statement like "nobody is perfect, and so, I am not perfect" has been used by many to defend serious wrong doing. Other sayings like "no condition is permanent," "nobody is a compendium of knowledge," "and nobody is above mistake" are not wholly true. So, under certain situations one cannot use them to defend a position. For instance, some mistakes and some acts of ignorance are inexcusable and as such are regarded as culpable mistakes or vincible ignorance. It is blamable because simple effort is the only thing needed to avoid such mistakes or ignorance.

STATISTICAL FALLACIES

Apart from the formal and informal fallacies, we also have statistical fallacies, and they are fallacies of a different kind. They result from inappropriate use of statistics. Statistics involves assessing and estimating the facts and figures about a population and making inferences on them based on samples drawn from the population. The fallacies under statistical fallacies include the following.

Fallacy of Biased Statistics

This fallacy occurs when we give a wrong estimation of a population. In this case, a small population is presented wrongly for a large population. It could happen in the delineation of political constituencies, wards, autonomous communities or counties.

Small Sample Fallacy

This fallacy is committed when we draw inference from a sample that is not actually representative of a population. This means that the sample is too small to represent the population. For example, if we sample two hundred people out of a population of three hundred million and drawn conclusion from the responses of the sample, we commit this fallacy. Most opinion polls during presidential elections commit this fallacy. Most of the polls do not indicate stratified sampling where only a segment of the entire population is sampled rather they take calls and responses from every part of the country. Statistically, representative sample has to be above twenty percent of the population.

Fallacy of Misused Data Quality

The fallacy results when we use data without considering how their qualities have changed over time and space. The quality of data has to do with how the particular data were collected, i.e., whether they were properly or wrongly done, the place the data were collected, the age of the data about to be used and changes in population affecting existing data. So, this fallacy is committed when we use the data drawn from entirely different population and apply them to another population without considering the differences in quality. The aim sometimes is to have a statistical filibustering effect on the audience. This means using a long statistical data to paint a different picture and obstruct truth of what actually exists. Some government ministers and secretaries use this fallacy in their annual budget defense to blind and confuse members of the congress or parliament and prevent them from knowing actually what the ministry has done or plans to do.

Fallacy of Unknowable Statistics

This fallacy is committed when we use inferences that are not intelligent guesses but something one made up and presented as statistics or a true picture of reality.

For instance, the popular belief that air transportation is safer than any other mode of transportation could not be proved statistically. This is because it is difficult to known the number that travels by road vis-à-vis that of air and the number of deaths on the road compared with the same of air travel. It is nearly impossible to check out certain figures.
For example: Ten million die on road accidents every year worldwide. This is meant to highlight a point to achieve a desired effect. It is not meant to paint a true picture.

FALLACY OF AMBIGUITY (LINGUISTIC FALLACIES)

A word is said to be ambiguous if it has more than one possible meaning or significance, hence an argument can move from one meaning of the word to another. This implies in one meaning it may be affirming and in the other meaning, it may be denying such affirmation. Also, arguments are sometimes flawed because they contain ambiguous words, phrases, statements or because they involve a subtle confusion between two closely related concepts. This kind of fallacy appears in a number of forms. Some of them are discussed below.

Fallacy of Equivocation

This fallacy occurs when in an argument a word or phrase is shifted in the course of the argument to take on new meaning, thereby creating the false impression that the reason for the conclusion is really a good reason, when it is semantically irrelevant. This fallacy occurs when two (or more) meanings of a word (or phrase) are used in a context in which validity requires a single meaning of that word (or phrase).

Example:

The end of a thing is perfection. Death is the end of life. So, death is the perfection of life.

The above argument is fallacious because there are two different senses of the word "end" and the two senses of end that is either "goal" or "last event" are confused in the argument.

Fallacy of Misplaced Concreteness

This fallacy is committed when we make what is abstract to sound like something concrete or real. This is often referred as reification which is an act of making something to be real or concrete. It involves bringing something into being. For instance, we commit this fallacy when we refused to take responsibility for a problem but rather attribute it to the society instead. We see the society as the cause of the problem and hold it responsible while in the actual sense the society is just an abstract term that indicates a collection of people. So, if we say the society is corrupting the youth we have committed this fallacy. Similarly, when we say "they" did this or "they" did that without mentioning the persons that did this and that we commit the fallacy of misplaced concreteness.

Fallacy of Incompatibility

The fallacy occurs when two terms or ideas which do not match are used together.

Example:

Damian: I waited for eternity before the ministry granted my request.

In this assertion by Damian, the words waiting and eternity are incompatible. Eternity is a concept of time that one cannot even imagine. Human waiting time can never run into eternity.

Even though it may be considered a hyperbolic expression yet it is a fallacy.

Fallacy of Amphiboly

The fallacy is similar to equivocation except that the double meaning is due to a syntactic deficiency in grammar construction such as grammatical error or a mistake in punctuation. This gives rise to two or more distinct interpretations which render the conclusion erroneous or irrelevant.

Example:
"The police were ordered to stop smoking in public." From the above statement, it could be inferred that policemen smoke in public or that the police should arrest any person smoking in public. And both are correct interpretations of the statement.

Fallacies of Composition and Division

The fallacy of composition consists in applying properties which belong to individuals to a group consisting of those individuals. This means that it is invalid to make inference from the nature of the parts to the nature of the whole.

Example:

Each senator in the Congress is corrupt. Hence, the Congress is corrupt. The fallacy of division is the opposite of that of composition. It is an invalid inference from the nature of the whole to the nature of the parts or from the nature of a group to the nature of its members.

Example:

America is a rich country Mr. Green is anAmerican Therefore, Mr. Green is a rich man.

Fallacy of Accent

This fallacy occurs in an argument whose deceptive and invalid nature depends on a change or shift in meaning as result of improper stress or emphasis in the premises or conclusion of the argument. Hence, the same sentence has a quite different meaning when different words are stressed differently. To avoid this type of linguistic fallacy in a speech, the speaker can give his statement an inflection that conveys the correct meaning. In written language, punctuations including the use of italics clarify a meaning which might otherwise be ambiguous.

Another common occurrence of the fallacy of accent arises when a statement is taken out of context leading to distortion in the original meaning. Journalists are usually guilty of this. The isolation of a statement gives it a stress it would not have had in the original context.

CONTEXTUAL FALLACIES

These are fallacies that result when statements are taken out the original context or when there is a shift in context in the process of an argument. They include the following:

Fallacy of Significance

This fallacy is committed when statement lacking in significance is made in a speech or writing that conveys little or no meaning to the listener or reader. For example twenty percent of those who use Cable TV watch CNN. The information did not tell the reader how many people use Cable TV and whether they watch only CNN or they also watch other channels on the Cable TV.

Fallacy of Emphasis

This fallacy is committed when emphasis is made on a word or group of words that is not so much important while the essential ones are not emphasized. This fallacy is most often found in advertisement or contract papers where important aspect of the advertisement or contract are written in tiny font while the less important are written in bold letters. Many people have signed contracts without reading the tiny words of the contract only to discover what they gotten themselves into later on. Check out TV and credit card contracts you will see fallacy of emphasis in the contract document. Politicians are sometimes guilty of this as they comment and emphasize the less important things said by their opponents and ignore the valuable ones. Preachers and commentators also commit this fallacy when they ignore important facts in the script before them and spend much time talking on less important facts.

Out of Context Quotation Fallacy

This fallacy is committed when a word or group of words in a statement or an entire statement is removed from the original context they were used. These changes are made in order to pass different message from the original one. Sometimes to quote a person out of context can be a kind of dubious manipulation that sends out diabolical meaning for a person's honest and sincere opinion. For example in a campaign speech in Roanoke, Virginia, on July 13, 2012, President Obama said among other things, "if you have got a business, you didn't build that."[12] This statement was immediately taken out of context by Mitt Romney and the conservative wing of the Republican Party, and it was used in a misleading campaign slogan against Obama's re-election in 2012 as someone against individual entrepreneurship and successful businesses. However, the remark was made in the context of his belief that wealthy citizens should pay higher taxes. According to Obama, "if you have being successful, you didn't get there on your own; somebody along the line gave you some help. There was a great teacher somewhere in your life. Somebody helped to create this unbelievable American system that we have, that have allowed you to thrive. Somebody invested in roads, bridges. If you have got a business – you didn't build that. Somebody else made that happen."[13]

SIGNIFICANCE OF FALLACY

It is important to mention that we could see fallacies in discussions we have in our various homes, offices and market places. It could be seen in other places where discussions and communication take place such as the mass media, print and electronic media, law courts, churches, mosques, schools and town halls. It is very much used in the household, in business, politics and governance. Fallacies could be seen in books, journals, magazines and newspapers.

Hermeneutics of Fallacy

Hermeneutics as the science of interpretations helps to detect fallacies in our language. The interpretation can be that of beliefs or worldviews, and these could be religious, cultural, political, social or economic in nature. The interpretation can also be of literary works and their concepts, principles, hypotheses, laws, etc.

Hermeneutics is a derivation from the name Hermes, the Greek god of message. He bears the messages of the gods and often makes them available to mortals. And as such Hermes is regarded as the god of security intervention, speeches, eloquences, art and writing skills. Plato and Aristotle articulated hermeneutics as act of making obscure expression clear and meaningful. It is a meaningful interpretation and enunciation of what is obscure and ambiguous. Thus, detecting fallacies is one of the concerns of Hermeneutics. For one to be proficient in the science of Hermeneutics, one should know all about fallacy in all its shapes and forms. The philosopher is therefore concerned with both hermeneutics and fallacy.

Fallacy as Sophistry

The term sophistry refers to the teachings of a group of philosophers in the 5th century BC called the sophists. The sophists were known to engage in subtle deceptive reasoning. Later, Sophistry became a method of advancing verbal attacks. It is not aimed at advancing the frontiers of knowledge. The sophists are most often interested in destroying the pillars of knowledge than building them. Fallacy as sophistry becomes apparent in arguments which appear to be correct and may be quite convincing, but are often incorrect and misleading. They are plausible but false and unsound reasoning. The fallacy has to do with deceptive nature of the arguments which may seem correct but on a close examination are faulty.

Example 1:

Consider the argument of a prominent sophist - Thrasymachus on Justice and Right. For him, one gains nothing from being just. Justice is not worth practicing because injustice pays more than justice, and unjust people are superior and stronger in character than those who are just. Justice does not pay; it is only the weak and simpletons who practice justice.
What is justice? He answers: "Justice is the interest of the stronger for might is right." For him, in every state the stronger establish their position and authority in power and their interests become "justice." They make laws to protect their interests which automatically are "right" within the state for as long as they are in power. Thus, justice in every State is the interest of the stronger or the most powerful, that is, the rulers. The state (with all its paraphernalia) is for him and many like him an ideological apparatus used by the rich, that is, the rulers to control the poor and the resources that belong to the whole people. If Thrasymachus is alive today, he would buttress his position more and argue that the rich apportion to themselves and their friends the wealth of the nation through tax cuts for the rich, the bail out of Wall Street and the banks. He would point to the failed trickle down economic policies that suggest if the rich are well taken care of, everybody else below will benefit. From the above, we can see that the sophist made use of fallacies that are psychologically persuasive but are flawed and unacceptable to many people.

Example 2:

Similarly, Hegesias of Cyrene (nicknamed Peisithanatos which means the Death Persuader) was a Cyrenaic in 290 B.C. who was influenced by some Buddhist teachings, and he took the hedonist teachings of the Cyrenaic School Founder, Aristippus to another level. Through his lectures, Hegesias made many of his listeners to commit suicide as he erroneously taught them that happiness is not the goal of life as it is impossible to achieve. According to him, the goal of life for every person is to avoid pain and sorrow. He taught them that the wise man's goal in life is to be free from pain and sorrow, and for him conventional values like wealth, freedom, security, etc. are all indifferent and produce no more pleasure than pain. He concluded that death is more desirable than life. He urged his listeners to escape life through suicide and move on to another plane of life full of attainable Cyrenaic pleasure. The high death toll from Hegesias' lectures and his book, *Death by Starvation* made King Ptolemy II of Philadelphus (284 – 246 B.C.) to ban him from lecturing in Alexandra.

Fallacy as a Technique of Persuasion: From Propaganda to Brain-Washing

As a technique of persuasion, fallacies are used in our homes, law courts, advertisements in print and electronic media, and in political and religious statements to change people's mind about certain beliefs. In these areas, the users try to play on the intelligence of their audience to make them see something where there is none. The aim of the user is to change the mind of the audience concerning the issue in question and for the audience to see the issue from the point of view of presenter. It is also aimed at making the audience to act according to the bidding of the presenter.

In its extreme forms, fallacies could be used in propaganda and brain washing of an individual or group of individuals. Whenever fallacies are persuasive, they do not normally only intend to attack the positions of their opponents, they also intend to make their opponents or the audience see reasons why the presenter's position should be seen as reasonable and acceptable. In some cases, they want the audience to see white as black, to see truth as falsehood or vice versa. Let us consider some uses of fallacies in different areas as a technique of persuasion.

As a Technique of Persuasion in the Household

Fallacy is frequent used in the household by parents and their children. It could be seen in the dialogue between parents and their children.

Example:

Father: "Mary, you have to stop going out at night. It is very dangerous for a girl."
Daughter: "Daddy, you know I can't stop going out at night just because of dangers that only exist in your mind."
Father: "I have finished! If you like go out of this house at night again, I will not pay your school fees anymore and you will find yourself out of this house too!"
Daughter: "I am sorry daddy. I will not go out at night anymore." In the above dialogue, the father uses the threat of force or sanctions to solve a particular problem in the house. Alternatively, the father could have explained the danger out there at night in a way that appeals to the rationality and understanding of the daughter rather than resorting to threats.

As a Technique of Persuasion in Business Organizations

Fallacy is also used in various business firms. The Manager of a business firm most often uses the threat of job termination or sack from work (i.e. fallacy of *argumentum ad baculum*) as a technique of persuasion to make workers increase production or avoid waste. The notions of "no work, no pay" and "a no call, no show" make many workers uneasy. Advertisers also employ many kinds of fallacies to make customers buy their goods. Most often fallacies that appeal to popular sentiment (argumentum *ad populum*) win customers and sell products.

Example:

"The secret of beauty: The all new Dove for every skin, soft and smooth, beautiful skin begins with Dove. With new exciting perfumes and richer creamier lather, Dove now comes in an international pack in three variants: Green Dove with lemon and herbs for oily skin; Beige Dove with cocoa butter for dry skin; and white Dove with natural moisturizers for normal skin. Choose the one that's right for you. There are no secrets to beauty. Not when you start with Dove."

You can see that the Dove advertiser is appealing to popular emotions to make the people choose Dove as the soap that could take care of their skin.

As a Technique Persuasion in Courts of Law

The court of law is not left out in the use of fallacies. The goal of every attorney is to win cases, hence fallacies are very important to the lawyers in the effort, and judges are mindful of this in court. It is not surprising that many hold the view that lawyers are lairs. Lawyers use fallacies to refute the positions of the opponents, or to make their own positions look strong. They as well use fallacies to extract truth from clients and opponent's clients during questions and cross examination in law courts. Such fallacies as used by the lawyer may include complex questions, false cause fallacies and *argumentum ad misericordiam* (appeal to pity), threat of force, hasty generalization, *petitio principii* (begging the question) etc.

Example:

A very good use of the fallacy of *argumentum ad misericordiam* is seen in Ileogbunam, in the paper "Juveniles on Death Row" in which a tribunal judgment stated: "The remaining part of the tribunal's judgment found the entire accused persons guilty on all four counts." The defense counsel proceeded to plead for the convicts that they were convicted on circumstantial evidence and asking for mitigation of their sentence because they are children.[14]

In the above citation, the defense counsel applied the fallacy of *argumentum ad misericordiam* as the last resort in a helpless situation of trying to reduce the sentence of the youths convicted of committing murder. The attorney pleaded with the judge to save the lives of the children because they are too young to serve a prison sentence let alone be executed, thereby attracting the judge's sympathy. Usually, lawyers resort to this kind of fallacy when the defense counsel feels that the battle to save their client might be lost.

Prosecutors also use the fallacy of *petitio principii* (begging the question) in court. In this case, instead of the prosecutors proving a case put to them by the court, they tend to assume what is to be proved.

Example:
Prosecutor: "This man is wicked."
Judge: "How do you know?"
Prosecutor: "Only a wicked person can do that kind of thing."

As a Technique of Persuasion in Politics and Governance

In politics and governance, fallacies have come to assume much significance and legitimacy. Politicians make use of fallacies to make their audience or the electorates see the qualities that make them more suitable for a political post than other candidates. Politicians use false cause fallacy to gain acceptance of their views.

Example: Todd Akin, a Republican candidate for the United States Senate used a false cause fallacy in trying to defend the party's position against abortion and to project his pro-life stance. He said, "In most cases of legitimate rape, the woman's body has ways of shutting the whole thing down to prevent conception and pregnancy."[15] He was criticized for wrong choice of words and false teaching of the Republican Party position on abortion. He was forced out of the Senate race because the false cause fallacy was very clear to all. A legitimate case of rape occurs when a woman says no to sex but the man ignores it and the act was carried through. The "Woman's Body" can't prevent conception if the act is carried through and all the necessary factors for conception are present. Many administrators use *argumentum ad baculum* such as; the threats of sanctions, of removing name from the work schedule, contract termination or no- work- no- pay policy in order to make contractors and civil servants under them comply with their wish. This carrot and stick module of getting things done is well known not only in business, but also in politics; it is used to instill fear in the audience that certain behavior will carry unpleasant consequences.

As a Technique of Persuasion in Amorphous Organizations

Fallacies also have been used as an instrument of persuasion, propaganda and brain-washing in many amorphous organizations like security agencies, false religions and terrorist organizations. It is also used by some secret service organizations. In the world of false teachings, propaganda, indoctrinations and deceitful prophecies; previous knowledge and beliefs of victims or followers are detonated, and their minds are wiped blank. The minds of the individuals or groups of individuals will become a tabula rasa, and fallacies are then uploaded to them. This is the means used by the masterminds to make an individual to commit suicide or for a group to commit mass suicide. Suicides are due to loss of the alternative mode of being. These are most often initiated by a fallacy absorbed hook and sinker by the individual or group.

The mastermind or the originator of a fallacy could be an inspirational teacher or leader like Presidents Obama, Donald Trump and Putin, or a dictator like the Nazis leader Adolf Hitler, a Communist leader like Stalin, and religious leader like Jim Jones of the Peoples Temple, terrorist leaders like Osama bin Laden of Al Qaeda and Abu Bakr al-Baghdadi of Islamic State- ISIS. The words and pronouncements of the mastermind are taken as gospel truth. His commands receive obedience in some quarters with immediate effect.

Again, in this era of military warfare and international terrorism, many cases of suicide bombings and mass murders are carried by brain-washed individuals acting under the influence of some established propaganda perpetuated as sound arguments by their leaders and superiors who are the masterminds. For instance, some Islamic families have refused to immunize their children because they were told by their masterminds that the system is being used by the Western world to sterilize their children and consequently to reduce their population. Some events sometimes help reinforce propaganda. Guess how secret agents gained access to Bin Laden compound for the first time, they acted as immunization officials. From the above review of the relevance of fallacy in human affairs, we can conclude that fallacies play a very significant role in human society. Sometimes and in certain situations, some of them appear to be indispensable in solving certain problems.

17

MAIN STREAMS OF PHILOSOPHY
Western and Eastern Philosophy

We want to enumerate and elucidate in this chapter the different types of philosophy. It is not meant to argue whether philosophy is one or many. Facts show that we have more than one philosophy, and since facts are sacred, they are not to be tampered with. Rather it is meant to acknowledge these philosophies that come from different parts of the world of thought.

In the different continents of the world, philosophy is at different levels of development. Philosophy cannot be compartmentalized into individual country's philosophy because it has moved beyond the boundaries of countries to reach out to as many other countries as possible. Even though in the strict sense, we can talk of Greek philosophy, American philosophy, British philosophy, German philosophy, and Russian philosophy, Chinese, Japanese philosophy and Indian philosophy, Bantu philosophy, etc. Instead of getting involved in the hair-splitting country by country typology, we could see philosophy as broadly typified into three major types:

Western philosophy;

Oriental philosophy;

African philosophy

THE WESTERN PHILOSOPHY

Western philosophy is regarded by many as the most developed and most progressive of all the types of philosophies. Even though it is not the oldest of all the philosophies, it has given to mankind more to think about than any other philosophy. Just as western civilization has yielded the greatest development dividend to humanity; it is also one of most dominant force in the history of thought. A force that shaped the development and progress of advanced nations, and helped to bring them to the state in which they are today.

On the other hand, some of the oldest human fossils were found in Ethiopia where the ancient kingdom of Kush is taken to be one of the oldest kingdoms of the world. Hence, Africa is believed to be the place where humans emerged as Homo sapiens. As we know, history had it that civilization started in Egypt and the Egyptian pyramids are taken as one of the seven wonders of the ancient world. The Hieroglyphic writing found in Egypt was one of the earliest acts of writing in the world, and one of the earliest libraries was founded in Alexandria, Egypt. Scholars and visitors from all over the ancient world went to Alexandria to memorize knowledge. This is why today knowledge based on cram studies and memorization are referred as Alexandrian knowledge. Hence, it is believed that Greek philosophy was an offshoot of the learnings which included mathematics and geometry that went on in temples of the Egyptian mystery religion many years before the rise of Greece as World Empire and center of learning.

The western philosophy has its origin from Greek philosophy. It reached its zenith in the British, American, German, French and Russian philosophies. Most western philosophers and scholars have denied the African origin of Greek or western philosophy. It would be totally incorrect to deny the possible African origin of Western philosophy as the cradle of civilization and learning was in Egypt Africa. The contribution of Oriental philosophy and African philosophy in shaping western philosophy cannot be denied without offending history. The refusal of the West to acknowledge the contributions of other regions to world civilization is one of the bases of underdevelopment, conflicts and international terrorism in the world today. The moment western civilization begins to recognize and pay tribute to the contribution of African and Eastern civilization, the world will begin to see genuine peace and most of the conflicts in the world will be resolved.

The position of dissenting western scholars on the contributions of other regions in general and African origin of Western philosophy in particular is not based on investigative research but purely a product of genetic fallacy, which canvasses the rejection, dismissal or non-acceptance of a claim because of the origin of the claim rather than on the wrongness of what is claimed. Naturally, it would be difficult for any proud westerner to accept Africa as the forerunner of his philosophy especially becauseAfrica and things African are considered to be primitive and backward. Okolo asserted that "this general skepticism was somehow understandable since many non-African scholars, the Europeans for instance had all sorts of prejudices and misconceptions about Africans, their thinking and traditional ways of life and consequently, could not bring themselves to think of African Philosophy side by side Greek, American, German or English philosophies, and not to talk of African origin of western philosophy."[1] The non-acknowledgement of the African origin of Greek philosophy by Western scholars is what some scholars, especially those like G.C.M. James, called *Stolen Legacy*.[2] Another zealous apologist for African origin of Greek philosophy, C.S. Momoh had this to say: First, that African philosophy exists is not in doubt. Second, that thisAfrican philosophy is ancient Egyptian philosophy ... that there could not have been Greek philosophy without Africanphilosophy.[3]

However, instead of talking of stolen legacy, we prefer to talk of unclaimed legacy. Africans have failed to claim the legacy laid down in Egypt as the cradle of civilization. It is not only in the area of philosophy but also in mathematics, geometry, science and technology. It is a well-known fact that Africa has lagged behind in every facet of development. The reasons for this backwardness of Africa, after being the cradle of civilization are not certain. Some scholars from different disciplines have suggested a number of reasons for this African condition. Some European scholars see it as African bondage while others referred to it as Blackman's burden. Some of the European scholars who criticized the African religious cum cultural movement known at its inception as Ethiopianism regarded the African condition as an outcome of religious cum cultural curse.

Ethiopianism was a religious cum cultural movement started in the 19th century by someAfricans, some of whom were the ex-slaves shipped from America to Monrovia Liberia and Freetown Sierra Leone. It was meant essentially to satisfy a quest by these Africans to identify themselves as among the chosen people of God based on the biblical role of Ethiopia and the reference to the country in the Bible as among the sons of Rachael. Probably included is the fact that the Queen of Sheba who gave King Solomon his first son Manasseh, was from Ethiopia. But some Western scholars rejected this claim and asserted the unpleasant fact that Africans, rather than being counted among the chosen people of God as recorded in the Bible, are the descendants of Ham, the cursed son of Noah who probably settled in Egypt after being cursed by Noah and sent away for having laughed at seeing the nakedness of Noah.

For these Western scholars, slavery and African underdevelopment could be traced the curse of Ham, and this curse has become the Blackman's burden ever since. Hence for them, there is need for Africa to be severed from the curse of Ham for it to realize that it has been left behind by the rest of the world in scientific and socio-economic development. This view is plausible but false. However, Africa needs to be unbound through education and investments in science and technology for the continent to get a sense of direction in technological development and achieve its own indigenous nobility as the rest of the world. But, it is laughable to see African problems from the spectrum of a religious curse. Nevertheless and strange enough, this erroneous belief has intermingled with other awful beliefs by some Whites that Africans are sub humans and uncivilized, and these partly account for the negative feelings some Whites have whenever a Black person is around them and some would treat their pets far better than they could treat a black person. These erroneous beliefs are also the basis of most police brutality and other hate crimes committed against black people.

What else could one attribute the failure of Africans to claim the ancient Egyptian legacy? Could it be the result of Western imperialism and colonialism of the last four countries? The Marxists maintained that slavery, the scramble for Africa, western imperialism, colonization and neo-colonialism are responsible for African underdevelopment. According to this development theory, Japan, China and Korea or any other developed country would not reach the state of development which they have now if they had experienced the subjugation and dispossession that Africa has gone through for more than four hundred years.

However, Modernist scholars rejected the above two positions and suggested that the reason for African underdevelopment was the inability of African leaders to manage the affairs of their countries in an efficient, effective and transparent way. This Modernist theory as presented by Western development philosophers asserted that the issue of corruption and lack of transparency and poor accountability are the main causes of African underdevelopment and the negative perceptions and feelings against Africans and things African.

We have so far presented in this work vivid account of Western philosophy. We offered a concise view of the major systems in Western philosophy, such as: Rationalism; Empiricism; Idealism; Pragmatism; Humanism; Materialism; Naturalism; Utilitarianism; Existentialism; and Phenomenology. Hence, we can now take a panoramic view of other world philosophies.

THE EASTERN OR ORIENTAL PHILOSOPHY

Oriental philosophy or Eastern philosophy, otherwise called oriental thought, is made up of Indian philosophy, the Chinese philosophy, Japanese philosophy and some Arabian philosophies. These philosophies are mostly ethno-religious philosophies of the Middle East and Asia, where religions like Islam, Hinduism, Buddhism and Confucianism are practiced. Most people of non-western cultures see religion as integrally related and inseparable from all the other areas of life and experience. For Asians as well as Africans, religion is taken to be essentially the basis of culture. Africans and Asians see religion as giving form and meaning to the rest of existence. There is no doubt that most of us who have followed the Western style of life are oblivious of the lifestyles and world views of the Orientals.

Nancy Wilson Ross acknowledges this view in her work, *Three Ways of Asian Wisdom* when she stated that the average westerner knows little or nothing about the powerful spiritual motivations, religious convictions and ways of worship of the people who live on the other side of the globe.[4] Our contention here is that it is possible to extract and abstract the philosophical world view of the people from their culture and religious doctrines. However, in the process we must make sure we do not take culture or religion to be philosophy. From this perspective, we shall briefly discuss the philosophies that make up oriental thought and world views, namely, the Hindu philosophy, the Buddhist philosophy, the Taoist philosophy and the Confucian philosophy.

Hindu Philosophy

The word "Hindu" means Indian. According to H.D. Lewis and Robert Lawson Slater, Hindu is an adjective which has been used to refer to what has been believed and practiced by some four hundred million people and their forebears for some five thousand years, none of whom refer to any single teacher acknowledged by all, or recite any one creed accepted by all.[5] Philosophy in Hindu tradition is known as *darsana* which means "seeing the truth" and applying this truth in solving the problems of everyday life.

For an Indian philosopher, the sole purpose for studying philosophy is not merely to gain knowledge for its own sake or to satisfy one's curiosity, but to discover and to live the highest kind of life, that is, the life that involves authentic existence, a life that will also bring permanent self-realization or bliss. For the Hindu philosopher, "just as many other true philosophers, unless one has convictions and lives in accordance with them, he is not really a philosopher."[6] Every philosophy gravitates around the basic ideas in the universe, namely: the idea of God, world/ matter, and man/ self. These are analyzed alongside human existence and experience. This fact could not be different in Hindu philosophy. Taking it discretely according to these denominations would give us at a glance the nature, orientation and horizon of Hindu philosophy.

The Absolute Brahman

In Hindu philosophy, Brahman represents the absolute and ultimate reality. If you call it God, you are not far from the truth. According to Hindu philosophy and cosmogony, the Brahman is the only one unchanging reality that transcends space, time, causality and all particular things. As a result, it cannot be comprehended by human thought or adequately expressed in words and concepts. This view is expressed in the Hindu *Upanishads* which contain the fundamentals of Hindu philosophy. This monotheistic view of reality further states that only Brahman is real, and the individual souls and the universe are illusory manifestations of Brahman. In other words, there is only one ultimate reality, one being and every other thing is part and manifestations of this one ultimate reality. These views look like what we have already seen in some western philosophers like Plato, Spinoza and Hegel.

On the Existence of Individual Self

For the Upanishads, the true self or the human person has no self-identity. The individual true self or soul, which in Hindu is known as *atman*, is identical with Brahman. For the Hindu philosopher, the greatest deception one could imbibe is to believe and live as though he is a separate and autonomous being with an individual self or soul quite distinct and free from the control of the absolute Brahman. In essence for the Hindu philosophy, the true self or soul is one identical with the Brahman, and it cannot exist independent of the Brahman.

On the Material World and its Existence

For Hindu philosophy, the material world is part of the Brahman, the absolute. So, this universe of animals, trees and non-living things like stones, mountains and rivers, fire and air as we see them or better as they appear to us, are just illusions. In Hindu parlance, they are called *Maya*. They are not substantial and distinct from the Brahman. This by implication connotes a pantheistic view of the world; the Brahman is everything and everything is Brahman. Emerging from this pantheistic position of Hindu philosophy is the view that history and time are circular and cyclic in nature. Everything including individual existence in the phenomenal sense repeats itself endlessly without purpose. However, from the transcendental standpoint of human existence, the true self is immortal, free and one with Brahman.

Even though, man is caught in the endless cycle of birth, life, death and rebirth (reincarnation and predestination), the true destiny of the self is the realization of the identity with the Brahman, which is often severed when the individual get immersed into the world of material things and their pleasures. The self, according to M. Hiriyana, "as we see it in the empirical world, is the Brahman appearing under the limitations which form part of that illusory universe."[7] It is in order to free itself from the limiting conditions of matter that self gets involved in series of rebirth. The fact is self-detachment and asceticism are prerequisite for attaining self-liberation during the series of rebirth and thus to attain oneness with Brahman. For this ethno-religious philosophy, life or existence is graded in the hierarchy of values. According to Hindu philosophy, values are in the ascending order: Wealth (Artha); Pleasure (Kama); Duty or righteousness (Dharma); Enlightenment or the release from finitude and imperfection (Moksha).

From this hierarchy of values, wealth and pleasure for the Hindu philosopher are worldly and secular values that are legitimate and good if they are given their appropriate place in human existence, but abuse of them reduces the chances of one achieving the true self and oneness with the absolute, and also heightens ones chances of rebirth. On the other hand, duty and righteousness which include the life of virtue such as sincerity, honesty, cleanliness, self-control, courage, prudence, justice, peace and love point to the highest value of enlightenment; a release from finitude and imperfection. These are eternal values which liberate man and put an end to the series of rebirth which every man faces in life. They also free the self from the Law of Karma; the law of retributive justice, the law of sowing and reaping which the Hindu conceives as operating in the world. At the point of liberation, the individual rests in oneness with the Braham.

The Buddhist Philosophy

Buddhist philosophy is the philosophy founded by Siddhartha Gautama (563 BC), who was a Hindu who achieved enlightenment and liberation to become known as Buddha - the "Enlightened One." As a result, Buddha was an idolized and deified person who is venerated or worshipped in the Far East and Asian temples where altars are erected in his honor.

The Buddhist Existentialism

As existentialism focuses on the human predicament in the conditions of life so also Buddhist philosophy dwells on the predicament of human existence. Thus, human suffering is a recurrent decimal in Buddhist philosophy. History has it that Buddha wandered for some years in isolation in the forest in search of the truth regarding human suffering. When he received beatific vision and struck cosmic consciousness, he repudiated some of the core teachings in Hindu philosophy and religion. Buddha made a fundamental break with Hinduism in his rejection not only of the Vedic scriptures but also of the concepts of Brahman and atman - the metaphysical absolute and the changeless self.

For Buddha, experience, gives no clear indication of such an all-inclusive World Soul. Buddha also rejected the authority ascribed to the ancient gods, and urged believers to rely mainly on the resources within themselves, namely: their reason and experience. He rejected the Hindu caste system, since wisdom and not birth or caste is of more importance in this life. Having reached the highest level of illumination and enlightenment – the apotheosis of perfection, the four noble truths were unveiled to Buddha regarding human condition. These noble truths are:

There is suffering all over the world.

The cause of suffering is selfish desires or "thirst."

Suffering can be stopped.

How to put an end to suffering

In summary, Buddha chose the austere and ascetic life instead of the affluence of the palace and the royalty which his father preferred and wanted him to live in. He meditated in the desert and reflected on human predicament especially enormous suffering raging among the people who have no opportunity to live in the palaces of his days. So, life outside the palace made him realize the first noble truth that suffering is all over the world. For him, unhappiness or pain accompanies the experiences of birth, illness, failure in one's endeavors or inability to satisfy desires. Old age and death are also part and parcel of suffering. According to Buddha, apart from the unavoidable suffering of age and death, most other sufferings are caused by selfish desires or thirst or craving. He rightly pointed out that the joy of having increases the desire to have more. This fact tends breed greed and unhappiness in the world. It follows that the only way to put end to suffering is the complete suppression and the extinction of this thirst through annihilation of desire, and banishing avarice by renouncing it, and allowing no place for it. The ability to do this brings one to the Buddhist paradise called *"Nirvana"* while the inability to exercise self-control over the cravings leads to an indefinite round of births, rebirths and deaths. The Buddhist philosophy went further to assert under the fourth noble truth that there are available eight noble paths, which if taken, one would gain enlightenment and achieve the Nirvana. These sacred paths are the path of:

i.Right understanding, ii. Right aspiration; iii.Right speech; iv. Right conduct; v. Right mode of livelihood; vi. Right striving or effort; vii. Right mindfulness; viii. Right concentration.

These paths are branches of a larger path of self-control and self-discipline in the face of illusory things of the world. Some scholars, including Joseph Omoregbe have asserted that "Buddha failed to explain or shed light on the nature of "Nirvana" rather he was more interested in explaining the paths that lead to it. As a result, the concept of Nirvana remains obscure and opaque."[8]

The only meaning that could be attributed to it is that it is a state of complete cessation of all desires, all cravings and thirst, and consequently, all suffering. In this situation, the law of Karma, the law of retributive justice which Buddha supports ceases to be in operation, and so no suffering takes place. Thus, in the Nirvana, there is liberation and freedom, peace and contentment, joy, insight, love and compassion for all living beings.

The Taoist Philosophy

The Taoist philosophy is a brand of Chinese philosophy that came with the Chinese civilization which was already old when western civilization was at its cradle. This philosophy was based on the concept of Tao. The protagonist of this concept was Lao Tzu, who made an ambitious effort to systematize the wisdom of his time – 6th century BC that was engulfed in turmoil. Tzu posited the Tao, which literally means "the way" as the focus of his philosophy. It epitomizes the way the universe works. In his book, *Tao Te Ching,* Tzu expressed the view that the Tao is the source of being;

it is superior to all things because it is the determinant of all things. It is transcendent yet immanent in nature and man.[9]

Over the centuries, inexhaustible ideas have been associated with the Tao. This falls in line with the belief of the adherents of Tao, that it takes no action and yet leaves nothing undone. It does not compete and yet it skillfully achieves victory. The ethical stance of the Taoist is that of moderation. According to them, extremes must be avoided. That is to say that the virtuous must stand in the middle - *virtuo in medio stat*. The two extremes are the life of indulgence, given over to pleasures, self-seeking and enjoyment with all the attendant vices such as hatred, corruption, man inhumanity to man which are ignoble, and the other extreme is life of austerity; this is wretched, unworthy and vain. The middle way is the life that does not deceive the eyes and spirit which leads to repose, serenity, knowledge, gentleness and kindness. There is also the Taoist paradoxical no action stance which holds that non-action is stronger than action, gentleness overcomes strength, and kindness conquers harshness possibly in the same way an enraged elephant is calmed by the sight of a lamb.

The Confucian Philosophy

Confucian philosophy is another Chinese philosophy drawn from the teachings of Confucius of China, who was born in 551 BC. Confucius was a contemporary of Tzu. Confucian philosophy has much in common with Taoist philosophy in trying to organize the wisdom of the time into a more orderly system. However, the Confucian philosophy differed from it in the sense that it laid less emphasis on the metaphysical orientation of existence. Confucius revised and systematized earlier classics and gave them practical over tone, in the sense that his philosophy was geared towards assisting the people to live well. So, he contributed immensely in making Chinese philosophy as a whole to be practical and this-worldly rather than being engulfed in metaphysical speculations.

The resultant philosophy was predominantly a system of ethical realism which constitutes the traditional Chinese philosophy. Confucian philosophy, as ethical realism goes with ethical code for human conduct. And a good man is the person who abides by and lives according to the code of ethics. The code emphasized that an ideal man should live above board despite the hullabaloos of life. The vicissitudes of human existence should not make him to depart from a virtuous life. He should not be egocentric, greedy, wicked, dishonest, etc. Rather he should be a man who is faithful, a man of love, which the code regarded as the test of greatness and wisdom. The Confucian philosophy has a great regard for the family as the foundation of the political and social structure of the state.

For Confucius, charity should start from the family. This is applicable to other virtues such as obedience to laws and constituted authority which gradually build up to make a stable and peaceful nation, with patriotic citizenry. The principle of moderation in life was advocated for the realization of individual personal fulfillment, peaceful family and a stable state.

The Maoist Philosophy

Maoist philosophy is a Marxist-based philosophy put together by Mao Tse-tung (1893-1976). Mao imbibed greatly Western ideas, and as a leader and statesman, decided to carry out radical transformation of the Chinese society of his days. He adopted and applied the 19th century Western liberalism as a background for his Marxist-Leninist collectivism. Irrespective of this fact, he did not repudiate the Chinese culture but laid emphasis on sustaining the valuable aspects of it that are not opposed to modernity and social revolution which are necessary for the development and progress of China and its dissatisfied elites.

However, the Versailles Peace Conference that took place after the World War I elicited from the Chinese public a feeling of general dissatisfaction with Western ideals. The Chinese people felt that Chinese interests were jeopardized and marginalized by the Western powers in the negotiations and settlements reached in the conference. The Chinese people became antagonistic to western culture and ideals and were predisposed to the Marxist-Leninist ideals of dialectical materialism which have proved successful and were being applauded in the neighboring Russia at the time. By 1949, Mao and his Communist party were able to proclaim the country, "The People's Republic of China" and the philosophy of conflict and class struggle as expressed in dialectical materialism was introduced as official policy of government. Having had experience of the Confucian traditional philosophy of China and its emphasis on elite consensus for harmony, the Chinese people found more realistic and appealing the Marxist-Leninist idea of development and progress through the struggle between contradictions in the society.

Consequently, Mao developed and advanced a philosophy of social change that still holds sway in China today. Mao espoused the philosophy that changes in society are due chiefly to the development of the internal contradictions in society, such as the contradiction between the productive forces and the relations of production, the contradiction between classes and the contradiction between the old and the new. For him, it is the development of these contradictions that pushes society forward and gives the impetus for the suppression of the old by the new and at the same time leaving behind vestiges of the old. He asserted unequivocally and irrevocably that the dialectical world outlook teaches us primarily how to observe and analyze the movement of opposites in different things and situations. And more importantly, Mao outlined in his writings the methods for generating and resolving contradictions in the society.[10]

Maoist philosophy was grasped and imbibed by the generality of the masses in China, and it has become source of strength and power which is behind China's world power status and second largest economy in the world after the United States. This power and strength from Chinese philosophy and culture have permeated neighboring countries like Japan, Korea, India and Malaysia although they have remolded these acquisitions and powers into something of their own that is distinctive and uniquely Japanese or Korean, Indian or Malaysian. Hence, the making of the Asian Tigers could be traceable to the impact bound Chinese development.

18

AFRICAN PHILOSOPHY
The Different Senses of the Concept "African"

There have been series of debates on the existence or non-existence of African philosophy alongside the Western philosophy. According to C. B. Okolo, both affirmative and negative answers appeared in the foremost African Philosophical Journal, *the Second Order* published by the University of Ife, Nigeria.[1] Over the years, however, the debate has shifted to the precise nature of African philosophy. This shift was a result of the off-shoot and growth of the Department of Philosophy in many African universities and various centers for African studies abroad. In this work, we shall consider what African philosophy is all about and the direction African philosophy should take in the 21st century, and in a world that has become a global village as a result of globalization, the internet and social media.

First of all, we may ask, in what senses can philosophy be called African? The concept "African" has more than one meaning. Hence, let us consider the different senses of the concept "African." As a result of the various usages of the term African, it has acquired somewhat an ambiguity that tends to be an absurdity – or as it were a *reductio ad absurdum*. An African scholar, Damian Opata in his scholarly paper *"What is African"* attempts a rescue and clarified the concept African in four senses, namely: geographical, racial or ethnic, ideological and epistemological.[2] We added the fifth term African as a cultural term.

African as a Geographical Term

If we take philosophy to be the general world view of a people, African is seen by Opata, as all the people and things that are localized to any of the countries in the geographical area known as Africa. As a geographical entity, Africa is the second to Asia as the largest of the seven continents. It has not less than fifty-five countries with an area about 11.7 million square miles, and is located squarely across the equator, with its northern and southern extremes nearly equidistant from the equator at 37 degrees, 21 minutes and 34 degrees, 51 minutes north and south respectively. Eighty percent of Africa's area, about nine million square miles lies between the tropics of Cancer and Capricorn, respectively. As a result of the above location of Africa in the world, a greater part of the vast land mass has a tropical climate of torrential rainfall, and sunshine usually witnessed during rainy and dry seasons, respectively. These seasons lack the fluctuations of temperature usually witnessed in Europe and America. And because of her thick rain forest and green vegetation, Africa has one of the most spectacular wild life and game reserves in the world – a tourist attraction for some African countries.

African as a Racial or Ethnic Term

Race depicts any of the subdivision of humanity having the same communal and physical characteristics like skin pigmentation, color and type of hair, eyes and nose pattern. According to the *New Encyclopedia Britannica,* "African(s) as a racial and ethnic term are people of Negro stock; brown to dark brown in color with characteristically woolly hair, broad nose and averted lips."[3] So, for the most part, the African is a Blackman. Africans in Diaspora are called African-American in the United States. And as such, an African could be a Briton, Australian, German, etc. Opata in his scholarly paper was of the view that "an African is also anyone whose aboriginal place is Africa and anyone who acquired the citizenship of a country in the African continent becomes an African, too."[4] In his opinion, a person who acquires the citizenship of these countries either by birth or naturalization is an African.

African as Cultural Term

Here, things African are juxtaposed with things western or oriental. African cultural artifacts are unique and quite different from the ones that are European, American, Arabic or Asian. African culture, tradition and customs say much about the African more than anything else. African beliefs, worship, music, cuisine, dress and ceremonies set the African apart from other people. And the African carries these things wherever he goes. Despite the dynamics of culture contact and change, and attempts by the western culture and civilization to run down African culture as backward and inferior, African culture has withstood the test of time and still stands unique in the midst of foreign cultures. African cultural artifacts still stand unique in British and other museums of Europe, America, Australia and Asia crying to be returned to their homestead; the African aborigine owners – 'a thing cries for its owner,' so to speak, *"Res clamat a domino."*

African as an Ideological Term

As an ideological term, African is taken to be the characteristics or manner of thinking/thought currents peculiar to or that originated from Africa. Horace Emeagwara in his work, *An Eclectic Philosophical Hermeneutics of African Personality,* asserts that some thinkers argue that it is within the juxtaposition of the African and the Whiteman/Caucasians that we can dramatically speak of the African in the ideological sense. For him, when this happens, the African is regarded as underdeveloped (at best developing), primitive, superstitious, weak, and unfortunate, less privileged if not hopeless and so on.[5] Hence, the African is often neglected, marginalized and is underrepresented and also is expected to play second fiddle in most things of life, such as in international stage, in the work places in Europe and America, and even in western movies especially of Hollywood origin, in recognitions like Oscar and Golden Globe nominations and awards.

On African as an ideological term, Opata is of the view that in the wake of hegemonizing European culture propagated in the instrumentality of western science and technology which parades value-free and objective ideas, it is important to call attention to things and ideas African, even if at the epiphenomenal level so that we Africans are not suddenly ideologically swept off our feet. Hence, African ideologies like communalism, Ujamaa, Negritude, Black Power and Black Pride, Black Lives Matter, Pan Africanism, NEPAD and African Union should not be forgotten.

African as an Epistemic Term

The African, through his experiences and knowledge, sees reality from African perspectives. This implies that he analyzes and interprets in the African sense to produce an African world view. The African, as an epistemic term, presupposes and precludes the notion that the African can have knowledge of any phenomenon, concept or event. So, for Pantaleon Iroegbu, African as epistemic term involves "the body of concepts, ideas and views that Africans as a people and as individuals have concerning different aspects of reality."[6]

This is why an African is known by the way he reasons and how he interprets reality, be it superstitious, religious, cultural, moral, rational or scientific. For instance, even before the coming of the Whiteman with his culture and religion, the Africans already have the concept of the Supreme Being – God, the creator and maker of the heavens and earth, and all that is in it. They have religion and liturgical ceremonies. They have ethical or moral sense of what is good, and what is bad. They also have laws and a system of administration, etc. At present, good literary works – fiction and non-fiction authored by African writers have been translated into many foreign languages and they are found in most libraries of the world. *Things Fall Apart* by Chinua Achebe and many of the novels in the *African Writers Series* are good examples.

The Meaning of African Philosophy

The five senses of the concept "African" could be grouped into two parts: The geographical, the racial or ethnic and cultural senses on one hand and the epistemic and ideological senses on the other. The first three are about the place and the person, while the other pair is about the knowledge, ideas, insights, experiences, judgment and the wisdom of the people. Okolo, in his work *African Social and Political Philosophy: Selected Essays* asserts that "most scholars would view African philosophy essentially as a critical and systematic reflection on African experience, the African himself, his prospects and mode-of-being in the world."[7] For him, in this essential definition and role, African philosophy distinguishes and distances itself from other philosophies or other systems of philosophy. Okolo went further to contend that in its deepest inquiry, African philosophy deals with the African subject, that is to say, the African precisely as an African, his ideas and insights.

In his other work: *What is African Philosophy*, Okolo further stated concisely that African philosophy articulates and critically reflects on the way or ways, for example, the African perceives reality. African philosophy thus places special emphasis on the African, his world, history, values, etc. It explores the particular way or ways the African experiences and interprets nature, society, religion, man, God, human conduct and so on.[8]

What differentiates philosophy from other fields of African studies is the fact that African philosophy is the fruit of rational discourse. It is logical and systematic in its inquiry. Thus, K.C. Anyanwu and E.A. Ruch conceive African philosophy as that which concerns itself with the way in which African peoples of the past and the present make sense of their existence, of their destiny and of the world in which they live.[9] This means that African philosophy in its critical role, seeks to understand, clarify and explain every aspect of the African experience, thereby it articulates the world view of the African, what or who the African is in the African environment, and his role and place in it.

Henri Maurier kicked off the debate on whether or not there is such a thing as African philosophy. He asked the question, is there an African philosophy? This he answered in the negative "No! Not yet."[10] Also, there are African scholars of western mentality such as Kwasi Wiredu and Leopold Senghor whom Frantz Fanon described with the phrase, "Black Skins White Masks,[11] who dance for the western gallery by expressing Afro pessimism about any good coming from Africa. They joined Maurier and other Western cohorts in denigrating or denying the existence of African philosophy. With the above definitions and elucidations of African philosophy, we believe there would be no room for, if they are still in existence, remnants of scholars like Maurier and Wiredu.

Communalism: The Background of African Philosophy

It is good and pertinent to know that the original world view and experiences of an African were conceived and expressed in African communalism. What is equally good to know is that the degree of the personality quest of the pre-colonial African, as unbound differs remarkably from the personality struggles of the colonial African as bounded. The pre-colonial African is the original uncorrupt African. It is the African before the Arab and European visitations. The predominant concept that summarizes the original and uncorrupt African as far as human nature is concerned is communalism. In his work: *What is African?* Okolo asserts that the past, of particularly, the traditional African as opposed to the modem urbanized African was very much community conscious since he is always related to and interacted with others as a community. Okolo describes the traditional African as a "being-with" the community, and observes that it is the community that makes or produces the individual such that without the community, the individual has no existence.[12]

In his own contribution on what communalism is all about, John Mbiti opines that it is the basis of authenticity in the traditional African setting. In his words, "those without firm roots in the community any more, are simply uprooted, who float in life like cloud who live as individuals but are dead to the corporate humanity of their forefathers."[13] Supporting this view, Oliver Onwubiko writes that "the community in the traditional African society is the custodian of the individual; hence, the individual must go where the community goes."[14] Under the same line of thought, Mbiti surmises that "the African existentialists approach to "I am" becomes "We are" and since we are, therefore, I am."[15] Thomas Mboya concludes that "in communalism, the individual is not emphasized. A person is an individual only to the extent that he is a member of clan, a community or a family."[16]

The summary of the above views is that the original African emphasizes community life and communalism as a living principle of which the basic ideology is the community identity. Its aim is to produce and present an individual as a community culture - protected. The community is the basis for joint security of all members with the traditional ruler, his ruling council and the Age grades as agents of community policing. An individual suffers alienation when he rejects the community and its paraphernalia, and stays away from his kith and kin. His existence remains inauthentic to a great extent as long as he remains outside the community. So, the philosophy of individualism seen in the West as an ideology and principle of life is not encouraged in African even though it is not destroyed.

On the place of factors of production and the relation of productive forces under communalism, Leopold Senghor says "in African communalism, there is almost never property in the European sense of the word, as the general means of production; the land and its wealth, the wealth of the soil were owned in common."[17] In the projection of this view, Uzodinma Nwala was apt when he said that "traditional communalism rested on common ownership of the means of production like land, forests, trees, minerals, and rivers as well as the fruits of labor."[18] The wealth produced collectively by the family was owned collectively by all its members. This means there was no property-less citizens in real communal African society. In essence, there was no class antagonism or class struggles.

This classlessness is not in the sense of not possessing functional differentiation or differentiation based on wealth, but class in the strict sense of capitalism. Most often, there was no one class monopolistically dominating the means of production or labor. The reason for nonexistence of class conflicts in communalism was given by the South African author, Steve Biko when he asserted that we Africans regard our living together not as an unfortunate mishap warranting endless competition among us but as a deliberate act of God to make us a community of brothers and sisters jointly involved in the quest for a composite answer to the varied problems of life.[19] Hence, for him, in all we do, we always place man first and all our actions are usually joint community oriented action rather than individualism.

Another reason for communalism is that the traditional African society places emphasis and premium on the freedom of labor. The worker in the traditional African setting was not tied to his work because of the necessity to earn his wage, or to fulfill his master's demands for productivity. In that work milieu, there were no conditions of service or work he had to abide by. He only had the natural atmosphere in which man expresses himself, creates and recreates the material basis of his existence through work. He works in a collective setting, and work is for him the expression of his human essence. He applied both his intellect and physical energy, and it was joy to work.

It must be acknowledged also that African communalism is propelled and sustained by certain African values. Samuel Sofola listed some of these values as emphasis on "wholesome human relations" among people; respect for elders; community fellow-feeling reflected in communal land tenure and ownership," "live-and-let-live" philosophy; altruism (including medical and economic variants of it); and hospitality.[20] For F. Okafor, these values include the "metaphysics of man," respect for elders, hospitality, kindness and brotherhood.[21] Oliver Onwubiko gave a comprehensive list of these values as (i) sense of community; (ii) sense of good human relations; (iii) sense of sanctity and sacredness of life; (iv) sense of hospitality; (v) sense of the sacred and holiness of religion, (vi) sense of time; (vii) sense of respect for authority and the elders; (viii) sense of language and proverbs as cohesion of the community based on the truth.[22] These values are still today the core values of any African community. They have become essential part of the living essence of the African man, and he carries them wherever he goes. Any African that loses these values loses his Africanity and his Africanness is put into question as well.

One of the above values which is worthy of acknowledgement is the African sense of hospitality. Africans are hospitable people; they welcome visitors and immigrants with open arms and smiles. They treat the immigrant as a person and not as a number. Africans give the immigrant a treat of a life time, and if he wants to go, the Africans would see him off carrying his luggage bulging with assorted gifts, and these gifts are not tax deductible and there is no tax return they can claim them as it is the Western world. But if the immigrant wants to stay, he is given the best of jobs in the country. He is not given dirty jobs many Africans wouldn't like to do. Africans would value his credentials and encourage him to succeed in whatever he intends to establish in Africa. They want to see the nice and good things he can do. They do not frustrate him or constrain him to do menial or dirty jobs or serve them as the case in Europe and America.

On the ideology that went along with communalism, we must assert that the African, like all other men is imbued with cognitive faculty, he thinks; he meditates and reflects on the world, his immediate environment and the universe. He builds up concepts, doctrines and ideologies. According to Stan Anih, the basic and most fundamental to African thought is its holistic nature, and its substantive ability to harmonize, unite and agree with the three levels of being constituting the African world – the inanimate, the animate and the spiritual being, the brain, the mind and soul in man. He went further to say that western thought pattern categorized reality as, "one and many," "universals and particulars," and formed these and many more as competing conceptions of metaphysics. But for the African, reality is a sum total of what is and what appears, what is seen and unseen, of life and death, light and darkness, truth and falsehood. However, there is always a greater preference for the good and the beautiful. For Anih, the sky we perceive, the mountains we climb, the streams we fetch, the rivers we swim... all inanimate beings we see; the various trees we plant, the various animals ... rational being and everything ensouled, the Supreme Being... all constitutes reality for us.[23] This means that reality for the communal African is not just empirical, concrete, material and temporal but includes all spiritual beings - intangible, immaterial beings and eternity. And there is a deep-rooted, inter-relationship between the three levels of being.

This position is supported by Emmanuel Obiechina when he said that the traditional (communal) African, whether in their folklore and mythology, in their symbolism and figures of language, in their religious and magical beliefs has a total view of the universe as a continuum and a perpetual flow of being and experience comprising the visible and invisible universe, the world of nature and the supernatural, and of the living and the dead.[24] In the same line of thought, Festus Okafor says that the traditional African more than any people of the human race, had never known any compartmentalization of the metaphysical. Among them, the world and the universe for that matter are ruled not by blind forces but by divine being.[25] Thus, for the communal African, man was never regarded as a mere economic animal or a mere conscious material entity whose home does not transcend nature, but rather an entity whose life transcends the material dimensions. Thus, African values and ideology point to that fact that the world and the universe are ruled not by blind forces but by divine being. And this world or universe is a world of inanimate, animate and spiritual beings, all acting together in a community.

Enslavement as an African Experience

The present African ideology and philosophy could be partly understood in terms of the African experience over the past four centuries. For Onwubiko, "the realities of African life must be defined in terms of existential postulates and explained in specific normative African concepts."[26] Slavery is one of the major African experiences that have tended to shape African world view and philosophy. Benign expression of slavery has existed in Africa before the coming of the Europeans. It was much like a house servant or house maid in the contemporary sense of the word. For many, being a servant is just an alternative of mode of being in a difficult situation and a stepping stone to something greater, as it were a survival strategy.

In the pre-colonial African milieu, a person who committed heinous crime or abomination could be sold into slavery. Captives of war could be taken as slaves as well. As in feudal societies, one could give up himself or herself to an African Lord for protection from his enemies who seek to kill him or her. It is also known that in pre-colonial African society a person could give up self or be given up by parents as a pawn for debts. The creditor takes the person as slave temporarily if the debt could be worked out by the slave or permanently if the debt owed could not be worked out. In similar cases, many young girls and women were given out in marriage to a creditor or benefactor of her family. This still happens today. The issue of self-enslavement was encouraged by indigenous feudal system whereby an individual who lives in isolation and in the face of danger to his life and family could seek or fly to the patronage of a powerful family or clan for security and protection from the perceived enemies. The individual could alternatively seek refuge in the shrine of a powerful deity in a neighboring village or town in which case he has to serve the deity for the security of his life and property.

On the other hand, there were cases where the individual is taken and dedicated to a deity to appease the deity on the belief that the gods would ward off dangerous diseases and such things like famine and drought from the community. The person so used could be a captive of an ethnic war or an individual given as a ransom or settlement by another community that had killed a member of the community inadvertently.

Of course, it is this deity related enslavement that gave rise to the caste system in some African communities. Members of the caste system are often regarded as being owned by the deity and as such they are set apart from other people as outcast and untouchables. Any attack or harm to them is an attack on the deity which according to the belief system often carries serious consequences in the form of retributive justice from the deity. Socially, there are a lot of relationship problems in most marriages between members of the caste system and the free - borne of another community. Perennial nature of some the problems have made the caste system to subsist up till today and have remained entrenched as it were a die-hard despite efforts by well-meaning individuals and groups to end it. The above types of domestic enslavements were abhorred by well-meaning people in the African communities but they did not impart negatively on the African mind as much as the trans-Atlantic slavery. The African masters worked in the farm beside and along with the slaves. Most often, the slaves lived as members of their master's households and occasionally they were married into or were formally adopted by their masters as family members. The case of King Jaja of Opobo is a good example. He was a slave who later became king of the land of Opobo. On the other hand, the trans-Sahara slavery, the European and the American slavery were quite different. These imparted most negatively on the African psyche because it involved an up rootedness of being of the individual. Trading in African human cargo may be dated back to ancient Egyptian and Roman days.

Daniel Offiong noted that during the period of Muslim ascendancy, it was practiced also among Muslims in Arabia, Turkey, Persia, and India. But the military subjugation of the continent of Africa in modern times, and the enslavement of some sections of its population, was begun by Portugal about 1445, the middle of the 15th century. The Portuguese introduced the Atlantic slave trade in the early 16th century when the discovery of the New World created a demand for more workers. Not long after this, the Spanish, French, Genoese, Dutch, and after 1560, the English also joined the trade, and merchants from Liverpool took it to unprecedented level, and were greatly involved. The Portuguese were mainly responsible for setting up a string of fortified trading factories along the West coast from Cape Verde to the Congo by the time the famous Vasco da Gama had sailed around the Cape in 1497.[27] The role of European nations in African slavery is remarkable as they are responsible for the surge for slaves. Jefferson Murphy acknowledged that sure enough, Europeans did not start the African slave trade but the sheer volume of the slave traffic across the Atlantic and the brutality with which African slaves were treated renders the European slave trade fundamentally different from anything that took place within Africa itself.

The European trans-Atlantic slave trade was triangular in nature. During the time, Britain, France and colonial America supplied the exports and ships for the trade. Africa, on the other hand, took care of the human merchandise while the colonial plantations provided the raw materials as well as the demands for slaves. So, the cargoes of manufactured goods came across the Atlantic and were exchanged for slaves with the European merchants making a huge profit out of it. According to Eric Williams, the triangular trade gave a triple stimulus to British industry. The slaves were purchased with British manufactures, transported to the plantations; they produced sugar, cotton, indigo, molasses and other tropical products, the processing of which created new industries in England, while the maintenance of the slaves and their owners on the plantations provided another market for British industry, New England agriculture and the New found land fisheries.

By 1750, there was hardly a trading or manufacturing town in England which was not in some way connected with the triangular slave trade. The profit obtained provided one of the main streams of capital accumulation in England which assisted in financing the Industrial Revolution of the 17th and 18th century. This could be regarded as one of the greatest transfer of wealth in the history of mankind and provided the qualitative leap to modernity in Europe and America. And that industrial revolution is still the bedrock of western development up to now. Those profits which we regard as 'old money' has intermingled with 'new money' but, they are still the basis of many investments that are yielding dividend in Europe and America today. If we follow the leads like the start-ups of old companies, mergers, name change and ownership, we can see them in Agro-allied companies, big banks and insurance companies, steel companies, real estate companies, railway corporations, Motor companies, construction and trading companies, oil and gas companies, etc. The old money still plays a role in the income gap between the Whites and the Blacks in Europe and America. The new money (investments and wealth that have no link to profits from slave trade) has not being able to bridge the gap.

It is on record that many merchants in Europe and America joined the Trans-Atlantic slave trade in one way or the other when they saw the lucrative nature of trade; in fact, they took the trade to another dimension. The trade became more of invasion of Africa and its interior hinterlands for human cargo. European slave raiders and their collaborators would swoop down on unsuspecting villages and hinterlands, and seize the victims who would command a good price on European Markets. This higher level of Europeanized and Americanized slavery played the shameful role of depopulating the African continent; the number of Africans taken for over more than four centuries of slavery is incalculable. The figure has been "estimated to be between 65 and 75 million able-bodied persons."[28] This constituted a central feature in the process of the western primitive accumulation of capital which was one of the basic components of the capitalism especially the Western capitalism. And for Africa it was "the beginning of massive brain drain which contributed to its underdevelopment up till today."[29]

So, the able-bodied men and women in their early twenties and mid-thirties were forcefully taken as slaves to work in the textile mills, tobacco factories, iron works, sugar refineries, and rice and grist mills. They provided labor for gold mines, lead mines, canal digging, turnpike and railroads construction as well as fisheries, lumber-gangs, street cleaning and worked as artisans, carpenters, draymen, barbers, common laborers, carriage drivers, and house and hotel servants.

The Africans taken away as slaves to the New World were quite different from the American Indians in the sense that the Africans were uprooted from their ancestral home and community to live in isolation in Europe and America where they were most often tortured with sophisticated instruments. A Brazilian, Arturo Ramos, represents the instruments and pains thus: There was the trouco of wood or iron, and instrument which held the slave fast at the ankles and in the grip of which he was often kept for day on end; the libambo which gripped the unfortunate victim fast at the neck; the algemas and the anjihos which bind the hands tightly crushing the thumbs ... Some plantation owners of more perverted inclinations used the so-called movenas and frezenas ... The slaves tied face down on the ground, were beaten with the raw hide whip. Apart from the physical torture that started from the beginning of their capture through their journey across the hinterlands and the Atlantic

Ocean, they also were tortured during their work in the plantations and mines. Their lives became a life of sickness, fear of being beaten, hunger and agonizing sense of loss of their country, culture and language. It is on record that "some slaves committed suicide for they believed that when they die they return home to their own fatherland. Some went on hunger strikes."[31]

Many others were killed during the slave raids, many died through suffocation in the camp at the Atlantic coasts and in the ships and during shipwreck or revolt.

B. Lalage and M. Crowther agreed that Camille Roussan created a significant picture and summary of the ordeal in the average life of a slave in his poem that heralds the invention of machines which assisted in no small measure (more than any human benevolence) in the abolition of slavery in Europe and America. His poem runs as follows:

Machines!
My father's dead!
He died of the diabolical effort,
He died in Santo Domingo,
My mother must have died in Conakry,
My brother died In New Orleans,
My sister died In Santiago,
All of them died.
Because they knew no sleep,
Whilst I did all your donkey work,
I am a docker in Brooklyn,
A storekeeper on all the seas,
A farmer in Cuba,
A shock trooper in Algeria,
My sufferings go by various names and liveries,
But I am still the big black slave,
Despite your presence there Messianic Machines,
Ready to do the big takeover.[32]

In the conscience and opinion of the West, they took Africa as a dark continent and had no doubt that this was a predetermined role that Africa had to play. But the growth of mechanized mines and plantations, automated industries and factories rendered most slave hands redundant and at a point unnecessary. As a result, the poet above described the machines as messianic machines because they did the big take-over from the slaves.

In the higher level of this dialectics, the West thought up the need to return some of the ex-slaves to Africa where they are needed to work and produce the badly need raw materials for industries and machines of Europe and America. The rest of them that were left behind suffered unimaginable marginalization and racism in Europe and America. They suffered segregation in terms of the neighborhood they could live in, the schools they could attend, the transportation they could use, where they could work and hotels they could lodge in. In fact, they were edged out of good housing and good businesses through restrictive clauses in the security deed of loan guarantee and mortgage contracts. Ultimately, they were constrained to live and do business in squalor and ghetto sections of the European and American cities; areas with little or no amenities, as it were, poor and insecure neighborhoods with little police presence, high unemployment and high crime rate.

This plight of African Americans still exists up to the present. Some scholars have therefore suggested that the abolition of slave trade was not actually the humanitarian gesture as many people were made to believe or a result of moral reawakening or a sense of guilt for that crime against humanity but a result of the growth of machines in Europe which rendered most slave hands redundant, and as such, were capable of replacing the slave hands in its entirety. This also precipitated urgent need for raw materials from Africa to keep the machines in Europe running at full capacity. The answer would be found in the direct intervention in Africa through the agency of colonialism.

Thus, for about four hundred years, the Europeans never bordered that the nefarious slave trade depersonalized and reduced the dignity of the Africans. For many Whites, Africans are sub-humans, and are to be treated as an object of possession or property. John Calhoun, a renowned slave master, once said that if he could find a black man who could understand the Greek syntax, he could then consider them part of our human race and his attitude toward enslaving them would therefore change.[33] T.U. Nwala says David Hume, on the same line of thought, opined that Africans are naturally inferior to Whites. According to him, there is scarcely ever was a civilized nation of that complexion, or even any individual eminent either in action or speculation. Among black slaves, none ever showed any symptoms of ingenuity.[34]

In any sense, the positions of Calhoun and Hume cannot be accepted because history had it that Greek Geometry, mathematics and philosophy had its origins from Egypt which is part of Africa. Again, the use of iron tools has long started in the Kingdom of Kush in Ethiopia before Western development. The impact of the Trans-Atlantic slave trade was not only that it depopulated Africa; it is responsible for Africa's underdevelopment, backwardness and the feeling of inadequacy.

Colonialism: The Enclosure and Dispossession of Africa

For Daniel Offiong, it is difficult to say where slave trade ended and where colonial imperialism began because before slavery was extirpated in Africa, colonial imperialism had established roots in the continent. "There was a perfect continuum between the two and the handover was thorough."[35] This means that the scramble for Africa was another evil that followed the abolition of slavery. Or rather, they intermingled and intertwined purposely. The colonial imperialism is pivoted on the some Western view that Africa was a dark continent, and that they were bringing the first light of civilization to a benighted people, lost in primitive barbarity. "These assumptions made some colonial administrators to adopt and enforce dehumanizing policies, claiming that Africans should regard colonialism as unqualified blessings."[36] These assumptions made Hugh Trevor-roper to say that perhaps in the future, there will be some African history to teach. But at the present, there is none; there is only the history of Europeans in Africa. The rest is darkness ... and darkness is not the subject of history.[37]

M. Perham toed this line of thought when she said that until the very recent penetration of Europe, the greater part of the continent was without the wheel, the plough or the transport animal, without stone houses or clothes except skins; without writing and so without history.[38]

However, Casely Hayford acknowledged in the work of Basil Davidson that before even the British came into relations with African people, Africans were a developed people, having their own institutions, having their own ideas of government.[39] Likewise, before the advent of Christian missionaries from Europe, Africans already have not only the idea of

God but also the concept of the Supreme Being- God, who they believe is the creator of the universe and African Traditional Religion has a unique liturgy of worship, ceremonies and music. It is even on records that colonial intruders signed treaties with kingdoms and empires of Africa, some of which were peace or secession treaties. Some kingdom like the Ancient Ghana, Mali, Sudan, Kush of Ethiopia (which produced the biblical Queen of Sheba that visited King Solomon) and Zulu Kingdom were not tiny principalities or states as some western observers might suggest. They were full-blown empires with a system of administration supported by organized military power.

The imperial colonialism was one of the greatest events of the 19th and 20th centuries which was so pervasive, and had a serious impact on the lives of Africans. It turned the lives of Africans upside-down and inside out – affecting from one generation to another the behavior, outlook, feelings, and beliefs of men, women and children. So, the colonial adventure in Africa could not be regarded essentially as a civilizing mission. Although there may have been individuals and institutions that worked hard and sincerely for the good of the African but the crux of the matter is that the colonial African, as a bounded person, was a sufferer of White supremacy. He was humiliated. He was stripped of his Africanity. He was neither truly black nor truly white.

In essence, White supremacy in Africa was the bane of colonial epoch. Colonial administration was based on "the rule by might doctrine." It also involves a political, social and economic oppression and exploitation of one country by another; the domination of the weak by the strong, the poor by the rich, the developing by the developed nations. Jack Woddis sees the essence of imperial colonialism as the direct and overall subordination of one country to another on the basis of state power being in the hands of the dominating foreign power.[40] The purpose of the exploitative philosophy of colonialism is to keep the colonized people in political subjugation, and to make possible the maximum exploitation of the people and the country's resources. Kwame Nkrumah, one of the foremost African nationalists articulated the purpose of colonialism as the policy by which a foreign power binds territories to herself by political ties with the primacy objective of promoting her own economic advantages.[41] So, during colonialism, a lot happened; there was forced labor, and able bodied men and women were forced to leave their homes to work hundred miles away for Europeans. Monetary taxes were imposed on peasants. Lands were taken from Africans and given to Europeans to established plantations. Africans were forced to plant export crops instead of their food crops. Ghana was known for cotton and gold and thus called the Gold Coast. Ivory Coast was known for ivory and was called Ivory Coast. In Nigeria, farmers have pyramids of groundnut in North, Cocoa in the West and palm oil in the East. These were products of forced labor. These were to be exported to Europe and America to run Western industries.

Also, as part of the strategy of keeping Africa perpetually underdeveloped, the colonial imperialists also monopolized all other economic activities, thus preventing the rise of an indigenous and noble entrepreneurial class. In all cases, the price Africans paid for the finished products was many times over the price for which they sold their raw materials because of the value added to the original raw material. By exporting the profits created by African labor to Europe, the development of Europe was assured, and at the same time this greatest capital flight in human history perpetuated the underdevelopment of Africa.

On colonial education, literacy among the Africans was necessary to the colonial master especially for communication and interpretation but too much literacy among the African was considered dangerous and undesirable, so to avoid competition with the West. High technical education was considered a treaty article forbidden for Africans. So, colonial education was not designed to benefit the African but to help prepare them to participate meaningfully in the economic and political exploitation and subjugation of their country. Culturally, Africans were treated as people having no worthwhile identity, and at times regarded as sub-human. Their culture was described as barbaric, savage and primitive. Their religions and shrines were rudely desecrated, and many were destroyed. For the colonial masters, the concept of the Supreme Being - God does not exist in African religions. African gods and morals were taken for fakes. They also denied or de-emphasized all African roles in world history, including the fact of the African origin of Hebrew and Greek thought, science and philosophy through the auspices of Ancient Egyptian mystery temples and religion. According to Emeagwara, when the Europeans acknowledged the pioneering role of Egypt, they argued, however, that Egypt was not a part of Africa, but of Southern Europe or the Mediterranean.[42]

Thus, African achievements in science and philosophy were appropriated as European achievements. We read about such African philosophers like St. Augustine, Origen and Philo as part of Western intellectual tradition and achievement. In his monumental work, G.M. James described the phenomenon as "stolen legacy." The overall effect of the above colonial situation is that in place of African cultural history and realities, European political, philosophical, economic, religious and cultural achievements were imposed. The only history, religion, morals, philosophy, logic, and science worth learning were those of the West. The introduction of organized formal European education and religion promoted the background and framework for the reproduction of European systems, beliefs and values. Africans were made to see the world from the perspective of European world, social and intellectual order. Colonial mentality took sway as Africans began to reject and deny their own cultural achievement. Some Africans who were privileged to be allowed to study abroad came back to extol the Western culture in their speeches and writings. Such African authors as Chinua Achebe and Wole Soyinka wrote works that received accolades, applause and laurels for dancing to European gallery. Literatures that are full of Afro-pessimism were made compulsory in primary and secondary schools in many African countries. *Eze Goes to School*, *Things Fall Apart*, and *The Lion and the Jewel* are good examples among many others. Thus, Euro-centrism triumphed in many departments of the African existence. The most critical element of Euro-centrism is its teaching that Africans have no philosophy. In fact, colonialism impacted negatively on Africans. It devalued the African and depersonalized him. It erected structure in which irrelevant skin color is used to determine who is inferior and who is superior. The colonialists indoctrinated the Africans to believe and accept that Africans were primitive, backward and if not for their presence, we would be living like animals.

In the words of Okolo, colonialism and its consequential master-servant relationship meant for the African a negation of self, a marginal role in his own destiny, object rather than subject of his own history.[43] As far as being or personality was concerned, the African remained inauthentic, untrue, "an invisible man" or in Fanon's phrase, "black skin - white mask." The reason for this African underdevelopment is well implied in the Lord Frederick Lugard's work, *The Dual Mandate*. According to this British colonial administrator in Nigeria, "the European brains, capital and energy would not be used for developing the resources of Africa from motives of pure philanthropy; that Europeans were in Africa was for the mutual benefits of her own industrial classes."[44]

Again, during the Berlin conference and that of Brussels that followed the scramble for Africa and its partition, and eventual colonization, no consideration was given to African interest, feelings and dignity. The communique from the conference only advocated that the colonialists should establish effective occupation of their territories to avoid conflicts among themselves. Thus, most of the treaties that followed this injunction were done by the colonialist either by force, persuasion, intimidation, bribery and deceit. African leaders that refused these treaties were either killed or forced into exile. Also, the boundary negotiations were between European pioneers; the Africans and their chiefs were most often not consulted. The result was that the new political boundaries cut across the old traditional ethnic brotherhood or groupings. For instance, Nigeria – Republic of Benin boundary splits the Yorubas into two; while the Ewes of Ghana were split between British Gold Coast and German Togoland. The same is the cause of the recent boundary dispute between Nigeria and Cameroon over the Lake Chad and Bakasi Peninsula, where some Nigerians from Cross River state were cut to Cameroon. Consequently, we have brothers or peoples with ancestral descent and communities living in separate walls of different European governments.

Furthermore, the Europeans imposed a big administrative superstructure on African economies, this means big governments with little economic base. This fact still exists in many African countries today. Thus, the economies were rendered backward and underdeveloped. The African economies lacked backbone by way of infrastructures, and as such could not carry the weight of the administrative superstructure up to today. The African cities of commerce became colonial administrative cities. Not much meaningful economic enterprise went on from year to year. White collar jobs and unskilled labor became the order of the day. What existed in form of industries were raw materials and their marketing boards. Imports from Europe were the focus of the African economies. Africa became a dumping ground for western finished products. The colonial masters were not interested in developing the hinterlands; they only built railways into the interior to make sure that the needed cash crops are conveyed to the coast for onward shipping to Europe. Thus, the colonial masters put up infrastructures in and around coastal towns and areas with major minerals such as gold, coal, diamond, and cash crops such as groundnuts, rubber, cotton, cocoa, tea, palm oil, etc. They refused to develop the hinterlands neither did they encourage the growth of new towns that could jumpstart industrialization. For them, technology development and industrialization would be counterproductive in Africa as they would use up the much needed raw materials for industries in Europe and America. They would also kill markets for foreign goods and nip in the bud African insatiable desire for foreign made goods.

The colonial masters also practiced racism within the colonies. They discriminated against the indigenes. Africans were not allowed to enter certain parts of the urban areas. The Government Reserved Area (GRA) was meant for the Whites and a few African collaborators. The colonial masters felt uncomfortable whenever native Africans were among them. They were also apprehensive to have their young ones interact with Africans. It was as if they would contact rabies or serious harm would be done to them. The schools they went to, the hospitals they are treated are well equipped and were quite different from the ones Africans went to. In most African schools pupils sat on the floor to learn. The school buildings were dilapidated, with licking roofs, without doors and windows.

It is also recorded that the colonial masters looted lots of valuable African arts. Religious shrines and king's palaces were raided, and treasures were looted and sent to Europe and America. It is their strong conviction and working principle that when an army captures a city, it loots it and that applies to colonization of one country by another. Thus, when the British army captured Benin in 1897, they looted about two thousand, five hundred ornaments and treasures from the Oba's palace. And many of the treasures are scattered throughout museums in Europe and America. We can now see even in the Middle and Far East stolen African treasures play a role in the life of museums as art lovers pay to see them. Onwubiko recalled that five of these Benin art works fetched £2,899 in a sale of African arts in London (1957-59) and that Benin ivory mask was sold to Nelson A. Rockefeller in 1958 for £20,000.[45] Thus, in the light of these, the enormous wealth lost by Africa can also be assessed. Also, during the 1977 All African Arts and Culture Festival (FESTAC) in Lagos, the Nigerian government had to pay Ten Million Pounds (£10m) to British government just to have a snap shot of the Benin arts after every move to restore them failed.[46]

At last, the nationalist movements came as the two world wars revealed the weaknesses of the Caucasian in the battle fields; that they, after all, were not stronger and better in body and mind. The nationalists were mostly African soldiers who fought side by side with the Caucasians during World War I and World War II. The Black Africans were frontline soldiers and they were courageous even under serious injuries and they were gallantry in the battle field more than their Caucasian counterparts. At the end of the war, the soldiers came home to their various countries in Africa to become nationalists. These nationalists fought to regain the independence of African countries, and recover their collective consciousness, freedom and human dignity. They were aware of the fact that they were being exploited and that they did not benefit from the exploitation of their natural resources and the surpluses they created. For Offiong, the nationalists embarked on all forms of radical action to compel their exploiters to return whence they came. But before they fled, the colonial powers imposed upon the people constitutions that would ensure conflicts among the different groups, as in Nigeria, Ivory Coast, Sudan and South Africa.[47] They worked hard to place in power those who would continue to promote their interests after they had gone. Most of these stooges were people they encouraged or sent to study in Europe. The colonialists were sure these Africans would return to be their stooges and act as their protégés. Nkrumah has noted in his work, *Neo-colonialism: The Last Stage of Imperialism*, that such compradors were not exposed to the kind of education that would liberate them mentally and otherwise. Their education was for the purpose of encouraging the culture of dependence after the ceremonial ending of colonialism.[48] This fact has hindered the progressive and development of many African countries up to the present.

Neo-Colonialism: The Unending Vestige of Imperialism

Neo-colonialism over the years has occupied a special place in African experience and world view. According to Green and Seidman, neo-colonialism results from "false decolonization," the preservation of the colonial relationship of western dominance and African dependence by means other than direct political control, after granting them pseudo-political independence." For Nkrumah, neo-colonialism is the worst form of imperialism. For those who practice it, it means power without responsibility and for those who suffer from it, it means exploitation without redress.

On the question of how neo-colonialism operates, David Wise and Thomas Ross recognized it as a kind of invisible government ... a loose amorphous grouping of individuals and agencies drawn from many parts of the foreign visible governments. It is not limited to the Central Intelligence Agency, although the CIA is at its heart. Nor is it confined to the nine other agencies which composed what is known as the intelligence community: the National Security Council; the Defense Intelligence Agency; the National Security Agency; Army Intelligence; Navy Intelligence and Research; the Atomic Energy Commission; and the Federal Bureaus of Investigation and the Federal Reserve Board. He continued that the invisible government includes also many other units and agencies (e.g., the World Bank, IMF, EU, NATO, G–8 conference, etc.) as well as individuals who appeared outwardly to be a normal part of the conventional government.[49] It even includes and encompasses business firms, multi-national oil and gas companies, big assembly plants, food and pharmaceutical multinationals, information technology and social media giants like Microsoft, Intel, Google, Yahoo, Facebook, Twitter, U-tube, and Instagram, the New York Times, the Wall Street Journal, Time Magazine, CNN, BBC and Voice of America, etc. Non-governmental organizations, non-profit organizations, aide agencies, community based organizations and foundations are sometimes insidiously a part of invisible government as it were "a hand of Esau and voice of Jacob" module.

The purpose of Neo-colonialism, among other things, is actually to keep the economic, political, military and other relations of developing countries within the framework of the capitalist or communist economic and political system. The resultant effect in practical terms is the continuing economic dependence of African countries on their former colonial overlords, superficial integration of the developing countries into the neo-colonial economic and sociopolitical blocs, structures and values. It includes also neo-colonial penetrations and infiltrations into African countries through marginal capital investments, aid, debts and technical partnerships. Most often, these lead to intermittent political instability, military coups, economic crises, and social dislocation, dependency and distorted development in Africa and third world countries.

Militarism: The Eclipse of African Freedom, Growth and Development

Militarism has in the recent past, formed part of the African experience. It is common knowledge that the colonial masters left behind stooges not only in the political circles but also in the military circles. Thus, the military formed part of the tentacles of neocolonial influence. Many African military officers were trained in military institutions like the Royal Military Academy, Sandhurst in England, where they were taught or rather they learnt the act of military violence and organized crime like coup d'états. Military coup d'états run contrary to the norm that the military institution should be subordinate to lawfully constituted civil authority. But, in Africa, since the independence of Nigeria in 1960, most African countries have witnessed more military inspired regime changes than the open and competitive transfer of political power from one group to another. According to Ayoade, as of April 1985, twenty-four African countries were under military rule and twenty-one under civil rule, two- Sierra Leone and Uganda - had experienced military rule and another, Cape Verde and Chad, were under militarized civilian administrations. Thus, by his estimation, sixty percent of African nations have had the experience of military rule, twelve percent offer their citizens some sort of electoral choice and the rest constitute the one-party or "president for life" states, where elections may be sporadically held, but merely to endorse the choice of political leaders.[50]

For Igwe, despite the preponderance of the military in the politics of most African countries, military rule is still considered an aberration by every well-meaning persons in Africa.[51] No matter the type of military that came to power, whether the military incursion into national politics and governance is the arbitrator-type or the ruler-type described by Amos Permutter in his article *"The Praetorian State and the Praetorian Army"*,[52] the aberration is not removed, and no matter how timely and pragmatic in the maintenance of the stability of the system, militarism is still not legalized. Coups are still a form of organized crime whether the coup plotters are caught or not. This fact is somehow well known to the army. Their awareness is amply illustrated by the instantaneous declaration of political transition agendas by new military leaders after they forcefully seized power from democratically elected government or in a counter coup.

The impacts of military incursions into the politics and governance of African countries have been tremendously negative. According to Babatope, since independence, every African country that has had a military intervention, with one or two exceptions, witnessed a concatenation of social and political aberrations; the worst forms of corruption, oppression of the masses, suppression of democracy and the voice of dissent, personal ambition for naked power, and morbid desire for self-perpetuation in office, physical elimination of political opponents and possible rivals, and so on.[53] The military perpetuated two forms of corruption: Corruption based on need, which exists among the masses the military has impoverished; and then corruption based on greed, which is found among the military leaders and civilians in power who enrich themselves from the public treasury and accumulate massive wealth they do not actually need.

So, we must emphasize here that the masses in Africa want to be ruled by a system that fully guarantees them the right to life, right to liberty, right to free education, the right to free health care, the right to decent housing, the democratic rights to express themselves under a very free atmosphere, the right to good economic well-being, the right to elect their leaders and be a part of the power that guides their lives. Whenever they took over power in any African country, the military negated all these things that bring growth and development.

Towards African Growth and Development Philosophy

African philosophy gravitates around monumental experiences of the people, and different philosophical concepts have emerged from these experiences and they tend to stand as African world view and interpretation of reality. These world views include the metaphysical, ethical, epistemological or the socio-political concepts. Some of these world views that have been used to periscope and project African philosophy are worthy of mention and acknowledgement. The major ones include: African Freedom; African Communalism and Socialism; African Personality; Negritude; African Nationalism and Patriotism; African Social Self and Self Help Philosophy; African Welfare-ism; Pan Africanism; Black Power and Black Pride, Black Lives Matter; Common Good and National Interest; African Union (AU) and African Security; Non-Alignment; African Union and the New Partnership for African Development

(NEPAD) and many others. Again, some of these concepts are worthy of brief explanation.

African Freedom

The African has never relented in his quest for freedom right through the four centuries of enslavement, colonialism and the decades of militarism to the present neo-colonialism and civil right infringements. African nationalism, civil rights agitations, non-violent resistance and protests are well known. For Okolo, "freedom has been a battle cry for the modern African since his pre-independence days, and has now become an integral part of his existential struggles."[54] One must admit that there is lack of proper understanding and articulation of African freedom. It is the role of African philosophers to clarify what African freedom is all about. African freedom has been classified into the following: Freedom from without, Freedom from within and Freedom to...

Freedom from without

Under Freedom from without, the African as a rational being resent all obstacles to effective choices on his part, more so when the obstacles are as a result of the free action of others. Usually, man regards himself as free in proportion to what he thinks or does, and what he chooses without any restraints from other people.

Freedom from within

On Freedom from within, the modern African is opposed to all forces which undermine his sense of worth, power, pride and dignity in his continent whether external or internal from the Whites or Blacks. Thus, the African regards colonialism, neo-colonialism, racism, terrorism, violence, exploitation, ethnicity and nepotism, abuse of power, illiteracy, racism, political disenfranchisement, social injustice and poverty as obstacles to his complete freedom.

Freedom to

Under Freedom to, in the philosophical sense refers to presence and abundance of opportunities for the African, and the ability of the African to actualize and master his own world. This is freedom to be what he wants to be; to control and shape his world in tune with his ideals and to be the main realizer of his dreams. It means being responsible, hardworking, independence, self-reliance, standing on one's own feet and being the subject of one's history. This is what Hegel called "Self-contained existence," and non-alienated existence, or simply authentic existence of the African in all facets of life. Consequently, we can talk of African political freedom, economic freedom, cultural freedom, religious freedom and psychological freedom, etc.

African Socialism

African socialism is all about African communalism and patriotism. It is African altruism as opposed to western individualism. African communities are well known for their extended family system than the western nuclear family structure. Ruch and Anyanwu asserted that African socialism has recorded series of exponents ranging from Nkrumah, Leopold Sedar Senghor, Tom Mboya, M.I. Okpara, Julius Nyerere, etc., but each of the exponents seems to endow the phrase with his own thinking and interpretations.[55]

The common denominator of these exponents is that African socialism has its essential elements as African communalism, African humanism and African welfarism. One other distinctive form of African socialism is the Ujamaa socialism of Julius Nyerere of Tanzania. Ujamaa socialism is more than a political system. It is at once a philosophy, a worldview as well as a gateway to Africa's true selfhood. It means familyhood, togetherness, or brotherhood. For Nyerere, it involves African personality per se - this is how we want to live as a nation. We want the nation to live as one family.[56]

African Personality

The concept of African personality was proposed first by Edward Wilmot

Blyden in May 1893, in a paper he delivered to the Liberia College titled *The Idea of an African Personality*. Nkrumah took up the concept and popularized it in his works and speeches. For Emegwara, African personality is a philosophical carpentry; an eclectic philosophical hermeneutics of all that is good and indigenous about the African and his historicity.

Blyden in his paper criticized African elites educated in foreign lands and who ridiculed things African and opted for foreign things. According to Blyden, no amount of training could transform an African into a European. He lamented that the great hindrance upon African development has been our unreasoning imitation of foreign things.

Furthermore, Nkrumah says "for too long in our history, Africa has spoken through the voices of others, now what I called an African personality in international affairs will have a chance of making its proper impacts and will let the world know it through the voices of Africa's own sons."[57] Okolo elucidated the concept by saying that African personality in action or in world affairs presupposes the state of freedom, independence, responsibility and control of African world by Africans.[58]

African Personality received a boost with the election of Barack Obama as the First African-American President of the United States in 2008 and with his re-election for a second term in 2012. It is regarded by many as the zenith of African Personality in world affairs. It came close to the heels of the elections and services of Kofi Annam of Ghana as the Secretary General of the United Nations, Chief Chukwuemeka Anyaoku of Nigeria as the Secretary General of the Common Wealth of Nations, and the selection of Dr. Mrs. Okonjo Iwuala of Nigeria as the Vice President of the WorldBank.

Pan-Africanism

Horace Campbell was of the opinion that Pan-Africanism emerged from the ravages of imperialism, racism, slavery and colonialism. For Esedebe, it is a feeling which was aroused and articulated in the New World around the time of the declaration of American Independence in 1776. The term simply means, all African(ism). As a movement it was geared toward the emancipation of Afro-Americans and self-government of African countries. Aforka Nweke sees it as a movement that provides a common ideological basis for the advancement both of African independence and collective security. Its primary goal is the unity of African peoples in one independent political community embracing all ethnic and national groups and free from political, economic and racial domination.[59]

Negritude

Negritude comes from the Latin word *"Negritudo"* meaning black or blackness. The concept was made manifest in the journal *"Presence Africaine."* The proponents of the concept and movement were Aime Cesaire a West Indian from Martinique, Leon Damas from Guyana and Leopold Senghor from Senegal. Negritude as a movement came into being in the mid-thirties with the meetings of African students and students from Haiti, Guyana, Martinique, etc. who were studying in France. It was born out of their common experience of racism, alienated consciousness, and of living in a white world without really belonging to it. Negritude was meant to assert, according to Cesaire that we were blacks and that we were proud of it, and that we thought that Africa was not some sort of black page in the history of humanity. In sum, we asserted that our Black African heritage was worthy of respect, and that this heritage was not relegated to the past, that its values were values that could still make an important contribution to the world.[60] In his exposition of what negritude is to the Africans, Senghor says it is African personality, or the cultural heritage, the values and above all, the spirit of Black African civilization.[61]

Furthermore, through his critique of Negritude, Prof. Wole Soyinka of Nigeria, the Nobel Laureate for Literature tried to energize the African to action on the belief that action speaks louder than voice, and that verbal glorification of great African past would not move the continent forward. He believes that Negritude should be action oriented. It should be a practical and pragmatic movement rather than an oration on great African past. He asserted that the tiger does not boost of its tigress-ness, it acts. In his work, *The Man Died*, he affirmed that the man dies in a person who keeps quiet and does nothing in face of oppression and subjugation not only of himself but also of his own people.

Black Power and Black Pride

The concept of Black Power and Pride came into being with a slogan made popular by an African-American, Stokley Carmichael in July, 1966 in a protest march in Mississippi against a black separatist movement in the United States. Carmichael started a chant: Black power! We want "black power." The black power slogan had been used before by Richard Wright and Adam Clayton Powell in 1965 in the Organization of Black Power, who gathered in Detroit to represent the ideas of Malcolm X, who was originally called Malcolm Little. For Richard Fruecht, black power basically means political power which used as a stepping stone, could lead to economic power so much needed for the Black survival as a race.[62]

Nkrumah summarized black power as the sum total of the economic, cultural, and political power (and technological power) which the Black man must have in order to achieve his survival in a highly developed technical society, and in a world ravaged by imperialism, colonialism, neo-colonialism and racism.[63] It must be noted that the propagators of black power rejected non-violence approach in the struggle for Black emancipation. The protagonists of black power opposed Martin Luther King Jr's non-violence method of emancipation. However, it must be noted and made clear that black power is not anti-White, but it is anti-anything and everything that serves to oppress the Blackman. They could be anti-White if White people align themselves on the side of oppression. Black power is opposed to white supremacy groups or individuals wherever they may be found, whether in government or in police force where they try to regain their loss imperial glory and display brutality and killing of blacks under the cover of law and duty.

Those who see black power as the sum total of the positive qualities of the Black man always conceive some factors as holding down the emergence of black power in Africa and in diaspora. In Africa, some of factors include high level capital flight, low level foreign investment, high level of unemployment occasioned by very low industrialization and technological development, huge debt burden, and unfavorable balance of trade with the western countries most of which are former colonial masters of Africa. According to them, the West has not committed much to alleviate the African condition brought about by their colonial and neo-colonial policies. There is no doubt the West is benefiting immensely from the African condition. Over the years, Africa has become a dumping ground for foreign goods, and Africans are now very much dependent on them. African leaders cannot oppose western policies in world politics and trade for fear of losing the token of foreign aids in existence.

In Diasporas, the problem faced by the Black Africans is crippling, it ranges from high unemployment rate among Blacks, which is greater than that of the Whites, Hispanics and other races in the American and European societies. The reason for this is not far-fetched. Blacks have the highest rate of dropout in schools, highest rate of divorce and broken families. Apart from these, by reason of history, Blacks are fundamentally marginalized in terms of ownership of the factors of production. They have the rear seat in the ownership of businesses, landed property, in commerce, in Civil service, in Military, in Police force, Air force, and Navy, in Congress and in the White House. For many companies which claim to be diversity employers, the nondiscriminatory rule or affirmation in employment means planting one or two Blacks in midst of hundreds of Whites in their company. This is symbolic employment rather than real employment of African Americans in the labor force.

The reason Blacks are behind in so many areas is not because Blacks are weaklings, no not at all. In competitive sports like football, basketball, boxing, athletics such as marathon and the 100-meter dash, Blacks are the torch bearers. Great sportsmen like Muhammed Ali and Floyd Mayweather in boxing, and Usain Bolt is the world fastest man, Magic Johnson, Michael Jordan and LeBron James in basketball, Tiger Woods in golf, Serena and Venus Williams in tennis, media mogul Oprah Winfrey, a nationalist like Nelson Mandela and music stars like Bob Marley, Michael Jackson, Kanye West, Jay Z and Beyoncé, Rihanna, to mention but a few, and all Black stars in the NFL, athletics and other areas of human endeavor are physical indices and practical indications that Blacks are not inferior at all. The list is not exhaustive. These African men and women are the toast of black power and pride. These personalities were successful partly because in these fields natural selection and survival of the fittest in terms of physical power and intelligence are the rules of the game as opposed to some discretionary application assessment used in many areas of employment that sideline African Americans.

Furthermore, black pride has recorded resurgence and a thrust to the future with the election and re-election of Mr. Barack Obama as the President of United States of America and Commander-in-Chief of the greatest of fighting force for good ever known to man. For many Africans, it is the summit of black power as well as the zenith of black pride. For others it is just a stepping stone to it if well used and harnessed not only by President Obama, but also by Africans.

Black Lives Matter

The concept has become a matter of controversy to many but it is a way to project and make it known to all that Blacklives matter in any environment Black people lives or work. Even though it does not mean or suggest that black lives should be or are more important than other lives. Rather it highlights that black people's lives are relatively undervalued in United States in particular and the world in general. In United States of America, police shoot black youths with reckless abandon. In Kenya and Nigeria, black people are being killed in large numbers by terrorist groups, and the international community keeps quiet and there is no solidarity march like they had in France after the Paris terror attacks. The same applied in the genocide in Biafra, Rwanda, Liberia, Sierra Leone, Sudan and Somalia, etc. The international community response was either lukewarm or non-existent. Thus, there is the necessity to recognize this inequality and bring an end to it for peaceful co-existence of all.

In the United States of America when we take a look at the bigger picture, we can also see some silent and latent reasons why Blacks are behind and the need for black lives matter advocacy; many Blacks are charged and are given unnecessary criminal records right at their prime, youthful age. Take a journey to the American prisons, and note the ratio of Black inmates to other races and you will be alarmed. It is on record that some white supremacy individuals in the law enforcement agencies venture into poor black neighborhoods and use new vehicles as baits to tempt and catch young Blacks who wish to have free ride in such vehicles with the keys left in the ignition and the doors open.

Many blacks are also known to have been followed and picked up after leaving night clubs and charged with Driving under Influence (DUI) by white police officers. The premises here are: he is from the nightclub, he is black, he must have tested alcohol, and therefore, he should be under the influence of alcohol. And the next thing a plea bargain or imprisonment is offered, and out of two evils, the black guy goes for the lesser – take a plea. The hard truth is he has a record and he is done and out of any good employment.

Sometimes, White blondes acting as prostitutes are set against black power - young Blacks. Some law enforcement agents use women in security to impersonate prostitutes in some dark corners of American streets. Unsuspecting young Blacks are lured into the act of soliciting with fake prostitutes and many have picked up criminal records as result, and their charge is soliciting for prostitution. Many are ruined for life in this way as they become unemployable in many sectors of the economy. The resultant economic and socio-psychological despair could account for the increasing crime rate among Black youths and the racial tension in America at present.

These facts raised above remind us a line in the Lord's Prayer in the Biblical Gospel of Matthew 6:9, Jesus said, "Our Father…lead us not into temptation but deliver us from evil." He went further to say in Matthew 18:6 -7, "But whoever causes one of these little ones who believe in me to sin, it would be better for him to have a great milestone fastened round his neck and to be drowned in the depth of the sea. Woe to the world for temptations to sin! For, it is necessary that temptations come but woe to the man by whom the temptation comes!" Because of the importance of this moral injunction it was repeated with more emphases in Mark 9:42 and Luke 17:2 of the Holy Bible. The law enforcement agencies should be guided by this injunction. This is not meant to condone in any form or guises such wrong doings by Black youths but at the same time two wrongs do not make a right.

What every young black person faces; the nightmare of every black person in America is epitomized in the 2014 Ferguson case where unarmed Michael Brown was shut by White officer Darren Wilson. Another example is the case of Trayvon Martin, an unarmed Black youth who died on March 26, 2012 as the result of a gunshot during a confrontation with George Zimmerman, a Hispanic-American man with white supremacy inclinations. Zimmerman was found not guilty of any crime by an all-white jury. The list of black people killed by the police and in hate crimes is inexhaustible. American police most often shoot to kill unlike their European counterpart who shoots to disable or incapacitate. Until they are made to use stun guns or modified tranquilizer bullets, white police officers will continue to kill Blacks in large numbers. Most of them are sure to get away with murder.

Another aspect of this nightmare is underscored in an article *"After Discrimination Finding, Jury's Out on Memphis Juvenile Courts."* In this article, Carrie Johnson asserted that "for people connected to the Memphis juvenile courts, April 2012 is unforgettable. That's when federal investigators determined that Shelby County juvenile court system discriminated against African-American defendants. The Justice Department said that the system punished Black children more harshly than Whites. In the most incendiary finding, investigators said the court detained Black children and sent them to be tried in the adult system twice as often as Whites." The report went further to assert, "Nine thousand children face delinquency charges in the red brick juvenile courthouse each year. Many are handled outside of court, but around three thousand are prosecuted by the district attorney's office." Furthermore, Carrie asserts that "the stark racial disparities that were highlighted in the DOJ's findings could also be found in the urban centers throughout the country. Lawyers say about ninety percent of those prosecuted in most United States courts are poor and Black. But attorneys as part of the above problem have been criticized for inadequate defense of their young clients. Consequently, there are more Blacks in prison than any other race. The reason for this negligence is that most often Black suspects are considered guilty until proved innocent. And race has become the defining characteristic not just of our juvenile court systems but also of our adult system as well."[64] In the present American society, class segregation has become racial segregation and hence life is worst of for you if you are black and poor. Dinesh D'Souza in his epic work, *The End of Racism* quoted Marian Wright Edelman as expressing similar view that it is utterly exhausting being black in America – physically, mentally and emotionally. There is no respite or escape from your badge of color.

African Union and African Security

The Organization of African Unity (OAU) was formed in May, 1963, after series of significant steps towards unification of independent African countries. The OAU had as its elements:

- a unique inclination to combine PanAfricanism with nationalism

- a quest for autonomy in solving African problems

- a drive to liberate the entire continent from colonization and racial discrimination.

The articles in the OAU charter project the objectives of the organization. For instance, Article 2 (i) of its charter says that the OAU undertakes to promote the unity and solidarity of the African States. Article 1 (ii) states that the OAU is to defend the sovereignty, territorial integrity and independence of the African States. Furthermore, Article III pledges that the OAU would observe scrupulously the following principles:

- Sovereign equality of member states

- Non-interference in the internal affairs of states

- Respect for the sovereignty and territorial integrity of each state

- Peaceful settlement of disputes by negotiation, mediation, conciliation or arbitration

- Unreserved condemnation of subversive activities

- Absolute dedication to the total emancipation of African countries and the policy of non-alignment with regard to all power blocks

In the 2002, the OAU metamorphosed to become the African Union (AU) after much deliberation. One of the reasons for the change was the fact that all the countries of Africa had become independent; as such, a major part of the objectives of the organization has been realized. Again, the transformation becomes necessary because of the global trend where continental organizations were forming unions. There is the European Union (EU) which has refocused to meet the challenges of the new millennium. Another reason adduced for the change was the need to change some of the articles of the OAU to meet the current demands for peace and security in Africa. As a result, AU has modified the articles that deal on non-interference in the internal affairs of states. This is to enable the organization to deal efficiently and effectively with crisis and conflict situations in African States. It will also enable the AU to move from peace keeping to peace enforcement in conflict or war situations.

Security is important to Africans, and this accounts for the reason why the issue received accolades of the African Union in their new Charter. The African leaders want peace and security both from within and without. Security as defined by the leaders in the AU emerges as a concept destined not only to protect the national integrity of States but also to defend those essential values that constitute specifically African dignity and identity. African security also entails the survival of African race at the encounter of the other parts of the world, be it the East, West, etc. African security for AU goes beyond merely safeguarding of territorial boundaries, to ensuring that the continent is industrialized rapidly and develops into a cohesive, egalitarian, technological society in which we could carry out researches and produce our own machines for our own industries and utilize our raw materials to produce finished products. Thus capital flight and brain drain from the continent would be reduced to the barest minimum. It was Gunder Frank who observed that in Latin America, the concept of national security has been elevated into a "doctrine." According to the doctrine, the security problems of Third World Societies can only be solved through the desideratum of science and technology under the aegis of the Armed Forces.[65]

Furthermore, Emeagwara asserts that to envision continental or national security as an ideology is to make a synthesis of political, economic, socio-psychological, military and geographical strategies in international politics. Economic and technological advancement remain, in the main, one of the essential elements toward continental security - that Africa may preserve its manhood, integrity, personality and security, there is a deep need to strengthen not only the economic, political and technological status, but also the power of military establishments. Africa, where necessary should nuclearize its arms; for African personality cum dignity is not a gift of charity obtained by kneeling and stretching of arms before the "powers that be." Ross Munro and Richard Bernstein in 1997 became bestsellers because of their work *"The Coming Conflict with China."* There is no doubt this possibility exists also for Africa with any global power that may to like to dictate to Africa how to live, or that would like to pursue an agenda of re-colonization of Africa or a country in Africa. Here, we are mindful of the module "the Pharaoh that knew not Joseph" that enslaved the Israelites. There could be a possibility of a US Congress or President that knows not the freedom and democracy of African nations or Russian and Chinese government that do not understand freedom and dialogue withAfrican nations or an European Union with Britain, France and Germany that could see non-nuclear African states as unviable states and muse the idea of benign recolonization. The case of Iraqi, Libya, Syria and Ukraine are eye openers. So, Africa should foresee these possibilities and be ready to wrestle power forcefully if need be with any power bloc. This is why nuclear arms race came into existence in the first place, and it is also what has forced some nations like India and Pakistan to nuclearize their arms, and the current bid by North Korea and Iran to have nuclear arms is for the same reason.

However, in 1964 the Heads of States and governments of the OAU adopted denuclearization of Africa as an approach to African security; they announced their readiness to sign all international treaty to be concluded under the auspices of the United Nations not to manufacture or acquire nuclear weapons. Commenting on this resolution by African Heads of State, Aforka Nweke says that those who believe in the practicability (or realization) of African Security through denuclearization are deceiving themselves.[66] There is need to reflect on the saying, *"Nemo dat quod non habet,"* that one does not dispose, transfer or give what he does not possess. We must submit that African security must hinge on African Unity under the auspices of African Union. Balkanization of the African continent would not do the black race any good.

Furthermore, African Union should also embrace the policy of Non-alignment. It should seek for positive contributions to make in every international body such as the United Nation, the Common Wealth, the Non-alignment Movement, now G77, G-18 or G20 etc. It should seek world peace, stability, security and wellbeing. They should avoid being used as a rubber stamp or stooges for perpetuating or supporting crimes against humanity or prosecuting unjust wars in any part of the world. These are essential part of the embodiment of nonalignment policy.And these are in line with the position of Azikiwe when he describes non-alignment as the prerogative of a state to preserve to itself the decision whether or not to associate with any power bloc or military alliance or concert of states or ideological school of thought.[67] Zik rightly acknowledges that non-alignment brings dignity and respect to any independent country as opposed to being tied to the apron of another country.

Also, non-alignment in the view of Colonel Nasser is not noncommitment; it does not mean that we isolate ourselves from problems of the African continent and the world. It means that we should contribute positively to the consolidation of understanding, and to the opening of channels for the deep chasms caused by crises.[68] This means that non-alignment does not mean sitting on the fence with hands akimbo and remaining in isolation or non-commitment or detachment or neutralism, be it in the secret race of armament, globalization, trade, war and the establishment of multi-national companies which have become the new agents of imperialism. We see it on the other hand as the search for and acceptance of whatever is true and just in the sum total of thinking. This is freedom to act in accordance with its own guiding spirit unhampered by any pressure from outside.

The New Partnership for African Development (NEPAD): As a Development Philosophy

This is the brain-child of the African Union in the 21st century. The guiding motives include among other things the global Black unification and advocacy. It promises to unite the continental Africans and the diaspora Africans wherever they may be; for a symbiotic welfare of the two. This symbiotic welfare was echoed by Malcolm X, in July 1964, when he called on the African Heads of State meeting for the then OAU Summit, to see the need for brotherhood between continental Africans and diaspora Africans. Malcolm X said, "We in America are your lost brothers and sisters, and I am only to remind you that our problems are your problems. As the Afro-Americans 'awaken' today, we find ourselves in a strange land that had rejected us, and like the prodigal son, we are turning to our elder brothers for help. We pray our pleas will not fall on deaf ears. He went further to say, your problems will never be fully solved until and unless ours are solved. You will never be fully respected unless we are also respected. You will never be recognized as free human beings until and unless we are also recognized and treated as human being."[69] The above call by Malcolm X was made within the racial environment of the 1960s; however, his call is still insightful and relevant to the New

Partnership for African Development under the auspices of the African Union. This is also true today because the plight of Blacks youths in America shows that Blacks are becoming endangered species. Police brutality and hate crimes against blacks are on the rise every day. This should not be the case in a country that exports democracy and parades itself as the land of the free.

At the same time, there is need to attract scientific knowledge, the technological know-how and the capital of diaspora Africans for the development of the continent for the wellbeing of all. What Africa needs to stand on its feet is the fundamentals of technological know-how. They need to use what they have to get microchip industries and machine tools industries to establish in Africa. Through apprenticeship, Africans will come know the building blocks of sophisticated technologies. The best faculty of Engineering and Computer Science in Africa cannot give Africa the practical knowledge this apprenticeship can give. To be able to do this, Africa needs the guild master services of the diaspora Africans many of whom work in high tech companies in Europe and America. What I am suggesting here has been done before and it is been done right now by many countries. This was how technology spread in Europe and America in the first place, this was how the Russians and the Chinese acquired their technological know-how; this is how the Israelis, the Koreans, the Indians, the Brazilians, the Pakistanis, the Iranians, etc. are having a breakthrough in technology. All of them liaised and used their Diasporas in one way or the other to arrive at where they are today in technology and industry. A number of these countries provided the land, factory, infrastructure and the whole capital and labor needed by a foreign technology to establish in their country. They know why they have to do that. If you call it technology transfer, you are not far from the truth.

Actually, African governments should realize that African strategy and path to industrial revolution should be "to build and privatize." These governments should build and sell to individuals or groups technologically advanced and market oriented industries. This is one of the ways to nurture and grow the private sector which is actually nonexistent inAfrican countries compared to the private sector in United States and other advanced countries. The governments should do that because they control most of the natural resources inAfrica and have the largest capital flow from taxation and import duties. Much more capital can be generated if African governments can remove entirely or reduce to the barest minimum the burden of big government by cutting down on the number of their states and governors, number of electoral constituencies, number of government ministries and ministers/ secretaries, number of senators, House of Representatives members, number of counties/local government areas, and number of councilors. The fund generated from these cuts and other 'sequestration' budget cuts will be put into capital projects and industrialization. African countries don't have to depend on imports from generation to generation; great things should be made at home and exported as other countries are doing. Imports are normally used to augment short-falls in local production of essential goods and to balance trade between two countries. This is how respect is earned by countries all over the world. Asian tigers do not 'boast of their tiger-ness,' they produce things – microchips and semiconductors, they build vehicles too. Nothing can be achieved in African countries under a large government because expenditures on personnel, overheads, logistics and corruption consume all the available resources of the nations.

With regard to the loyalty and support of diaspora Africans to Africa as their motherland, we know their interest in Africa is not lacking as they are today proud to be addressed as African Americans in America for instance. The only problem is nobody has recognized them and what they are capable of doing. It has always seemed as if they are standing alone in their problems and achievements. Many of them work with high tech companies like Boeing, Northrop Grumman Corporation, General Electric Company, American Steel companies, oil and gas companies, Microchips and semiconductors companies like Intel, Microsoft and Apple among others in the Silcom Valley, motor companies like General Motors, Chrysler, Ford and Tesla Motors, and many general electronic companies in the industrial parks scattered all over United States and Europe. And these guys have a wealth of knowledge that can make a great impact and as such continental Africans cannot afford to ignore them. Tapping their wealth of knowledge and experience is not done through espionage; it can be done through mobility of labor, joint venture partnership and counterpart funding in a few selected technologies.

Foreign Aids/Grants for NEPAD

In the past, many scholars see reparation as a necessity which Europe and America should be forced to accept for the development of the African continent and Africans in diaspora which they have plundered for more than four centuries through the agencies of slavery, colonialism and neo-colonialism. This plundering of the Africa continues in the present through the offices of the multi-national corporations and other secret agencies. In this 21st century, some leaders like Obasanjo of Nigeria surmised that AU wishes to change the tune from reparation to a kind of development partnership in which the African States under the aegis of African Union would contribute their own quota especially in terms of providing the enabling environment for investment and development in Africa. This enabling environment also includes peace and stability, financial transparency, democracy and good governance devoid of corruption. On their part, the developed countries especially of Europe and America would contribute in terms of investment capital, stoppage of capital flight from Africa by urging multi- nationals to plough back some of their profits made in Africa into industrialization and other social corporate responsibilities. Industrialization would give employment to the growing army of unemployed African youths and at the same reduce the influx of migrants to Europe and America.

The advanced countries through the UN should also make resolutions and laws to send back to Africa ill-gotten and stolen monies and wealth - in form of money laundering and shares or investments abroad made with stolen monies from Africa. It must be stated that the African continent is no longer interested in manipulative aids and grants from developed countries. We submit that indiscriminate aids, grants or charity from abroad should be channeled through NEPAD. This is to ensure that aids are no longer "crumbs" from the developed world, and they should command justice and fair deal and not for subjugation of the Africa and her people.

There is need for NEPAD to seek for a reformation of the idea of General George Marshall, the founder of the Marshall Plan and the brain behind American and European aids to other countries. Marshall was of the view that should America fail in carrying out aids, it will affect her international trade.[70] In other words; Marshall sees international aids as a stimulant to American exports and as such a weapon and an incentive for opening up new markets for American businesses. It is therefore not surprising when President John F. Kennedy in 1963 asserted: "I wish American business men who keep talking against the foreign aid programs would realize how significant it has been in assisting them to get into markets where they would have no entry and no experience and which has traditionally been European ... and the importance of this aid to our export is increasing."[71] This means that aids from developed countries are not all charity as many think. They are not yet philanthropic gestures from a big uncle to pathetic nations of the world like those of Africa and the thirdworld.

More still, some scholars do not see it as aids in any form; they see it as incentives to trade; more or less a payback for a favor done to the advanced world. It was Panel Hoffman who said after x-raying American aids effort to other countries: doesn't it badly distort reality to call something that creates large numbers of jobs for American works foreign aids? Is it foreign aids when we help to secure for ourselves new sources of essential raw materials? Is it foreign aids when we follow a course that could eventually lower the cost of goods and services Americans need every day? We earned our first sizeable dividends from that pioneering cooperative venture known as the Marshall Plan.[72] This just tells us that foreign aids and grants have the major goal of serving, not the overall economic interest of the recipients, but the political and economic interest of the donors and their collaborators in the recipient countries.

It is on record that most of the foreign aids and grants to Africa are meant for specific projects instead of a comprehensive or sectoral development plan. This makes NEPAD a deserved development philosophy that should aim at engaging and fostering the advanced countries to offer disinterested aids/ grant to Africa. The hosting of the inaugural United States–African Leaders Summit, August 4-6, 2014 by President Obama in Washington is a welcome development for trade, investment and security of the African continent. During the summit the first ever U.S.–Africa Business Forum was established and we believe these two events could be made a biannual get-together for the benefit of the partners.

NEPAD should also have within its fold an agency that would function as a debt buying arm of African Union. Its function should be to buy back African debts and to renegotiate and sell them to well-meaning countries, individuals and corporate bodies who want to assist in the management and reduction of Africa's debt burden. The debts are to be put up for sale in NEPAD's web site and cable networks. We suggest this because the cost of debt reschedules and debt servicing negates whatever advantage Africans intended to get from foreign aids or loans. A good example of debt renegotiation, cancellation and relief involving a discounted buy- back was the case of Nigeria which after many years of futile debt servicing decided in October, 2005 to pay Twelve Billion Dollars to the Paris Club to offset about Eighteen Billion Dollars of the debt owed to the club. Hence, Nigeria earned an overall reduction of her debt by Thirty Billion Dollars and became the first Africa nation to clear the debt she owes her official lender in April 2006. The then-Nigerian Finance Minister and former Vice President of the World Bank, Dr. Mrs. Okonjo Iwuala, and the CGD Fellow, Todd Moss played a pivotal role in the deal. We can proudly say that this idea of debt sale or discounted buyback as a solution to African debt problem was recommended to African countries and NEPAD in this book when it was first published in 2004.

Africa's external loans are most often used directly or indirectly to service her foreign debts. Most of African debts and the money used to service them are no longer cost effective for Africans. The opportunity cost/loss is great if we consider the things Africa could do with the monies in terms of providing development programs and democracy dividend to the people. Most well-meaning individuals and corporate bodies are now aware that humanity has failed in Africa. In the words of the former World Bank Senior Vice President, Ernest M. Stern: we have failed in Africa, along with everybody else i.e., other charity foundations and world bodies such as International Bank for Reconstruction and Development (IBRD), International Monetary Fund (IMF), Overseas Development Fund of the European Union and Development Assistance Committee (DAC), etc. We have not fully understood the problems of Africa. We have not identified priorities. We have not always designed our projects to fit the agro climatic conditions of Africa and the social cultural and political framework of African countries. Everyone else is still unclear about what can be done to Africa.[73] We must conclude by recommending that if NEPAD is to achieve its aim of Africa renaissance, the advanced world should hid the advice of Rene Dumont that for Africa to be rescued from strangle hold of underdevelopment, the world should offer disinterested aids/grants without stringent clauses. In his words, he asserted... and what have we done up till now to give Africans more effective help? It is high time that we give Africa truly "disinterested" aid, concerned above all with Africa's development, and not with prolonging abuses and privileges.[74]

This disinterested aid should include free movement not only of African finished goods but also of responsible African citizens in and out of the developed world. These two factors help to bring about even development in such a way that African countries would begin to catch up with the rest of the world in standard of living and cross fertilization of ideas. In this direction, the African Growth and Opportunity Act (AGOA), a legislation enacted by the U.S. Congress to encourage the export of African Agricultural products and textiles to America, and the U.S. Migration Visa Lottery, which allows annually about 55,000 people from different countries of the world to win a Green Card are commendable policies for they have increased foreign investment and monetary remittances in U.S. dollars to many African countries. But the overall value of these two United States' programs is still small if compared to the value of U.S. goods that are exported to all parts of Africa and the Third world, and the number of Americans that could enter other countries of the world if they wish to travel. So, restrictions on the movement of responsible African people and quality African products especially to the advanced countries should be reduced to the barest minimum to encourage African development drives.

Chapter 1

Understanding Philosophy: Demythologization of Philosophy

1. Herbert Spencer quoted in Galina Kirilencho and Lydia Korshunova, What is Philosophy? (Moscow: Progress Publishers, 1980), 26, 32-33.

2. Merriam Webster, " Religion" in Webster's Encyclopedic Unabridged Dictionary of the English Language (New York: Gramercy Books, 1989)

3. A.S. Hornby, Advanced Learner's Oxford Dictionary, (London: Oxford University Press, 1982), 712.

4. Ibid., 48.

5. Ibid., 96.

6. Melvin Rader, The Enduring Questions: The Main Problems of Philosophy (New York: Holt, Rinehart and Winston, 1969), 1 - 5.

7. Ibid.

8. Ibid.

9. Ibid.

10. Plato, The Symposium (London: Oxford University Press, 1945)

11. Plato, The Republic, Trans. F.M. Cornford (London: Oxford University Press, 1945)

12. Aristotle, Metaphysics, Trans. Philip Wheelwright (London: Odyssey Press, 1935), 3b-19.

13. George Santayana, The Three Philosophical Poets (Cambridge: Harvard University Press, 1927)

14. Cicero quoted in Rader, The Enduring Questions, 532 - 550.

15. Epicurus, Adversus Mathematicos, Xi 169.

16. Curt John Ducasse, Philosophy as an Art (New York: Dial, 1929), 3.

17. John Dewey, Experience and Nature (Chicago: Open Court, 1925), 398.

18. Jack Maritain, An Introduction to Philosophy (New York: Sheed and Ward Inc., 1954)

19. William James, Some Problems of Philosophy (New York: Longmans, Green, 1911), 5.

20. Martin Heidegger, in John Stone: What is Philosophy? (New York: Macmillan, 1965), 111-115.

21. Alfred Jules Ayer, Language, Truth and Logic (London: Routledge, 1961), 49.

22. Ludwig Wittgenstein in Kirilencho and Korshunova, What is Philosophy? 26.

23. Rader, The Enduring Questions, 5.

24. Kirilencho and Korshunova, What is Philosophy? 26.

25. Ibid.

26. Ibid.

27. Nicholas Ikhu Omoregbe, Knowing Philosophy: General Introduction (Lagos: Joje Publishers Ltd., 1990), 3.

28. Kirilencho and Korshunova, What is Philosophy? 41.

29. Ibid.

30. Ibid.,42.

31. Ibid.

32. C.D. Broad, Scientific Thought (New York: Harcourt Bruce and World, 1923), 148-153.

33. Titus Harold, Marilyn Smith and Richard Nolan, Living Issues in Philosophy, 7th Edition (New York: Litton Educational Publishing Inc., 1979), 9-13.

34. Ibid.

35. Ibid.

36. Broad, Scientific Thought, 152.

Chapter 2

The Nature and Significance of Philosophy

1. Merriam Webster, "Science" in Webster's Encyclopedic Unabridged Dictionary of the English Language (New York: Gramercy Books, 1989)

2. Ibid.

3. Aristotle, Metaphysics (London: Indiana Uni. Press. 1966), 15.

4. Cicero quoted in Galina Kirilencho and Lydia Korshunova, What is Philosophy? (Moscow: Progress Publishers, 1988), 28-29.

5. Melvin Rader, The Enduring Questions: The Main Problems of Philosophy (New York: Holt, Rinehart and Winston, 1969), 4 - 5.

6. Albert Sidney Hornby, "Art" in Advanced Learner's Oxford Dictionary, (London: Oxford Uni. Press,1983)

7. Kirilench and Korshunova, What is Philosophy? 12.

8. Rader, The Enduring Questions, 9.

9. Chukwudum Barnabas Okolo, Problems of African Philosophy, (Enugu: Cecta Ltd., 1992), 7-8.

10. Henri Maurier, "Do we have an African Philosophy?" African Philoso-

phy, Ed., Richard A. Wright (Lanham: University Press of America, 1984)

11. Erik A. Ruch, Is There an African Philosophy? Second Order, Vol. III, No. 2, (July, 1974), 3.

12. L.C. Onyewuenyi, "Is there an African Philosophy?" Journal of African Studies, Vol. III, (1971), 521.

13. C.S. Momoh, "African Philosophy... Does it exist?" Diogenes, 130, 1988, 75.

14. Nicholas Ikhu Omoregbe, Knowing Philosophy: General Introduction (Lagos: Joje Publishers Ltd., 1990), 6-7.

15. William H. Halverson, A Concise Introduction to Philosophy (New York: McGraw-Hill Co., 1980), 26.

16. Rene Descartes, Discourse on Method (London: Macmillan, 1952), 119.

17. Thomas J.M. van Ewijk, Gabriel Marcel: An Introduction (New Jersey: Dens Books Pantist Press, 1965), 6.

18. C.D. Broad, Scientific Thought (New York: Harcourt, Bruce and World, 1923), 152.

19. William James, Problems of Philosophy (New York: Longmans, Green, 1911), 5.

20. D.D. Raphael, Problems of Political Philosophy (London: Macmillan, 1981), 3.

21. Rader, The Enduring Questions, 1.

22. Ibid., 2.

23. Titus Harold, Marilyn Smith and Richard Nolan, Living

Issues in Philosophy, 7th Edition (New York: Litton Educational Publishing Inc., 1979), 6.

24. Chinua Achebe, The Trouble with Nigeria (Enugu: Fourth Dimension Publishing Co. 1985), 10.

25. A.C. Prabhupada, Consciousness: The Missing Link (Los Angeles: Bhaktivedanta Book Trust, 1980), Back Cover.

26. Ibid.

27. Max Planck, on Mind as the Matrix of Matter, retrieved from the World Wide Web, Today in Science, Jan. 7, 2015.

28. William Barett, The Illusion of Technique (Garden City: Doubleday, 1978), xv.

29. Jacques Maritain quoted in Harold, Smith and Nolan, Living Issues in Philosophy, 7.

30. Aristotle, Metaphysics, 1.

31. Fredrick Nietzsche, The Joyful Wisdom, Trans. Thomas Common (New York: Macmillan Co., 1924), 167-168.

Chapter 3

Philosophical Methodology: Types of Philosophical Methods

1. Melvin Rader, The Enduring Questions: The Main Problems of Philosophy (New York: Holt, Rinehart and Winston, 1969), 10.

2. Ibid.

3. Jeremy Stangroom and James Garvey, The Great Philosophers: From Socrates to Foucault (New York: Metro Books, 2007), 9 – 10.

4. Friedrich Hegel, The Spirit of Modern Philosophy, Trans. Josiah Royce (Boston: Houghton, Mifflin Co., 1982)

5. Hegel quoted in Rader, The Enduring Questions, 358 - 359.

6. Immanuel Kant, Critique of Pure Reason (New York: Harper and Row, 1960)

7. Karl Marx and Friedrich Engels, Collected Works, Vol. III (Moscow: Progress Publishers, 1975), 187.

8. Rene Descartes, Philosophical Works of Descartes, Trans. E.S. Haldane (London: Cambridge Uni. Press, 1911), Rule 1.

9. Ibid.

10. Henri Bergson, Introduction to Metaphysics, Trans. E. Hulme (London: Putnam and Sons, 1912)

11. Rader, The Enduring Questions, 131-136.

12. Ibid.

13. Ibid.

14. Bergson, Introduction to the Metaphysics, 1912.

15. Gilbert Ryle, Scientific American, Vol.197, September, 1957.

16. Kant, Critique of Pure Reason, 1960.

17. Ibid.

18. Quentin Lauer, Phenomenology: Its Genesis and Prospects (New York: Harper and Row, 1958)

19. R. McHenry, The New Encyclopedia Britannica, Vol. IV, 15th Edition (New York: Encyclopedia Britannica, Inc., 1991)

20. V.M. Martin, "Eclectism", The Catholic Encyclopedia, Vol. V, Ed. G.M.

Sauvage,(London: Mcgraw-Hill, 1967)

21. Nnamdi Azikiwe, Ideology for Nigeria: Capitalism, Socialism or Welfarism (Ibadan: Macmillan Publishers, 1980), Preface.

22. Horace Emeagwara, Eclectic Philosophical Hermeneutics of African Personality (Nsukka: UNN, 1998) 1-3.

Chapter 4

Fundamental Problems of Philosophy and their Solutions

1. Fredrick Copleston, History of Philosophy, Vol. 1(New York: Image Books, 1962), 55.

2. Stephen Greenblatt, The Swerve: How the World became Modern (New York: W.W. Norton and Co., 2011), 5 - 6, 73.

3. Ibid., 5 and 74.

4. Karl Marx, Selected Writing in Sociology and Social Philosophy, Ed. T.B. Bottomore (London: Watts and Co. Ltd., 1956)

5. George Berkeley quoted in Titus Harold, Marilyn Smith and Richard Nolan, Living Issues in Philosophy, 7th Edition (New York: Litton Educational Publishing Inc., 1979), 253.

6. Friedrich Hegel, The Spirit of Modern Philosophy (Boston: Houghton Miffling Co.,1952)

7. C.S. Seely, Modern Materialism: A Philosophy of Action (New York: Philosophical Library, 1960), 7.

8. Rene Descartes, The Philosophical Works of Descartes, Trans. E.S. Haldane and G.R. Ross (London: Cambridge Uni. Press, 1931) 11 and 64.

9. John Locke, An Essay Concerning Human Understanding (London: Cambridge Uni. Press, 1957)

10. CERN 2011 Findings on Antimatter Experiment, Retrieved from World Wide Web, Antimatter-experiment, November 11, 2014.

11. Canon Fernand Van Steenberghen, Ontology, Trans. Martin Flyn (New York: Harper and Row, 1963) 80.

12. Martin Flyn quoted in Steenberghen, Ontology, 81.

13. Aristotle, Metaphysics, (London: Indiana Uni. Press. 1966), 1001-1052.

14. Nicholas Ikhu Omoregbe, Knowing Philosophy: General Introduction (Lagos: Joje Publishers Ltd., 1990), 80.

15. Greenblatt, The Swerve: How the World became Modern, 75.

16. Ibid., 103.

17. S. Alexander, Space, Time and Deity (New York: Macmillan Press, 1920)

18. David Hume, A Treatise of Human Nature, Ed. L.A. Selby- Biggie (Oxford: Clarendon Press, 1896), 212.

19. Omoregbe, Knowing Philosophy: General Introduction, 160.

20. Ibid., 167.

21. S.E. Stumpf, Philosophy: History and Problems, (New York: McGraw Hill Inc., 1994), 63.

22. Ivan Frolov, Dictionary of Philosophy (Moscow: Progress Publishers, 1984), 238-239.

23. Bertrand Russell, The Problem of Philosophy (New York: Oxford Uni. Press, 1976), 53.

24. Steenberghen, Ontology, 80.

25. W. Brugger, Philosophical Dictionary (Washington D.C: Washington Press, 1984), 299.

26. M.T. Clark, Aquinas Reader: Selections from the Writings of Aquinas

(New York: Image Books, 1972), 395.

27. Richard Henry Popkin and Avrum Stroll, Philosophy Made Simple (London: Heinemann, 1981), 92.

28. Bertrand Russell, History of Western Philosophy (London: Hazell Waston & Viney Ltd.1979), 69.

29. Ibid., 59.

30. Will Durant, The Story of Philosophy (Garden City: Clarion Press, 1943), 473.

31. Ibid., 420.

32. Ibid., 424.

33. Stumpf, Philosophy: History and Problems, 423.

34. Ibid.

35. Ibid., 14.

36. Ibid., 17.

37. Copleston, History of Philosophy, Vol. 1, 55.

38. Ibid., 177.

39. Titus Harold, Marilyn Smith and Richard Nolan, Living Issues in Philosophy, 7th Edition (New York: Litton Educational Publishing Inc., 1979), 31-32.

40. A.R.Lacey, Dictionary of Philosophy (London: Routledge,1996)

41. Hume, A Treatise of Human Nature, 212.

42. Louis de Raeymaker, The Philosophy of Being: A Synthesis of Metaphysics (London: 1954), 267.

43. A.C. Fraser, The Works of George Berkeley (Oxford: Clarendon Press, 1971), 13.

44. Melvin Rader, The Enduring Questions: The Main Problems of Philoso-

phy (New York: Holt, Rinehart and Winston, 1969) 393-395.

45. Space – Time in Einstein's Special Relativity Theory, Retrieved from the World Wide Web, www.einstein- online.info, November 11, 2014.

46. Stephen Greenblatt, The Swerve: How the World Became Modern (New York: W.W. Norton and Co., 2011), 6 and 185 – 197.

47. Ibid., 5.

48. Ibid., 8-10.

49. Fredrick Nietzsche quoted in Rader, The Enduring Questions, 503.

50. Jeremy Stangroom and James Garvey, The Great Philosophers: From Socrates to Foucault (New York: Metro Books, 2007), 116-119.

51. Ibid.

52. Rader, The Enduring Questions, 503.

53. Stangroom and Garvey, The Great Philosophers, 92 – 95, 116 - 119.

54. G.P. Klubertanz, Introduction to the Philosophy of Being (New York: Appleton Century-Crofts, 1963), 221.

55. Greenblatt, Swerve: How the World Became Modern, 76.

56. Stangroom and Garvey, The Great Philosophers, 124.

57. Ibid., 38-39.

Chapter 5

Metaphysics: The Horizon of the Question of Being

1. Marcel Onyeocha, Metaphysics: Cycle A – Theory (Owerri: Seat of Wisdom Press, 1987), 1.

2. Melvin Rader, The Enduring Questions: The Main Problems of Philosophy (New York: Holt, Rinehart and Winston, 1969), 197 – 198.

3. Marcel Onyeocha, Metaphysics: Cycle A – Theory, 2.

4. William A. Wallace, The Elements of Philosophy (New York: Alba House, 1977), 90.

5. Ibid., 91.

6. Catholic University of America, "Unity", in New Catholic Encyclopedia, Vol. 14 (Washington DC, 1981), 448.

7. Ibid., 332.

8. W. Brugger and K. Baker, Philosophical Dictionary (Washing on: Gonzaga University Press, 1974), 112.

9. Rader, The Enduring Questions: The Main Problems of Philosophy, 178-202.

10. Ibid.

11. Nwachukwu, An Aid to B.Phil. (Calabar: B.M.S Press, 1982)

12. Rader, The Enduring Questions, 175.

13. Ibid., 241-242

14. Rene Descartes, Philosophical Writing, Trans. L.J. Lafleur (New York: Bobbs-Merril Pub. Co. Inc., 1960)

15. Ibid.

16. Copleson, History of Philosophy, 100.

17. Rene Descartes, Philosophical Writings, Trans. Norman Kemp Smith, 186.

18. Descartes, Philosophical Writing, Trans. Haldane and Ross, 166.

19. Ibid., 168.

20. D.J.B. Hawkins, A Sketch of Medieval Philosophy (New York: Sheed and Ward, 1947), 33.

21. Rader, The Enduring Questions, 262.

22. Descartes, Philosophical Writing, 190-191.

23. George Berkeley, The Works of George Berkeley, Trans. Campbell Fraser (Oxford: Clarendon Press, 1971)

24. Rader, The Enduring Questions, 360.

25. Ibid.,358.

26. Alfred North Whitehead, Science and the Modern World (New York: Macmillan Co., 1953), 106-107.

27. Lovejoy, The Revolt Against Dualism (Chicago: Open Court Pub. Co., 1932)

28. David Hume quoted in S. E. Stumpf, Philosophy: History and Problems, (New York: McGraw Hill Inc., 1994), 275.

Chapter 6

Epistemology: The Search for the Meaning of Truth

1. C.N. Bittle, Reality and the Mind (Milwanke: The Bruce Publishing Co. Ltd., 1936), 14-15.

2. Richard H. Popkin and Avrum Stroll, Philosophy Made Simple (London: Heinemann, 1982), 172-173.

3. D.W. Hamlym, The Theory of Knowledge (London: Macmillan Press, Ltd., 1971), 79.

4. A.D. Woozley, Theory of Knowledge (London: Hutchinson & Co. Ltd., 1966), 14.

5. Titus Harold, Marilyn Smith and Richard Nolan, Living Issues in Philosophy, 7th Edition (New York: Litton Educational Publishing Inc., 1979), 42.

6. William Hannaford and Gene Blocker, Introduction to Philosophy (London: D.Van Nostrand Co., 1976), 68.

7. Thomas Aquinas quoted in B. O. Eboh, Basic Issues in Theory of Knowledge (Nsukka: University of Nigeria, 2004), 9.

8. Galina Kirilencho and Lydia Korshunova, What is Philosophy? (Moscow: Progress Publishers, 1988), 13.

9. Woozley, Theory of Knowledge, 13

10. Irving Copi, Introduction to Logic, 5th Edition (London: Collier Macmillan Publishers, 1978), 4.

11. Melvin Rader, The Enduring Questions: The Main Problems of Philosophy (New York: Holt, Rinehart and Winston, 1969), 81.

12. John Locke, An Essay Concerning Human Understanding, Bk IV, (London: Clarendon Press, 1950) Chap. 2.

13. Hannibal Retrieved from the World Wide Web, Ancient History , November 12, 2014

14. A.J. Ayer, The Problem of Knowledge (London: Penguin Books, 1956), 143.

15. Norman Malcolm quoted in Eboh, Basic Issues in Theory of Knowledge, 10.

16. Hamlyn, Theory of Knowledge, 212.

17. E.W. Carlo, Philosophy, Science and Knowledge (Milwaukee: The Bruce Publishers, 1978), 24.

18. Ibid.

19. John Dewey, Creative Intelligence (New York: Henry Holt, 1917), 65.

20. Dewey, The Influence of Darwin on Philosophy and Other Essays (New York: Henry Holt, 1910), 160

21. Hamlyn, Theory of Knowledge, 112.

22. L.M. Regis, Epistemology (New York: Macmillan Co., 1959), 338-339.

23. Bertrand Russell, The Problem of Knowledge (New York: Oxford Uni. Press, 1976), 5

24. C.N. Bittle, Reality and the Mind (Milwaukee: The Bruce Publishers, 1936), 291.

25. F.H. Bradley, Essays on Truth and Reality (London: Clarendon Press, 1914)

26. William James quoted in S.E. Stumpf, Philosophy: History and Problems, (New York: McGraw Hill Inc., 1994), 401.

Chapter 7

Ethics: The Morality of Human Actions

1. A. Fagothey, Right and Reason: Ethics in Theory and Practice (New York: Mosby Co., 1959)

2. Thomas J. Higgins, Man as Man (Maryland: The Prince Publishing Co., 1956)

3. E.M. Kirkpatrick, Chambers' 20th Century Dictionary (London: Cambridge University Press, 1986), 272.

4. A. Appadorai, The Substance of Politics (Madras: Oxford University Press, 1975), 68.

5. J. Donceel, Philosophical Anthropology (New York: Sheed and Word Inc., 1967), 396.

6. J. Laski, A Grammar of Politics (London: Allen and Unwin, 1962), 142.

7. B.F. Nwankwo, Authority in Government (Enugu: Almond Publishers, 1990), 104.

8. Higgins, Man as Man, 3.

9. Fagothey, Right and Reason, 10.

10. Higgins, Man as Man, 3.

11. Melvin Rader, The Enduring Questions: The Main Problems of Philosophy (New York: Holt, Rinehart and Winston, 1969), 513.

12. Ibid.

13. Aquinas on "the Meaning of Law" quoted in Studies in Ethics (Owerri: Seat of Wisdom Press, 1988), 24 - 25.

14. Ibid.

15. R.M. Hare, Freedom and Reason (New York: Pine wood Publishers, 1978), 20.

16. James Wesley Ellington, Immanuel Kant: Grounding for the Metaphysics of Morals, 3rd Ed., with on a Supposed Right to Lie because of Philanthropic Concerns. (New York: Hackett Publishing, 1993), 30 - 37.

17. Bergson, Introduction to Metaphysics, Trans. E. Hulme (London: Putnam and Sons, 1912), 59.

18. Aristotle, Ethics of Aristotle, Trans. J.K. Thomson(London: George Allen and Unwin, 1953)

19. Ibid.

20. Marcus Tullius Cicero, The Laws, BK 1 &2, Trans. Clinton W. Kayes (Cambridge: Harvard University Press, 1943)

21. Rader, Enduring Questions, 548 - 550.

22. Thomas Hobbes, Leviathan, Trans. J. Plamentz (London: Fontana Books,1956)

23. Jeremy Bentham, Introduction to the Principles of Morals and Legislation (London: Oxford Uni. Press, 1968), Chapter 1.

24. John Dewey, Reconstruction in Philosophy (New York: Henry Hort Co.1920), 26.

25. Rader, The Enduring Questions, 638 - 642.

Chapter 8

Aesthetics: The Criteria for Value Selection

1. George Santayana, The Sense of Beauty (New York: Scribner Press, 1959), 18-19.

2. D.H. Parker, Human Values (New York: Harper and Brothers, 1931), 20-21.

3. Titus Harold, Marilyn Smith and RPhilosophy, 7th Edition (New York: Litton Educational Publishing Inc., 1979), 107.

4. Melvin Rader, The Enduring Questions: The Main Problems of Philosophy (New York: Holt, Rinehart and Winston, 1969), 637.

5. Harold, Smith and Nolan, Living Issues, 107.

6. John Dewey quoted in Rader, Enduring Questions, 637.

7. Dewey, "The Pragmatic Acquiescence", New Republic, Vol. 49 (Jan. 5, 1927), 189.

8. Dewey quoted in Rader, The Enduring Questions, 638.

9. John Dewey, Experience and Nature (Chicago: Open Court, 1929), 2.

Chapter 9

Branches of Philosophy: Thoughts on Society, Law, Religion, Science and History

1. D.D. Raphael, Problems of Political Philosophy (London: Macmillan, 1981), 3.

2. William Blackstone, Political Philosophy: An Introduction (New York: Thomas Y. Crowell Co., 1973), 18.

3. Thomas Aquinas, Summa Theologae, Vol. 11 (London: W. Benton Publishers, 1982)

4. H.J. Paton, The Moral Law (London: The Anchor Press Ltd. 1976)

5. J.L. Austin, Philosophical Papers (Oxford: Clarendon Press, 1961), 129.

6. S.E. Stumpf, Philosophy: History and Problems (New York: McGraw Hill Book Co., 1983)

7. Austin, Philosophical Papers, 129.

8. C. Savigy, On the Vocation of Our Legislation and Jurisprudence (London: Hill Top Press, 1956), 20.

9. M.H. Fisch, Classic American Philosophers (New York: Appleton-Century Crofts, 1951), 7.

10. Immanuel Kant, Critique of Judgment (New York: Harper and Row,1960)

11. David Hume, Dialogue Concerning Natural Religion, Trans. Norman Kemp Smith (London: Oxford University Press, 1935)

12. Ibid.

13. William Pepperell Montague, Belief Unbound (New York: Yale University Press, 1931)

14. Blaise Pascal, Thoughts, Trans. O.W. Wights (Boston: Mifflin Co., 1935)

15. William James, The Will to Believe (New York: New World Press, 1967)

16. Melvin Rader, The Enduring Questions: The Main Problems of Philosophy (New York: Holt, Rinehart and Winston, 1969), 482 - 484.

17. Anselm, The Proslogium, Trans. S.N. Deane (London: Open Publishers Co., 1903)

18. Rader, The Enduring Questions, 484 - 489.

19. Ibid.

20. Thomas Aquinas, Summa Contra Gentiles, 1, 13, Trans. T. Gilby (London: Oxford University Press,1951)

21. Rader, The Enduring Questions, 490.

22. Ludwig Feuerbach, The Essence of Christianity, Trans. G. Elliot (New York: Harper and Ross, 1957)

23. Ibid.

24. Ibid.

25. Fredrick Nietzsche, The Joyful Wisdom, Trans. T. Common (New York: Macmillan Co., 1924), 167-276.

26. Harvey Cox, The Secular City (New York: Macmillan Co., 1965), 2.

27. Rader, The Enduring Questions, 483.

28. Humanist Manifesto, Retrieved from the World Wide Web, americanhumanist.org, November 16, 2014.

29. Martin Buber and M. Friedman, The Knowledge of Man, Trans. R.G. Smith (New York: Harper and Row, 1965.)

30. J. Donceel, Philosophical Anthropology (New York: Sheed and Word Inc., 1967)

31. Titus Harold, Marilyn Smith and Richard Nolan, Living Issues in Philosophy, 7th Edition(New York: Litton Educational Publishing Inc., 1979)

32. Jeremy Stangroom and James Garvey, The Great Philosophers: From Socrates to Foucault (New York: Metro Books, 2007), 141 – 143.

33. G.O. Friel, Punishment in the Philosophy of St. Thomas Aquinas and Among the Primitive Peoples (Washington: Catholic University of America Press, 1939), 100.

34. Harold, Smith and Nolan, Living Issues, 30 and 253.

Chapter 10

Human Thought Patterns: Naturalism, Materialism and Supernaturalism

1. Harold, Marilyn Smith and Richard Nolan, Living Issues in Philosophy, 7th Edition (New York: Litton Educational Publishing Inc., 1979), 249.

2. Ibid., 39.

3. Democritus, Epicurus and Lucretius articulated in Stephen Greenblatt, The Swerve: How the World Became Modern (New York: W.W. Norton and Co., 2011), 183-202.

4. Robert T. Pennock, Methodological Naturalism, Retrieved from the World Wide Web, November 17, 2014.

5. Ibid.

6. Ibid.

7. C.S. Seely, Modern Materialism: A Philosophy of Action (New York: Philosophical Library, 1960), 7.

8. Harold, Smith and Nolan, Living Issues, 249-250.

9. George Santayana, Philosophical Poets (New York: Harvard University Press, 1927)

10. Melvin Rader, The Enduring Questions: The Main Problems of Philosophy (New York: Holt, Rinehart and Winston, 1969), 228.

11. Rene Descartes, Discourse on Method in the Philosophical Works of Descartes, Trans. E.S. Haldane and G.R.T. Ross (Cambridge: Cambridge University Press, 1939), 111: 39.

12. Descartes quoted in Rader, The Enduring Questions, 56.

13. Thomas Hobbes, Leviathan, Ed. Plamenatz, 59.

14. Galina Kirilencho and Lydia Korshunova, What is Philosophy? (Moscow: Progress Publishers, 1985), 235.

15. Ibid., 229.

16. Greenblatt Stephen, The Swerve: How the World became Modern, 17.

17. Rader, The Enduring Questions, 548.

Chapter 11

Schools of Philosophy: Empiricism and Rationalism

1. Titus Harold, Marilyn Smith and Richard Nolan, Living Issues in Philosophy, 7th Edition (New York: Litton Educational Publishing Inc., 1979), 171.

2. D.W. Hamlym, The Theory of Knowledge (London: Macmillan Press, Ltd., 1971), 35.

3. John Locke, Essay Concerning Human Understanding (London: Fontana & Collins, 1976), 68.

4. Ibid.

5. Ibid.

6. Locke quoted in C. Mascia, A History of Philosophy, 4th (New Jersey: Anthony Guild Press, 1961), 290.

7. Harold, Smith and Nolan, Living Issues, 171.

8. Ibid.

9. Mascia, History of Western Philosophy, 291.

10. Nwachukwu, An Aid to B. Phil., Ikot Epkene: BMS Press, 146.

11. F. Leibniz, New Essays Concerning Human Understanding, Trans. A.G. Langley, (New York: Lasalle, 1949), 20.

12. Robert McRae quoted in M. Buttler, Cartesian Studies (Oxford: Basil Blackwell, 1971), 49.

13. Harold, Smith and Nolan, 172.

14. Ibid. 173.

Chapter 12

Schools of Philosophy: Idealism and Realism

1. Titus Harold, Marilyn Smith and Richard Nolan, Living Issues in Philosophy, 7th Edition (New York: Litton Educational Publishing Inc., 1979), 269.

2. Ibid.

3. Melvin Rader, The Enduring Questions: The Main Problems of Philosophy (New York: Holt, Rinehart and Winston, 1969), 357.

4. Bertrand Russell, The Problem of Philosophy (London: Oxford University Press, 1976), 19.

5. Harold, Smith and Nolan, Living Issues, 269.

6. Ibid. 271.

7. Campbell Fraser, The Works of George Berkeley (Oxford: Clarendon Press, 1968), 313.

8. George Berkeley, Three Dialogues between Hylas and Philonous (Oxford: Clarendon Press, 1967)

9. Rader, The Enduring Questions, 360.

10. Russell, The Problems of Philosophy, 20.

11. Ibid. 21.

12. Berkeley, The Three Dialogues, 343.

13. Harold, Smith and Nolan, Living Issues, 274.

14. Rader, The Enduring Questions, 352-359.

15. Harold, Smith and Nolan, Living Issues, 297.

16. Ibid., 297-298.

17. Ibid., 310.

18. Ibid.

19. Alfred North Whitehead, Science and the Modern World (New York: Macmillan, 1925), 106-107.

20. Rader, The Enduring Questions, 309-311.

21. D.W. Gotshalk, quoted in The Enduring Questions, 310- 311.

22. Herold. Smith and Nolan, Living Issues, 297-299.

Chapter 13

Schools of Philosophy: Existentialism and Marxism

1. Walter Kaufman, Existentialism from Dostoevsky to Sartre (New York: World Publishing Co., 1956), 12.

2. Titus Harold, Marilyn Smith and Richard Nolan, Living Issues in Philosophy, 7th Edition (New York: Litton Educational Publishing Inc., 1979), 325.

3. Paul Tillich, "Existentialist Aspects of Modern Arts" Christianity and the

Existentialism, Ed. Carl Michaelson (New York: Scribner, 1956), 129-130.

4. R. Bretall, A Kierkegaard Anthology (Princeton: Princeton University Press, 1946), xx.

5. Soren Kierkegaard, The Point of View, Ed. Walter Lowrie (London: Oxford University Press, 1939)

6. Bretall, A Kierkegaard Anthology, 196.

7. Ibid.

8. Ludwig Feuerbach quoted in Rader, The Enduring Questions, 717.

9. Karl Marx, Selected Writings in Sociology and Social Philosophy, Ed. T.B. Bottonmore and M. Rubel (London: Watts and Co. Ltd., 1956)

10. Ibid.

1. Rader, The Enduring Questions, 717.

12. Jeremy Stangroom and James Garvey, The Philosophers: From Socrates to Foucault (New York: Metro Books, 2007), 104-107.

13. Ibid.

14. Ibid.

Chapter 14

Schools of Philosophy: Pragmatism and Logical Positivism

1. Titus Harold, Marilyn Smith and Richard Nolan, Living Issues in Philosophy, 7th Edition (New York: Litton Educational Publishing Inc., 1979), 304.

2. Ibid. 306.

3. Jeremy Stangroom and James Garvey, The Great Philosophers: From Socrates to Foucault (New York: Metro Books, 2007), 108-115.

4. Harold, Smith and Nolan, Living Issues, 306-307.

5. Ibid.

6. Melvin Rader, The Enduring Questions: The Main Problems of Philosophy (New York: Holt, Rinehart and Winston, 1969), 111 - 136.

7. Ibid.

8. Ibid.

9. Ibid.

10. Stangroom and Garvey, The Great Philosophers, 112-115.

11. John Dewey's Creative Intelligence quoted in Rader, Enduring Questions, 158.

12. Ibid.

13. Ibid.

14. Harold, Smith and Nolan Living Issues in Philosophy, 304.

15. Ibid., 306.

16. Wittgenstein, Philosophical Investigations, Trans. G.E.M Ancombe (Oxford: Blackwell, 1953)

17. Rader, The Enduring Questions, 153-157.

18. J.L. Austin, Philosophical Papers (Oxford: Clarendon Press, 1961), 129.

19. Bertrand Russell, "Cult of Common Language" Portraits from Memory (London: George Allen and Unwin, 1956), 154-159.

20. Rader, The Enduring Questions, 155-157.

21. Ibid., 156.

22. A.J. Ayer, Language, Truth and Logic (New York: Dover, 1946)

23. M. Schlick, "The Turning Point in Philosophy" Logical Positivism, Ed. A.J. Ajer (Chicago: The Free Press, 1959), 56.

24. F. Waismann, "How I See Philosophy" Contemporary British Philosophy, Ed. H.D. Lewis (London: George Allen and Unwin, 1956), 482-483.

25. C.D. Broad quoted in Rader, The Enduring Questions, 1- 3.

Chapter 15

Logic: The Instrument of Philosophy

1. J.J. Sanguineti quoted in Fabian Agudiosi, Introduction to Philosophy and Logic: A Supplementary Guide (Enugu: Faba Communications Press, 2003), 161.

2. G.H. Joyce, Principles of Logic (London: Longmans, Green and Co.,

1908), 3.

3. Agudiosi Fabian, Introduction to Philosophy and Logic, 162.

4. Irving Copi, Introduction to Logic, 5th Ed., (London: Macmillan Publishing Co., 1978)

5. Stephen Layman, The Power of Logic (New York: Mayfield Publishing Co., 1999)

6. Ibid.

7. William Pepperell Montague, Belief Unbound: A Promethean Religion for the Modern World (New York: Yale University Press, 1931)

8. Layman, The Power of Logic, iv.

9. Ibid.

Chapter 16

Fallacies in Logic: The Errors of the Human Mind

1. Sydney Herbert Mellon, An Introductory Textbook of Logic (London: William Blackwood and Sons, 1992), 313.

2. Roland Munson, The Ways of Words: An Informal Logic (New York: Doubleday, 1976), 256.

3. Daniel Okezie, Fallacies in Logic: A Critical Evaluation (Nsukka: UNN, 1999)

4. Baum Robert, Logic (New York: Holt Rinehart and Winston Inc., 1975), 463.

5. Kahane Howard, Logic and Philosophy: A Modern Introduction, 4th Ed. (Londoichard Nolan, Living Issues in Wordsworth Publishing co., 1982), 207.

6. Robert Rafalko, Logic for an Overcast Tuesday (California: Wordsworth Publishing Co., 1989), 470.

7. Ibid.

8. Irving M. Copi, Introduction to Logic, 5th Ed., (London: Macmillan Publishing Co., 1978), 78-79.

9. Sarah Palin, "Death Panels" The Wire: News from the Atlantic. Retrieved from the worldwide web, The Wire, 12 January, 2015.

10. Bertrand Russell, Has Religion made useful Contributions to Civilization? (New York: Watts and Co., 1930)

11. Philip Emeagwali: Inventor of the World's fastest Computer, retrieved from worldwide web, Black Inventor, 12 January, 2015.

12. Barack Obama, "You didn't build that" Washington Post, July 18, 2012.

13. Ibid.

14. Chuks Iloegbunam et al, "Juveniles on Death Row", Newswatch Magazine, Lagos, Sept. 12, 1988, 10.

15. Todd Akin, "Legitimate Rape Comment" retrieved from the worldwide web, Slate, January 12, 2015.

Chapter 17

Main Streams of Philosophy: Western and Eastern Philosophy

1. C. B. Okolo, Problems of African Philosophy and One Other Essay (Enugu: Cecta Publishers, 1992), 7.

2. G.C.M. James, Stolen Legacy (New York: New York Philosophical Library, 1954), Chapter VI.

3. C.S. Momoh, "African Philosophy...Does it Exist?" Diogenes 130, 1988, 91.

4. N.W. Ross, Three Ways of Asian Wisdom (New York: Simon and Schuster, 1966), 7.

5. H.D. Lewis and Robert L. Slater, World Religions (London:

   C.A. Watts, 1966), 22.

6. Titus Harold, Marilyn Smith and Richard Nolan, Living Issues in Philosophy, 7th Edition (New York: Litton Educational Publishing Inc., 1979), 398-399.

7. M. Hiriyanna, The Essentials of Indian Philosophy (London: Allen and Unwin, 1949), 158.

8. Nicholas Omoregbe, Knowing Philosophy: General Introduction, (Lagos: Joje Publishers Ltd., 1990), 65-66.

9. Chang Chung-Yuan, Tao Te Ching, Trans. (New York: Harper and Row Publishers, 1975)

10. Mao Tse-tung, Selected Works of Mao Tse-tung (Peking: Foreign Language Press, Vol. 1, 1961), 314.

Chapter 18

African Philosophy: The Different Senses of the Concept "African"

1. C.B. Okolo, What is an African? (Nsukka: University of Nigeria Press, 1996), 3.

2. D.U. Opata, "What is African?" Seminar Paper Presented at the William Amo Center for the Study of African Philosophy(Nsukka: University of Nigeria, 6 Feb. 1992)

3. R. McHenry, "African" The New Encyclopedia Britannica, Vol. VIII, 15th Ed. (New York: 1982)

4. Opata, What is African? 6 Feb., 1992.

5. Horace Emeagwara, An Eclectic Philosophical Hermeneutics of African Personality (Nsukka: University of Nigeria, 1998), 26.

6. Pantaleon Iroegbu, Enwisdomisation and African Philosophy (Owerri: International Uni. Press, 1994), 119.

7. C.B. Okolo, African Social and Political Philosophy: Selected Essays (Nsukka: Fulladu Publishers, 1993), 4.

8. C.B. Okolo, What is African Philosophy? (Nsukka: University of Nigeria, 1992)

9. K.C. Anyanwu, and E.A. Ruch, African Philosophy: An Introduction, Ed. (Rome: Catholic Book Agency, 1981), 17.

10. Henri Maurier, "Do we have an African Philosophy?" African Philosophy: An Introduction, Ed. Richard A. Wright (Washington D.C.: University Press of America, 1977)

11. Frank Fanon, Black Skins White Masks (New York: Grove Press, 1967)

12. Okoro, What is an African? (Nsukka: University of Nigeria, 1996)

13. John Mbiti, African Religion and Philosophy (London: Heinemann Publishers), 286.

14. Oliver Onwubiko, African Thoughts, Religion and Culture (Enugu: Snaap Press, 1991), 14.

15. Mbiti, African Religion, 141.

16. Tom Mboya, Freedom and After (London: Andre Deutsch, 1963)

17. L.S. Senghor, Selected Poems, Trans. and Intro. J. Reed and Clive Wake (Ibadan: Oxford University Press, 1964), 254.

18. T.U. Nwala, Igbo Philosophy (Ikeja: Literamed Publishers, 1997)

19. Steve Biko, I Wrote What I Like (New York: Random House Publishers, 1978), 43.

20. J.A. Sofola, African Culture and the African Personality (Ibadan: 1982), 52.

21. Festus Okafor, Africa at Crossroads (New York: Heinemann Publishers, 1974), 14-24.

22. Oliver Onwubiko, Wisdom Lectures on African Thought and Culture (Owerri: Totan Publishers Ltd., 1988), 20.

23. Stan Anih, Third Millennium God-Talk (Enugu: Snaap Press Ltd., 1995), 94.

24. E. Obiechina, Culture, Tradition and Society in West African Novels (London: Cambridge University Press, 1973), 131.

25. Okafor, Africa at Crossroads, 4.

26. Onwubiko, Wisdom Lectures on African Thought, 17-18.

27. D.A. Offiong, Imperialism and Dependency: Obstacles to African Development (Enugu: Fourth Dimension Publishers, 1980), 85.

28. Ibid.

29. Ibid., 91.

30. Jauretche Arturo, The Negro in Brazil (Washington: Associated Press, 1939), 34.

31. Kenneth Burke, Africa: Selected Readings, Ed. (Boston: Houghton Mifflin Publishers, 1969), 129.

32. B. Lalage and M. Crowder, The Proceedings of the First International Congress of Africanists, Ed. (Illinois: Northwestern University Press, 1964), 214.

33. T.U. Nwala, Discourse on African Philosophy and Identity in the Twentieth Century (Nsukka: University of Nigeria Press, 1997)

34. Ibid.

35. Effiong, Imperialism and Dependency, 85.

36. M. Crowder, West Africa under Colonial Rule (London: Hutchington and Co. Ltd., 1976), 10.

37. H. Trevor-roper, The Listener, November, 28th, 1968.

38. M. Perhum, The Colonial Reckoning (New York: International Publishers, 1957)

39. Basil Davidson, Which Way Africa? (Baltimore: Penguin Books, 1965), 285.

40. J. Woddis, Introduction to Neo-Colonialism (New York: International Publishers, 1967), 14.

41. Kwame Nkrumah, Autobiography (London: Nelson Publishers, 1967), 14.

42. Emeagwara, An Eclectic Philosophical Hermeneutics of African Personality, 49-54.

43. Okolo quoted in Emeagwara, 55.

44. K.B.C. Onwubiko, The School Certificate History of West Africa, Bk II, (Lagos: Africana Educational Publishers, 1978), 246.

45. Ibid.

46. Ibid.

47. Offiong, Imperialism and Dependency, 115-116.

48. Kwame Nkrumah, Neo-Colonialism: The Last Stage of Imperialism (New York: International Publishers, 1966), 1.

49. D. Wise and T.B. Ross, The Invisible Government (New York: Random House, 1964)

50. John A. Ayoade, "African Search for Democracy: Hopes and Reality" Democracy and Pluralism in Africa, Ed. Dov Ronen, Colorado: Lynne Rieneer Publishers, 1986), 19- 33.

51. Igwe I., Democratization in Africa: Nigerian Perspectives, Vol. I (Abuja: CDS, 1994), 100.

52. Perlmutter Amos, "The Praetorian State and the Praetorian Army" Comparative Politics, 1, 3, April 1969, 381-404.

53. Ebenezer Babatope, Coups: Africa and the Barracks Revolt (Enugu: Fourth Dimension Publishers, 1981), VII.

54. C.B. Okolo, Africa Social and Political Philosophy: Selected Essays (Nsukka: Fulladu Publishers Co., 1993), 10.

55. E.A. Ruch and K.C. Anyanwu, African Philosophy (Rome: Catholic Book Agency, 1981), 343.

56. K.J. Nyerere, Ujamaa - Essays on Socialism (Dares – Salaam: Oxford University Press, 1968), 89.

57. Kwame Nkrumah, I Speak of Freedom (London: Praeger Publishers, 1961), 125.

58. C.B. Okolo, African Social and Political Philosophy, 53.

59. A.G. Nweke, Africa Security in the Nuclear Age (Enugu: Fourth Dimension Publishers, 1985), 12.

60. A. Cesaire, Discourse on Colonialism (New York: Monthly Review Press, 1972), 72.

61. C.P. Onwuachi, African Identity and Black Liberation (Buffalo: Black Academy Press, 1972), 123.

62. R. Fruecht, Black Society in the New World (New York: Random House, 1971), 384.

63. Kwame Nkrumah, Revolutionary Path (London: Panaf Books Ltd., 1980), 420.

64. Carrie Johnson, "After Discrimination Finding, Jury's Out on Memphis

Juvenile Courts" Retrieved from Flip Board November, 2014.

65. Emeagwara, An Eclectic Philosophical Hermeneutics of African Personality, 1998.

66. Nweke, African Security in the Nuclear Age, 65.

67. Nnamdi Azikwe, Ideology for Nigeria (Ibadan: Macmillan Publishers, 1980), 4.

68. Gamal Abdel Nasser, Speech on the Ninth Anniversary of the Egyptian Revolution, July 22, 1961.

69. Malcolm X, Pan Africanism, Ed. P.O. Esedebe (Enugu: Fourth Dimension Publishers, 1980), 233.

70. Chinweizu Ibekwe, The West and the Rest of Us (Lagos: Pero Press, 1987), 268.

71. John Kennedy, quoted in G. Kolko, The Roots of American Foreign Policy (Boston: Beacon Press,1968)

72. Paul G. Hoffman, "The Two Ways Benefits of Foreign Aid," Fortune Magazine, (March, 1972), 118.

73. Ernest M. Stern quoted in Lloyd Timberlake, Africa in Crisis (London: Earthscan Publishers, 1985), XIV.

74. Rene Dumont, False Start in Africa (London: Earthscan Press, 1988), 260.

INDEX

Achebe, Chinua, 39, 40, 415
  on cargo cult mentality, 39
Aesthetics, 225-229
  meaning of, 225
  values of, 226
Absolutism, 79, 107
African philosophy, 10-11, 28, 29, 412-454
  Communalism, 417-418
  concepts of, 415
  existence of, 415
  freedom, 437
  meaning of, 415
  personality, 438
  role of, 436-438
  slavery and, 421-425
  socialism, 438
  values of, 419
  writers' series, 39, 417-418
  and Black power, 441
  and Pan-Africanism, 439
  and Black lives Matter, 443
  and Development, 436
African Union, 445
  African security, 445
  and OAU, 445
  NEPAD: brain child of, 449
Agnosticism, 136
  meaning of, 136
Algebra of Revolution, 56
Altruism, 152
Analogy, 156
  of proportionality, 157
  of attribution, 157
Analytic Method, 66-71

Analytic Philosophy, 36, 326, 327-329
Anthropology, 252-254
Appardoria, A., 196
Aquinas, 15, 21, 46, 53, 75, 89, 103
  and existence, 133
  and knowledge, 176
  and values, 262
  as father of eclecticism, 75-76
  on degrees of abstraction, 46
  on being and things, 80
  on change and permanence, 104-107
  on laws, 204
  on senses, 176-177
  on participation, 100
Arguments, 344-357
  valid and invalid forms of, 350-357
  types of, 350-357
  sound and unsound forms of, 346-350
Aristotle, 11, 14, 15, 17, 26, 36, 54, 55, 83, 88, 94, 110, 182, 202, 213
  and doctrine of the mean, 11
  and the five causes of things, 163
  on natural law, 236
  on change and permanence, 104-110
  on happiness, 159
  on metaphysics, 154
  on philosophy, 11, 17, 26
  on plurality in reality, 84, 110
  on potentiality and actuality, 161-162
  on substance and accidents,

159-160
  on theoretical knowledge, 181
  on truth, 36
  on good, 202
Austin, J.K., 237-239
Authentic existence, 315
  see also self-alienation, 315
Authority, 179
Atheism, 5, 128
  and the death of God, 128-132
Atomism, 86, 95
Avicenna, 18
Axiology, 225
Ayer, A.J., 18, 67, 33, 180, 331, 332
Azikiwe, Nnamdi, 75-76
  and neo-welfarism, 76
  on eclecticism, 75
  on non-alignment, 449-450

Bacon, Francis, 6, 38, 330
  on idols of the mind, 38-39
Baruch, Spinoza, 134
Being, 85-91, 153-156
  analogy of, 156
  transcendental attributes of, 158
  concept of, 153-156
  definition of, 153-156
  division of, 157
Bentham, Jeremy, 146, 152
Bergson, Henri, 63-67, 106, 211
  intuition for, 60
  on analysis, 66
  on change, 154
Berkeley, George, 82, 92, 95, 170-171, 290-294
  on empiricism, 280

  on idealism, 290
  on immaterialism, 170-171
Bill, Clinton, 40
Blyden, Wilmot, 438
  and African development, 436
  on African personality, 438
Braham, 404-407
  in Indian philosophy, 404
Broad, C.D., 19, 22, 34, 35
Buddhist Philosophy, 406-408
  and existentialism, 406
  Nirvana in, 408
  Noble truths, 407
Bush, W. George, 383

Causality, 112-115
  and five causes of things, 163
  and theories of, 113-118
Camus, Albert, 142
  and the Myth of Sisyphus, 142
  see also Theatre of the Absurd
Categorical propositions, 341
  elements of, 342
CERN, 120
  and trilogy of reality, 83
Change, 104-110
  and permanence, 107-110
  as feature of reality, 107-110
  meaning of, 104-110
Cicero, Marcus, 18, 26, 27, 202, 214-217
  and natural law, 214
  on nature, 214
  on philosophy, 18
  utility from justice, 276-278
Civil freedom, 197

Coherence theory, 186
  See also truth, 184
Colonialism, 427-433
  and African lives, 327
  purpose of, 327
  and neo-colonialism, 433-454
Communalism, 417-421
  reasons for, 417-421
Confucius, 409
  and philosophy, 409-410
Conscience, 211-212
  kinds of, 211-212
  as moral standard, 212
Correspondence theory, 184
  see also truth, 184
Cosmic Evolution, 110-118
  differentiation of, 111-113
Creationism, 112

Darwin, Charles, 6, 60-64
Deductive Method, 60
  Charles Pierce's attack on, 61, 62, 65
  See also intuitive method, 60
Delphic Oracle, 49-52
Democritus, 17, 80, 82, 86, 165, 271
  and materialism, 272
  on existence, 80
  on philosophy, 17, 18
  on reality, 80, 87
Deontology, 219-220
Development theories, 402-403
Descartes, Rene, 32, 61-66, 83, 90, 94, 127, 149, 167, 273,
  and Henri Bergson, 63

  as protagonist of dualism, 83, 166-168
  on being as a concept, 166-168
  on deduction, 60-62
  on existence of God, 168-170
  on intuition, 60-62
  on knowledge, 169
  on philosophy, 62, 83
  on reality, 166-168
Determinism, 274
Dewey, John, 18, 183, 222, 229, 325
  experimental naturalism of, 149
  on philosophy, 18
  on pragmatism, 189, 325
  practical knowledge, 183
  selection of values, 229
  truth and, 325
  valuation of self, 126
Dialectic, 53
Dialectical materialism, 308
  see also economic determinism, 308
Dualism, 83, 166-170
Dun Scotus, 89
Duty, 219

Eclecticism, 75
  essence of, 76
  eclectic method, 75-76
Egoism, 152, 215
  forms of, 215
  meaning of, 215
Einstein, Albert, 71-72, 117-118
Empiricism, 280
  and knowledge, 280
  defect of, 284

forms of, 282
Empiricist theory, 280
  see also regularity theory,
Engels Friedrich, 309
Energism, 82
En-soi, 199
  see also Sartre, Jean Paul, 299
Entailment theory, 113
Epicurus, 18, 81, 86, 88, 118-122, 266
  founder of Epicurean school, 145
  on existence, 86
  on philosophy, 18
  on pleasure, 145
Epistemology, 173-190
  and the theory of knowledge, 174
  goals of, 186
  and truth, 186
Euclid, 116
Evolution, 111
  and kinds of, 111
Essence, 96-99
  nature of, 96
Ethics, 191
  forms of, 191-194
  meaning of, 191
Ethiopianism, 401-402
Existence, 92-93
  essence of existence, 92-93
Existentialism, 253, 299-307
  and abstract universals, 302
  and capitalism, 303
  and features of, 300
  and rationalism, 303-304
  and the recovery of man, 305-306
  and Western Philosophy, 400
  and on existence, 299-307
Experiment, 125, 128, 138, 140, 222

Fagothey, Austin, 202, 192
  see also Right and Reason, 192
Fallacy, 358-398
  classification of, 360
  meaning of, 358
  significance of, 392
  as technique of persuasion, 394-398
  from propaganda to brainwashing, 394
False Alternative, 383
False Analogy, 384
False Cause, 377
False Dilemma, 384
  see also fallacy,
Feuerbach, Ludwig, 308, 250
  and Hegel philosophy, 308
  and Marxism, 250, 309
  and materialism, 309
  on humanism, 250, 305
  on God, 250, 305
  on religion, 250-305
Freedom, 195-198
  and types of, 196-198

Gandhi, Mahatma, 6
Globalization, 223-224
God, 11, 12-13, 14, 49, 95, 103-104, 128, 133, 150, 179, 242, 245, 247
  and all ideas about, 13-14, 179
  and the cosmos, 1103-104
  belief in, 133-135, 150
  conscience as, 211
  death of, 128-132

essence of, 100-104
existence of, 168, 242
knowledge of, 168, 179
language of, 168
proofs of existence of, 168-170, 242
man with, 242
revelation of, 242
sceptics and, 242
Greenblatt, Stephen, 24, 80-81, 87, 118-122, 124-125, 278

Habit, 202
Hamlyn, D.W., 53, 54, 281
Hegel, 53-54, 82, 92, 281
324-326, 349, 490
and dialectics, 53-54
and the universe, 293
attack on, 55
on constituent of reality, 293-294
on truth, 176
on self-contained existence, 315
Hedonism, 144
and utilitarianism, 144-145
meaning of, 144
Heraclitus, 80, 103-105
Hermeneutics, 18, 77, 392
meaning of, 77
Heidegger, 18, 75, 89, 211, 89, 98
and being as *dasein, sein* and *seindes*, 89
on philosophy, 18
Higgins, Thomas, 193, 202,
Hindu Philosophy, 404
Braham in, 404
values in, 404-406

History, 259-261
Hobbes, Thomas, 18, 150, 214
and dictates of reason, 150
and egoism, 152
on natural law, 214
and mechanistic materialism, 82, 263
on philosophy, 18
and reality, 82
Holmes Oliver Wendell, 240
Hornby, Sidney Albert, 12
Human act, 192, 198-202
classification of, 198
constituents of, 193
freedom in, 195
knowledge, 193
modifiers of, 200
morality of, 202
object of, 203
voluntariness of, 194-195
Human conduct, 191
problems of, 191-192
Humanism, 247-252
and kinds of, 248-252
Hume, David, 69, 93, 106, 172
and God, 172, 243
and knowledge, 172
on analytic judgements, 66
on cause and effect, 113-115, 243
on change, 113-115
on perception and objects, 113-115
Husserl, Edmond, 42
and phenomenology, 72-75, 98
on philosophy, 72-73
on truth, 72-75
Huxley, Thomas, 41, 253

Idealism, 92, 170, 288
  meaning of, 288-289
  types of, 290
Induction, 62, 347-349
Instrumentalism, 189
Intention, 199
Intuition, 60-66, 178, 211
  and knowledge, 60-66
  as moral standard, 211
  definition of, 60-66
  function, 60-66
Intuitionism, 216-217
  forms of, 216-217
Intuitive method, 60-66
  see also deductive method, 60-66

James, William, 18, 35, 189, 243-244
  and pragmatism, 319-325
James, G.C.M., 401, 429-430
  see also Stolen Legacy, 429-430
Judgements, 68-71
  suspension of, 68-71
  types of, 68-72
  value, 68, 73
Jurisprudence, 235
  concept of, 235
  meaning of, 235
  schools of, 235-241
Justice, 213

Kant, Immanuel, 56, 66-72, 94, 97, 106, 110, 116, 147,
  and God, 72, 243

on analytic method, 66-72
on being as a concept, 116, 159
on dialectics, 72, 56
on judgements, 68-72
on respect of moral law, 147, 219
on space and time, 71, 116
on synthesis, 66
synthetic a priori of, 69-70, 287
Kaufmann, Walter, 301
Kierkegaard, Soren, 299, 185
  and individual existence, 299, 302-307
  and truth, 185, 299
  on existentialist ideas, 299-301
  on God, 303
  on stages of life, 304
Kirilenko and Korshunova, 10-14, 19
  on philosophy, 19
Knowledge, 136-138, 175
  and human act, 171
  definition of, 136, 175
  empiricists and, 280
  human mind, 175
  intuition and, 60-66
  kinds of, 182, 137, 181
  origin of, 175
  practical, 182, 181
  sources of, 138, 175-183
  theory of, 136
  truth in, 184-190

Lao, Tzu, 408
Laws, 204, 230-235, 335
  and the people, 335

divisions of, 205
examination of, 234
functions of, 205, 234
kinds of, 204-206
meaning of, 241
philosophy of, 234
qualities of, 258-260
Layman, Stephen, 339, 346, 357
Leopold, Senghor, 10
  on black emotions, 10
  on negritude, 440
Leibniz Gottfried, 95, 75, 143
Locke, John, 64, 83, 281, 282
  and intellect, 281-282
  and knowledge, 281-282
  and natural law, 281
  on constituent of reality, 83
  on ideas, 83
Logic, 335-357
  and forms of inferences, 334
  definition, 338
Logical Positivism, 231, 329- 334
  characteristics of, 329
  kinds of, 330-334
  theory of verification and, 331
  meaning, 331
Love, 14
Lucretius, 14, 17, 81, 88, 92, 118-121, 165, 266-268
  as disciples of Democritus, 165
Luther King, Martin Jr., 6, 7, 115
  and non-violent resistance/protest, 7, 58,

Machiavelli, Niccolo, 147-149

and political strategies, 148
Mao, Tse-tung, 410
  and utilizing early warning signs, 411
  of conflict, 410-412
Marcel Gabriel, 91
  being as a mystery, 91
  on blind intuition, 91
Maritain, Jacque, 18, 42, 106- 107
Marx, Karl, 56, 57, 82, 254, 262, 307-308, 314-318
  on change, 307-318
  on constituent of reality, 262, 308
  on dialectical materialism, 314-318
  on task of philosophers, 314-318
Marxism, 307-318
  and authentic existence, 315-318
  and communism, 313
  and core of, 309-310
  and Feuerbach, 308
  and Hegelian philosophy, 307
  and ideas, 307-310
  and self-alienation, 315
Materialism, 262-263
  and the naturalism, 265
  meaning of, 274, 313
  types of, 271
  and forms of, 271-274
Maoist philosophy, 410-411
Matter, 83
Maurier, Henri, 28
Max, Planck, 41
  on matrix of matter, 41
  and Intelligent design, 41

and Big Bang theory, 41
and Quantum theory, 41
Meliorism, 143
Memory, 180-181
  and remembering, 181
  and knowledge, 181
  divisions of, 181
Metaphysics, 153-172
definitions of, 153
  divisions of, 154
  idealism in, 170-171
  organicism and, 171-172
  schools of, 163-172
  skepticism, 172
Militarism, 435-436
  African philosophy and, 435, 436
  African Development and, 437-436
  in Sierra Leone, 435
  in Uganda, 435
Mill, John Stuart, 218
  and private morality, 218
Mind, 82, 92, 165, 166
Modern dialectical Method, 53
Montague W. Pepperell, 243
  God and the problem of evil, 355
Morality, 192, 202-225
  and standards of, 204
  and schools of, 212
Motivation, 151
Mysticism, 12
  and philosophy, 11-12
  meaning of, 12
Myths, 9-12

Naturalism, 214, 262-270

and supernaturalism, 275-279
  meaning of, 275
Negritude, 440
  and African personality, 414, 438
Ngugi, James, 39 see also "Weep not Child"
Neo-colonialism, 433
  and African worldview, 434
  militarism and, 435-436
  purpose of, 433
New Partnership for African Development (NEPAD) 449-455
  brain-child of African Union, 449
  foreign aids for, 452
  functions of, 449-455
  motives of, 451
Nietzsche, 43, 97, 106, 128-132, 249-251
  and the death of God, 128-132
  and democracy, 97, 249-251
  as mastermind of the superman, 97, 249
  on existentialism, 97-98
  on change, 106
  on Christianity, 97, 128-132
Nkrumah, Kwame, 433-434
  on African personality, 439, 441
  on colonialism, 427-433
  on knowledge, 427-433
  on neo-colonialism, 433

Obama, Barack, 40, 60
  on guns and religion, 40
  and sophistry, 60 see also fallacy: "You didn't build

that", 391
Ockham, William, 102
  and Ockham's razor, 102
Okolo, Chukwudum Barnabas,
  28, 401, 415
  on African freedom, 401, 415
  See also the African as a
  being-with-the-community
Omoregbe, Joseph, 19, 29, 32, 84, 96
  man's essence, 96
  on philosophy and being, 29, 86
  on existence, 84
Optimism, 143
Oriental philosophy, 399, 403- 411
Organization of African Unity,
(OAU), 445
  and African Union, 446
  and denuclearization of
  Africa, 448
  articles of, 446
  elements of, 446
  principles of, 446
Organicism, 171

Pan-Africanism, 439
  and colonialism, 427
  and emancipation of African
  Americans, 427
  goals of, 428
  nationalism and, 427
Palin, Sarah, 380, see also
  fallacy: Obamacare and the
  death panels, 380
Parmenides, 85, 86, 104, 107
  on being, 104
  on change, 104
  on permanence, 104, 107
Participation, 100
  meaning of, 100
Pascal, Blaise, 150, 244
  see also Pascal's Wager, 150
Passion, 201
Permanence, 104, 107-110
  change and, 104
  reality of, 104-107
Perfectionism, 146
Phenomenological method, 72- 74
Phenomenology, 253, 217
  fundamental rule in, 72-74
  in ethics, 217
Philosophy, 9
  and Africans, 10-11
  and as an art, 27
  and God, 13
  and demythologization of, 11-12
  and as a profession, 31
  and other sciences, 25
  and scientific knowledge, 25
  and theology, 13
  branches of, 230
  conceptions of, 20-24
  definition of, 17-24
  divisions of, 153
  epistemology in, 173
  meaning of, 9
  methods for use in, 45
  motives for, 42-44
  mysticism and, 12
  myths and, 9-13
  problem of, 78
  rationalism in, 178
  religion and, 12-13

types of, 399
uses of, 36-42
universality of, 28
value of, 36-42
Peirce, Charles Sanders, 64-66
see also pragmatism, 319-325
Pessimism, 141-143
Plato, 6, 12, 14, 17, 35, 36, 53, 101, 110
and ultra-realism, 101
doctrine of participation of, 100
on philosophy, 18
on reality, 100
on truth, 100
on values, 100
Pleasure, 210
see also pain, 210-211
Plotinus, 101
see also creation by emanation, 101
Pluralism, 84-85, 103
radical, 103
Popper, Karl, 55-56
Potency and Actuality, 162-163
divisions of, 162-163
Pou-soi, 103 See also
Sartre Jean Paul, 98-99
Practical Knowledge, 182
and theoretical knowledge, 180
Pragmatism, 189, 319-326
and truth, 323
characteristics of, 320
meaning of, 321
nature of, 320
Prescriptive philosophy, 35
Privation, 144

and evil as, 144
Propositions, 341
and types of, 341-344
Putin, Vladimir, 60
Pythagoras, 31, 80, 85, 108
mathematical doctrine, 108
on relativism in reality, 109
reality of permanence, 108-110

Rader, Malvin, 15-17, 26, 28, 36, 48, 51, 65, 66, 106, 132, 161, 178, 214, 245, 247, 284-287, 290
and idealism, 290
on corrupt civilization, 132
on cosmic order, 214
on God, 132
on law of nature, 178
Raphael, D.D., 35, 231
Rationalism, 284-287
and knowledge, 285
criticism of, 287
faith in, 284-287
forms of, 286-287
Realism, 294-298
and matter, 294-298
forms of, 296-298
meaning of, 298
Reality, 79-85, 165
aspects of, 110-135
change and, 104
nature of, 110-135
Reason, 15, 139-140, 177-178
and thinking, 207
man in, 126
morality based on, 207

as moral standard, 207
uses of, 277-278
primacy over law, 277
Rationalism, 284
forms of, 286-287
Relativism, 79
Religion, 11-12, 179, 242
meaning of, 242
on God, 243
philosophy of, 242
Revelation and inspiration, 179
Right, 278
Rodney, Walter, 59
Russell, Bertrand, 39, 67, 105, 284, 289, 290, 292, 329
and idealism, 284, 290
on analytic method, 66-71, 326
on ordinary language, 329
on value of philosophy, 326-330
on religion, 380
Russell, Leo, 40
Ryle, Gilbert, 67, 94, 127

Satischandra, 18
on philosophy, 18
Sartre Jean Paul, 98-99
and freedom, 98-99
man's essence, 98
on existence, 98
Schopenhauer, Arthur, 141
and pessimism, 141-143
Scientific Empiricism, 281
see also Empiricism, 280
Science, 25, 254
and philosophy of, 254

Scientific Method, 257, 269
limitations of, 258
Senghor Leopold, 10
on African communalism, 417
and Negritude, 440
Self, 126-128, 166
and nature of, 126-128
see also mind and body,
Skepticism, 92, 93, 136, 172, 221
and agnosticism, 92, 136
Situation ethics, 220
Spencer, Herbert, 10
Spinoza, Baruch, 95, 134
Socrates, 6, 12, 15, 17, 28, 36, 48
and the natural law, 36, 48
on justice, 52
on philosophy, 17
technique of, 46-53
Socratic Methods, 46-49
kinds of, 46
Speculative philosophy, 34
objects of, . See also philosophy, 34-36
Speculative knowledge, 34
See also theoretical knowledge, 181-182
Stangroom Jeremy and James Garvey, 46-49, 55-5, 128-132, 141-143, 249, 324
Substance, 159, 161
as essence, 93-94
as material stuff, 94
characteristics of, 160-165
kinds of, 160
Supernaturalism, 275-279
and existence of God, 275-279
Syllogism, 350

forms of, 350-353
  meaning of, 350
Synthetic a posteriori, 69
Synthetic a priori, 69
Synthetic method, 66

Taoist philosophy, 408
  and Confucian philosophy, 409
Teleology, 118, 122, 123, 164, 247
  non-teleological views, 118-123, 164-247
Theism, 133-135
  pantheism, 133
  monotheism, 133
  polytheism, 133
Theology, 12-13
  and philosophy, 12-13
Theoretical knowledge, 181-182
  and practical knowledge, 180
  Kant's synthetic a priori and, 69
Titus, Smith and Nolan, 19-23, 37, 174, 227, 229, 271, 280, 289, 295, 301
  functions of philosophy, 19-23
  on conceptions of philosophy, 19-23
Todd, Akin, 397 See fallacies
  and legitimate rape comment, 397
Transcendental Aesthetic, 71
Transcendental Dialectic, 72
Trilogy of reality, 83
Truth, 174, 184
  and epistemology, 184
  and knowledge, 184
  meaning of, 184

pragmatist and, 189, 323
theories of, 186-190

Universals, 100-103
  concept of, 100
  problems of, 100
  and values of, 100-103
Universalibility, 146-210
  forms of, 208
Universe, 110, 118
  and experimentalist views of, 125
  and non-teleological views of, 118-123
  and teleological views of, 123-125
Utilitarianism, 146, 218
  and money, 146
  forms of, 218
  on happiness, 218

Values, 15, 140, 225
  aesthetic, 225
  in Ethics, 141
  kinds of, 226
  nature of, 140, 228
  selection of, 228
  theories of, 140-141
Virtues, 15
Voluntariness, 194-195
  types of, 194-195

Weak Rationalism, 286
  and knowledge, 284 See also Rationalism, 284-287

Webster, Merriam, 11, 25
Weep Not Child, 39-40
Western Philosophy, 399
  origin of, 400
  systems in, 403
Whitehead, Alfred North, 171, 296-297
Wiredu, Kwasi, 10, 28
Wisdow, 15-17
Wittgenstein, 18, 67, 326-329
  on philosophy, 326-329
Woozley, 174-175
  on epistemology, 174
  on memory, 174

Zeno, 85
  on pluralism, 85

www.ingramcontent.com/pod-product-compliance
Lightning Source LLC
Chambersburg PA
CBHW031128160426
43193CB00008B/73